AN INTRODUCTION TO SOCIOLOGY

ELIZABETH J. WILKINS, B.A.(Soc.) M.A. (Leeds)
*Lecturer in Sociology at Hitchin College and Moderator for Sociology
for the Associated Examining Board*

SECOND EDITION

MACDONALD AND EVANS

MACDONALD AND EVANS LTD
Estover, Plymouth PL6 7PZ

First published 1970
Reprinted 1971
Reprinted 1972
Reprinted 1973
Reprinted 1975
Second edition 1976
Reprinted 1978

©

MACDONALD AND EVANS LIMITED

1976

ISBN: 0 7121 0937 4

Printed in Great Britain by Butler & Tanner Ltd,
Frome and London

PREFACE TO THE FIRST EDITION

IT is necessary for all students of sociology to have a wide generalised knowledge of their subject, although it is usual nowadays for those who eventually become professional sociologists to specialise within the field.

The purpose of this work is to provide a systematic and comprehensive introduction to sociology for students whose needs are as yet not of a specialist nature. It is hoped that those who are looking for a textbook covering the whole subject at the level required by the various bodies which set examinations in sociology at the present time will find it of use to them. This work is primarily designed for use by students in sixth forms, technical colleges and colleges of education, but undergraduates in universities may also find that it provides them with a satisfactory foundation upon which they can base further study. For all who wish to develop their knowledge in this way, the recommendations for further reading which are included at the end of each chapter should be of service.

Also at the end of each chapter there is a selection of questions on the material covered. Many of these questions—those followed by an abbreviated attribution—have been reproduced with permission from recent examination papers of the Associated Examining Board ("A" Level), the Oxford Local Examinations Board ("A" Level) and London University (External Diploma in Social Studies). These will enable the student both to test his knowledge of the chapter and to anticipate the type of question with which he is likely to be faced in an examination. All students would be well advised to make use of these exercises.

January 1970   E. J. W.

PREFACE TO THE SECOND EDITION

THE book has been revised to take account of the changes that have taken place since the first edition was published. Some sections have been completely rewritten and some new material has been introduced, although the main body of the text remains unchanged.

As far as possible I have tried to preserve the continuity of the statistics which are the major indicators of trends in many areas of sociology. Unfortunately this was made extremely difficult by the discontinuity of presentation of statistics by the various government departments responsible. For this reason, some of the tables and graphs included in the first edition could not be updated and have therefore been omitted. Wherever possible, alternative material has been substituted.

I am very grateful to those who have written to me since the book was first published, and also to colleagues who have assisted me by making constructive comments on many of the topics considered in the text. Their help and encouragement have been of great value.

August 1975   E. J. W.

ACKNOWLEDGMENTS

To produce a textbook of this kind it is necessary to draw on numerous sources and publications, and for permission to include copyright material I am indebted to the following.

George Allen and Unwin Ltd., for extracts from *The Science of Society* (S. Cotgrove), *English Social Differences* (T. H. Pear), *Prisoners and their Families* (Pauline Morris) and *Education and the Social Order* (Bertrand Russell); Associated Book Publishers Ltd., for extracts from *Psychology and Social Problems* (Michael Argyle), *Family and Colour in Jamaica* (F. Henriques) and *Industrial Accidents, Sickness and Other Absences* (Tavistock Pamphlet No. 4) (J. M. M. Hill and E. L. Trist); Anthony Blond Ltd., for a quotation from *Class—A Symposium*, edited by R. Mabey; the British Broadcasting Corporation; Cassell and Company, for a quotation from *Tomorrow We'll Be Sober* (Lincoln Williams) (reprinted as *Alcoholism Explained* (Evans Brothers)); the Central Board of Finance of the Church of England; Chatto and Windus Ltd. and Mrs Laura Huxley, for a quotation from *The Doors of Perception* (Aldous Huxley); the Community Relations Commission; the Conservative Political Centre; the *Daily Telegraph* and the *Sunday Telegraph*; J. M. Dent and Sons Ltd., for an extract from the Everyman's Library edition of *Rousseau's Dissertation on the Origin and Foundation of the Inequality of Mankind*; Faber and Faber Ltd., for quotations from *A Troubled Area: Notes on Notting Hill* (Pearl Jephcott) and a table from *Politics in England* (Richard Rose); Gallup Poll; Victor Gollancz Ltd., for an extract from *Middle School* (John Partridge) (reprinted under the title *Life in a Secondary Modern School* (Penguin Books Ltd.)); D. C. Heath and Co., for an extract from *The Concept of Sociology* (E. E. Eubank), Copyright ©,1932, by D. C. Heath and Co. Boston, Mass., U.S.A.; Heinemann Educational Books Ltd.; the Controller of Her Majesty's Stationery Office; Holt, Rinehart and Winston, Inc.; Hutchinson Publishing Group Ltd.; the *Illustrated London News*; the Independent Broadcasting Authority; the Institute of Practitioners in Advertising; William Kimber and Co. Ltd., for an extract from *Long to Reign Over Us?* (Leonard Harris); Leonard Hill Books, London, for a quotation from *The New Towns* (Sir F. Osborn and A. Whittick); Longmans Green and Co. Ltd.; Methuen and Co. Ltd., for passages from *Dark*

Strangers (Sheila Patterson) and *Social Psychology* (W. J. H. Sprott); *New Society*; the *Observer* Ltd.; Penguin Books Ltd., for quotations from *The Family and Marriage in Britain* (Ronald Fletcher), *Risinghill* (Leila Berg), *Child Care and the Growth of Love* (John Bowlby), *Communities in Britain* (Ronald Frankenberg), *Human Groups* (W. J. H. Sprott), *Discrimination and Popular Culture* (Denys Thompson) and *Voters, Parties and Leaders* (Jean Blondel); Pergamon English Library, for extracts from *The Magazines Teenagers Read* (Connie Alderson); Political and Economic Planning; Routledge and Kegan Paul Ltd., for extracts from *The Changing Social Structure of England and Wales 1871–1961* (David Marsh), *Society: Problems and Methods of Study* (edited by A. T. Welford and others), *The Captive Wife* (Hannah Gavron), *Workers, Unions and the State* (Graham Wootton), *Down Stream: Failure in the Grammar School* (R. R. Dale and S. Griffith) and *Family and Class in a London Suburb* and *Family and Kinship in East London* (Peter Willmott and Michael Young), also for material from articles by Raymond Aron, W. J. M. Mackenzie and Mark Abrams which have been published in the *British Journal of Sociology*; the Joseph Rowntree Charitable Trust; the Scottish Council for Research in Education; S.C.M. Press Ltd.; Times Newspapers Ltd.; the Trades Union Congress; the Centre for Urban Studies, for a quotation from *British Towns* (C. A. Moser and W. Scott) (Report No. 2 in the report series of the Centre); the University of Nottingham; C. A. Watts and Co. Ltd., for an extract from *Broadcasting and the Community* (J. Scupham); the executors of Sir James G. Frazer and the executors of H. G. Wells.

Permission to include examination questions was kindly given by the Associated Examining Board, the Oxford Delegacy of Local Examinations and the University of London.

I should like to express my appreciation to the staff of the libraries of Letchworth College of Technology and Hitchin College of Further Education for the invaluable assistance they have given me and the patience they have shown in dealing with my many requests for material; also to Mrs Mary Harris, who had the unenviable task of turning a very difficult manuscript into an admirably presented typescript.

Last, but by no means least, I wish to thank my family for their co-operation and forbearance during the time that this book was in preparation. My husband gave me a great deal of practical help by checking the script and reading the proofs for me, and both he and my children made it possible for me to devote time and attention to the book which they might justifiably have expected that I should devote to them.

ACKNOWLEDGMENTS TO THE SECOND EDITION

Once again, my husband has given me a great deal of practical assistance by producing the new graphs that are included, by checking the typescript and the proofs with me, and just as important, by relieving me of many of the household tasks that might have made it difficult for me to concentrate on my writing.

I also wish to thank Mrs. Shirley Morris who has done all the necessary typing so accurately and so speedily

CONTENTS

PART ONE

THE STUDY OF SOCIOLOGY

CHAPTER

The social theories of the Greeks. The Roman view of society.
The theologians of the Middle Ages. The Renaissance and the
Reformation. Contributors to sociological thought, 1600–
1850. The founding fathers of modern sociology.

Sociology and the physical sciences. The need for information.
The application of knowledge. The need for a distinctive
vocabulary. How scientific is sociology?

The field of study. The functions of sociology. Sociological
concepts. Society. Social consciousness. Groups and communities. Associations and institutions. Social structure and social
systems. Culture and civilisation.

The use of historical documents. Sampling. The questionnaire.
The measurement of attitudes. Opinion polls.

PART TWO

THE SOCIAL SYSTEM

The interaction of heredity and environment. Groups. Leadership. The development of a hierarchy. Deviant behaviour.

The concept of class. Social classes in Britain. Social mobility.
The functions of class. Class and culture.

Marriage. Divorce. The family. The extended family. The
family in Britain. The functions of the family.

LIST OF ILLUSTRATIONS

LIST OF TABLES

THE STUDY OF SOCIOLOGY

CHAPTER I

THE HISTORY OF SOCIOLOGY

THE word *sociology* was first used during the nineteenth century by the French philosopher Auguste Comte, who said that its purpose was "to discover the nature, the natural causes and the natural laws of society." Although Comte invented the term, many years passed before it came into general use and before the study of sociology developed as a separate discipline.

It should not be inferred from this, however, that sociology is a very new subject. From the first moment that people began to question and think about the societies in which they lived, which must have been many thousands of years ago, they began to think in the way of sociologists, although they regarded themselves as philosophers. Plato was thinking in sociological terms when he considered the social systems which existed in his day, and compared one with another. He decided that none was perfect, and this led him to formulate his theories concerning the ideal state.

The Social Theories of the Greeks

PLATO

Plato (427–348 B.C.) was born in Athens, and spent most of his life there except for a period of travel after the execution of his friend Socrates. By reason of his parentage and interests, Plato might well have devoted himself to politics, but instead he spent his days in study, teaching and philosophy. One reason for this was probably that, when Socrates was condemned to death for "corrupting the young men and not believing in the city's gods," Plato's disgust at the low level to which politics had sunk caused him to renounce all political activities.

In the course of his travels, Plato visited southern Italy and Sicily, and made many friends amongst those who were interested in scholarship and politics. By the time he returned to Athens he was convinced that his only opportunity to influence politics was to found a school where he could explain his ideas to a new generation and create a different type of political character.

Plato was the first western philosopher to examine the relationship between the individual and the state, and from this examination he derived his *organic* theory of society. He believed that the state, being a collection of individuals, must itself be a reflection of the individual organism, and he therefore based his theories of society on his assumptions and beliefs about the nature of the individual. Plato lived long before scientific experimentation was known, so his assumptions and beliefs appear rather fanciful and far-fetched in the light of present-day knowledge.

He believed that the "soul" of an individual was composed of three elements—reason, spirit and appetite—and that no person could achieve perfection, and therefore happiness, unless there was complete harmony and balance between these three divisions within his soul. Since the state was but a reflection of the individual, Plato reasoned that it could not be perfect either, unless there was a similar balance between its three divisions. He likened the rulers, who were the thinkers and organisers, to the rational element of the soul, the soldiers and administrators to the spirited element, and the servile people, or slaves, to the appetitive element. Each of the elements had its own particular virtue, but justice, or righteousness, he held was the virtue of the whole soul and could be defined as "every part doing its own work and not interfering with the others." Plato argued that in the ideal state philosophers would be the proper rulers, and they would be responsible for controlling the breeding and training of all citizens in order to achieve the necessary harmony between the elements.

Plato's philosophy of the state was no doubt just as startling to his contemporaries as it is to us today, but it indicates very clearly that he was not concerned with the interaction of individuals within a society. He believed that people behave as they do because they are taught the roles they have to play.

ARISTOTLE

Although he continued to uphold the organic view of society, Aristotle (384–322 B.C.) based his theories on his study of biology, and the analogy which he drew between the body and the state was even closer than that shown by Plato. Aristotle, who was the son of a physician, went to Athens when he was about 17 to further his education, and he became a student in Plato's academy, where he remained until Plato's death. Although much of his thinking was obviously influenced by his master, his views regarding individual behaviour were opposed to those expressed by Plato since he believed that behaviour was not something which was taught but was instead derived from the nature of the individual himself.

Aristotle considered that, because an individual is able to think, he is also able to control his behaviour by reason, so that a good man is not only intellectual but moral as well. The ideal man is the one who does things regularly, without ulterior motive and gladly. Aristotle argued that doing a thing gladly is important because the virtuous life is one which is pleasant, and a virtuous person will do what he ought because he wants to.

The theories put forward about the nature of man and society by the classical Greek philosophers might have differed to some extent, but they all considered that the individual was of greater importance than the state. In their attempts to describe an ideal society, they sought to establish an efficient, stable and happy society within which all its members would be assured of leading worthwhile and contented lives.

The Roman View of Society

The Romans were more concerned with the state itself than with individuals, and their concept of law and morality was directed towards maintaining the stability of the constitution. It was the Roman view that the state and its institutions did not exist for the benefit of man, but man existed for the benefit of the state. Cicero (106–43 B.C.) discussed the form and principles of the perfect state in his treatise *De Res Publica,* and it was on his assumption that people behave as they do in order to incur reward rather than punishment that the Roman legal system was based.

Cicero's philosophy developed from his belief that there is a universal law of nature under which all men are equal—not in terms of learning or wealth but in the possession of reason, instincts and the ability to distinguish between what is right and what is wrong. He averred therefore that justice, or right, is not based upon the opinions of man but upon nature, and because all men are subject to nature they are fellow citizens bound together in communities for the advantages of helping each other and receiving just government.

The second and third centuries after the birth of Christ were marked by the continuous development of Roman political philosophy, although much of what was written was simply an elaboration of Cicero's theories. His views of the state and morality continued to influence thought about society and the reason for man's existence until the Middle Ages.

The Theologians of the Middle Ages

The letter of St Paul to the Romans explained the attitude that Christians should adopt towards those in authority over them:

"Let every soul be subject unto the higher powers. For there is no power but of God: the powers that be are ordained of God. Whosoever therefore resisteth the power, resisteth the ordinance of God: and they that resist shall receive to themselves damnation. For rulers are not a terror to good works, but to evil. Wilt thou then not be afraid of the power? Do that which is good, and thou shalt have praise of the same: For he is the minister of God, a revenger to execute wrath upon him that doeth evil. Wherefore ye must needs be subject, not only for wrath, but also for conscience sake . . . Render therefore to all their dues: tribute to whom tribute is due; custom to whom custom; fear to whom fear; honour to whom honour." (Romans 13: 1–7.)

Both for the early Fathers of the Church, and for the theologians of the Middle Ages, there was no real conflict between the concepts of secular justice and the nature of the state and the concepts of Christianity. The Roman view of the state and the philosophy of the universal law of nature could be encompassed by Christianity simply by substituting God for nature. The effect of this was to regard society as being completely subordinate to divine rule. The theologians still adhered to the organic theory of society according to which each individual was assigned a specific role and status within the state, or body, but now not only was the individual considered to be subordinate to the state, but the state itself was believed to be controlled by divine rule. This rule was constant and immutable because it was perfect. The medieval theologians claimed that their authority was derived from the Church, and it was therefore extremely powerful because it had to be accepted without question. As a result, the societies influenced by Christian theology became very rigid, and a fatalistic attitude was adopted by the individuals within them. This whole period was one in which ideas stagnated, and little progress was made.

The Renaissance and the Reformation

During the four centuries of the Renaissance, the spirit of enquiry, which had for so long been forced to remain dormant, was revitalised. There was a great desire for knowledge and understanding, and much emphasis was placed on the importance of learning. The theory which now developed as an explanation of social behaviour was one based on knowledge and logic. The individual was not moral or good because the society taught him to be good, or because, by being good, he fulfilled his role of enhancing the stability of the state, nor was he good because the Church told him to be good; he was good because it was logical to behave in such a manner, and illogical to behave badly or to be immoral. This view caused the study of politics, or the machinery of government, to become separated from the study of morality. Little attempt was made during this period to investigate the way in which society was organised, but the fanciful organic theories of the Greek and Roman philosophers and the medieval theologians were replaced by more realistic and factual discussion.

The growth of free criticism and individualism in the latter years of the Renaissance period was accompanied in Europe by the emergence of nationalism. This encouraged philosophers to turn their attention once again to a consideration of the structure of society.

It was the Reformation which really provided the necessary stimulus for a complete re-examination of power and authority, and caused the attitude towards spiritual power as opposed to temporal power to be rationalised. Both were acknowledged to have their rightful place within the society, and in the new nation states, the concept of the *Divine Right of Kings* was introduced. The sovereign not only represented the state as the ultimate source of secular authority, but, as God's agent within society, he was also the ultimate source of spiritual authority. The two forces became fused; the king's right to rule was derived from God, and was therefore indisputable. As the king and the state were one and the same—"*L'état c'est moi*" —his power was absolute.

Contributors to Sociological Thought, 1600–1850

THOMAS HOBBES

Thomas Hobbes (1588–1679), the first great English philosopher, was personally involved in the upheavals of the Civil War, and he became intensely interested in politics. He attempted to show in *De Cive* the proper relationship between the Church and the state and the true purpose of civil authority. While he considered it necessary to have an absolute sovereign, he thought that the right to rule should be derived from the consent of those whom the sovereign governed, and not from Divine Right. In his greatest work, *Leviathan*, Hobbes developed his theory of *social contract* as the basis of popular representation embodied in the sovereign. He argued that human beings are naturally selfish, but that knowledge had made them reasonable.

Originally they had been motivated by purely personal appetites and desires, and they were constantly fighting with each other as individuals sought to achieve their own ends. The state of nature was a state of anarchy. However, they had gradually learned the benefits of a peaceful existence, and in order to enjoy these benefits they had been prepared to forgo their separate rights and enter into a contract with an authority which would guarantee to provide and safeguard the security which they desired. In return for providing security, the authority was given absolute power, which the individual had no right to question. In Hobbes's view, the authority could be a king, the state or a parliament; the form it took did not matter so long as it was established by popular agreement.

The value of Hobbes's contribution to sociological thought was enhanced because it paved the way for an entirely new view of social structure. No longer was it believed that power was imposed from above, but instead that it was something that developed from within the society, and was dependent for its existence upon the mutual agreement of the members of that society. Inherent in this theory was the idea of some form of interaction between individuals, which was a possibility that had not been explored previously. Hobbes's approach was still entirely subjective and it was not until the eighteenth century that more objective methods were used in the attempt to understand the nature of society.

The last thirty years of Louis XIV's reign in France was a period of social and political decadence. After his earlier military successes, the tide of fortune turned for Louis and his grandiose schemes brought nothing but defeat and humiliation for the French. The excessive costs of his numerous campaigns virtually bankrupted the country; unemployment and poverty resulted from the extremely high rates of taxation; and even the Church was alienated by his policies. Not only did he offend the Catholics, but the Protestants were persecuted to such an extent that everybody of a humane mind was horrified and disgusted.

This corruption and decadence of absolute government resulted in an upsurge of social philosophy, which had been repressed during the long years of personal or bureaucratic autocracy which France had experienced, but which could now be repressed no longer. Consequently, during the eighteenth century, that country became the centre of political theory and discussion, and Montesquieu was one of the most notable philosophers to emerge.

MONTESQUIEU

Unlike his predecessors, Montesquieu (1689–1755) did not base his reasoning entirely on conjecture, but made a very careful examination of the evidence provided by history about societies. By comparing all the information he collected about different societies and their institutions, he came to the conclusion that they depended for their structure upon the particular conditions under which people lived. Montesquieu mentioned specifically the relationship between the number of people within a society and the nature of its government and institutions. He argued that the relationship between these factors was so close that the structure of any society would change in response to any excessive increase or reduction in the size of population. While he was correct in his observations that family, law, ethics, religion and so on cannot be the same in a very large society as in a very small one, he failed to observe that the decisive factor is not the number of people who are subject to the same authority but the number who are bound together by some kind of relationship. It is now known that if one authority governs a large number of people who are scattered over a very extensive area, the distance between the separate groups will be so great that there will be little or no relationship between them, and their structure will not be affected by the overall size of the population.

Montesquieu mentioned several other conditions which influenced the nature of societies, and commentators have unfortunately tended to place undue emphasis on certain of these aspects of his work. While it is true that he described a relationship between climate and society, he did not, as is commonly thought, reach the conclusion that climate is the factor primarily responsible for producing the characteristics of one society which makes it distinguishable from another. His observations about climate and soil were only a part of his study of the circumstances in which people live, and he examined also the state of the arts, trade, methods of production, national mentality and temperament, long-established customs and habits and political constitutions. Montesquieu considered that all these factors were part of a society's circumstances and had to be mutually adjusted if the social structure were to remain organised and stable.

The publication of Montesquieu's *Esprit des lois* in 1748 made a great impact on sociological thinking. While he defined a law as "the necessary relations arising from the nature of things," which implied that there were certain uncontrollable factors which influenced the structure of any one society, he also showed that societies did not come into existence in an absolute form, but changed as they were influenced by changing circumstances. Once his view that social institutions were liable to change had become widely accepted, the study of society took on a new interest. The desire for knowledge was insatiable, and the second half of the eighteenth century produced many writers who sought to shed more light on the various aspects of social life. Economics, law and politics all provided matter for special investigation and deliberation.

Side by side with the growth of learning about society, rapid strides were being made in the study of the natural sciences. Achievements and discoveries in the fields of mathematics, chemistry and physics were so great that students of the social sciences were prompted to adopt the same method of approach to their own work. As new theories were put forward to explain natural phenomena, so they were taken up and adapted to explain social phenomena, and during the first decades of the nineteenth century more consideration was given to the adaptation of theories than to the development of social science as a separate discipline. The *evolutionist school,* drawing a parallel between physiology and society, which was once again conceived of as an organism, expounded the view that society had developed by stages from savagery through barbarism to civilisation. They similarly argued that each of the social institutions had followed an evolutionary pattern. For example, religion had progressed from idolatry to polytheism and thence to deism, and marriage had evolved from a state of general promiscuity, which had changed to polygamy and finally reached monogamy. From this school of thinking the fanciful *law of the three stages* was handed down to the next generation of social theorists.

AUGUSTE COMTE

Auguste Comte (1798–1857) was much influenced by the law of the three stages, although he attempted to develop the idea by establishing a relationship between intellectual development and social development. He distinguished three stages in intellectual development—the fictive, metaphysical and positive stages—and explained how these were reflected in society.

In the first, the *fictive stage*, man had to come to terms with his physical environment, which was hostile and insecure. Things that he could not understand he explained in terms of some external power beyond human control, and this gave rise to the belief in spirits

and gods. The fictive stage in the development of the intellect cor-
responded with the stage of militarism and savagery in social development. According to the law of the three stages, each stage was
superior to the one which preceded it, so that Comte's *metaphysical*
stage, the second in the development of the intellect, was an advance
on the fictive stage. This second stage was a period of reasoning and
thinking during which the mind was exercised, and the intellect
became more disciplined. No attempt was made to discover universal
laws of nature at this time, because the metaphysicists held that all
things had their own "essences" or inherent truths, and for this
reason everything had to be considered in isolation if that "essence"
were to be revealed. The metaphysical stage produced societies that
were better ordered and less brutal; they were still primarily militaris-
tic, but there was a sense of discipline that had been lacking in the
days of savagery. The third and last stage is reached with the introduction of *positivism* in thinking, and industrialism in society.

It was as the founder of the "positive" movement that Comte
achieved recognition as a philosopher, and, although modern sociologists do not consider his theories as anything other than a series of
interesting speculations, they recognise that he was responsible for
demonstrating the need for an objective, systematic study of society.

Comte chose the word *positive* to indicate the relationship between
the theoretical and the practical aspects of a study, or, as he called
them, the "philosophy" and the "polity," which, he thought, should
never be separated. His ambition was to find a way of linking and
organising all knowledge about the world, man and society into a
consistent whole, so that the basis for a new way of life could be
established. This new way of life would be the result of a *positive
religion*, which had for its creed the love of all humanity whether
past, present or to come, and would bring about complete moral and
social reorganisation.

The aims of positivism, Comte contended, were: to subject all
knowledge to scientific investigation; to extend the fields in which
the scientific method was applied; and to bring together the results
obtained within the separate sciences in order to formulate a single
doctrine. The search for a single doctrine was the important factor
in the positive philosophy, and Comte considered that the necessary
unity was only to be found by science. He divided science into two
categories—the *concrete*, which dealt with definite objects in all their
different aspects, and the *abstract,* which dealt with the general laws
manifested by all the objects within any particular class. Comte also

classified the abstract sciences, and set out a hierarchy based on their dependency upon each other and their increasing complexity. He put them in the following order: mathematics, astronomy, physics, chemistry, biology, sociology.

Sociology was the name devised by Comte for the new science of society which he envisaged, and he believed that social relations are capable of being analysed, interpreted and controlled. He made no direct contribution in the form of new knowledge to the study of society, but demonstrated the need to replace mere speculation about its nature with empirical methods of approach. His philosophy marked a turning point in sociology, and paved the way for a modern, systematic science of society to develop.

The Founding Fathers of Modern Sociology

EMILE DURKHEIM

Emile Durkheim (1858–1917) was born in France of Jewish parents. His father was a rabbi and was anxious for his son to follow the same vocation, but while he was still at school the young Durkheim became very interested in Catholicism. This he later rejected when he became an agnostic and showed that, as well as being a brilliant intellectual, he was also completely independent of traditional philosophical influences.

In 1887 the University of Bordeaux created a lectureship in social science for Durkheim, and while he held this post he continued his struggle to free the study of sociology from the conservatism and prejudice inherent in French academic circles at that time. In this he was greatly influenced by the positivism advocated by Comte, and he devoted much time and thought to formulating rules of sociological research, which he based on his contention that social phenomena are only "things" which have to be observed and investigated objectively. He regarded sociology as a search for causes, which might be discovered from the examination of social phenomena, and he decried the obsession of his predecessors with the need to find some underlying purpose. In this he differed from Comte, who had been content to generalise from history and had not made any precise observations of particular societies or undertaken any field-work to verify his generalisations.

Durkheim was largely preoccupied with the problem of social integration, of discovering what holds societies together, and with establishing the fundamental principles of social solidarity. He gradually reached the conclusion that the structure of any society rests on patterns of behaviour developing from commonly held beliefs and values becoming institutionalised in the social system and being reflected in the personalities of the individual members of the society. The sense of unity which this would provide was referred to by Durkheim as the *conscience collective*, and he indicated by this concept that social solidarity is dependent upon the degree to which individuals feel committed to the society and their willingness to conform to institutionalised behaviour patterns. The actual way in which an individual behaves can be interpreted in terms of the processes by which he adapts himself to the existence of social norms and the sanctions supporting their continuation.

Earlier theorists held the view that the goals of an individual could be traced to some motivation within his personality, and social norms were something outside and apart from individuals to be located in the society as a whole. For this reason, they argued, personal goals and social norms were disconnected and at times liable to conflict. Durkheim, however, believed that this assumption was not viable, and showed that personal goals only become meaningful when they are related to the norms and values of society. This was the reasoning behind his brilliant recognition of the concept of *anomie*, which he explained in his famous *Du suicide,* published in 1897.

An apparent paradox led Durkheim to undertake his study of suicide, a subject which has always proved fascinating to sociologists. The utilitarian theory that a rising standard of living would bring about a general increase in happiness was not supported by the evidence of what was happening in those countries where the standard of living was rising most rapidly. The suicide rate showed a marked rise in these countries, which was concomitant with the change in the standard of living, and Durkheim carried out a detailed statistical analysis in the attempt to explain why suicide rates should vary. He claimed that the suicide rates reflected the integration of individuals within social groups, which, he reasoned, was why the unmarried, the divorced and the widowed are more likely to commit suicide than people who are married. He also claimed that, when some event occurs which upsets the established norms and values of a society, there is a breakdown of the *conscience collective* and the individual finds himself in a state of normlessness, or *anomie*. Durkheim maintained that anomie could exist in times of economic prosperity as well as in times of depression, which explains why suicide rates are higher amongst people in the upper income groups and why they show an increase when the economic cycle is nearing the peak as well as when it nears the depth.

Durkheim left many aspects of anomie still to be investigated, but his formulation of the concept cleared the way to a better understanding of social control. This, when supported by the findings of modern psychology about personality and the motivations underlying conformity and deviance, led to our own greater knowledge of the processes by which social solidarity is established and maintained.

Largely as a result of his work on suicide, and his valuable contributions to the study of society, Durkheim was given the chair of sociology at the Sorbonne in 1902—the chair which had been founded for Auguste Comte. While he was at the Sorbonne, Durkheim investigated the nature of religion in primitive societies, his studies being based on the material provided by observation of the tribes in Central Australia. He did not undertake any field-work himself, but nevertheless produced a very influential work based on the evidence available from other travellers which enabled him to reach the enlightening conclusions he set out in *Les Formes élémentaires de la vie religieuse* (1912). In this book he described society as something "existing exclusively within the minds of individuals," and showed how culture can be separated from simple social environment. Religion, being a cultural phenomenon, can be severed from morality, but where morality becomes a matter of secular ethics rather than a by-product of religion it is necessary for it to be just as deeply rooted and as satisfying. Unless this is so, its value will be diminished as a process by which social integration and solidarity can be achieved. Of special interest in this field was his analysis of religious ritual as a mechanism by means of which social solidarity is reinforced.

More important than this, however, was his work on education. Durkheim was very anxious to promote practical reforms in the French social system, which he felt were necessary because it was fashionable at that time to look, not forwards, but backwards to the period of Descartes and Racine which was regarded as the heyday of France and the century setting a shining example to the country's young people. Durkheim considered that only through education could modern western societies reach a proper understanding that "to be free is not to do what one pleases; it is to be the master of oneself, to know how to act with reason and to fulfil one's duty."

Through his work on education, Durkheim made the first major contribution to the understanding of the processes by which the child becomes socialised. In his *L'Education morale,* he developed his theory about the personal aspects of values and norms by examining the way in which constraint or moral authority is exercised through the conscience of the individual. He clarified further the concept that the moral element in the *conscience collective* is social, and therefore external to the individual; that it arises from values that are shared by the members of the society. By the processes of socialisation, these values are assimilated by new members of the society and gradually become internal in the form of individual consciences. Durkheim contended also that there are subconscious, non-rational components within the structure of personality which are the special mechanisms supporting commitment to these values. These are the mechanisms which counteract any tendencies to deviate.

During the First World War, the last years of his life, Durkheim, like many other intellectuals, became committed, in an academic sense, to the war effort. After the war broke out, he wrote a number of pamphlets which were intended to explain France and the French to outsiders.

For most intellectuals in Western Europe, the war had a stultifying effect, and, unfortunately, Durkheim died before the war ended. His health had been gradually deteriorating for some time, but his death was no doubt hastened by the grief he felt when his son, Pierre, was killed in the Balkans in 1916, and his despair at the seemingly senseless slaughter of so many of his most brilliant and promising young students.

The outstanding achievement of Durkheim's academic career was that, during a very important phase in the development of sociology as a scientific discipline, he was able to penetrate much more deeply into the nature of social integration and solidarity than any of his predecessors. Consequently, he formulated the main principles on which sociologists have been working since his death. Some aspects of his work were undoubtedly crude, and needed a great deal of extension and refinement as new knowledge became available, and other aspects have become obsolete, but this does not render his theories any the less important. They were the foundation stones on which the fruitful study of social integration has since been built.

MAX WEBER

Max Weber (1864–1920) was a contemporary of Durkheim, but had a very different background and upbringing, so that his work developed along rather different lines. Weber was born into a highly cultured German upper-middle-class family. His father was a politician, and an influential member of the Reichstag as a National Liberal. The family lived in Berlin, and Max, who was a brilliant scholar, eventually entered the university there to study law. His attention was, however, fairly soon redirected towards economics, and after a short period, spent in lecturing in law at the University of Berlin, he moved first to Freiburg and then to Heidelberg as Professor of Economics.

Weber's health was very poor, and, after a complete breakdown, he was forced to resign his professorship and spend most of his life as a private student in Heidelberg. Being a semi-invalid, he was unable to do any continuous teaching, and during his most productive years as an intellectual he devoted himself to his personal research.

Although Weber's theoretical work covered a number of different aspects of the social system, and included studies of legal, economic and political institutions, he focused his attention upon religion. He was particularly concerned with the relationships between religious beliefs and practices and other forms of human behaviour, especially behaviour in the economic sphere. His first essay on the sociology of religion, "The Protestant Ethic and the Spirit of Capitalism," posed the questions which he later set out to answer in his comparative studies of the religions of China, India and Judaism. He wanted to discover whether or not beliefs in the supernatural, including God, and practices associated with such beliefs, could materially affect secular social behaviour in general and economic behaviour in particular. In order to do this by means of analysis and comparison, Weber had first to determine which of the factors, economic organisation or religious orientation, would remain constant. He decided that religion was the independent variable.

After making a careful survey, he reached the conclusion that in Europe, China and India the existence of factors likely to favour the development of capitalist systems were approximately the same, so that the fact that the three civilisations displayed very different characteristics might be at least partially attributable to the differences inherent in their religious systems. At no time did Weber suggest that all differences in the development of societies could be explained in terms of differences in their religions, but he attempted to show that religion is at least one causal factor in determining the path along which a society will progress.

Weber was strongly critical of the use of historical methods, which were so widely advocated for the study of the social sciences by many of his contemporaries. He insisted that the problem of causation in the study of society is entirely dependent upon empirical, analytical techniques, as it is in the natural sciences, but, nevertheless, he made use of certain historical conceptions himself. He used a "subjective" approach in his attempts to understand the motives underlying individual behaviour, and suggested that a sociologist might usefully try to analyse how he would behave in the same situation as the individuals concerned. However, he held that it is not necessary to consider everything in terms of individuals, since there are typical behaviour patterns which can be recognised within a society when it is studied as a whole. This led to the formulation of Weber's concept of the *ideal type,* and his more general theory of social behaviour, which would take subjective factors into account.

As well as attempting to explain the behaviour of individuals in terms of the society's ideal types, Weber emphasised the importance of the *cultural complex of meanings.* By this he meant the ways in which social ideals are made realistic for the individual and affect his perception of situations, so that his actions are, in a sense, directed by the society. Weber was really outlining the psychological problems of personal motivation, and trying to show how the interests of the individual, which are primarily responsible for causing him to act in a certain way, could be related to the general system of behaviour within the society. The reasons why Weber emphasised economic activities in his studies are not difficult to comprehend; the relationship between the basic needs of an individual and the steps he takes to satisfy them are of great importance to the basic structure of all societies. Weber's approach was very much a *behavioural* one, and he considered all aspects of the social structure as reflecting different types of social behaviour. This approach has since developed into the *action-theory* method adopted by many sociologists today.

Weber repeatedly argued that, in the development of any social structure, there are numerous stages at which two alternative movements might be made, and in his analysis he sought to explain the differences between these alternatives and the factors responsible for determining which of them was adopted by the society under investigation. By this *differentiation* in the process of social evolution, he indicated not only the different activities which characterise each particular aspect of the total social structure—law, politics, economics, religion—but also the ways in which, within each of these spheres, situations are perceived differently and so produce different types of behaviour.

The concept of *breakthrough* was essential to Weber's understanding of differentiation. At each "turning-point" in a society's development, he suggests, there are two directions in which it could progress. If it were to proceed in one direction, the society would undergo radical changes in the established system, but, if it were to take the other, the existing order would be reinforced. The breakthrough points in social progress are associated with the idea of *charisma*—a word which was not originated by Weber but which has become part of the terminology of sociologists largely as a result of its key role in his theories.

In the sociological sense, charisma refers to the qualities of those who possess, or are believed to possess, powers of leadership either by virtue of exceptional personality or derived from some unusual inspiration such as a magical, divine or diabolic source. Charismatic leadership is, according to Weber, the means by which breakthroughs are achieved in the evolution of society. He was largely concerned with the influence of religion on society, and so regarded prophets as the prototypes of such leaders, although he was careful not to exclude the purely secular leaders from his studies.

Two important points have to be considered in association with the concept of charisma. The first is the role of the individual who first conceives and initiates the breakthrough, and challenges the legitimacy of the established system. Weber contended that at each critical stage in a society's evolution it is possible to pinpoint the person responsible for rejecting the existing system and suggesting an alternative. We do not need to look far for examples of charismatic leaders; Moses and Mohammed, or, more recently, Lenin, Hitler and Mao Tse-tung, are all typical of individuals who have been responsible for changing the course of development of whole societies.

The second point to note is the emotionalism which surrounds charismatic leadership. This is concerned not with the individual as the focal centre of such movements but with the level of commitment to the new ideas which is found in the other members of the society. In other words, a charismatic leader can emerge only if the total situation is one which is conducive to change. Visionaries may be present all the time, but they will be nothing more than "voices crying in the wilderness" unless conditions within the society are such that people will respond emotionally in support of their ideas. Weber said that, in some cases, the emotional fervour and dedication of the members of a society to new ideology can be so intense that it comes very close to being pathological.

Different societies and different institutional elements within a particular society will contain different propensities for change, and will not, therefore, all respond in the same way to a suggestion that they should break away from the established system. Those groups which are strongly conservative and rooted in traditionalism will be most likely to resist "prophetic" movements. Weber instanced peasant groups and feudal systems as cases where the propensity for change is particularly low, because, in different ways, individuals in both these situations identify themselves with the existing order, and have good reasons for wishing to preserve it. Weber laid emphasis on the regularity with which "prophetic" movements have originated in urban communities which are less traditionally biased than rural communities, and he also took care to show that the desire for change does not usually stem from the "underprivileged" strata of society. Protests against the existing order, which are largely associated with disaffection for the political and economic systems, are more likely to be made by members of the middle classes, who, if anything, stand to lose rather than gain should their protests be successful in promoting change. Certainly in our own society, middle-class intellectuals such as the Webbs, Hyndman and Morris were very influential in the early days of the socialist movement which sought to improve the conditions of the working classes, and this could only be achieved at the expense of the upper and middle classes.

To some extent, the very wide range of sociological concepts introduced by Weber make his work difficult to understand. Unfortunately, his untimely death, which occurred when he had reached the peak of his intellectual power, meant that he did not complete all that he had inaugurated in the theoretical field. His eminence as a sociologist has probably been chiefly recognised in the United States, despite the difficulties met with on account of language, which are the greater because Weber used German in a peculiarly individual way. It must be remembered, too, that he was frequently dealing with aspects of human behaviour which were very "near home," and his treatment of the evolution of European society tended to arouse cultural resistance amongst those who recognised themselves in his analysis and felt uncomfortable at what he revealed. Weber lived at a time when many intellectuals were unrealistically optimistic about the future, and seriously thought that social development would always be towards a brighter and progressively better state. Whilst Weber was not the prophet of doom, he was not content either to live in what he would have regarded as a fool's paradise, and he recognised trends in the western world which he considered could lead to radical changes in the very foundations of European civilisation.

Weber, like Durkheim, made a contribution of major importance to the development of sociological theory. Each tended to emphasise different aspects of social life, and together they can rightly be regarded as the founding fathers of modern sociology. Durkheim focused his attention on the factors responsible for integration and solidarity, and tended, therefore, to be mainly concerned with analysing the more static elements in society, whilst Weber was primarily interested in the dynamics of social change. Both approaches are of equal value in any comprehensive study of society, although more attention is possibly paid currently to the problems of progress and change.

Amongst British sociologists at the present time, Weber's influence would appear to be greater than Durkheim's, and there is a tendency for investigations to be directed more towards discovering what is wrong with our society that needs changing than towards studying what is right with it that is worth preserving. In the minds of a great number of laymen in this country sociology is frequently under-stood to be synonymous with socialism, and this demonstrates effec-tively that distortion can become a very real possibility if proper consideration is not given to each aspect. Distortion due to bias of this kind can only be harmful to the standing of a discipline, and may be held partially responsible for the fact that, even today, sociology is still treated with a certain amount of suspicion.

EXERCISE 1

1. In what ways did the Roman philosophers' view of the state differ from that of the Greeks?

2. Explain why Christian societies during the Middle Ages became very rigid and non-progressive.

3. During the eighteenth century France became the centre of social and political discussion. What factors in French society caused this to happen?

4. Why did achievements in the fields of the natural sciences during the first half of the nineteenth century hinder progress in the social sciences?

5. "The philosophy of Auguste Comte marked a turning-point in the history of sociology." Comment upon this statement.
6. Write short notes on the following:
    (a) The "conscience collective."
    (b) Anomie.
    (c) Social isolation.
    (d) Social integration.
7. Explain the reasoning behind Durkheim's argument that society exists "exclusively within the minds of individuals."
8. What do you understand by the "behavioural" method of social theory?
9. Write short notes on Weber's concepts of:
    (a) Breakthrough.
    (b) Alienation.
    (c) Charismatic leadership.
    (d) Differentiation.
10. "At the present time there is a tendency for investigations to be directed more towards discovering what is wrong with our society that needs changing than towards studying what is right with it that is worth preserving." Discuss.
11. Why should *sociology* be so frequently confused with *socialism* in Britain today? How would you distinguish between them?
12. Outline briefly any major perspective in sociological theory (such as functionalism or social behaviourism) and illustrate its use and/or influence. (*A.E.B.*)
13. Comment upon the contribution made by sociology to our understanding of the process of socialisation.

FOR FURTHER READING

Raymond Aron. *Main Currents in Sociological Thought.* Penguin Books, 1968.
George Holland Sabine. *A History of Political Theory.* Harrap, 1963.
Emile Durkheim. *Montesquieu and Rousseau.* University of Michigan, 1960.
Max Weber. *The Theory of Social and Economic Organisation.* English translation, The Free Press, 1947.
Percy S. Cohen *Modern Social Theory.* Heinemann, 1968.
Talcott Parsons. *Sociological Theory and Modern Society.* The Free Press, 1967.
R. K. Merton. *On Theoretical Sociology.* The Free Press, 1967.

CHAPTER II

SOCIOLOGY AS A SCIENCE

Sociology and the Physical Sciences

WHAT IS A SCIENCE?

The definition of science is a simple one; science is knowledge, and all those things about which we are certain, because they have been proved to be true, constitute our stock of knowledge. Although we learn a great deal from experience, it is not necessary, indeed it would not be possible, for us to prove everything for ourselves before it becomes part of our knowledge, but it is necessary for us to be absolutely sure that our sources of information are reliable in order for us to accept what we are told.

If a doctor tells us that it would be dangerous to take more than the prescribed dose of the tablets which he has given us, we know that he is basing his instructions on his own knowledge of the effects of this drug, and therefore we accept what he says. We do not need to experiment ourselves in order to discover if he is right, and it would obviously be very foolish of us to do so.

The possession of knowledge gives us a feeling of security, because it enables us to assess the risks involved in a particular course of action, and to take steps to avoid endangering ourselves. Knowledge is also a comforting thing to have, because it helps to reduce worry and anxiety. If the newspapers carry reports of a particularly brutal murder, the readers may be shocked and disgusted, but they are unlikely to feel afraid, because statistics show that the number of murders committed in Great Britain each year is about 150, so that the chances of any one person out of the population of nearly 55 million being murdered are so slight that they are hardly worth considering. People are reassured by the knowledge that they are unlikely to become the victims of murder themselves.

It is not the known, but the unknown, which causes people to be afraid. To overcome their fears, either individually or collectively, they may become superstitious, or trust in the power of magic and charms to protect them against all those things of which they are unsure and cannot understand. But, as the stock of knowledge is increased, so the need to rely on false notions and misinformation declines.

However, the conclusion should not be drawn from this that there is no value in anything which has not been proved, because, without new ideas, progress would be impossible. Knowledge depends upon ideas, although not all ideas become knowledge. Some ideas, if put into practice, will prove to be true, while others will turn out to be wrong, but, unless we experiment with new ideas, we cannot increase our knowledge.

THE NEED FOR INFORMATION

A very large number of ideas, or theories, may be put forward in an attempt to explain a particular phenomenon, and, in order to discover which of them, if any, is correct, it is necessary to collect information to support them. The scientist is concerned not only with the theory but also with collecting the evidence to prove that the theory is right or wrong. Only when all the evidence is available can this decision be made, and the original theory be accepted or rejected.

The physical scientist is in a much stronger position than the social scientist, because he can usually collect his data and carry out experiments in a laboratory under controlled conditions, but the social scientist has to look much farther afield for his information, and he will probably be unable to experiment. He has to rely upon statistics, observations made during field-work and all the books and papers which he can find relating to the matter which he is studying. The importance of seeking and recording such information was often not realised in the past, so that much historical evidence may be lacking. For all these reasons, the social scientist is often hampered because his information is incomplete, or else it does not prove conclusively that his theory is correct.

Unfortunately, the cost of social research is very high, and in order to keep the expenses down there is always a risk that the sociologist may be urged to make a judgment when, perhaps, he has insufficient evidence to support his theories.

THE PROBLEM OF OBJECTIVITY

Many of the matters with which the social scientist has to deal are those which necessarily arouse strong feelings within us, and to which we can hardly avoid responding emotionally. Not one of us is likely to be completely indifferent when such subjects as sex, crime, racial discrimination or religion are discussed, and, because we so easily become emotionally involved, it is very difficult for us to remain unbiased. It is even more difficult to reach a decision about these things if we do not have sufficient information at our disposal, and, because we are biased, we may be tempted to jump to conclusions. We are all liable to indulge in a certain amount of self-deception, and to delude ourselves into believing something which is untrue: because we are prejudiced, it is sometimes much easier for us to see things as we should like them to be, rather than to face up to reality. Very few drivers seem willing to admit either to themselves or to others that they are anything but experts, and yet there is a great weight of evidence to show that the majority of road accidents are caused by careless or inexpert driving.

The physical scientist's approach to his work is completely impersonal, but the social scientist is studying society, of which he is himself a part. It is difficult for him to remain entirely objective, and it is natural for him to set personal standards by which he assesses the information which he receives. There is always the possibility that he may be able to present his data in such a way that they fit in with his own preconceived notions of what should happen in a particular situation.

One of the biggest problems with which the social scientist is faced, then, is that of being able to hold himself completely aloof, and of ensuring that reality is not being distorted by personal bias or prejudice.

THE APPLICATION OF KNOWLEDGE

In the physical sciences, a great deal of research is undertaken for its own sake. Although the stock of knowledge is thereby increased, little or no importance is attached to the possible practical applications of this new knowledge. This type of work is pure science.

The social scientist is less likely than the physical scientist to consider research worth undertaking unless the knowledge which he discovers can be used as the basis for social engineering; that is, for changing or improving the society. Certainly, a considerable amount of information has been collected by sociologists about primitive societies and about situations which existed in the past which, at first sight, might appear to have no significance at the present time; but with this knowledge we may be in a better position to understand, and to deal with, problems which arise now. In the world at the moment, not all societies have reached the same stage of development, and it is much easier for those which have progressed more rapidly to assist those which are backward, if they are equipped with as much knowledge as possible about such societies.

It has been found that the members of many illiterate and primitive societies are quite ignorant of the connection between sexual intercourse and conception, believing that spirits place babies in their mothers' wombs while they are bathing, or during a propitious shower of rain and so on. Giving contraceptive advice and appliances to the backward peoples of India, where such beliefs are widely held, is therefore unlikely to prove very effective in reducing the birthrate, and much money would be wasted in any such attempt. However, the knowledge of their beliefs shows that the first and essential step which must be taken, if the birth-rate is to be controlled, is that of teaching the people concerned the true facts about conception. If this can be done, they can afterwards be taught how to use contraceptives with some hope of success.

THE SELECTION OF MATERIAL

A very large amount of the knowledge which has been accumulated by sociologists consists of description based on observation, or derived from statistics obtained by making surveys, but, because the social scientist's field of study is so wide, and the material available for description is so diverse, he could easily collect a large volume of information which may have relatively little value. Unless he selects very carefully from amongst the numerous possibilities the subject-matter which he sets out to describe, he may waste a great deal of time and energy producing an amorphous mass of data which is nothing more than a collection of unrelated facts and figures.

Scientific research has to be well organised and systematic, so that its limits must first be clearly defined.

THE IMPORTANCE OF OBSERVING CORRECTLY

Once the sociologist has selected the material he wishes to study, it is necessary for him to observe correctly, and to do this he will need training. Although an amateur may well be able to select his subject-matter and to describe it clearly, it is likely that he will make mistakes that a trained observer can avoid, and which would reduce considerably the value of his work. He will probably choose to study something in which he is particularly interested personally, so that he will have difficulty in remaining completely objective, and he is also likely to be unaware of the extent to which he is influenced by his own feelings, so that his observation may well be biased. If he sets out to find the answer to a question with a preconceived idea of what that answer should be, it is probable that he will, quite unwittingly, notice those things which show his idea to have been right, and he may minimise the importance of, or even overlook completely, those things which contradict it.

Two independent accounts of the same phenomenon may differ considerably if they are made by people with different attitudes and values. The description of a day in the hunting-field given by an enthusiastic huntsman would, in all probability, be very different from that given by a member of an anti-blood-sports association, and yet both accounts might be accurate.

OPINION AND FACT

Whether he is studying biology or some aspect of society, the scientist must record his observations in such a way that they can be checked to ensure that they are correct. However much information he may collect, it can only be regarded as scientific if he sets it out so that it can be verified by others. There is a great difference between stating an opinion and making a statement of fact, and it is the factual statement which is scientifically valid.

If I say, "The number of prisoners who escaped from gaol increased alarmingly during the last year," that is simply expressing an opinion, since the word "alarmingly" cannot be measured or verified. Would-be gaol-breakers might, in fact, consider the same increase "encouraging." If, however, I say, "The number of prisoners who escaped from gaol in 1965 was 503 and the number who escaped in 1966 was 692, which represents an increase of 37.7 per cent," I am stating a fact, which can be verified.

HOW PERMANENT IS KNOWLEDGE?

Much of the search for scientific knowledge has been concerned with the attempt to discover laws which are everywhere applicable at all times: the so-called universal laws of nature. The physical scientist can repeat the same experiment as many times as he wishes in order to test his theories, and the knowledge which he acquires as a result is lasting, because he is dealing with constants. On the other hand, the social scientist is dealing with phenomena which are subject to change, and, despite what is commonly said, history does not repeat itself, although some events may be similar. No two revolutions, for example, are ever exactly alike, although there may be certain features which are common to some or all such incidents. For this reason, the social scientist may often be unable to generalise, or to provide us with a complete explanation of the phenomena which he is studying. He may be able to show why certain kinds of things are likely to happen, but he may not be able to explain why specific things actually do.

Some sociological knowledge can be generally applied, because it seems to be true of all kinds of society at all times throughout history. The society does not exist where wealth and power are equally divided, or where some form of class distinction is unknown. However, other knowledge is limited in its application, because it is not always true in all situations. While we know that a large number of young offenders are the children of broken marriages, this does not mean that all children whose parents have separated will become criminals. We can say only that these children are more "at risk" than the children of united parents.

Even though sociological knowledge sometimes has only a limited application, it is not rendered useless, and, as the store of such knowledge is increased, more general laws may be discovered.

THE COMPLEXITY OF SOCIAL PHENOMENA

The work of the social scientist is often complicated by the fact that he is seeking to establish a relationship between two or even more social phenomena. He might set out to show that the average age at which people marry in a certain society has lowered during a given period of time. He can do this by collecting all the relevant statistics, and writing a straightforward description, which would provide us with some interesting facts. It is likely, however, that he will wish to go further than this, and try to find out why the people within this society are getting married at an earlier age than their parents.

In the attempt to establish relationships, there is always a danger of over-simplifying explanations, and seeking only one cause for a particular phenomenon. Social phenomena are not usually simple, though, and their causes are likely to be many and various, although some will be more significant than others. The sociologist studying the age at which people marry may find that the factors influencing this are biological, economic and psychological, and each of these factors is, in its own turn, not necessarily constant. If it is found that the main influence on the age of marriage is economic, this may well be due not only to a general rise in the incomes of young people, but also to a change in the society's attitude towards buying on credit, to the availability of more comprehensive benefits under the social security schemes, which reduce the necessity to make provision personally for unforeseen emergencies, to improvements in contraceptive techniques which enable young people to marry without expecting to incur the expense of becoming parents within the first year, and to the progressive emancipation of women which allows the young bride to contribute financially to the partnership.

COINCIDENCE AND CORRELATION

That there is a relationship between two variables may be indicated if it is found that there is a proportionate and simultaneous variation in them both, but thorough investigation is necessary in order to ascertain whether or not these variations are purely coincidental, or to establish that there is a causal connection between the phenomena. For example, we know that each year there is an increase in the number of students entering British universities, and each year too there is an increase in the number of eggs that are consumed in this country, but we should not deduce from this that eating eggs causes students to go to university, or that going to university causes people to eat eggs. On the other hand, if we find that during a period of time there is an increase in cigarette smoking, and, during the same period, there is also an increase in the incidence of lung cancer, we may suspect that the two phenomena are related. If after careful investigation, cigarette smoke is found to contain carcinogens, then we may fairly safely assume that cigarette smoking is a contributory cause of lung cancer. However, we may also have evidence to show that the incidence of lung cancer amongst smokers is higher in densely populated industrial areas than it is in rural areas, and that some non-smokers in both these areas contract the disease, which suggests that smoking is not the only cause of cancer, and we must then continue our investigations to find out what the other causes are.

Correlation should not be confused with causality. There may be a relationship between two, or more, phenomena without that relationship being a causal one. Two phenomena, which may be directly related to each other, such as an increase in the consumption of beer and a larger number of cars on the road, may share common causal factors so they are not completely independent. In this case, both phenomena are reflections of a general increase in prosperity, as well as of an increase in the size of the population. Although neither of them is a cause of the other, there is a correlation between them; they are linked, albeit indirectly.

Even if we are able to establish a causal relationship between two phenomena we may sometimes have difficulty in finding which of them is the cause and which is the effect, because this may not always be obvious. It would be absurd, when considering the relationship between cancer of the lung and smoking, to suggest that having cancer causes people to smoke, as, in this case, cause and effect are easily distinguishable. If we were to consider the relationship between a change in moral standards and the illegitimacy rate, it might not be immediately possible to determine whether a more permissive attitude within the society causes the illegitimacy rate to increase, or whether a continuous rise in the illegitimacy rate eventually causes the society to become less rigid in its attitude.

THE USE OF WORDS

For the purposes of general, everyday life, people with shared backgrounds and experiences are unlikely to have much difficulty in understanding each other, although we must all have been aware, on occasions, that what we have said has been misunderstood or "taken the wrong way," and there are times when we have to indulge in quite lengthy explanations, or to use analogies and comparisons, before we are satisfied that other people understand what we are trying to convey. Sometimes the fact that common speech is rather imprecise can be an advantage, because it enables us to make statements which are deliberately ambiguous.

In order to communicate with other people, we use words. Nouns are words which refer to things, and when we use a noun it is not necessary for us to point to the thing in order to convey what we mean. We should not, in any case, be able to do this if we are using an abstract noun. However, it is because words are referents that we cannot always be certain that other people understand precisely what we mean by them. People often have differing referents for the same word. The noun "house," for example, refers to a building in which people live, and, although no one is likely to confuse a house with a car, it may well be that for some the word conjures up a mental image of a large mansion, for others that of a semi-detached, three-bedroomed villa, and for yet others that of a middle-of-terrace dwelling with two rooms upstairs and two downstairs. Each person is likely to think first of his own house when the word is used.

It can be seen, therefore, that even when concrete nouns are used people have very different referents, which are largely based on their own knowledge and experience, but the problem of referents becomes much greater when abstract nouns are used to convey concepts and ideas. Our understanding of abstract nouns is very much influenced by personal attitudes and values, and the meaning we attach to words such as poverty, fascism, family, stability and morality may differ considerably from the meaning attached to them by somebody else.

The sociologist, being mostly concerned with abstract, as opposed to concrete, phenomena, must be careful to make clear what he means by the words he uses. If his work is to be accepted as scientific, he must define his terms, so that other people can be sure that their referents are the same as his.

THE NEED FOR A DISTINCTIVE VOCABULARY

Unlike other scientists, sociologists are sometimes hampered because they have no vocabulary of their own, and with few exceptions all the words which they use in connection with their work are borrowed from our everyday language. Because there is no distinctive terminology at their disposal, social scientists often have to adapt these borrowed words to suit their particular purpose, and it sometimes happens that a different connotation is given to the same word by different sociologists, or that different words are used to convey identical ideas.

Physical scientists, too, borrow many words from common speech, but they have overcome the possibility of confusion by assigning arbitrary definitions to these words, so that there is no opportunity for questioning their precise meaning. Horses and candles are no longer our chief sources of energy and light, and a man's foot is no longer considered a reliable gauge of length, but "horse-power," "candle power" and "foot" have all been accorded precise mathematical meanings, so that the terms which were originally used as somewhat rough and ready measurements can now be used to convey exact information.

Sociologists have, from time to time, attempted to produce a dictionary of concise definitions. As early as 1905, in the United States, Small produced a glossary containing forty-eight concepts and terms which he considered to be the terminology of the social sciences, and in 1931 Professor Eubank, in *The Concept of Sociology*, compiled a list of 332 such terms and concepts, but found himself bound to comment that:

"The very extent of such a list as this is confusing; but it is indicative of an underlying confusion that is still more significant. It reveals strikingly how far the sociologists are from agreement upon the very terminology itself. The youth of this science is nowhere more clearly shown than in the indefiniteness and lack of uniformity of its vocabulary."

Eubank examined the works of ten leading American sociologists, and tabulated lists of concepts and terms which each used. There was a total of 146, but of the total only 63 were used by more than one sociologist, and not one of the terms was used by all ten.

Much more recently, a *Dictionary of the Social Sciences* was compiled under the auspices of UNESCO, and was published in Great Britain in 1964. The stated aim of the Secretariat of UNESCO was to "find synthetic scientific definitions that would constitute a common denominator to the different usages" of sociological terms and concepts, but the editors, in their preface, remarked upon the difficulties of compiling a volume of this nature. So often the views of the contributors were at variance, and in some instances it was found necessary to express a number of different views on single items.

Sociologists have invented very few words of their own, although they quite frequently coin words—something which tends to arouse feelings of suspicion, or even of amusement, in outsiders—but coined words are generally no more precise than those from which they are derived, so that they contribute very little to the development of a special phraseology.

John Madge suggests in his book *The Tools of Social Science* that although:

"The failure of social scientists to mend their ways, and their inability to emulate the 'exact' definitions of natural science, are often regarded as yet further signs of the backwardness of social science ... the straining after scientific precision may not be as important and rewarding as at first appears."

The lack of a distinctive terminology may sometimes present problems, but these problems are not major stumbling-blocks capable of impeding all progress in the field of sociology. This science has now been established for a sufficiently long period, and has achieved so much, that it might well prove a waste of valuable time and effort to devote too much attention at this stage to constructing a language for the use of professional sociologists.

How Scientific is Sociology?

We are now in a position to consider the question, "Is sociology a science?" and this can best be decided if we apply the same criteria as

those which can be used to test the scientific nature of any study:
(*a*) the reliability of its knowledge, (*b*) its organisation and method,
and (*c*) the extent to which its knowledge is capable of being
generalised.

THE RELIABILITY OF ITS KNOWLEDGE

Sociology, if compared with physics or chemistry, is a relatively new
discipline. For this reason, its stock of reliable knowledge is as yet
somewhat limited, although it is being increased all the time, and
in some areas of study a great deal of progress has been made in a
comparatively short period. For example, we now know a great deal
about human relations and its importance not only to the world at
large but, more especially, to industry. It is really only during the
last twenty years that the term "human relations" has been in general
use, and attention has been paid to establishing the relationships
between the mental attitude of the worker—his adjustment to those
with whom he works, to authority and to his actual job—and his
efficiency and productivity.

Science and technology have both advanced so rapidly that an
increasing sense of urgency has been given to the work of the sociologist, as people are continually having to deal with the new or
changing conditions which result from these advances. Elton Mayo,
whose book, *The Social Problems of an Industrial Civilization,* was
published in 1945, summed up the situation when he said: "The
consequences for society of the unbalance between the development of
technical and of social skill have been disastrous." Since this book
first appeared, considerable progress has been made in sociological
research, but, unfortunately, there is still a strong body of opinion
which, though in favour of spending money on investigating scientific
and technical phenomena, which produces tangible results, at the
same time fails to understand the need for parallel research into the
social repercussions of scientific and technological advances.

There still remains a very wide gulf between the amount of knowledge which has been accumulated in the fields of the physical sciences
and technology and that which pertains to the social sciences, but
this gap is gradually being narrowed.

ITS ORGANISATION AND METHOD

We generally assume that any discoveries made by primitive
peoples were purely accidental or were the results of very hit-or-miss
experiments. Today the methods used by scientists of all kinds are

much less wasteful, and are usually much quicker to yield the answers which are being sought. This is because the knowledge already in existence has been organised in such a manner that it is not simply an amorphous mass of data, but a collection of factual information in which relationships between one part of the information and other parts have been established. Once relationships and inter-relationships have been found, it is possible to use existing knowledge as the basis for further investigation and experiment, so that progress in increasing knowledge becomes more rapid and, probably, easier.

Within the sphere of sociology, the collection of information and its subsequent organisation have been undertaken in a relatively short time in comparison with that of the physical, and even the technical, sciences, but, now that the need for more knowledge has been generally recognised, the way is clear for advances. More reliable methods are being devised for collecting information which, not so long ago, defied systematic investigation, and, as sociologists increase their stock of knowledge, it becomes possible to organise it more efficiently.

THE GENERALISATION OF KNOWLEDGE

The knowledge acquired by physical scientists is applicable at all times, and, as a result, so-called "universal laws" have been established. Very little of the social scientist's knowledge can be applied so generally, since he is dealing, not with constants, but with variables, and it is for this reason that sociology is commonly considered to be less scientific than chemistry, physics or mathematics. It would, however, be foolish to dismiss sociology as being unscientific on these grounds alone, and the possibility always exists that, as the stock of knowledge is increased, a greater number of general laws will be discovered.

EXERCISE 2

1. By what standards is it possible to decide whether or not a study is scientific?

2. A scientist is concerned not only with the formulation of theories but also with collecting information to support them. Why is a physical scientist in a stronger position when he requires information than a social scientist?

3. Why is it difficult for a social scientist to remain entirely objective in his approach? Why is it important to adopt an objective approach in any scientific study?

4. What is meant by a "causal relationship"? How might *correlation* be confused with *causality*?

5. Social scientists are sometimes hampered because they have no vocabulary of their own. Explain the advantages of a distinctive terminology to a scientific discipline.

6. "The consequences for society of the unbalance between the development of technical and of social skill have been disastrous" (Elton Mayo). Discuss.

7. How does knowledge gained about primitive societies and situations which existed in the past help us to understand and deal with problems which arise in the present?

8. Explain why the high costs of social research might adversely affect the results obtained.

9. It has frequently been suggested that sociologists waste a great deal of time trying to justify their existence as scientists, and that they are unduly sensitive to suggestions that their work is less scientific than chemistry, physics or mathematics. Do you consider it necessary or valuable to compare the social sciences with the natural sciences?

10. Examine the similarities and differences between sociology and *two* of the following: history, psychology, economics. (*A.E.B.*)

11. Examine some of the problems involved in applying the perspectives of science to the study of societies. (*A.E.B.*)

12. Can sociology properly be described as a science? (*Oxford*)

FOR FURTHER READING

J. Madge. *The Origins of Scientific Sociology*. Tavistock, 1963.
P. Berger. *An Invitation to Sociology*. Penguin Books, 1971.
D. Willer. *Scientific Sociology: theory and method*. Englewood Cliffs, 1967.

CHAPTER III

THE NATURE AND SCOPE OF SOCIOLOGY

The Field of Study

It is not difficult to define "sociology," and compilers of dictionaries obviously have no qualms when they include such snappy definitions as "the study of human society," but it is questionable how many of them pause to consider the implications of so simple a statement.

Ideally, sociology has to deal with the whole scope of human activities and relationships; with the reasons for them and their consequences; with the rules and regulations by which they are organised and controlled; indeed, with all the numerous and infinitely varied aspects of the behaviour of man in society. Any sociologist, undertaking such a study, would be faced with a task of such gigantic proportions that he would find himself quite overwhelmed, probably even before he started it. His first problem would be that of deciding where to begin, and, even if he managed to reach a decision on this point, he would quickly discover that the possibilities of such a study are so great that his task would never be completed, and such a discovery is enough to prove a very strong deterrent to progress.

To be of value, then, the scope of sociology has to be limited, although the focal purpose of studying human society has to be retained. How can this limitation be achieved?

Sociologists, faced with the need to set a limit to the scope of their field of study, have answered this question in two different ways, and this has given rise to somewhat divergent schools of thought. German sociologists, at the beginning of the century, amongst whom Max Weber was a notable exponent of the "behaviourist" concept of sociology, sought to confine their studies to certain clearly defined aspects of human behaviour, and to make a distinction between sociology and other social studies.

Weber considered that the aim of sociology is to interpret or explain social behaviour, and he defined social behaviour as deliberate activity carried out by an individual or a group which is occasioned by and refers to the behaviour of others. Interactions which are brought about by chance or accident, in which people are involved without any consideration of each other's behaviour, do not constitute social

behaviour by this definition, so that a very large part of the field
of human relations is necessarily excluded. Weber held that, if the
motives behind intentional activity of this kind were discovered and
understood, it was possible to generalise about social behaviour, and
to formulate sociological laws, and he attached much importance to
establishing a general method of sociology by which all social entities
could be explained in terms of predictable types of behaviour. By this
means, he thought, sociology could justifiably be regarded as a valuable empirical study of society, and by it sociologists would be able
to avoid personification of social groups, which he decried as anathema
to good sociological method. Weber considered that the historical or
inductive study of actual societies was only of interest in so far as it
served to illustrate particular types of social behaviour.

While it is apparent that the investigation of these forms of social
relationships must play a valuable part in sociological enquiry, such
a narrow delimitation of sociology will give rise to a somewhat barren,
theoretical discipline, which will yield little knowledge or assistance
to progress unless its manifestations in everyday life are also followed
in detail.

This should lead us to the conclusion that the scope of sociology is
too great for the subject to be defined as a specialism in the way that
the behaviourists defined it, and this was the conclusion reached by
the second, more widely acceptable, school of thought. Sociologists
in this school regard the study of human society as an encyclopaedic
study, which allows for specialisation within the general field. It is
a well-established fact that all aspects of social life are closely linked
and interwoven, so that societies must be studied as wholes, and no
one part selected for particular attention, since any change in one
part will necessarily affect all the others. For obvious reasons, sociologists will be forced to specialise in the aspect of society which
interests them most, but they must be aware that they are studying,
not the whole of sociology itself, but a small part of it; for example,
the sociology of education, of religion or of industry.

Sociology does not differ from any other science in this respect.
It seems incredible today that there was once a time when a clever
man could acquire all the knowledge that had been accumulated
about everything, but, as the general stock of knowledge increased
through the ages, separate disciplines came to be marked off from
the original science—philosophy—and, as these disciplines developed
their knowledge, they too became subdivided in their turn. Nowadays
a man may call himself a chemist, a physicist or a mathematician,

but he will be a specialist in only a part of the field of chemistry, physics or mathematics, and, apart from his awareness of the underlying principles of the general science, he will have a detailed knowledge only of his own chosen aspect of it.

The Functions of Sociology

An important function of the general science of society is to analyse and classify the different types of social relationships which give rise to phenomena such as institutions and associations. In co-operation with each other, individuals have greater chances of survival and perpetuation, which is why societies are formed. Although superficially individuals may appear to differ greatly, fundamentally they are the same, since they are motivated by the same desires and appetites. Human beings express their nature by creating and re-creating organisations which will affect their social relationships, or behaviour based on mutual awareness, in a myriad ways. Such expression is the fulfilment of every condition of life, and provides the basis for the organisation of authority and power, of usage and procedure. However, sociology does more than the investigating of social relationships of this type. It also seeks to determine the relationship between the different elements of social life. There is, for example, a close link between the political and economic systems, and between moral and religious and legal systems, and sociology will attempt to establish and explain exactly what these relationships are.

Another, and even more ambitious, function is to discover the fundamental factors governing continuity and change in social life, so that universally applicable sociological laws may be established, and so that the science may progress, if possible, from one which has to rely on rudimentary empirical generalisation, which, while being useful, cannot be wholly satisfactory.

Last, but by no means least, sociology has to bring together the findings of the other specialisations within the social field such as history, economics, politics and anthropology, to relate them to each other, and to consider the concepts underlying the whole of life in society—concepts which are likely to be disregarded by the specialists unable to see the wood for the trees.

Sociological Concepts

As we have already seen, difficulties have arisen because sociologists do not have their own distinctive terminology. For this reason, it will be useful at this stage to devote some space to defining the sociological terms that we shall be employing, so that there will be less chance of confusion later.

SOCIETY

This is obviously the broadest and most inclusive term, and it is used to cover the whole network of human relationships which result from individuals coming together in response to their basic urges towards self-preservation. Society is based on the desire in man to live in company with his fellows, but this does not mean that this is his natural state, as many writers contend. Solitary confinement is certainly a very dire form of punishment, but this is not because the social desire is innate but because it is instilled and acquired during early life. Only a potentiality to be socialised is inborn.

Some sociologists have tried to limit the term "society" so that it includes only organised relationships, and excludes all those which are not obviously structured or brought about by recognisable associations and unions. While it would be quite impossible for sociologists to study all the numberless haphazard personal relationships which occur, we must remember that social organisations develop from casual relationships in the first place, so that logically they cannot be ignored.

Again, other sociologists have tried to restrict the meaning of "society" in a different way. They hold that "society" implies mutual awareness and a sense of belonging together, but again this appears to be taking too limited a view. Indirect relationships are in many cases just as important as those which are direct. The lives of all of us may often be seriously affected by things or actions over which we have no proper control, and sometimes by factors of which we have no proper knowledge, but all of which occur because man seeks man in order to survive.

If we disregard these attempts to restrict the concept, and use the term "society" in its widest sense, we shall include all relationships which arise because man is a social creature, and accept that "society" has no definable limits.

We must, however, make a distinction between the evasive and unbounded properties of society in general and "a society." "A society" is a collection of individuals who are joined together by relationships, or patterns of behaviour, which distinguish them from other individuals who do not share these relationships, or who have different patterns of behaviour; it is an organisation of mutually adapted personalities.

An important aspect of a society is the idea of reciprocity, or give and take, because a society is founded not only on the awareness of likenesses but also on the awareness of differences. This fact not only gives rise to the development of different societies, but is responsible, too, for the divisions which occur within a particular society.

The physical basis of a society is an aggregate, but integration of the individuals within an aggregate into a society takes place at the psychological level. An essential factor in the formation of a society is the persistence of the aggregate in time, because only by such persistence is a social consciousness developed. A crowd of people attending a football match may develop a common response to a particular set of stimuli, but, once the game is over, the crowd will break up, and there will be nothing left. Alternatively, a number of people may be brought together in just such a haphazard way, and, if the aggregate is then isolated for a time from contacts with other people through some quirk of circumstance, then common interests and methods of living and working together will emerge, so that the members will begin to develop into a society.

Psychological integration is never so complete as that which is achieved at the physical level by an organism. Individual organisms of the same group will always react in exactly the same way when they are subjected to the same stimuli, but, however high the degree of integration within a society, the reactions of its members will always remain on the individual level. For example, if a society is faced with some calamity such as an earthquake or a flood, all the members may feel frightened, but the manifestation of their fear will take many forms.

A society is incapable of producing an idea; ideas remain the property of individuals.

Two major factors are involved in the transformation of an aggregate into a society: the organisation of behaviour and the development of social consciousness. The beginnings of these are to be found in the division of labour and those activities which are essential to the group's welfare. At first, there may be no conscious recognition or direction, and individuals may proceed on a trial-and-error basis until some acceptable pattern is established. As the division of labour continues, members of the group will become increasingly interdependent, and as this happens organised patterns of behaviour will emerge. With this emergence, a social consciousness will come into existence.

SOCIAL CONSCIOUSNESS

The existence of social consciousness is an essential element in a society, because it ensures the common emotional responses of the members. It is the factor which can cause an individual to sacrifice his own personal inclinations and selfish interests for the good of the whole, and will make certain that he carries out essential activities and fulfils necessary responsibilities, even when there is nobody supervising him or forcing him to do so. This emotional unity is sometimes referred to as the *"esprit de corps."*

A crowd may sometimes display spontaneously a violent form of this emotional response, as when demonstrators turn on the police without any directions being given if one of their number is roughly handled, but this is a purely transitory response. In a much less noticeable form, emotional unity is found in a society, because individuals who are co-operating with each other over a period of time develop common emotional responses.

In our society, we have practised a monogamous form of marriage for many generations, and a well-established pattern of emotions has developed in conjunction with this system. If it were to be suggested now that we should practise a polygamous form of marriage instead, the common emotional response would be one of aversion and disgust.

This does not mean that new ideas can never be introduced into a society. In many instances the process begins with the acceptance of a new idea by a small group, which is followed by a gradual passing on of the idea to the rest of the society, and it sometimes happens that many individuals will refuse to accept it. The recent discussion about capital punishment in Britain provides us with a good example of this type of partial acceptance by a society. Only a minority of the population of Britain accept that capital punishment is abhorrent and unnecessary, and there are still large numbers of people who would like to see the decision to abolish it reversed. On the other hand, when the idea of the welfare state was first conceived, many people disliked it, but if they were to be asked now to revert to the previous system they would dislike this idea equally as much.

Such behaviour as this clearly indicates that, however strongly a society is integrated, there is no such thing as a "mind of society." While an individual may be dominated and influenced by the society in which he lives, he is not extinguished by it, and he always retains the capacity to change his social environment.

GROUPS

These are collections of people who enter into distincti
ships with each other, because they are in regular cont:
munication, and groups possess a structure which can be
There are many different types of group, reflecting numerous and
varied aspects of social life, and they may be classified in several ways
according to size, persistence, the manner in which they were formed,
the systems by which they are organised and so on.

Not every collection of individuals will form into a group, because
there exist certain segments in a society which, although their members are interested in the same pursuits or indulge in similar patterns
of behaviour, have no recognisable structure. Such collections as
these are sometimes referred to as "quasi-groups," and these aggre-
gates of people are the portions of a society from which the members
of proper groups will be recruited. Social classes provide a good
example of quasi-groups, as does any collection of people who have
common aims and interests, who share certain modes of behaviour, or
who have similar physical or intellectual characteristics. Like proper
groups, quasi-groups vary greatly. They differ according to size,
and in the degree of cohesion within them, which also means that
some have a greater potential to form into proper groups than
others.

COMMUNITIES

The actual population which occupies a given area is referred to as
a community, and the members of a community will be bound to
each other by a shared system of rules and regulations which control
their relationships with each other. Communities can exist within
larger communities, and a society is made up of groups of communities, each of which inhabits a certain area.

Although an individual can live the whole of his life within a community, there is no such thing as a self-contained community within
society today, because no community can exist which does not have
relationships with the rest of society.

Communities come into being to satisfy the varying needs of the
individual.

ASSOCIATIONS

Associations are formed in response to the particular needs of
a community, and they comprise groups of individuals who are
organised for the achievement of a common purpose. They may be

deliberately planned, or may form as the result of environmental pressure which more or less forces men to co-operate with each other. Trade unions, agricultural associations and choirs or drama groups are examples of social entities of this type.

An association may have a great deal of power, which its individual members acting alone could not hope to possess, and it is able to operate in a distinctive way; a way which is often different from that in which its members operate. If we consider a group of farmers who form an association for the purpose of pooling their funds in order to buy expensive capital equipment which they can all share, we will see that, whereas each farmer acting alone will have to use whatever machinery he can afford, and will be forced to make do with implements that are old-fashioned and inefficient, by joining others like himself he will be able to enjoy the advantages of much more labour-saving modern equipment.

The existence of associations presupposes the existence of institutions, since one cannot exist without the other, and the two concepts are so closely linked that in everyday parlance they are frequently confused. However, it is important that we should understand the distinction between them.

INSTITUTIONS

An institution may be defined as the established practices and usages which govern the relationships between individuals or groups, or the established forms or conditions of procedure which are characteristic of group activity.

Institutions are formed and maintained by communities and associations, which could not function without them. For example, the Church is an institution; it is the set of established procedures and usages which regulates the relationship between individuals in terms of practising their religion.

The reason why institutions are commonly confused with associations is that both terms are frequently used with reference to the same phenomenon, but the term "institution" should properly be used in an abstract sense, while the word "association" should be used in a more concrete sense with reference to the people who have joined together to form it. If we consider again the example of the Church, we can see that in the first sense it is an institution, but the same word is also used with reference to a group of people, or a congregation, who associate with each other in order to give expression to their religious beliefs.

Similarly, marriage is an institution, if we think of it in the abstract sense that it is the system by which sexual relationships are controlled and regulated within a society, but in the "concrete" sense it is also an association between the partners involved in the union.

SOCIAL STRUCTURE

Social structure consists in part of all those relationships which are person to person, or *dyadic*. The kinship structure of any society is based on relationships such as those which exist between husband and wife, father and son, or, in many primitive societies, the relationship between maternal uncle and nephew.

Another factor which determines social structure is the differentiation of individuals and groups according to their roles or status—royalty and commoners, masters and servants, employers and employees, teachers and students, etc., are all features of the structural system. Any one person may have many roles—citizen, businessman, husband, father, treasurer of his golf club and so on—and these may change during his lifetime, but the total number of roles at any given moment gives him a recognised status within society. We can only study persons in connection with the social structure, and social structure cannot be studied except in terms of the persons who are the units of which it is composed.

Differentiation is the result of division of labour, and is an essential ingredient in the formation of a social structure, which comes into being and persists by means of a complex mechanism, of which law, morals and government are all a part. These are not disconnected phenomena, but all depend upon and influence the relationships between persons and groups.

Social structure is not static, although the actual form which it takes may remain constant over a very lengthy period, and any changes which take place within its framework will only have a very gradual effect on the structure itself. However, a particular event such as a revolution or a war may serve to bring about an abrupt and violent change.

SOCIAL SYSTEMS

The sum total of all the *ideal patterns of behaviour* within a society makes up its social system.

Ideal patterns of behaviour are generally quite distinct from actual behaviour, and form part of the culture of a society to be handed down from one generation to the next. These ideal patterns serve as a guide to the society in its attempts to train the individual, and also guide the individual if he has to cope with a situation for which he had not been trained specifically. Ideal patterns are, as it were, "precedents" to which reference may be made if necessary.

These ideal patterns gather around them a stock of emotionalisms, and so, despite the great disparity which often exists between them and overt behaviour, a society will be reluctant to discard the ideal for the actual and approve new patterns. In our own society, we hold rigidly to the ideal behaviour which we expect from relationships between the sexes, and frown upon sexual intercourse between couples who are not married, so we turn a blind eye towards all the promiscuous and extra-marital relationships which we cannot deny exist.

A "permissive" society is one in which the overt behaviour has become so far divorced from the ideal that the social system has really undergone a radical change, although the members of that society refuse to acknowledge the fact.

The many and varied activities which are carried out in society each have their own prescribed pattern of behaviour, which serves as a model for the participants, and these patterns are genuine entities which can be studied separately. However, individuals have to act within more than one pattern at the same time in the course of everyday life, so that these patterns as wholes have to be adjusted to each other, otherwise individuals will find that conflicting demands are made upon them, and a great deal of confusion will result.

However close the adjustment between various patterns may be, the possibility of conflict can never be entirely ruled out, and some form of compromise has generally to be reached. This compromise is made easier to achieve because, as we have seen, overt behaviour often differs considerably from the ideal. Thus it is possible in our society for a man whose religion requires him to lead a life of loving kindness and self-sacrifice to be accepted as a good Christian and also as a successful businessman, even though, in the sphere of economics and commerce, personal ambition is much admired, and, to achieve his success, he may have to be completely ruthless.

All the prescribed patterns, then, which control life within a society form its social system, but the members of a society are usually quite unaware that their behaviour constitutes part of a prescribed pattern; they act mainly by habit, as they have been taught to act, without stopping to think first.

Very occasionally, social systems are brought into being as the result of conscious social planning, but social planners always are faced with the problem that the individuals who are to form the new society have already been trained by, and have become adjusted to, another society, and have therefore accumulated a wealth of unconscious habits which may be incompatible to the new system. Such habits are capable of being changed if the new system offers, in exchange, patterns which can be easily assimilated, and which are not too much at variance with those with which the individuals are familiar. If such patterns do not exist, individuals may revert to those of the societies from which they have been drawn, and they will then form themselves into cliques in order to preserve their own system, so that they will not become completely integrated.

CULTURE

The behaviour of an individual is composed of three parts: behaviour which is instinctive and of biological origin, behaviour which is the result of personal experience, and is gained by solving problems without guidance or assistance, and behaviour which is learnt from others. This learnt behaviour includes ideas, techniques and habits which are passed on from one generation to another, and which are virtually a set of solutions to problems that, in the course of time, others have met and solved before. This learnt behaviour, or social inheritance, is what is called *culture*.

Because human beings have a great ability to transmit what they have learnt to others, they are capable of developing a number of behaviour patterns which are just as recognisable as those provided by instinct, but are much more easily modified to suit particular environments. This flexibility has led to culture, in general, being broken up into numerous local varieties. Therefore, just as we need to distinguish between the terms "society" and "a society," so we need to make a distinction between culture in general and parti-cular cultures. "A culture" is the combination of those social charac-teristics which distinguish one society from another; it is the essence of a society.

Although the basic material and companionship needs of all human beings are exactly the same, the ways in which these needs are satisfied vary considerably. In the first place, the members of a particular society will use for food, building materials and clothing whatever is available for these purposes within their natural environment. We find that the Eskimo hunter eats mostly fish and seal-meat, makes his summer tent of skins and his winter shelter of blocks of snow, and dresses himself warmly in the furs of animals which he traps, while in a completely different part of the world the Polynesian islander has a wealth of fruits and vegetables to eat with his fish and meat, thatches his wooden house with the leaves of the coconut palm, and makes what little clothing he requires from vegetable material. Even in the most advanced societies, such differences as these can still be observed.

Unlike other mammals, however, human beings are not completely dominated by their physical environment; they have the inventive and creative ability to improve upon nature by making tools, clearing forestland, making irrigation systems and so on. But man is not content simply with becoming more efficient in obtaining food, his house or his clothes; he generally goes much further than this, and develops all manner of rituals and ceremonies in connection with them. Food, for example, is prepared, served and eaten in numerous different ways, and, although it satisfies hunger if it is simply pushed into the mouth by hand, man has produced a variety of utensils and implements which he uses for this purpose. Think of how much importance we attach, in our own society, to laying the table with elaborate china- and glass-ware and special spoons, knives and forks for different dishes, yet most of us would admit that fish and chips eaten out of a newspaper can taste just as good as the most delightfully served meal.

But man has other needs to satisfy as well as the basic material ones. He seeks the company of others like himself, and to help him to meet these social needs other behaviour patterns have been developed. Again, these patterns vary from one society to another, being learned as part of an individual's cultural inheritance. Amongst some peoples it is customary to greet each other by pressing noses together, amongst others to embrace and kiss each other on both cheeks, while, in this country, we shake hands, but all these different forms of behaviour are means by which individuals know what to do in a particular social situation; they are part of the technique of living together, and there are similar "correct" ways of behaving in all the different social situations which an individual may be called upon to face.

It sometimes happens that two societies use the same behaviour to meet different situations, and when individuals from these societies meet each other, misunderstandings may occur. In Britain, when we are introduced to a stranger, we say "How do you do?", to which he should reply "How do you do?" or "Pleased to meet you"—even if he is not. If we then wish to become better acquainted with him, it is usual to pass some remark about the weather, and continue then towards more general conversation. In France, however, the polite way to bring a conversation to an end is to make some comment about the weather, and this is perhaps why an Englishman, meeting a Frenchman for the first time, might be baffled by his moving away from him just as he was making some friendly overtures, while the Frenchman might regard the Englishman as very churlish indeed, because he dismissed him so quickly after they had been introduced.

Human beings are able to develop and pass on their culture by means of language, which is itself a product of culture. Language has to be learned in the same way that other cultural techniques are learned, and, once this has been accomplished, the individual can acquire the rest of his culture.

The lack of this means of communication is very obvious amongst animals. Although an animal can instruct other animals by its example when danger threatens, it cannot convey warnings from a distance, because its presence is essential, nor can it teach its young what it has learned from its own experience. Human beings, however, with their superior mental equipment, have a great advantage over other mammals, because, through language, they can profit by the wealth of experience which is passed on to them by preceding generations, and they are thus prepared for, and know how to deal with, all manner of eventualities.

Language is also essential because only through this channel can new ideas be introduced, and the existing culture be enriched. Unlike animals, humans are not content to remain at the utilitarian level of survival, and man is all the time elaborating and adding to his cultural inheritance to the extent that the improvement of culture has become an end in itself. Because of this, the over-elaboration of culture has in some instances progressed so far that it appears to place an intolerable burden on the individual, and, far from helping him to feel at ease in a particular situation, it may be the cause of his feeling acutely embarrassed, or even of jeopardising his life. The Jews of the Classical period carried their observance of the Sabbath to such extremes that they refused to defend themselves if they were attacked on that day, and, nearer home, we are all bound to be at least a little worried at some time or another about saying or doing the wrong thing; our rituals have become so complicated that the subject of correct etiquette can fill any number of books on the matter, and we cannot possibly know it all.

Much more serious in its implications at the present time is the extent to which certain cultural phenomena, such as religion, can still reduce the individual's chances of survival, as is evidenced by the Hindu Indian's refusal to eat the meat of the cow, even though he may be dying of starvation.

CIVILISATION

"Civilisation" is another word which is used in a very wide sense in everyday speech. In its literal sense, the term properly refers to all those human achievements which are connected with living in an organised city or state, but the word has become broadened to include not only all such social achievements, but also all achievements which make human beings different from animals. Although we frequently hear people talking about "civilised," as opposed to "primitive," societies, when they are referring to peoples who have rather different habits and customs, "civilisation" is used by sociologists to distinguish between societies at different stages on the scale of human progress.

It is important to make a distinction between "civilisation" and "culture," because the two concepts appear to be closely linked, and are often confused, although they are essentially different; the most civilised societies are not necessarily the ones with the most complex cultures. Professor McIver, in his book *Society: its Structure and Changes,* explains very clearly that civilisation is the means to an end, and culture is that end. As he understands it, civilisation includes all the techniques which man uses to control his environment, both physical and social, while culture is concerned with intrinsic values and things which are desirable for their own sake.

The technical ability to master the environment, and the social ability to organise and control human behaviour, are continuing coherent processes in the evolution of society, which are valid at all times and in all places. They are the processes which enable two different societies, without reference to each other, to reach the same conclusions, and achieve the same purposes, so that both can be said to be equally civilised, but the cultures of the two societies may be quite different. In other words, civilisation proceeds along the same lines, but the development of culture can take any number of paths. Russian scientists and technologists are developing their skills in exactly the same way that American scientists and technologists are developing theirs, and Russian society is just as well organised as American society, but the two have widely divergent cultures.

CONCLUSION

Defining the major concepts which make up the subject-matter of sociology indicates clearly the vast field of this study. It must be realised that, while these concepts may be investigated in isolation, and each may follow its own pattern of development, these different aspects of human society do not vary independently, nor does one assume any greater importance than the rest. The sociologist tries to isolate as many of these variables as he can, but, having isolated them, he must proceed to examine the relationships which exist between them.

The progress which has been made so far in the field of sociology has tended to concentrate on some aspects of life in society to a greater extent than on others. A vast wealth of knowledge has been accumulated in the study of social institutions, and much has been written about different religious and marriage practices, and different political and legal systems. More recently, sociologists have shown an increasing interest in the economic institutions, which, despite their importance, had previously been rather neglected— probably because they do not have the immediate general appeal that other less prosaic aspects of society possess. Also, in this connection, it must be borne in mind that the study of society remained the province of the layman until the end of the last century.

Many of the social conditions created during the process of civilisation are now being studied in the most advanced countries of the world, and, with the development of reliable techniques for investigating these conditions, sociologists are being provided with a rapidly increasing supply of data. Much more information is still required, but, as the available material is analysed, and comparative studies are undertaken, sociology will be getting nearer to the point at which it may be possible to determine the fundamental principles which govern social continuity and change.

EXERCISE 3

1. What is sociology?
2. Explain the meaning of the following:
   (a) Social behaviourism.
   (b) An encyclopaedic study.
   (c) Sociological laws.
   (d) Empirical generalisations.
3. Assess the importance of culture in a social system.
4. What does a sociologist mean when he uses the term "institution"? Distinguish between an *institution* and an *association*.
5. "Civilisation is a means to an end, and culture is that end." Discuss.
6. Explain the part played by social consciousness in the transformation of an aggregate into a society.
7. Write notes on the following:
   (a) Communities.
   (b) Social structure.
   (c) Culture.
8. "A permissive society is one in which the overt behaviour patterns are divorced from the ideal." Explain and discuss.
9. Examine the limitations of a behaviourist concept of sociology.
10. "Sociology is of academic interest only and provides no guidance for the conduct of social policy." Discuss. (*Oxford*)
11. "Organisations change mainly as a response to institutional strain, rarely as a result of individual initiatives." Discuss with reference to *either* the Churches in Britain *or* British trade unions *or* the British penal system. (*London*)

FOR FURTHER READING

Stephen Cotgrove. *The Science of Society*. (Revised edition.) Allen and Unwin, 1972.

T. B. Bottomore. *Sociology: a guide to problems and literature*. (Second edition.) Allen and Unwin, 1971.

K. Thompson and J. Tunstall. *Sociological Perspectives*. Penguin Books, 1971.

C. Wright Mills. *The Sociological Imagination*. Penguin Books, 1970.

M. A. Coulson and D. S. Riddell. *Approaching Sociology*. Routledge and Kegan Paul, 1970.

G. D. Mitchell (ed.). *A Dictionary of Sociology*. Routledge and Kegan Paul, 1970.

CHAPTER IV

THE METHODS OF SOCIAL INVESTIGATION

AFTER reading the preceding chapters, you will have discovered that sociology is a very broad subject, and that in studying it we are not so much concerned with describing social phenomena as with trying to establish the causes and explanations of them. Because social phenomena are the products of human behaviour and inter-action, they are always less predictable than the phenomena with which the physical scientist is dealing, and therefore the methods which the social scientist uses are many and various. There is no one way in which to tackle the unravelling of complex social pheno-mena, and different groups of social scientists will have different ideas about how this can best be done, which will be reflected in the different techniques which they adopt.

The Use of Historical Documents

The historian concentrates almost entirely upon documents which have been preserved through time; in fact, history began only when people started to record events in which they were personally con-cerned, and to produce tangible evidence of their existence in the form of documents. For all our information about past events, whether they occurred last year or hundreds of years before the birth of Christ, we must rely heavily on the documents of the time. Geologists and archaeologists may be able to tell us a lot about what happened in prehistoric times, but they cannot tell us much about the people who once inhabited the areas which they have studied, or about what prehistoric societies were actually like. Just imagine for a moment that one of the men who took part in the final stages of building Stonehenge had kept a diary, and recorded what his job entailed, why the magnificent structure was being erected, and, perhaps, what happened at the inaugural rites which he described in detail; a subject which will remain for ever a matter for pure conjecture would instead have become part of our knowledge about life in Britain many thousands of years ago.

Archaeologists have unearthed a great deal of material evidence of prehistoric settlements—remains of dwellings, cooking utensils, weapons and tools—but of the people who inhabited these settlements and used the various items found on the sites we know next to nothing. As it is, our first factual information about the tribes who long ago inhabited the British Isles comes to us through the accounts of the Roman invaders, who, for one reason or another, recorded what they observed when they reached these barbarian shores, and whose writings have survived the passage of time.

Historians may be concerned purely and simply with events, but these events occurred, and are still occurring, as a result of human action and interaction. To overlook the contribution that the historical method can make to the social scientist's work would be to deny him an understanding of those processes which enrich his study of the contemporary scene. It would be foolish indeed to attempt to divorce the present from the past, as society today is to a very great extent a reflection of what has been happening within it over many hundreds of years.

Historians have developed their own techniques for the collection, verification and analysis of documentary material, and social scientists, who rightly believe that the study of contemporary society without reference to the way in which it has evolved would be only half a study, are likely to rely heavily upon the historical method.

Documents, which to the historian are quite indispensable, can be divided into two easily distinguishable categories, which, for the sake of convenience, we may call *personal documents* and *public, or official, documents*.

PERSONAL DOCUMENTS

In this group we may include all those documents whose writers are recording events in which they actually took part, and which are therefore eye-witness accounts of things which happened as recently as yesterday or many hundreds of years ago. Autobiographies, diaries and letters provide a wealth of this type of material, but we must bear in mind that these writers were not usually concerned with producing systematic, impersonal records, so that their descriptions are generally completely subjective, and will be influenced by their personal experiences, attitudes, beliefs and prejudices. These authors may also rely to some extent on memory, and, unlike elephants, human beings do sometimes forget things which, had they been included, might have proved valuable to students seeking information.

For the social scientist, personal documents are both valuable and almost as necessary as they are to the historian, but, in making use of them, certain precautions must be taken with regard to their interpretation.

The representative nature of the documents must be considered

Not every one of us has the inclination or even the ability to put our thoughts into written words, so that the material available in the form of personal documents is bound to provide a somewhat unrepresentative picture of the subject being studied.

A simple experiment was carried out by the author at a college of further education with two classes of students to show how this lack of inclination and ability could reduce the value of personal documents as a source of information. The students were all in the same age group—16–18 years old—and had left school fairly recently. Both classes contained approximately the same number of students, but one class (group A) included those who were pursuing a purely academic course of studies and were drawn from the sixth forms of local grammar schools, and the other class (group B) comprised craft apprentices, most of whom had spent their years at school in the lower streams of secondary modern schools. All the students were asked, without prior warning, to write for an hour about themselves; not a seemingly difficult task.

The results were interesting, although possibly not surprising. In group A, only one student completed the task in the allotted time; of the rest, most asked to be allowed to finish their essays for "homework." In group B, who nearly all grumbled about doing any written work, all had finished the task within 40 minutes, slightly more than half of them within 30 minutes, and during this time they had all been easily distracted. The essays produced by the two groups were of such different standards that only those written by the students in group A were of any real value when it came to analysing their content matter.

Until the Acts of the 1870s and 1880s were passed, which made the education of all children compulsory, by far the greater part of the population was either barely literate or completely illiterate, so that the personal documents which have survived from the days before formal education was made available for everyone are, with few exceptions, the writings of only a small minority within the society—the work of a few people with some literary inclination. For this reason, these documents, while of great interest to the

c

historian, are not as representative as the sociologist would wish, and other material will almost certainly be required to supplement personal documents.

It must be remembered that personal documents are personal

It is necessary to examine carefully the motives which induce people to put pen to paper and write about themselves, because these motives may influence the content of the documents produced, and so introduce some distortion of fact.

G. W. Allport, in his book *The Use of Personal Documents in Psychological Science* (1942), classifies the motives behind the writing of personal documents into thirteen separate categories: the need for self-justification, exhibitionism, sheer literary delight, a desire for order, the attempt to secure personal perspective, the relief from tension, the possibility of monetary gain, being given a specific assignment, the use of writing as a therapeutic exercise, the need to confess in the hope of absolution, scientific interest, a sense of serving the public and a search for immortality. Allport suggested that these motives might operate independently of each other or in combination in any one particular case.

We must bear in mind that every writer is largely the product of one particular culture, and his attitudes and opinions will be formed by the society into which he has been born. For the sociologist, this fact might sometimes be an advantage rather than a disadvantage, since it is the society as a whole, rather than any particular individual, in which he is interested, and much information may be gleaned about a society by noting the attitudes and opinions of its writers.

But there are times when an author might well be inhibited in the expression of his thoughts because to put these thoughts into words would be considered immoral or unconventional by society were they to be made public. For this reason, autobiographies, letters and diaries whose authors anticipate the scrutiny of the public must always be regarded as "suspect" to some extent, because there may well be deliberate omissions.

Diaries are the most intimate of all personal documents, unless the writer intends them to be published at some time in the future. They may be useful as sources of material for this reason, but diarists, like anyone else, tend to be more concerned with unusual and dramatic events than with the humdrum happenings of daily life; their records may therefore place undue emphasis on certain outstanding happenings while providing only scant mention of routine matters.

It is difficult to obtain enough documents on which to base hypotheses

Because personal documents are not always very representative, and may be biased, it is necessary to have a very large number if they are to be used in formulating theories. While it is not completely impossible to obtain this great quantity of documents, it is unlikely that sufficient will be available from which to generalise without reservations.

Many documents of this kind which were produced in the past have obviously been lost, and others such as letters, which would surely have yielded much valuable material for the historian and sociologist alike, must obviously have been destroyed either because they were not considered important or because the writers or recipients feared that the nature of their contents would provide incriminating evidence.

It is possible to introduce distortion

Distortion of fact may be introduced when using personal documents as a source of information, not by the informant himself, but by the investigator. The latter may have formed a hypothesis, and it is sometimes possible for him to shape the information which he receives to fit the hypothesis. This is most likely to occur where the sociologist rather than the historian is using contemporary personal documents, because there are times when it is necessary for the investigator to record information on behalf of the informant, who may be illiterate or have language problems. This is often the case where personal information is sought from immigrants in this country at the present time, and the investigator has to record statements made by them.

If the investigator has to prompt or guide his informant, the document which is produced may well be distorted. Subjects may be discussed at length which, left to his own devices, the informant would have ignored, and false attitudes and opinions may be assumed for the benefit of the investigator, who in these circumstances is in the same position as any interviewer. Unsolicited personal documents are likely to provide a more reliable indication of an individual's genuine thoughts, attitudes and beliefs.

THE ASSESSMENT OF PERSONAL DOCUMENTS

There are no scientific tests by which we are able to judge the distortion of fact that may exist in the type of documents which we have been discussing, but this does not mean that the historian has to rely entirely on intuition or guesswork when assessing the value of his material. He can apply certain external corrective tests.

Can the information be corroborated?

There may be a great deal of material drawn from other sources with which the information in a particular document corresponds, and corroboration such as this is the best indication of all that any one writer produced an accurate account. Historians have made it a general rule to accept as correct any information about an event which is provided by two or more completely independent sources.

However, it is not always possible to obtain substantiative evidence, and if it is not available some other tests for credibility will have to be used.

Are the circumstances in which the documents were written likely to favour reliability?

There are a number of conditions under which writers are likely to produce truthful documents, and it is a fairly simple matter to recognise them. Louis Gottschalk outlined some examples of these conditions in his critical essay on "The Historian and the Historical Document." He said that an informant is likely to give an accurate account when:

1. The matter recorded is a matter of *indifference* to him.
2. A statement is *prejudicial* to him, to those whom he loves, or to his own ambitions.
3. The facts recorded are so much *matters of common knowledge* that there would be no point in lying about them.
4. The part of the statement which is of interest to the investigator is purely *incidental,* as far as the informant is concerned, but probable in the circumstances.
5. Statements are made which are clearly *contrary to his expectations and anticipations*.

PUBLIC OR OFFICIAL DOCUMENTS

In this category we can include a number of documents such as records, reports, newspaper editorials and articles by "our own correspondents," pamphlets and other sponsored publications. These will all vary in credibility and accuracy according to whether they are documents conveying specific instructions, such as military commands, or the publications of organisations with propagandist interests.

Records

The investigator has a great wealth of these documents available as it is customary for statutory bodies, from Parliament downwards, firms, societies and committees to keep records of their proceedings. Documents such as *Hansard,* and the verbatim records of court proceedings, are obviously very reliable, but the minutes of any meeting do not usually contain significant errors.

Probably the best record of all is an unedited tape-recording, since that reproduces not only what was said but also the manner in which it was said, and this can very often be of equal importance. If you have not proved this for yourselves before, you can carry out a very simple experiment. Write down a straightforward statement such as "Our cat doesn't chase birds," and then read it over five times emphasising each word in turn. You will then find that even a seemingly innocuous statement can be made extremely provocative or have several implications, according to how it is said.

However, since the purpose of official records is usually that of providing useful, factual information, and since they are not intended to influence opinion, we can regard such sources as reliable and subject to only a very low level of distortion, if any.

Reports

Such documents are produced retrospectively, even if notes were taken at the time the event being reported actually occurred, and, unlike records, they are often intended to convey an impression, or justify the events being reported.

The reports produced by official committees of enquiry set up by Parliament to investigate matters of public concern are likely to be more reliable than newspaper reports, which are usually to some extent propagandist when dealing with the same matters. These propagandist reports are, however, valuable since they not only will contain a great deal of factual information but will also indicate the attitude being adopted by the newspapers publishing the reports. Since newspapers are extremely influential, it is useful for the sociologist to know of these attitudes.

Miscellaneous sponsored documents

As well as records and reports, all published documents are of interest to the sociologist, because they help to reveal attitudes and opinions, although contemporary publications are likely to be the most useful, since current trends in the climate of opinion are of greater concern than historical changes. Such sponsored documents as pamphlets and newspaper articles may well contain a considerable amount of factual information, but they are also likely to be biased, so that this information might be incomplete or presented in a manner which unduly emphasises just a part of the whole matter. Fortunately, the extent of such bias as this is not usually difficult to estimate, because, if the sponsor of this type of document is known, the investigator should be able to discover in what way the information is most probably weighted.

The use of case histories

Official social case-workers, such as probation officers, health visitors and school welfare officers, and voluntary social workers, such as marriage guidance counsellors and members of the Women's Royal Voluntary Service, are all first-hand observers of many kinds of social behaviour, and, in the course of carrying out their duties, they amass a great deal of information relating to the people whom they attempt to assist. This information, for the sake of convenience, is recorded in the form of *"case histories."*

At first sight, it would seem to be a sensible arrangement for social scientists to use material provided by these case histories in their investigations, and in exchange they could assist the practical social workers towards a greater understanding of the problems with which they have to deal. However, at the present time, there are certain difficulties which stand in the way of a working partnership of this kind.

In the course of time, social science has developed along rather different lines than those taken by *social studies*. To outsiders, the subtle distinction in nomenclature must seem to be a rather unnecessary example of hair-splitting, and they can hardly be blamed if they take it as an indication that there is something rather odd about studying society. What has happened is that *social science* has come to be accepted as a theoretical study concerned primarily with the systematic classification and analysis of social phenomena, while *social studies* are subjects in which people are trained so that they may become welfare workers of one kind or another.

To some extent the social scientists can be held responsible for the rather uneasy relationship which now exists between social science and the social studies. In the past they have tended to remain somewhat aloof and academic in their approach to the study of society, and have given the impression that to use their findings for the purposes of social engineering is somehow inferior. Fortunately, this attitude is gradually becoming less apparent, and the theorists are looking longingly towards the mass of material in the possession of the case-workers.

On the other hand, being concerned chiefly with trying to help those members of the society who are for many reasons unable to cope with their environment, social case-workers have devised their own methods of dealing with the problems they meet. They keep their records mainly as *aides-mémoire*, and they are obviously much more interested in people as individuals than in people as statistics. The case histories are not recorded in any uniform way, and the observations noted in them are generally too subjective to make the data as valuable as they could be for the social scientist. We must remember, too, that case-workers are dealing with the casualties of society, so that their records, if used without reference to other material, would present a rather biased picture to the investigator.

Sampling

Although sociologists make use of material such as we have been discussing, they are more likely to investigate contemporary social phenomena than that which has happened in the past, however helpful and interesting this may be. In order to discover facts about the present, they have devised the method which is called the *social survey*.

In his *Social Surveys and Social Action*, Mark Abrams, who is a leading exponent of the modern social survey, has described it as "a process by which quantitative facts are collected about the social aspects of a community's composition and activities." He says that there are three characteristics of a social survey:

1. The desired information is obtained by questioning directly the members of the group which is being studied.

2. The findings which emerge can generally be expressed quantitatively.

3. The information is usually sought for a practical purpose— to find out the cause and extent of a social problem, so that steps can be taken to overcome it.

For the simple reasons of economy and practicality, observation has to be selective; it is possible to observe only a part, or *sample*, of all the relevant data which are available, and on what is found to be characteristic of the sample are based the generalisations about the whole. The extent to which the generalisations are accurate and valid will depend entirely upon the extent to which the chosen sample is representative of the whole.

The degree to which this can be assumed depends upon the following criteria.

The nature of the matter being studied

If the individual items which make up the whole are homogeneous, or differences between the units are only very slight, it is obvious that any single item or group of items will be representative of them all. Where there is this high degree of homogeneity, the selection of a sample is very simple and can be made by *rule of thumb*. For example, any spoonful of soup taken from the pan by a cook will give an accurate indication of the flavour and seasoning of all the soup that happens to be in that particular pot at the time. Similarly a chemist has to deal with materials which display a correspondingly high degree of homogeneity, so that he can be certain that an experiment which he carries out using any sample of a particular chemical will yield the same results as an experiment in which he uses any other sample.

In the field of social research, however, the phenomena being studied will not usually have this homogeneity, and where it is not possible to carry out a full census—the cost and effort of which for most purposes would be prohibitive—it is necessary to rely upon observation of a sample. The sociologist will have to select his sample in such a way that it is representative.

The method used to select the sample

A representative sample must contain, in relative proportions, all the significant characteristics of the larger whole of which it is a part, but the sociologist has to accept that a sample cannot possibly reproduce the characteristics of a whole population with complete accuracy. If, however, the sample is properly selected, the errors can be reduced to a minimum, and they are then often of less importance than the errors which would result from faulty methods of carrying out the survey.

There are two major errors which are very often found when

samples are selected. The first of these is the error which results from *bias*. This should be avoidable, although it frequently occurs because the people chosen to provide the sample are wrongly assumed to be representative. For example, people might be selected from the names in a telephone directory, but, since only a certain section of the population has the telephone installed, people chosen in this way could only be representative of those with telephones. In the same way, stopping people in the street during the daytime would not provide a representative sample, since people at work would obviously be excluded.

Another error due to bias, which is not so readily apparent, occurs where selection is made according to some characteristic which happens to be correlated with another characteristic, and this has been overlooked by the investigator. Suppose a survey of the eating habits of people in Great Britain were to be carried out, and the sample were to be selected by means of surname. The investigator might decide to include surnames beginning with the letter M, since that is the middle letter of the alphabet, but this would produce a very biased sample, since it would include a disproportionate number of Scotsmen.

The second type of error is the *sampling error*. Chance differences between members of the public included in the sample and those who are excluded are almost certain to exist, and the existence of these differences will have to be considered when any sample is selected. Sampling errors can be measured and regulated by methods which will be discussed later.

METHODS OF SAMPLING

Random sampling

Many techniques of sampling are based on the principle of random selection. In everyday speech, the word "random" is used to suggest something which is haphazard, casual, unorganised and without any specific purpose, but, obviously, if such a method were to be employed when selecting a sample for observation, the results would be far from scientific. The sociologist using the word "random" simply means that each individual within the whole of the group about which he is seeking to generalise will have the same chance of being selected as every other individual.

The simplest method of random sampling is for the whole group to draw lots, but this is only possible where the numbers are small, and people involved are near to each other. In most cases it would be far too tedious, if not completely impossible, so it is usual to adopt a procedure known as *stratification* to make the selection of samples easier.

By means of stratification, the population as a whole is divided into blocks, or strata, on a particular specified basis such as age, education, income or occupation. Each of these blocks can then be sampled at random. Since many social surveys are concerned with a particular stratum of the society, the value of dividing the population in this way is obvious.

This system can also be used for *proportional sampling,* as stratification is based on known characteristics of the whole population, and this knowledge can be used to secure a proportionate distribution of these characteristics in the sample. Such weighting as this is important, because it provides a means of ensuring that a sample is representative. For example, a sample which contained more than 5 per cent of university graduates would not be representative of the whole population of this country, because only this proportion receives a university education.

Stratification may be used where the completely random selection of members for a sample group from the whole population would not provide enough subjects for the purpose of a particular investigation. This would be the case if the investigation were concerned only with a small minority group, such as millionaires or coloured immigrants. When stratification is employed in this way, according to the characteristic being investigated, it is referred to as *purposive sampling.*

Frequently a *two-stage* sampling technique is used to make the selection easier. In this case, the members of the final sample group will be selected at random from groups that have already been selected at random out of the total population. This method is very often employed when surveys are carried out in this country, and the procedure is to take as the first stage a sample of the administrative areas, or local authorities, and at the second stage to take a random sample of the people who live in the selected areas.

Further stages may be added in order to reduce the size of the group to be questioned if this is necessary. This is called *multi-stage sampling,* but, if further stages are added, more accurate results will be obtained if a large *sampling fraction* of the proportion of the whole population under consideration is used in the first stage. This will almost certainly make the field-work less convenient, as it will be dispersed over many areas, even though the actual numbers of the final sample group may be small.

Systematic sampling

The technique of systematic sampling is rather less reliable than any random method, but there may be occasions when random sampling is not practicable or is too expensive, and a very simple method of selection has to be used. This might be the choosing of every twentieth name on an alphabetical list, or picking out every tenth file from a drawer. Whatever the system decided upon, it could provide an acceptable sample for many purposes so long as certain precautions are taken. For example, if files are taken from a drawer it is essential to ensure that no files are missing when the selection is made, because "active" files might be "active" for a reason that could considerably affect the sample.

The main drawback of systematic sampling is, however, that it is not possible to make an accurate estimate of the sampling error.

Quota sampling

The quota sampling method is generally used by the commercial survey organisations where maximum speed and minimum cost are the primary considerations. The designers of these surveys allocate to each field-worker a quota of people to be questioned, and this quota is intended to contain the right proportion of individuals who have certain given characteristics—age, sex, social class, etc.—which correspond with the characteristics of the whole population as indicated by the Census reports or some other similar source of information about the people of the country.

The actual selection of people to be questioned is left to the field-worker, and this of course means that the accuracy of such a survey really depends upon the way in which he or she tackles the task of interviewing. As a practical exercise in the difficulties to be encountered in interviewing on a quota basis, the author recently set a class of students the job of each questioning fifty people in four hours. They soon found that some people are much more approachable than others, that amongst the women, old-age pensioners are generally more amenable to being interviewed than busy housewives with toddlers in tow, and that it is often simpler and quicker, when one is in a hurry, to ask one's friends to "help out" by completing the questionnaires.

These students quickly realised that there are too many dangers inherent in quota sampling to make it a sufficiently reliable method for use where really accurate results are necessary. There is too great a risk of bias and distortion creeping in to make this method suitable for establishing anything other than the most general trends.

TERMS USED IN SAMPLING
Population

The word "population" is one which has a rather different meaning in everyday speech from that which is given to it by statisticians, and those carrying out surveys in which statistical methods are used. We think immediately of a population as being the total number of men, women and children who inhabit a particular geographical area such as a town or a country, but, for the rather special purpose of sampling, "population" denotes the whole of the large group from which the members of a sample are selected.

If a survey were to be conducted which was concerned with nurses or policemen, then the population would be the total number of nurses or policemen engaged in their particular occupations at that time. In the same way, it would be possible to have a "population" of churches, prisons or schools, if these institutions were under investigation.

The sampling unit

This term is used to indicate the entity which is selected to form the sample. It is perhaps easiest to illustrate this term with examples. If a survey is carried out to investigate the actions or characteristics of individuals, then the sampling unit will be the individual; if, on the other hand, the survey is concerned with families or households, then families and households will provide the sampling unit. Similarly, a survey of youth clubs or hospitals would be based on a sample of youth clubs or hospitals, rather than the individuals within them.

The sampling frame

The sampling frame is the source from which the sampling units are selected. If the survey is concerned with individual adults, the most common source is the *electoral roll*, which provides a record of all people over the age of 21 who are resident in each electoral district. This is the best source available at present, although it is not absolutely complete because it is certain to exclude a number of people in an area at a particular time such as those who have only recently moved or who are never, for various reasons, in any place for very long.

There is no "ready-made" frame from which families can be selected, as no list is kept of family units in this country. Households, too, are not recorded, although the *rating records* which list independently rated houses are sometimes used for this purpose, despite the fact that quite often more than one household share a single house.

It will be seen from this that the first step in carrying out any survey is to devise a frame, suitable to the matter being investigated, from which the sampling units can be selected. The importance of this is generally disregarded by the planners of commercial surveys, and this is another reason why the findings of this type of investigation are not considered sufficiently reliable by sociologists, who need more accurate information.

Multi-phase sampling

Sometimes, when the size of the sample is very large, general information is collected from all the units, while more detailed information is collected from a sub-sample of those units. This happens, for example, in the case of the census of the population of Great Britain which is taken every ten years. All households are required to provide certain general information, but one in ten is asked to complete a more detailed questionnaire.

The findings of a survey of a sub-sample can also provide a useful means of checking that the whole sample is representative. If significant differences come to light, then there has been an error in sampling.

THE PILOT SURVEY

Before the main survey is carried out, it is often found helpful to conduct a pilot survey. This can perform a number of useful functions apart from that of providing the investigator with a certain amount of prior information collected from a sub-sample of the group to be studied. Such prior information is often necessary in the planning of a research project, as it assists the investigator to decide whether or not his original idea was basically correct.

The pilot survey can also be used to find out which is the best way of collecting the information required to support the theory. Some preliminary work will enable the investigator to establish what type of questionnaire or interview will be most suitable for his particular purpose, and it will also provide the opportunity for training the field-workers who are actually going to carry out the survey.

This is the stage in an important project at which the wording of a formal questionnaire, the techniques of interviewing and the method of recording answers can all be considered and discussed. In the light of what is learned from conducting a pilot survey, it may be possible to carry out the main survey with much greater efficiency. Far from increasing the cost of a major project, this type of groundwork is most likely to reduce the overall expenditure, by indicating at an early stage in the proceedings whether or not the survey has been properly planned and is being conducted in the best possible way for the investigator's purposes. Several pilot surveys may be necessary before a good result can be assured from the main survey.

THE SIZE OF THE SAMPLE

The method used for carrying out a modern social survey is based on *statistics,* and, although it is not necessary for a social researcher to have a detailed knowledge of statistics, it is important that he should have some idea of the principles involved. He will, in any case, almost certainly have to seek the assistance of an experienced statistician in designing and analysing the results of a survey of this type.

The normal distribution of a characteristic

By the distribution of a characteristic is meant the manner of its dispersal throughout the population.

Let us suppose that the characteristic being investigated was that of the height of adult males in the population, and we took a random sample of a hundred men. We could measure the men, and divide them into *classes,* with *class intervals* of three inches; the men under 4 ft 6 in. in height would be placed in class 1, the men between 4 ft 6 in. and 4 ft 9 in. in class 2, and so on up to the men over 6 ft 9 in., who would be in class 11. Having measured the men, we could show our findings in a table (Table I), and ascertain the frequency with which certain heights are encountered in the sample.

From Table I we could produce a *histogram*, or frequency polygon, to show the distribution of height diagrammatically (*see* Fig. 1). We would see immediately that the distribution is symmetrical

Table I—Frequency of Heights in a Sample

Height	Class	Frequency	Class × Frequency				
Under 4 ft 6 in.	1	1	1	×	1	=	1
4 ft 6 in.–4 ft 9 in.	2	3	2	×	3	=	6
4 ft 9 in.–5 ft 0 in.	3	7	3	×	7	=	21
5 ft 0 in.–5 ft 3 in.	4	12	4	×	12	=	48
5 ft 3 in.–5 ft 6 in.	5	17	5	×	17	=	85
5 ft 6 in.–5 ft 9 in.	6	20	6	×	20	=	120
5 ft 9 in.–6 ft 0 in.	7	17	7	×	17	=	119
6 ft 0 in.–6 ft 3 in.	8	12	8	×	12	=	96
6 ft 3 in.–6 ft 6 in.	9	7	9	×	7	=	63
6 ft 6 in.–6 ft 9 in.	10	3	10	×	3	=	30
Over 6 ft 9 in.	11	1	11	×	1	=	11
	Total	100	Sum of Class × Frequency				600

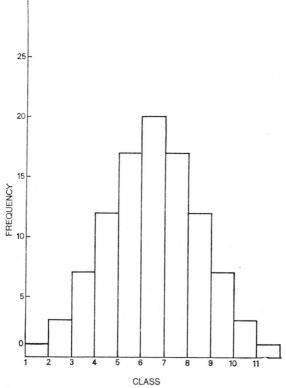

Fig. 1—Histogram produced from Table I.

about the *mean* (class 6), which is found by dividing the sum of the frequencies (100) into the sum of the products of the frequencies and classes (600).

However, since we know that height does not vary in steps of three inches, we can justifiably smooth out the steps in the histogram and produce a curve (*see* Fig. 2). Because this curve is symmetrical, we can say that height has a normal distribution in our sample. If further investigations using other samples provided similar

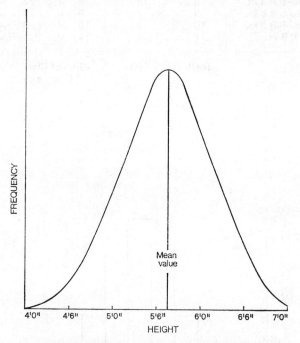

Fig. 2—Distribution curve produced from Table I

results, we could assume that the characteristic of height is distributed normally in the whole population and that any completely random sample would be representative *provided it was large enough*.

It is a very useful fact that distributions of a characteristic in so many samples are approximately normal, because the nature of normal distribution is precisely known. The characteristic is distributed symmetrically around the mean with a large number of small deviations and only a small number of large deviations from the mean. The *standard deviation* can be calculated mathematically, and approximately 68 per cent of the population comes within one standard deviation of the mean, approximately 95 per cent within two standard deviations and approximately 99 per cent within three standard deviations.

It should be remembered that there is no specific proportion of a total population that will be sure to provide a truly representative sample. This is because the composition of any random sample will differ to some extent from the composition of the population from which it is drawn owing to the operation of chance in selection. The actual size of a sample has to be fixed according to the number in the population and the level of accuracy required, or, to use the statistical term, according to how large a *sampling error* the investigator is prepared to accept. It is possible to measure the sampling error by calculating the *standard error*.

Calculating the standard error

The standard error depends not only on the size of the sample but also on the extent to which the units that comprise the population vary from each other. This means, therefore, that the researcher must know something about the findings he will get before he can commence his survey, so, unless this information can be obtained from an existing source in a sufficiently accurate form, it will be necessary to carry out a pilot survey. However, provided that such prior information is available, there should be no difficulty in deciding what size the sample for a survey should be.

If the survey is being undertaken to find the incidence of a particular characteristic within a population—*e.g.* the proportion of wage earners who earn less than £20 per week—the following formula can be used:

$$\text{Standard error} = \sqrt{\frac{pq}{n}},$$

where p represents the proportion of the population which displays the characteristic (*i.e.* earns less than £20 per week), q represents the proportion not displaying the characteristic (*i.e.* the proportion earning £20 or more per week) and n represents the number of units in the random sample.

The standard error can also be expressed as a percentage:

$$\text{Standard error } \% = \sqrt{\frac{p\% \times q\%}{n}}.$$

If prior information indicates that in the population of wage earners 10 per cent earn less than £20 per week, the standard error in a random sample of a hundred wage earners will be:

$$\sqrt{\frac{10 \times 90}{100}} = 3\%.$$

This does not mean that all random samples will contain the same degree of error. If a number of different samples were selected, some would be more in error and some less. In fact, in a series of such samples, approximately one-third would contain sampling errors larger than the standard error, and about one-twentieth would contain errors more than double that of the standard error.

If we were to take the same example as before, and select a large number of different samples to find out how representative they were of the wage-earning population, we would find that two-thirds of these samples would produce results showing that between 7 and 13 per cent ($10\% \pm 3\%$) of wage earners earn less than £20 per week, and nineteen-twentieths would produce results showing that between 4 and 16 per cent ($10\% \pm 6\%$) earn less than £20 per week.

Perhaps the most important fact which the formula shows is that the standard error is related to the size of the sample. The standard error is halved if the number in the sample is quadrupled. Using the above example once again, if we were to increase the number in the sample to four hundred, the standard error would be 1·5 per cent. Now, in a large series of samples, two-thirds would produce results between 8·5 and 11·5 per cent ($10\% \pm 1\cdot5\%$) and nineteen-twentieths would produce results between 7 and 13 per cent ($10\% \pm 3\%$).

The actual derivation of statistical formulae which are based on the theory of probability is, in view of its complexity, too specialised a subject for any detailed examination of it to be included in this book. When a sociologist needs to employ statistical methods, unless he is also a skilled statistician, it is advisable for him to seek the assistance of someone who is properly qualified to help him.

However, when the population is large and the characteristic being investigated has a *normal distribution*, it is usually sufficient to use the simple formula provided above to calculate the size of the sample.

Calculating the size of a representative sample without prior information about the population

As we have seen, provided that some information about the characteristics of the population under investigation is available, it is possible to determine mathematically the size a sample needs to be if it is to be representative of the whole to a measurable degree of accuracy. However, it sometimes happens that no such knowledge exists and then it becomes necessary to adopt empirical methods to test the adequacy of a sample.

Even the simplest empirical method is a fairly lengthy one, since it necessitates selecting a number of different samples of the same arbitrary size, and comparing the findings from them. If the findings from these different samples vary greatly, it can be assumed that the size chosen is too small to be representative of the whole population, so it will have to be increased until the variations in each successive sample selected are only very small and deviate as frequently in one direction as the other from the mean, or average, distribution of the characteristic under investigation. The extent of the deviation acceptable in such samples will, of course, be determined by the level of accuracy, which is decided upon for the purpose of a particular survey.

The Questionnaire

FACT-FINDING SURVEYS

In Britain, until fairly recently, surveys have usually been conducted only for the purpose of obtaining factual information. In the past there has been something of a reluctance on the part of the British public to become involved in the subjective type of survey, which attempts to measure attitudes and opinions, although, with the rapid developments in commercial surveys since the Second World War, we have become more accustomed to this type of investigation.

Professor A. L. Bowley, in his *Elements of Statistics,* outlined the general principles which should be taken into consideration when designing a questionnaire for an objective fact-finding survey. According to him the questions should:

1. Be as few in number as is necessary to produce the required information.

2. Require an answer of "Yes" or "No" or a number or measurement which is precise.

3. Be phrased in such a way that the informant can easily understand them.

4. Be such as can be answered honestly and without bias.

5. Be not unduly inquisitorial.

6. Be corroborative as much as is possible.

7. Directly and obviously be related to the information being sought.

SURVEYS TO INVESTIGATE ATTITUDES AND OPINIONS

The Americans have always shown less "respect" for tradition and authority than the British, who for a long time resisted the canvassing of opinions, which was generally considered to be "not quite nice" and in some way an invasion of one's privacy. However, the idea of carrying out opinion polls and market research has spread to Britain from the United States, and, since about 1950, we have seen the steady growth of surveys of this type run on a commercial basis. We have seen, too, the establishing of survey organisations which are officially sponsored, such as the Social Survey Division of the Central Office of Information, and Listener Research, which makes investigations for the British Broadcasting Corporation. The officially sponsored survey organisations are rather more objective in their approach than the commercial organisations, and their main object is to obtain information which can be used for the purpose of planning future policy.

The investigation of attitudes and opinions is very difficult, because they involve our emotional responses or feelings towards certain ideas and suggestions, and there is no means whereby feelings can be measured accurately. To ask someone how strongly he feels about a concept—racial discrimination, for example—will produce a purely subjective response which cannot be categorised in terms of a precise measure of intensity. The feelings of one person cannot be properly compared with those of another, except in a general manner, when it could be said that one feels very strongly against a particular idea while another is completely indifferent.

It can be said that the findings of these surveys can be useful if they are carried out to investigate trends or changes in attitudes, opinions and beliefs, but the findings should not be regarded as accurate.

The problems encountered in designing a questionnaire for this type of survey are much greater than designing one which is intended to obtain factual information. Sometimes the informant is supplied with a series of *multiple-choice* or *cafeteria* questions—that is, questions to which a number of answers are provided—and he is required to select the answer which he considers appropriate. This method makes for easy analysis of the responses, but it also introduces the possibility of an informant not finding the answer he would give if left to his own devices, and therefore having to choose the one which comes nearest to it. This is sufficient to make the findings only a rough approximation.

Where *open-ended* questions are asked, and the informant is given the opportunity of answering them in his own way, the task of analysing the responses may be extremely difficult. It is likely, in the event of a very large number of varied answers being given, that the system of coding them will be to canalise all those that are roughly the same into one category. Once again, gradations will be disregarded, and the findings will be somewhat distorted as a result.

It is not by any means easy to frame questions which are suitable for each and every informant to answer. Those which can readily be understood by those of low intellect or of a poor educational status might well prove to give too little scope to the highly educated or intellectual informant. When questions are framed which use technical terms or words with which many people are not familiar, there is always the possibility that a large number will reply "Don't know," whereas, if the questions were put in another way, an entirely different response might be elicited. This indicates that, unless great care is exercised, the actual phrasing of a question could well influence the findings adversely.

When asking people about their attitudes, there is always the possibility that they will give the answers which they think they ought to give, rather than those which disclose their real feelings. People may be tempted to answer according to what they preach rather than what they actually practise, and what they preach is likely to conform to what is generally considered to be right or respectable in the society. Many people are understandably reluctant to admit that they hold opinions which might label them as "anti-social" or "immoral," so they are liable to be cautious if they feel that their views are unconventional. This problem may be encountered when an informant is asked to write his answers to the questionnaire, but it is emphasised if he is interviewed by a field-worker, because then he might easily become embarrassed if he thinks he is giving an "unpopular" answer.

To counteract these difficulties, the questionnaires for a survey of attitudes and opinions need to be considerably longer than those for a factual survey if the results are to be at all reliable.

THE OMNIBUS QUESTIONNAIRE

The idea of the omnibus questionnaire was originated by the American George Gallup, who has given his name to the commercial survey organisation. This type of questionnaire is so called because it generally contains between two hundred and three hundred questions.

The very large number of questions is necessary because, although they may not always appear to the informant to be related to each other, they are designed to assess the credibility of the material. A series of searching questions will generally be a more effective means of obtaining a realistic statement than one question would be, because the responses given enable a skilled investigator to build up an overall picture. The responses given to each question can be compared with each other, and any inconsistencies can be seen.

A lengthy questionnaire like this will take a considerable time to complete, and it is therefore likely that many of the people who have been selected to form the sample may refuse to answer it. This is particularly a risk where the survey is being conducted through the post, because a large number of the questionnaires will most probably be consigned to the waste-paper basket.

This type of questionnaire also increases the possibility of bias being introduced into the results, since the people who feel strongly about the matter under investigation are more likely than others to give up the time required to answer it.

THE QUINTAMENSIONAL OR FIVE-STAGE PLAN

The quintamensional plan for designing questions to investigate public opinion is considerably more elaborate than the omnibus questionnaire. It can be briefly summarised as follows:

Stage 1. This is the "filter" stage which is intended to discover if the informant has previously considered the matter being investigated. Even if he replies that he has, he will probably be asked more questions to establish how seriously he has thought about it.

Stage 2. An open-ended question is asked which gives the informant the opportunity of answering in his own way.

Stage 3. The informant is asked a question, or several questions, to which a specific answer—"Yes," "No" or "Don't know" —can be given. At this stage, if specific-answer questions are not practicable, multiple-choice questions may be provided instead, although these are rather less satisfactory.

Stage 4. At this point a series of questions is given which are intended to find out the reasons why the informant holds his opinions.

Stage 5. This final stage is devoted to questioning the strength of the informant's opinions.

THE PROBLEM OF NON-RESPONSE

Theoretically, by use of technical expertise and the application of random sampling principles, it should be possible to select a sample which is as representative as funds will allow, and also to produce results of which the accuracy can be precisely tested. However, the social scientist is less fortunate than the statistician, because he has to put theory into practice, and there is one problem which he cannot easily overcome. Whereas the statistician bases his calculations on textbook situations such as the tossing of unbiased coins or the selection of coloured balls out of a barrel, the social scientist has to take his sample from a human population. Some of this population may simply not be available when the sample is taken and others may refuse to co-operate for a variety of reasons.

The problem of non-response is one which the social scientist cannot legitimately disregard, and it is also one which he is almost certain to encounter, particularly if the survey is conducted by post. Because non-response is an inherent difficulty in social surveys, methods have been devised for keeping it down to an acceptable level in most cases, and for estimating broadly the bias it may produce in the results.

Experience has shown that the part of a sample which refuses to provide the required information often differs considerably from the rest. For this reason, if 85 per cent of the people selected co-operate, there is no justification for regarding them as a satisfactory sample and simply omitting the other 15 per cent, even if a very large number of individuals were chosen in the first place.

It is possible to distinguish different categories or causes of non-response:

Unsuitability for questioning

Any large number of people selected at random from the population either of the whole country or of a geographical area are likely to include some individuals who are not suitable for interviewing. They may be deaf, seriously ill, mentally handicapped or unfamiliar with the language. The field-worker will have to decide whether there is a genuine reason of this nature for an individual's failure to co-operate. He will obviously not regard a headache or over-tiredness as a reasonable excuse, and, in these circumstances, he should make a further attempt at another time to obtain the information he requires.

Mobility of the population

When people are pre-selected from a sampling frame such as an electoral roll or a list of ratepayers, the sample will almost certainly contain a number of individuals or households who have either moved to another address in the area or left it altogether. This is a cause of non-response which cannot be overcome, because very few of the lists suitable for use as sampling frames are absolutely up to date.

Absence from home or work

It is not always possible to interview the people selected, because a survey has to be conducted within a specified period. It frequently happens that people are not available either at home or at work during the time when the field-work is undertaken. Some people are always bound to be out at the time when an interviewer calls.

Straightforward refusals

When certain official surveys, such as the population census, are carried out, people are legally compelled to supply the required information. In the vast majority of cases, however, no such statutory power is available to those who are conducting surveys, and they are entirely dependent on the willingness of members of the public to co-operate. No matter how carefully the purpose of the survey is explained or how tactfully the interviewers approach their task, there will always be some people who refuse to answer a questionnaire.

To some extent the refusal rate is related to the length of the questionnaire and the amount of time and labour the informant is required to devote to completing it.

THE SIZE OF THE NON-RESPONSE PROBLEM

The size of the problem is very largely governed by the number of calls which can be made on each person selected before all hope of obtaining an interview is given up. The funds available for the research may enable eight or more calls to be made, but usually the cost of each call means that only three or four are possible.

By comparing the non-response rates of a very large number of surveys, it appears that between 10 and 20 per cent of any sample selected will be non-responsive where the survey is conducted by means of personal interviews, and very much higher than this if the questionnaire is sent through the post. In surveys which require informants to keep records over a period of time, such as enquiries into family expenditure, the level of non-response may be as high as 40 per cent or more.

Generally, people who are unsuitable for questioning form less than 2 per cent of any sample, and these, together with the 3 to 5 per cent of persistent refusers, will have to be discounted.

In those instances where people selected have moved, it may be possible to trace the ones who are still in the area, but it is not usually practicable to try to find the others on account of the expense and time involved. In surveys using households as the sampling unit, a solution to this problem can often be found by substituting the new household for the one which has departed. The number of houses left empty owing to people moving is likely to be very small.

When individuals are the sampling units, the problem of removals is greater, because substitution of one individual for another is a dangerous procedure where random sampling techniques are used.

The level of non-response due to people being unavailable at the time an interviewer calls can be kept to a minimum if appointments are made in advance, or field-workers make use of any previous knowledge they have about the sample members. For example, it can be safely assumed that men and young people will not be at home during the daytime, and that housewives with a large family spend more time in their homes than the ones who have only one or two children or none at all.

Moser and Stuart have found that refusal to co-operate is not spread evenly throughout the whole population. In an experimental survey they obtained the rates of refusal shown in Table II:

Table II—Refusal Rates by Sex, Age and Social Class (Percentages)

Sex		Age-group		Social class	
Males	6·1	20–29	4·6	Upper	12·2
Females	8·9	30–44	6·1	Middle	9·7
		45–64	11·0	Lower	6·3
		65+	7·5		

Source: C. A. Moser. Survey Methods in Social Investigation.

Although these findings relate to quota sampling, Moser suggests that the differentials are typical. The refusal rate, therefore, will to some extent depend upon which sectors of the community provide the members of a sample. For example, a survey conducted amongst middle-aged females in the upper class is likely to have a greater number of refusals than one conducted amongst young males in the lower class. These are somewhat extreme cases, but the example is useful since it indicates the way in which bias due to non-response of this type can be introduced into a survey covering all sectors of the population.

ESTIMATING THE EFFECTS OF BIAS FROM NON-RESPONSE

This is only possible if some knowledge, however scanty, can be obtained about the members of the sample who fail to provide the required information. Field-workers are often able to collect certain facts; they can find out whether the people selected are suitable for interviewing; they can make a note of the sex, approximate age and social class of people they see but fail to interview; they may be able to find out something about a person's job and family circumstances from other people in the household. Individuals who refuse to complete the questionnaire are sometimes willing to provide answers to a few simple questions.

If some knowledge about non-respondents is available, it is possible to compare them with the respondents in the sample, and to discover whether there is any obvious difference between them on the basis of sex, age or social class, etc. If the two groups are broadly similar, the researcher may consider that the element of non-response in the sample will not seriously bias the findings.

"Follow-up" procedures where non-response is extensive can often reduce the effects of bias where there are notable differences between the respondents and non-respondents. If the initial request for information is unsuccessful, it may be possible to persuade a proportion of the non-respondents to reply to a second enquiry. The people who then co-operate could be used as a sub-sample for investigation of the non-respondents. Subsequent enquiries might be made and findings compared with those from the first sub-sample to establish any particular trends amongst the non-respondents in the main survey.

The importance attached to non-response, the efforts made by the researcher to reduce it and to assess the element of bias it produces, will depend upon the accuracy which is required in the results of a survey.

The Measurement of Attitudes

Since the Americans have been concerned for far longer than we have in Britain with the measurement of attitudes, they have made considerably more progress in the development of the special techniques which are necessary. Two of these techniques, *Latent Structure Analysis* and *Scalogram Analysis,* are particularly important, and show some promise that it will eventually be possible to discover the distribution of attitudes, to find out how they originate and to measure their intensity more exactly.

Both these techniques were developed by sociologists as part of a programme initiated by the Research Branch of the Information and Education Division of the United States War Department during the Second World War. Similar work had been going on almost since the beginning of the century, but it had not had official sponsorship and really adequate financial backing. Most of the earlier work had been done by social psychologists, but only during the last war were its implications fully recognised, and the advice of sociologists and psychologists was then sought by the United States Government.

Some of the really early work on attitude measurement was done by Bogardus, who evolved the *social distance method,* which was purely subjective and was intended to discover the "social distance" between an informant and people belonging to different nationalities or ethnic groups from himself. The same technique could also be used in relation to occupations, religions, interests or any other social phenomenon. The main difficulty in Bogardus's method was that of constructing a scale which could adequately represent degrees of "distance" so that data could be measured and compared.

Thurstone developed a more objective method of constructing scales, and *Thurstone Scales* have since been produced in great variety. The following, from his article "Attitudes can be Measured," is Thurstone's own account of this method:

> "Several groups of people are asked to write out their opinions on the issue in question, and the literature is searched for suitable brief statements that may serve the purposes of the scale. By editing such material a list of from 100 to 150 statements is prepared expressive of attitudes covering as far as possible all gradations from one end of the scale to the other. It is sometimes necessary to give special attention to the neutral statements. If a random collection of statements of opinion should fail to produce neutral statements, there is some danger that the scale will break in two parts . . . there will be perhaps 80 to 100 statements to be actually scaled. These statements are then mimeographed on small cards, one statement to each card. Two or three hundred subjects are asked to arrange the statements in eleven piles ranging from opinions most strongly affirmative to those most strongly negative . . . The task is essentially to sort out the small cards into eleven piles so that they *seem* to be fairly evenly spaced or graded. Only the two ends and the middle pile are labelled. The middle pile is indicated for neutral opinions."

Latent Structure Analysis

Under the guidance of Lazarsfeld, this method was developed along somewhat similar lines to the Thurstone Scale, but it attempts to overcome the problems met with in the earlier type of scale.

In this case, the existence of a uni-dimensional scale is assumed, which represents a continuous range of attitudes towards a specific issue. For example, there could be a scale to cover the whole range of attitudes towards drug-taking. It is further assumed that everyone can be placed on this scale at a particular point, and this point can be found by questioning them. Informants are given a number of *test items,* which are usually simple statements, and they are required to indicate whether they agree with them or not. All the test items are chosen because they are considered to be relevant to the matter under investigation.

Although the mathematical calculations involved in the analysis of the answers is extremely complicated, and really widespread use has not yet been made of this method of investigating attitudes, its chief advantage over earlier methods is that it requires far fewer questions or test items. This makes it less onerous to those people who are selected to form the sample for investigation, and it is therefore easier to enlist their co-operation.

The big disadvantage of Latent Structure Analysis is that it assumes that the answers to a series of questions on a particular issue will be influenced by only one latent attitude. This is seldom likely to be a correct assumption, because in most cases there is a complex inter-relationship between a number of attitudes held by a single individual, and this would produce inconsistencies in a method based on the idea of a one-attitude scale.*

Scalogram Analysis

At the same time as Lazarsfeld was developing his technique of Latent Structure analysis, Guttman, another American sociologist attached to the Research Branch of the Information and Education Division of the War Department, was evolving a rather different method for measuring attitudes—the *scalogram*.

Guttman was concerned with the observable responses of people towards certain emotional issues (as he defined attitudes) and not with fitting these attitudes into a preconceived latent structure pattern. This means that the method is not based on the rather unrealistic assumption that uni-dimensional attitude scales exist, but deals only with the material obtained from the informants.

One type of scalogram can be constructed by listing the physical symptoms which are produced by an emotional situation and asking the informants to state whether or not they have experienced these symptoms. The items in this type of scalogram are accorded points, both positive and negative, and they are also of a cumulative nature; *i.e.* a person stating that he has experienced the symptoms with the highest number of points could also be expected to have experienced all those with a lesser number. This person would therefore have a higher positive score than another who had only experienced a less strong symptom.

Where it is not possible to list the physical reactions to an emotional situation, another type of scalogram may be constructed by offering an informant a series of multiple-choice questions and according positive and negative points to each of the possible responses. For example, the questions could be framed along the lines

* For a fuller description of this technique, see P. F. Lazarsfeld, S. A. Stouffer *et al., The Logical and Mathematical Foundation of Latent Structure Analysis.* 1950.

"How good at his job would you say the Prime Minister is?" and the choice of answers could be "Very good," "Fairly good," "Average," "Fairly poor," "Very poor." In order to bring in the cumulative factor in scoring, a dividing line could be drawn to separate the positive scores from the negative. In our example, positive scores could be given for the answers "Very good," "Fairly good" and "Average," and negative scores for "Fairly poor" and "Very poor."

The greatest difficulty in constructing either type of scalogram is to find a series of items which can be scaled in a satisfactory way, and to decide how the cumulative system of scoring can be achieved.

Probably the most useful feature of Guttman's technique is the method he devised for analysing the data. This is done manually by placing a piece of lead shot for each point scored in the appropriate pocket provided on a slat. A slat is used for each informant, and the slats fit on to a frame. When all the points have been awarded, the frame is inverted over a second frame which also contains pockets, and in this way all the shot representing the responses to a particular question is brought together. It is then very easy to count the shot in each pocket on the second frame, and to assess the results of the survey.

PARTICIPANT OBSERVATION

Participant observation was at one time regarded as the method chiefly used by anthropologists for collecting information, but it now appears to be gaining greater popularity with sociologists. This may well be because it has become increasingly apparent that there is frequently a wide divergence between what people *say* they are doing and what they are *really* doing; between the official norms and the unofficial norms operating within a group; between the stated aims and purposes of an organisation and the effective goals within it.

The participant observer generally seeks to become a member of the group which he is studying and, by taking part in its activities, he hopes to view the situation from the point of view of his subjects. He develops a much closer relationship with his informants over a longer period of time than is the case with more formal methods of research, and in this way it is possible for him to obtain information which would almost certainly not otherwise become available.

Although participant observation is generally spoken of as a single research method, sociologists who make use of it usually draw upon a number of techniques in order to discover as much as possible about the particular groups that they are studying. As well as directly participating in activities and playing their own role, observers are likely to collect documents, carry out interviews, question key members of the group about particular aspects of it, watch closely how their subjects behave, and also make use of a certain amount of self-analysis, recording their own feelings and reactions to events as they occur.

Researchers will develop their own styles to suit the requirements of their particular line of research; they will devise their own systems for recording information and making notes while in the field, because there are no hard and fast rules of participant observation which can be learned. There are, however, some specific problems associated with this method of research which are generally recognised, and which have to be considered.

The first of these has to do with *gaining entry to the group* to be studied. This is not always an easy problem to overcome, because there is very often a great deal of suspicion about the activities of researchers, and a reluctance to allow an observer into a group or an organisation. Refusal to co-operate in a research project is less likely to be encountered if investigators explain the exact nature of their work and the type of information which they are seeking.

Secondly there is the problem of *establishing and maintaining relationships* with the members of the group once entry to it has been gained. In this instance, the personality of the researcher will be an influential factor, and the success or failure of the project will be entirely dependent upon the ability of the observer to get himself or herself accepted by the others. The observer must take into account that not all members of the group will be equally friendly and communicative. It is therefore important that the effort should be made to involve as many subjects as possible to reduce the risk of bias and distortion that might result from concentrating only on the more forthcoming and articulate amongst them.

In the third place, because they become involved in the activities of the people they are studying, participant observers are very likely to *alter the behaviour of their subjects* by their presence. Although this cannot be avoided entirely, as far as possible the observer should attempt to play a neutral role in the group.

Fourthly, the researcher will have *to maintain an objective position*, and this may well prove to be the most difficult problem that is encountered. Many participant observers have found it useful to withdraw from the field at fairly regular intervals in order to preserve the necessary degree of detachment from their subjects. Over-close involvement in the activities of a group may make it difficult for the observer to keep his own feelings from colouring and possibly distorting his perspective.

Fifthly, there are problems associated with *recording* and, later, *analysing* the data that have been collected. These can be very daunting, because a great mass of information will inevitably be accumulated over a period of time in the field. Just as researchers will generally devise their own systems for keeping records and codifying material so they will also devise their own systems for categorising and interpreting the information. The analysis of non-quantitative data is extremely difficult.

Lastly, there are the technical and ethical problems of *presenting and publishing the findings* of this type of research. Typically, there will be a large number of conclusions to be drawn and frequently an excessive amount of space will be required if all the qualitative evidence to support them is to be included.

When using participant observation, the researcher develops ties with his subjects and much information is gained in confidence. The problem inevitably arises as to how much of this information should be divulged. It may be extremely difficult to hide completely the identity of the group or individuals studied, and the researcher may feel that by publishing his findings he is betraying a trust that has been placed in him. As well as having responsibilities to his inform-ants, the observer also has to consider his responsibilities to sociology, to the people who will treat his findings as a contribution to knowledge and to other social scientists who may wish to conduct similar research projects. Because of the very nature of participant observation, these responsibilities may often conflict.

SOCIOMETRY

Sociometry is the method which is increasingly being used by sociologists and psychologists to explore the structure of social groups and to examine the role, status and personality traits of group members. The method is based on the measurement of attraction and rejection between the individuals in groups, and it has been used successfully to investigate not only groups as such but also group processes such as leadership and morale, social adjustment and deviance.

The basic principle of sociometry is the *sociometric test*, which requires each individual within the group being studied to select from amongst the other members those with whom he would prefer to associate in particular situations. Each person is also asked to state those with whom he would least like to associate in these situations. The selections and rejections of the group members are always considered in terms of the specific circumstances under which the group exists, such as living together, working together or associating for any other purpose.

There are, therefore, two preliminary stages in the use of sociometric techniques—establishing the criteria for a group's existence, and ascertaining the patterns of selection and rejection within the group in terms of situations connected with these criteria.

From the information obtained about selection–rejection patterns within a group, it is possible to produce a *sociogram*, which can be

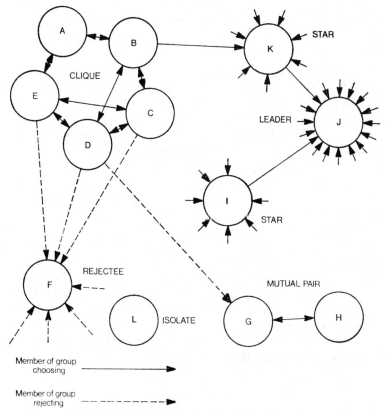

Fig. 3—Example of a sociogram

used to depict graphically various aspects of the group's structure. This makes it relatively easy to discover and analyse such structural phenomena as cliques, rejectees and isolates (*see* Fig. 3).

Sociometric tests have shown that in some groups the same individuals are preferred in all situations, but in others different members are selected for each different activity which the group undertakes. Sociometric tests will reveal, for example, whether leadership of the group is a constant factor at all times, or whether different individuals will perform this role as the group has to deal with different circumstances.

By supporting sociometric tests with personal interviews conducted amongst the members of the group being studied, it is possible to establish the emotional basis of the pattern of relationships—whether the pattern is founded on sympathy, fear, envy, anger or any other of the numerous emotions which might hold individuals together. These tests can therefore also be applied to assess the degree to which a group is integrated—whether there are many ties which hold the members together, or whether the group forms only for the purpose of carrying out one particular activity.

At first sight, it might appear that sociometry is a simple technique. Certainly the principles of sociometric tests are easy to comprehend, but in many instances they are no more easy to apply than any of the other methods which have been developed for measuring attitudes and opinions. Sociologists who have made use of sociometric techniques have discovered that there is an inherent danger of arousing antagonism when investigating rejection patterns, and they have therefore frequently had to confine their research to the investigation of preference patterns, which has immediately reduced the possible value of their work.

Since J. L. Moreno first set out the principles and methods of sociometry in his book *Who Shall Survive?* (1934), more sophisticated statistical techniques, such as indices and scoring devices, have been developed for use in conjunction with sociometric tests. These are valuable when a mathematical analysis of group behaviour is required for scientific study, but they are subject to the same limitations as all methods so far devised for recording numerically such concepts as preference, morale or emotion.

EXERCISE 4

1. Give a brief outline of the different methods which may be used to carry out social investigations.

2. What difficulties are encountered when measuring opinions? What attempts have been made to overcome these difficulties?

3. Describe the different methods used for the selection of samples. Explain how the size of a representative sample is decided.

4. Examine the value and limitations of questionnaires as a tool of social research. (*A.E.B.*)

5. *Either*: (*a*) Give an account of any enquiry you have undertaken as part of your studies, including a discussion of the methodology of the project, any theoretical perspectives used, and its contribution to your understanding or to sociological knowledge, *or*: (*b*) Examine critically the methodology of any one sociological enquiry. (*A.E.B.*)

6. Compare the advantages and disadvantages of interviews and questionnaires as research tools. (*A.E.B.*)

7. The problem of non-response in a survey cannot legitimately be disregarded. Comment on the reasons for non-response, and explain the steps which may be taken to overcome it.

8. Outline the principles of sociometry, and suggest a situation in which sociometric tests would provide a useful method of analysis.

9. Explain the difficulties encountered when measuring attitudes, and examine critically at least *two* methods which have been devised to overcome these difficulties.

10. Explain the meaning of the following terms used in sampling:
    (*a*) Population.
    (*b*) Sampling unit.
    (*c*) Sampling frame.
    (*d*) Sampling error.

11. What are the major difficulties in the analysis and interpretation of social survey data? How may these difficulties be overcome? (*Oxford*)

12. What is "sampling"? Illustrate your answer by reference to any sociological investigations with which you are familiar. (*Oxford*)

13. What are the principal problems encountered in the construction of survey questionnaires? How may these problems be overcome? (*Oxford*)

14. What are the principal difficulties in interviewing in social research? How may these difficulties be overcome? (*Oxford*)

FOR FURTHER READING

J. Madge. *The Tools of Social Science*. Longmans, 1963.
George A. Lundberg. *Social Research*. Longmans, 1942.
Mark Abrams. *Social Surveys and Social Action*. Heinemann, 1951.
C. A. Moser. *Survey Methods in Social Investigation*. Heinemann, 1958.
J. Galtung. *Theory and Methods of Social Research*. Allen and Unwin, 1967.
J. L. Moreno. *Who Shall Survive?* (Revised edition.) Beacon, New York, 1953.
Freda Conway, *Descriptive Statistics*. Leicester University Press, 1967.
N. K. Denzin. *Sociological Methods: A Sourcebook*. Butterworths, 1970.
T. G. Connolly and W. Sluckin. *An Introduction to Statistics for the Social Sciences*. Macmillan, 1971.

PART TWO

THE SOCIAL SYSTEM

CHAPTER V

THE INDIVIDUAL AND SOCIETY

The Interaction of Heredity and Environment

EACH new baby that is born comes into the world with certain inherited characteristics that are transmitted through his parents, who are themselves the products of a long line of ancestors. The baby will grow up in the material and social surroundings which make up his total environment, and the person he becomes and all that he does will be determined by the complex interaction of heredity and environment. These two factors are responsible for shaping the personality of the individual.

HEREDITY

At the beginning of the century, biologists rediscovered the work done by Gregor Mendel, an Austrian monk, more than thirty years earlier. Mendel had originally been interested in cross-breeding red- and white-flowered peas, and had stumbled across the fact that some intangible "elements" determined whether the offspring of cross-bred parent plants would be red or white. He observed, too, that these "elements" maintained consistent ratios between red and white offspring in successive generations. Mendel wrote about his experiments in a little-known scientific journal, and it was this article which was found, after many years had passed, by biologists studying the nature of heredity.

Biologists all over the world followed up Mendel's discovery, and, in the United States, Morgan and Pearl, amongst others, developed the theory of heredity by means of *genes* and *chromosomes*—the factors which, for want of a better name, Mendel had referred to as "elements."

Each cell of a living organism consists of a dark nucleus surrounded by a jelly-like substance known as *cytoplasm*. Within the nucleus are contained a number of thread-like structures, *chromosomes*, which are strings of genes—the carriers of hereditary characteristics. The number of chromosomes within the nucleus is constant for each species, and in man there are forty-six. Growth and development takes place by means of cell division, each nucleus splitting into two before the cell itself divides. In the course of this nuclear division, each chromosome also divides lengthways, one half passing to each of the new nuclei, and in this way each of the divided cells contains a full complement of chromosomes. However, in the case of germ cells—the female ova and male sperms—the division of the chromosomes is followed by two divisions of the nucleus before the new cells are formed, which means that each human germ cell contains only twenty-three chromosomes instead of forty-six as in other body cells. At the moment of conception, when the sperm enters the ovum, the two nuclei fuse and a fertilised cell is formed, which now contains the normal twenty-three pairs of chromosomes, but one of each pair is contributed by the father and one by the mother. In this way children will inherit characteristics from both of their parents.

Physical characteristics which may be inherited include the colour of skin, hair and eyes, the shape of skull and a tendency to be short or tall. Certain physical defects such as colour-blindness, pre-senile cataract, haemophilia and brachydactyly—the absence of one bone in each finger—are also inherited. With the exception of diabetes, no common diseases are transmitted from parents to children, although the predisposition towards certain allergies, tuberculosis and cancer may be passed on.

In the case of mental characteristics, the role of heredity is difficult to assess; firstly, because there are no completely accurate methods by which mental aptitudes and abilities can be measured, and, secondly, because it is virtually impossible to separate the hereditary and the environmental influences from each other in order to establish which of them is responsible for certain characteristics. Most psychologists agree, however, that the level of an individual's intelligence is probably inherited, if by intelligence is meant a general reasoning ability. More is known, in fact, about the inheritance of some mental abnormalities such as certain types of deficiency and disease than is precisely known about the transmission of normal psychological features.

Each baby, then, is born with certain physical and mental characteristics which he inherits from his parents, and he will also have some innate *biological needs* which give rise to hunger, thirst, tiredness, sexual urges and so on which will require satisfying. These needs are commonly referred to as *instincts*. A combination of these characteristics and instincts, however, does not make the baby a "person" but rather a "potential person." As Sprott states in his book *Social Psychology*: "It is a mistake to think of the 'person' as a pre-fabricated structure waiting at birth to be erected, well or ill, by the adults in charge of it. Prior to an infant's earliest contacts with other human beings it simply does not exist as a 'person' at all."

ENVIRONMENT

It would be a senseless undertaking to spend time discussing the personality of any individual as though he or she existed as an isolated entity. Human beings do not live independently of others, but are invariably part of a group, and, as a result of the consequential interactions within the group, each individual will be shaped and moulded, and will acquire his own personality. This personality will be the result of a complex combination of physiological and environmental forces. Whether physical or environmental factors contribute more to personality is still a matter of much debate, but we know that both are essential.

The individual's first encounter with other human beings is through his family, and for a considerable time he will remain completely dependent upon his parents, particularly his mother, for the satisfaction of his basic biological needs. From the very beginning he will experience the emotions associated with these needs; if they are not satisfied, he will be unhappy and will express his unhappiness by crying persistently and making his discomfort obvious; if the needs are satisfied, he will be contented and comfortable, and will make "agreeable" noises or sleep peacefully.

Gradually, as his awareness of others develops, the child will experience more complex needs which are associated with the fact that he is a social being, and, in order to survive, must live with other people. These *companionship needs* will lead him to feel neglected, lonely and unhappy if they are not satisfied, and he will learn what to do if he is to be accepted by other people. He will assimilate the simple rules of give and take, the beginnings of co-operation and emotional restraint which are necessary if the most simple social order is to be maintained.

The individual will, however, feel the desire for recognition as a person, and, in order to achieve this, he will have certain needs which are, perhaps, best referred to as *ego needs*. All his attempts to make some impact on his environment, however trivial, his ambitions to reach even the easiest of goals and his wish to demonstrate superiority over others will all reflect the need to assert individuality.

These needs are common to all human beings and are therefore regarded as part of human nature, but, although this successfully explains *why* people do certain things, it does not answer the question as to *how* they do them. The way in which they do these things is wholly determined by their total environment. In our discussion of culture in Chapter III, we noted that each society will have its own ways of coping with the contingencies of living, and these will be passed on from one generation to the next, so that each individual will learn how to do things according to an established system. During the 1930s, the anthropologists Margaret Mead and Ruth Benedict demonstrated very clearly how adaptable human nature is to a wide variety of social conditions, and Ruth Benedict concluded, in *Patterns of Culture*, that:

". . . most of the organisations of personality that seem to us most incontrovertibly abnormal have been used by different civilisations in the very foundations of their institutional life. Conversely, the most valued traits of our normal individuals have been looked upon in differently organised cultures as aberrant. Normality, in short, within a very wide range, is culturally defined."

Culture patterns are assimilated within the home, the neighbourhood, the school and all groups of any kind to which an individual belongs, whether formal or informal in their organisation. These agencies will all help to influence attitudes and so also assist in shaping personality. If we compare the attitude of American parents towards their children, for example, with that of British parents, we find that the former generally expect their children to be much in evidence and to assert their individuality from a very early age. They appear to enjoy the company of their children, to whom they give the maximum amount of freedom and the minimum amount of discipline. A child's "goodness" is judged according to his achievements. British parents, on the other hand, expect their children to play a very subordinate role within the family, and to adapt themselves to the established routine. Discipline is more strict, and much attention is paid to such matters as keeping to a set pattern of meal times and bedtime. The children's "goodness" tends to be measured in terms of how little they interrupt the well-ordered life of the parents. Mothers proudly remark that their children are so good "you'd hardly know they were in the house" —a boast that would be anathema to American mothers.

From such simple differences as these the growing child will begin to assume certain personality traits which will help to make him acceptable as a member of a particular society and also frequently make him distinguishable from members of another society. Americans, probably largely on account of their experiences in the earliest formative period of their lives, tend to be more pragmatic, confident and self-assertive than their British counterparts, and they also have far less respect for traditional types of authority.

Within the social environment of the neighbourhood, the child will absorb more of the attitudes and beliefs shared by those amongst whom he lives. People of similar socio-economic status tend to be drawn together and to live in areas which reflect the type of resident. This, of course, is the reason why certain districts or regions become labelled as "good-class residential areas," "stockbroker belts," "slums," "tough areas" and so on.

Children will base their standards and expectations almost entirely upon those which they encounter and accept within the small family and neighbourhood community in which they live. They do not have the capacity for reasoning and questioning the situations which they meet, but tend to take their somewhat limited social environment for granted, and this environment is likely to influence their personalities profoundly. Although as they grow up their horizons will be widened, and the children will take up the attitudes, beliefs and behaviour patterns which are shared by the whole society, differences in their sub-cultural backgrounds will almost certainly remain a part of their make-up to a considerable extent.

INTER-PERSONAL PERCEPTION

Family, neighbourhood, school, youth clubs, possibly religious organisations, and eventually the job he takes up, will all present the individual with social situations within which interaction with others will assist in personality development. One important part of this development is the process of *inter-personal perception*—the process by which social situations are interpreted and made meaningful for the individual. As he becomes aware that other people respond to him as a separate and autonomous being, the individual will gradually evolve a concept of himself as an entity. George Mead, upon whose studies in psychology a whole school of psychotherapy has been based, contended that the concept of self is of vital importance in the development of personality and social adjustment, and that the individual's evaluation of himself will change in response to changes in other people's evaluation of him.

There is a chameleon-like quality within all of us which makes it possible for us to adapt ourselves in this way. The feeling that other people have little confidence in our ability to perform a particular task may undermine any self-confidence we possess, whilst knowing that others think we are very capable may provide us with just the boost to our morale that makes us determined to do the job well and successfully. Also, the desire to conform that is inherent in us makes us adopt the values and norms of those with whom we associate, and, where it is necessary, alter our behaviour to fit in with new social situations which we encounter. Many children, for example, "grow away" from their parents if they receive a different type of formal education and take up occupations which carry with them higher prestige on the social scale. Children of working-class parents may move upwards in the social scale and eventually take on the attributes and mannerisms of middle-class citizens.

In the United States recent studies of military and college groups have shown that individuals who regard themselves as being similar to the other people with whom they are in regular contact, and are also perceived as similar by the other people, are better adjusted socially than those whose concept of themselves conflicts with others' perception of them.

The way in which the individual perceives other people is closely linked with his attitudes towards them. He will tend to agree with the people whom he likes, and like those with whom he agrees. Conversely, he will tend to disagree with those whom he dislikes, and dislike almost "on principle" those people with whom he disagrees. The patterns of mutual attraction or rejection on the grounds of agreement and disagreement are of fundamental importance to personality development and individual adjustment to social situations, because they provide the bases upon which groups come into being, and groups are the essential elements in social life.

We have already discussed in an earlier chapter how the individual does not have to flounder helplessly as he meets social situations for the first time, but instead gradually learns the prescribed patterns of behaviour forming the culture of the society into which he has been born, and is thus able to adjust to his environment. He learns what to expect of others and what will be expected of him in return. Associated with the cultural behaviour patterns are the concepts of status and role.

STATUS AND ROLE

The type of behaviour which is advocated by the society, and is therefore acceptable to it, is centred around the different positions of individuals within the system—males, females, children, adults, employers, employees, parents, teachers and so on. These positions are called *statuses*, and assigned to each status is its own appropriate behaviour. There is, therefore, a kind of behaviour which is expected of a child but may not be expected of an adult; another kind of behaviour which is expected of a man, but maybe not of a woman.

It is also possible to make a distinction between types of statuses, since some are biologically determined and some are *achieved*. Every individual will naturally be assigned certain statuses during the course of his life simply because, as he passes through the various stages from the cradle to the grave, he will progress from the status of an infant through those of childhood and adolescence to adulthood and old age, and his behaviour will be expected to reflect his changing status.

Statuses which are not determined naturally, but result from special ability and the personal effort made by an individual, can be regarded as achieved rather than prescribed statuses. Those positions which are achieved will depend on the society itself, and will vary to some extent from one society to another. For example, no individual can achieve the status of an industrial employer in a purely agricultural community. The individual will need the stimulation of opportunity to achieve this second type of status, and the opportunities provided will be derived from the particular characteristics and specialisms of the society to which he belongs.

Even where a very wide range of opportunities is presented by the society, the statuses actually available to each individual may be limited by such factors as sex, class, wealth and education. As yet, in British society, women are not eligible for membership of the Stock Exchange; the son of a manual labourer is less likely to become Archbishop of Canterbury than the son of an upper-class academic; the son of a wealthy businessman is more likely to become a company director than the son of a factory floor-sweeper.

The behaviour patterns which are associated with the different statuses are the *roles*. As we have already noted, in any society there are *ideal* patterns of behaviour to which the *actual* behaviour approximates, and we are therefore all aware of the way in which people in different roles ought to behave in our own society. Individuals who carry out their roles in the way we think they should are regarded as "good," and are accorded general approbation by those who know them, although frequently the approbation is tinged with guilt when people feel that they are failing to measure up to the same standards quite so well themselves. The person who is "too good to be true" is very often rather unpopular. If we consider the roles of husband, wife, parent, teacher, vicar, doctor or Member of Parliament, to take but a few of the innumerable examples, we can conjure up a mental picture of the ideal image in order to decide whether individuals fulfil their roles well or badly.

Roles, however, are not independent entities. The role associated with any status has to be linked with that of others. The status and role of a parent exist because there exist the status and role of a child; the employer obtains his status only because there are also employees; the role of the professor is linked with that of the student. The appropriate behaviour of one status is reciprocated by the appropriate behaviour of another, and in this way a sense of security and order is maintained because everybody "knows where they are."

One of the major problems facing our society in Britain, as well as others, at the present time is that of the speed with which roles change; this has largely resulted from the acceleration of scientific and technological development. In little more than a century, the nature of our society has altered radically, and it takes time for the system to become adjusted. Slow, gradual changes can be much more easily assimilated and accommodated than the sudden, revolutionary changes to which society has been subjected in recent times, and, consequently, there is an element of insecurity in the present and uncertainty about the future. Members of the older generation tend to look backwards, somewhat despairingly, and say "Things were never like this in our young days," while the generation which has been born and grown up during the disruptive period following the Second World War largely lacks a sense of purposefulness because nobody knows what to expect. Too much happening too quickly means that roles do not have an opportunity to become stabilised before they are called upon to change yet again.

Another important point that must be taken into consideration in the discussion of roles is that a single individual is required to fill a number of roles either simultaneously or in succession. It is possible to isolate these roles. For example, we could say that when a man gets out of bed in the morning, washes, shaves and dresses, he is playing the role of an adult male; when he has breakfast with his family he acts as a husband and father; once he has left his house and reached his place of work, he becomes a bank manager, a shop assistant, a factory worker or a bus driver; when he returns home in the evening he is a husband and father again until, perhaps, he proceeds to be a member of a golf club or a darts team, or a guest in someone else's home. However, we must remember that, although we can separate these different roles in this way, they are not independent of each other in practice. For instance, the way in which a person dresses will be influenced by his own perception of his job and other people's perception of it; he may possibly have to wear an official uniform, but, even if he does not, he will dress in what we might well think of as an "unofficial" uniform. In some occupations people will wear a well-pressed dark suit; in others pin-striped trousers and black coat; some people will wear more casual clothes to work, and some will wear overalls and a cloth cap. The way in which a man does his job will also be very much influenced by the responsibilities and attitudes he acquires in his other roles as adult, husband and father.

The sum total of all the multiple roles which an individual fills, and the way in which he perceives them and is perceived by others in them, make the individual a person with his own characteristics and qualities which we call *personality*. Allport, in his *Personality*, has provided us with a useful definition of this concept. He says that it is "the dynamic organisation within the individual of those psycho-physical systems that determine his unique adjustments to his environment."

Groups

Human beings are invariably organised into groups of one kind or another, and the individual will be related to the society as a whole through the groups of which he is a member. Small groups are the basic units which interweave and overlap to form the vast network of social relationships which enable a society to exist and persist.

PRIMARY GROUPS

The groups which are of fundamental importance are those which are small enough to enable intimate face-to-face relationships to be maintained. Families, play-groups, neighbourhood groups, occupational groups and recreational groups are all examples of the type of unit known as a *primary group*. Within these units all the group processes of co-operating, fighting, imitating, loving, helping and so on are carried out in the ways determined by the culture of the society of which they form a part. Such groups play the most significant role in the development of character and personality.

SECONDARY GROUPS

The larger, less intimate, groups which are deliberately organised for a specific purpose are referred to as *secondary groups*. They are generally more formal than the primary groups, but, although the hierarchy is as a result more clearly defined, co-ordination and communication between members of these groups may be difficult to achieve in practice. As more individuals are involved, the possibility of maintaining close physical relationships between them is reduced, and so is the sense of being directly concerned with the overall aims of the group. This is particularly appropriate in industry, where it has repeatedly been revealed that an individual's loyalty and interests are likely to be more strongly directed towards the informal primary group of workers with whom he regularly and closely associates than they are towards the less personal objectives and policies of the firm as a whole.

All groups are formed in order that human needs may be satisfied, and they also enable many activities to be undertaken which it would be impossible for the individual to achieve alone. This is as true of such enjoyable activities as participating in team games as it is of more essential activities such as industrial production based upon division of labour and specialisation.

All social groups are also characterised by the interaction of their members and by shared aims, beliefs and values, although they vary immensely in size from a dyad to a whole society comprising many million members, and may differ in their organisation from very informal friendships to extremely formal associations.

NORMS

The sharing of aims, beliefs and values will give rise to the development of *norms*, that is common patterns of behaving, think ing and feeling. All groups will develop norms which relate parti cularly to the purposes for which the group was originally formed, and if members deviate from those norms they will be subjected to various forms of persuasion, pressure and sanctions by others within the group to make them conform. Any member of a group who consistently refuses to conform will eventually be rejected by the group and probably excluded from its activities. People who are anxious to remain within the group will therefore conform to its norms, as will those who are keen to enter into a group but are as yet not fully accepted.

An interesting problem remains to be solved, and that is why members of a group always want *deviates*—those who refuse to conform to the norms—to accept its norms. Michael Argyle, in *Psychology and Social Problems,* suggests that:

> "In rare instances the group goals may be threatened, as in the case of the rate-buster in industry. In others the group as a whole might be thrown into disrepute. In matters of belief it has been suggested that those who are uncertain of their views get emotional satisfaction from them, feel threatened by the presence of those who hold other views, and want to create social support for their own."

Some individuals can be regarded as somewhat "two-faced" where conformity to norms is concerned. When they are with the other members of the group they are observed to conform apparently wholeheartedly, but once away from the group they reject its norms. In other words the norms remain external to the individual, and may only become "internalised," as Durkheim expressed it, after a fairly long association with the group during which the norms are considered, interpreted and rationalised by the individual. The process of internalisation is part of what Durkheim referred to as socialisation.

GROUP INTEGRATION

This refers to the amount of cohesion between the members of a group—to the number of ties which bind them together. The cohesion may vary in intensity so that the level of integration which exists may range from the loosest of associations to very close-knit groups. Integration may occur as a result of only one common bond or tie between the members of a group or because there are numerous bonds, but, the more bonds that exist, the more closely integrated the group will be. Members of a cricket team, for example, may have no ties except the common desire to play cricket, and the group will only form in order to take part in a game or to practise. The individual members will not identify themselves with each other or feel a sense of involvement as a group on any other occasions. At the other end of the scale, however, a group of coloured immigrants may form their own little community in an English town within which numerous ties exist based on ethnic, economic and cultural characteristics, and members of that community will identify themselves with each other at all times.

It is possible to distinguish three different types of group integration: mechanical or organic, normative and socio-psychological.

Mechanical integration

This may occur where the members of a group become dependent on each other as a result of division of labour. Individuals within the group may be prevented from withdrawing because they recognise that they will be less able to satisfy their particular needs outside the group. This type of integration is most common amongst occupational groups and economic organisations of all kinds.

People who share the same characteristics, particularly physical defects or abnormalities which mark them off as being different from others, may also become integrated into a group in this way. The members of the group may have nothing in common except the particular characteristic which they share, but they will feel sympathy for each other, and this emotional bond may provide the basis of group solidarity.

Normative integration

The strongest reasons for a group to hold together, apart from economic necessity and dependence, are consensus of opinion and shared attitudes. Common patterns of behaviour and value systems will bind people to each other because they are able, through the group, to give each other emotional support and to reaffirm their individual beliefs and feelings.

Within a small group there must be normative consistency, because, if norms were to conflict, a disruptive situation would develop and the group would almost certainly disintegrate. A very large group, however, is capable of containing conflicting norms, provided that the majority of the members conform. While the group as a whole may tolerate some inconsistencies, individual members may have difficulty in compromising and adjusting, although they will generally be prepared to concede that the advantages of belonging to the group outweigh the disadvantages of being outside it.

A group which shows a very high degree of integration will usually also be one in which the members have a strong sense of *discipline*. If the group is placed in a critical situation which calls for determined or even courageous behaviour in order to surmount it, the presence of discipline will be particularly marked. A crisis in a marriage, such as the loss of a child or a sudden reduction in the economic circumstances, may draw a husband and wife closer together, but if the individuals concerned are selfish and lacking in discipline, such a crisis might well cause the marriage to break down. On a much larger scale, the threat of attack may unite a nation, but unless the individuals within the nation are prepared to accept that discipline is necessary, and to put the interests of the whole group above their own individual concerns, a threat of this kind will produce chaos and disruption.

Discipline depends upon the observance of meaningful rules and regulations which provide a code of behaviour. In formally structured groups, the principles by which the conduct of members is controlled are likely to be laid down in a constitution or at least in an agreed set of rules. The willingness of individuals to abide by the regulations depends, however, on the purpose underlying them. Motorists, for example, are generally willing to accept that, unless they drive according to the rules, the roads will be too dangerous for people to use. Traffic laws can be seen to have a purpose that is easily recognised and understood. It sometimes happens, however, that rules and regulations are made in the first place for a very good reason which individuals can understand and accept, but, over a period of time, circumstances change, and the conditions which made the rules necessary no longer exist. If the rules are not abolished or altered to reflect the new situation, they may fall into disrepute and be broken repeatedly, or else, if those in authority try to enforce them, a great deal of resentment is aroused in the people who are expected to submit to them.

The reason why the observance of a common code of behaviour is more in evidence in a small, highly integrated group than in a very large group is partly to be found in the fact that members are more easily able to communicate with each other, and any rules that they devise can be adapted much more quickly to suit the changing situations encountered by the group. The rules are likely, therefore, to remain meaningful.

In order to protect themselves against disruption and disintegration, groups may bring pressure to bear on their members to ensure that discipline is maintained. If individuals refuse to adhere to the established code which regulates behaviour, they may be subjected to sanctions. At one end of the scale, the state may punish people who break its laws, and, at the other end, members of a small informal group will reject those who refuse to comply by bringing social pressure to bear on them. Isolating criminals from the rest of society by putting them in prison is only a more extreme form of the punishment which is meted out to a non-conformist in a small informal group by means of "cold-shouldering" and bringing pressure to bear on the individual, which causes him eventually to remove himself from the group.

Socio-psychological integration

This takes place within a group because of the *mutual satisfaction* members derive from being part of it. Groups form for a purpose, and where there is a sense of achievement the people will want to continue in those groups. A few individuals who decide to form themselves into a small group one evening each week to listen to gramophone records which they all enjoy will want to continue doing this all the time they derive a common satisfaction from it. In just the same way, a football team or a number of people engaged on a particular project at work will be held together if they feel that they are playing well or making progress as a group. Sometimes, a group which has formed for one purpose may want to tackle another task together although the original purpose has been achieved and no longer gives them any reason to remain with each other.

The desire to remain together as a group will depend to a great extent on the *mutual attraction* of members. Morale will be higher and the stability of the group enhanced where the members like each other and "get on well" together. This applies largely to primary, face-to-face, groups, and is the aspect of social integration to which J. L. Moreno and his followers have paid particular attention. Moreno looked at groups as being a series of links between person and person based on *tele*: "a feeling which is projected into distance; the simplest unit of feeling transmitted from one individual to another"; this feeling could be one of like, dislike or indifference. Each of these attitudes transmitted from one individual to the others within the group will be met with one or other in return, and the most harmonious grouping will be that in which the attitude of like is transmitted and reciprocated between the members.

DIFFERENTIATION WITHIN THE GROUP

During the existence of a group members will assume different roles and perform different functions within it. In the first place, differentiation will reflect the purpose of the group. Formal groups may be brought into being by sponsors, or the agents of sponsors, to perform specific tasks, and, in this case, those responsible for bringing the group together will also be responsible for its structure and for assigning individuals to specific roles within it. Examples of this type of group are those employed by a firm to carry out its objectives, and members will be selected from amongst people who are considered best able to perform the functions necessary to reach these objectives. Differentiation will be based on specialisation and division of labour within the group, and differences between members will be recognised by the members themselves and respected and maintained by them.

Some formal groups come into existence as a result of social pressure. The society as a whole may evolve a system which can only be put into practice by organised groups. For example, in Britain it is now considered essential for the sake of the society that all children between the ages of 5 and 16 should receive a formal education. In order to make this possible it is necessary to provide schools in which the required subjects may be taught. As a consequence organised groups have been formed within which a recognised structure is maintained, and differentiation is based firstly on the role of the teacher and the pupil, and secondly on the division of labour between the teachers which makes it possible for them to perform their functions as teachers in the most efficient way. In this manner the society's desired objective—educating its children—is achieved.

LEADERSHIP

Leadership is of fundamental importance in any group, but the type of leadership which exists will be largely determined by the social structure of the group itself. Some groups, particularly informal ones, are more democratic than others, being member orientated rather than leader orientated. In very formal groups with clearly defined regulations and methods of procedure, there may be a strongly autocratic organisation or one in which the amount of authority vested in members of the group at different levels is precisely established by some agency outside the group and imposed on it.

A major problem encountered when discussing the nature of leadership is that of deciding what is meant by the term. A certain amount of confusion is caused by the fact that the words "leader" and "leading" are used somewhat loosely and imprecisely in everyday speech. We speak of a person who is a "leader" in the particular field in which he specialises when really we mean a person who has discovered some new knowledge or whose ability is superior to that of others engaged on the same work. We also talk about "leading scientists" or "leading surgeons" when we are referring to the eminence of such people, and not to any role which they perform as members of a group.

There is also a certain amount of confusion between "domination" and "leadership." Both terms refer to supremacy and ascendancy, but domination relies on the submissiveness of those who are controlled, while leadership relies on their acquiescence. There is an obvious and important distinction, therefore, between these two concepts.

Dominance implies the assuming of superiority, and there are many aspects of social life in which superior status has traditionally been assigned to certain roles, so that, to some extent, dominance and submission are methods of conduct which are learned during a complex cultural training. In this society, for example, the superiority of the male has been "taken for granted" for so long that only comparatively recently has the idea of sexual equality even been considered, and children have been taught to accept the pattern of male dominance and female submissiveness. This particular pattern was developed from biological differences in the first place, but cultural processes may encourage other differences between members of the society, such as in class, age, occupation, intelligence and so on, to be recognised and accepted as the bases of dominant or submissive roles. Dominance is somewhat rigid and inflexible and it will almost certainly be maintained by means of aggression or compulsion which will control the behaviour of others, but only for as long as they are prepared to submit. Domination of a group does not provide an integrative element within it, but may instead cause it to disband, since those who are subjected to the will of the dominator may decide to leave if they are in a position to do so. It is interesting to note that aggression tends to provoke counter-aggression, and, if the members of a group which is being dominated cannot leave it, they will generally find ways of retaliating. Individuals or groups who dominate others do so for their own purposes and do not heed the interests and ambitions of those who are forced to submit to them. On a small scale, people who "get too big for their boots" or start "chucking their weight around" will arouse feelings of antagonism, and, on a much larger scale, occupying armies have to contend with acts of sabotage and underground resistance movements.

Leadership, on the other hand, is an integrative element within a group, and is more flexible since it is dependent upon co-operation. Co-operation and acquiescence differ from mere submission, because they rely upon the willingness of individuals to follow their leader, and therefore leadership implies psychological interaction. A leader influences his followers but he is also influenced by them in return. It is a reciprocal relationship, but one in which the ability of the leader to influence others is greater than that of others to influence him so that the leader is in a position of supremacy.

Leadership is essentially a group function, and, in informal groups, different individuals may emerge as leaders in different situations. In formal groups, it is sometimes found that the "official" leader is not, in fact, the "real" leader. The appointed person may be followed by the rest of the group to a limited extent by virtue of his official status, but the person who influences the group by his personal qualities rather than his position in the formal hierarchy may be regarded as the true leader by the other members, and may be given more support and co-operation by them. The ability to elicit a desired response from others cannot be derived purely and simply from the possession of an official title and status, but must depend to a great extent on the personality traits of the individual who becomes a leader.

Since leadership is a two-way process and is a function of the group as a whole, the qualities looked for in a leader will be determined by the needs and purposes for which the group has formed. It is therefore quite possible for an individual who possesses the particular qualities to make him a leader in one group to play a very minor role or even be an isolate in another. It is possible, however, to generalise to some extent and say that versatility is an essential characteristic for any leader since he will have to be initiator, planner, organiser, judge, expert, social psychologist, external liaison officer and so on, all rolled into one. A great deal of research has been carried out to try to determine the qualities which make for good leaders, but Charles Bird, who in *Social Psychology* compared the findings of some twenty enquiries, was able to extract from them no less than seventy-nine personality traits which were regarded as being desirable in a leader. He listed the traits mentioned in each enquiry and found that initiative was mentioned six times, extraversion and a sense of humour five times, and fairness, sympathy, enthusiasm and self-confidence four times.

Leaders may be elected or appointed; they may reach the position by a system of promotion according to seniority, or they may be self-chosen. Again, the way in which a leader is established will depend to a large extent on the nature of the group. Some methods of selection are more appropriate to formal groups than informal groups. Some are more appropriate to democratic organisations than to groups which have an autocratic structure. Professor Sprott, in *Social Psychology,* remarks that the motivation of the self-chosen leader is of great importance to his group:

> "These motives are obviously very varied. In a co-operating group, the leader may put himself forward because he knows something which the whole group wants to know and which it is necessary for them to know if their project is to be successful. More interesting is the leader who puts himself forward more persistently, because any such will be men who find in leadership a compensation for inferiorities which rile them. They will be of the more domineering kind and will tend to resent criticism and avoid discussion. Their insecurity displays itself in a sensitivity about their position and the marks of deference that go with it."

Professor Sprott also states that it is necessary to draw attention to those cases where the selection of a leader by appointment is accompanied by some formal examination:

> "Such examples of formal leadership are of interest because the appointing body only has before it candidates already selected by examination, and the type of examination—usually a written one—may eliminate candidates who would in point of fact be good leaders in the posts for which they would like to apply."

We must bear in mind that the personality traits displayed by leaders may not necessarily be associated with any ethical considerations. The leader of a gang of hooligans and vandals, the pimp who procures prostitutes and runs a brothel or the head of a group of criminals may perform the same functions within their groups and be just as effective as the director of a team engaged in scientific research, the headmaster of a school or the captain of a cricket team.

THE DEVELOPMENT OF A HIERARCHY

When a new group forms, some type of hierarchal structure will come into existence within a relatively short period, even where a formal structure is not imposed on the group by some external agent. The way in which the differentiation of roles occurs will, of course, be determined by what the group is and what it does, but it is possible to analyse the various types of structure and role relationships within them very broadly according to differences in terms of task activities and division of labour, of power and influence or of position in the communications network.

The nature of a group's task will influence *the way in which the activities are apportioned* amongst its members and the level of integration and co-ordination required. The work on which the members of a group are engaged may not demand that everyone has the highest possible degree of ability; it is much more likely to need a mixture of degrees and types of ability, and this will be reflected in the different roles of the individuals who form the group.

In a formal group the roles of individual members are frequently clearly defined in terms of *authority or power,* which thus provides the group with a hierarchy of superordinatory and subordinatory positions. In less formal groups a similar power hierarchy may develop on the basis of the prestige attached to the different roles. It is interesting to note that an individual may possess such prestige quite independently of his position within the group, and his "external" status may be carried over into the group as a result. For example, his general status based on occupation, wealth, age or education and the position he holds in the wider field of society may accord him a similar status within the much narrower limits of any primary group of which he is a member.

It is somewhat irrational to assume that, because someone has a particular ability in one area, he will be equally able in many others. We even talk rather disparagingly of the person who is a "Jack of all trades and master of none," and yet we pay a great deal of attention to the pronouncements on any subject made by an individual who is eminent in his own field. The proof of this can be found in the practice of inviting such people as leading politicians, university professors, famous athletes and well-known journalists to take part in television and radio broadcasts during which they are asked to discuss a very wide variety of topics. The knowledge on which such people base their deliberations and contributions is unlikely to be any greater, in most cases, than that of many millions of viewers and listeners, and yet what they have to say carries considerable weight on account of their general position in the society and the prestige attached to it.

The *network of communications* within a group is also an important basis for determining the pattern of role relationships. It is possible to examine the position of each individual in terms of links with other individuals, and to assess whether a particular role is central, intermediary or peripheral in the communications structure; the high-status members of a group are likely to initiate and receive many more messages than the low-status members.

In 1950 and 1951 Thilbault and Kelley conducted some laboratory experiments in which they found that, in groups which had no externally imposed restrictions on communications, not only are the direction and frequency of messages passed important in assessing the relative status of different members, but also the content of the communications they exchange. High-status members communicate more than low-status members and all members direct more messages upwards to those of higher status than downwards. Low-status members who had no chance of moving up in the hierarchy tended to spend more time in discussing matters which were quite irrelevant to the group's main task than low-status members who anticipate promotion.

To a considerable extent, the network of communications also influences and is influenced by the pattern of friendships which evolves within a group. With few exceptions we do not develop either positive or negative feelings towards people unless we regularly associate with them, and, once we have got to know them, we tend to avoid those whom we dislike while looking for opportunities to mix with those whom we like. Within a group, the pattern of friendships may cause subdivisions, or cliques, to come into being and, although the task on which a group is engaged may itself produce activity-orientated subdivisions within it, there is always the possibility that friendship groupings may not correspond with the way in which task activities are divided. The friendship structure in a work group may not always enhance its efficiency, because hostilities and attitudes of indifference between members may cause problems in the communications network and be generally disruptive. We must remember, however, that for many people there is very little satisfaction to be derived from the job they are doing, and friendships provide compensation for this, so that the social relationships may take precedence over the formal aims of the group.

There are many people who lack the desire or ability to interact with others. They appear to be indifferent to the people with whom they come into contact, and, in return, other people make little or no effort to associate with them. Generally, these *isolates* tend to be somewhat introverted and self-centred, and, where they do not deliberately avoid relationships with others, they may also be unhappy. Most of us experience a sense of isolation at some time or other during our lives—when we join a new school, move into a neighbourhood far away from our previous home or start work for a different employer, for example—but usually we quickly become familiar with our new environment and begin to establish relationships with the people with whom we come into contact. The true isolate, however, through inability or preference, will make no attempt to establish and maintain communications with the people he encounters, and may even rebuff any friendly approaches made to him.

Sometimes isolation from mutual contact is a prescribed form of behaviour in certain sectors of the society, and a person may be an isolate in one group because he is conforming to the norms of another according to which it is not "the done thing" to associate with the members of this second group. This type of isolation is an important element in social organisation, because social distance as well as social nearness is an essential structural principle.

DEVIANT BEHAVIOUR

Behaviour which is different from, or conflicts with, the standards which are accepted as normal within a group or social system is referred to as *deviant behaviour*. What is considered to be normal or deviant behaviour can only be gauged in terms of the social context in which it is observed, because what is regarded as quite normal in one group or culture may well be regarded as very abnormal in another. Professor Sprott, in his *Science and Social Action*, argues that: "the concept of deviance implies the concept of order. We have at the back of our minds the notion of a social system with its normative regulations, and deviance is the departure on the part of participants from culturally expected rules of conduct."

A number of experiments have been conducted in order to

establish the extent to which deviant behaviour is disapproved of, and it has been found that the degree of disapproval tends to vary according to the level of integration which exists within the group where it occurs. The more highly integrated groups and those with an authoritarian structure generally reject deviant members most readily, and in circumstances which appear to threaten the existence or well-being of a group the members will be intolerant of deviant behaviour.

Much attention has been paid to the possibility of reintegrating deviant individuals into society, and to making them into conforming members of it. Delinquents, mentally maladjusted patients, criminals, alcoholics, drug addicts and so on have been the subjects of a great deal of sociological and psychological research, and many attempts have been made to find effective methods of remedial treatment. It has been found that the isolated individual who displays symptoms of maladjustment is easier to treat than the deviant who seeks out others like himself and joins with them to form a group of non-conformists. Once this occurs, and the group provides the satisfaction its members seek, the deviants will become integrated and conforming members of it, and their reintegration into the larger community, which they perceive as rejecting them, becomes much more difficult to achieve.

The deviant or delinquent individual is just as much a product of his social environment as the most highly integrated and conforming person. It could be said that society creates its deviants because it frequently expects its members to do things which, left to themselves, they would have no inclination to do, and it also often refuses to allow them to do many of the things they very much wish to do. In our society, it is taken for granted that people will work in order to earn a living, and although there are many occasions when people would prefer to do something else, shirking these responsibilities is regarded as a form of deviance so that pressure is brought to bear on them to make them conform. Similarly, while it is customary to go about either nude or very scantily dressed in many parts of the world, however high the temperature soars in Britain we are not permitted to be undressed in public, despite the discomfort we may feel as we swelter in factories, offices and shops, and the obvious relief that shedding our clothes would bring.

The interesting question which arises in the discussion of deviant behaviour is why so many other individuals who are subjected to the same kind of stresses and frustrations are not maladjusted or delinquent. By far the greater number of people find it very easy to conform and adjust themselves to the society in which they live. As yet, despite the research that has been undertaken in the attempt to establish the cause or causes of deviant behaviour and the numerous theories that have been put forward to explain it, there is no wholly satisfactory answer available. Heredity, poverty, broken homes, overcrowding and lack of parental discipline have all been named as possible contributory elements, but any detailed examination of these factors only reveals that none of them can be held entirely responsible. Many delinquent children have quite normally adjusted brothers and sisters; poorer members of very wealthy and competitive societies do not by any means all resort to crime; a large number of children from broken homes grow up to be perfectly adequate adults.

There is, however, an increasing amount of evidence that many of the individuals who show symptoms of deviance have difficulty in forming satisfactory relationships with other people. Dr John Bowlby, who has made very detailed investigations of the case histories of delinquent children in London, suggests in his book, *Child Care and the Growth of Love,* that:

"There is a very strong case indeed for believing that prolonged separation of a child from his mother (or mother substitute) during the first five years of life stands foremost among the causes of delinquent character development."

Many retrospective studies made into the backgrounds of different categories of deviants—criminals, prostitutes and psychopathic personalities—give support to the hypothesis that the seeds of maladjustment are sown very early during the formative years of life, and have their roots in the parent–infant relationship. John Gittins, in his report on *Approved School Boys,* remarks that:

"Where a home is described as 'apparently normal' there is no guarantee that it may not have very unsatisfactory features. It will be noted that little mention has been made [in a list provided by the court 'records of information' about boys sent to approved schools] of the physical conditions of the homes. Usually they are untidy and cramped, comfortless and depressing. Often they are filthy and sometimes they are insanitary beyond description. Nevertheless we find that the emotional atmosphere of the home is the vital matter. A respectable and very clean house tenanted by parents at loggerheads often presents a problem that is insuperable. The happy-go-lucky and affectionate family living in squalor is a much more promising proposition from our point of view . . . Most of the boys come from fairly large families and frequently their brothers and sisters are—so far as is known—not delinquent. There is no doubt that both constitutional and environmental factors unite to cause delinquency but our ignorance on this subject is profound."

Considerable progress is being made in increasing our understanding of deviant behaviour, but our knowledge is still too limited for us to be able to deal satisfactorily with all the problems it creates in the society, and it is not always practicable at present to make use of such knowledge as we do possess in the retraining of deviants. There is a hard core formed by the more serious non-conformists who appear at present to be completely resistant to all forms of influence, and, whilst we may suspect that they are "more sinned against than sinning," there is an obvious necessity for the rest of society to be protected from them.

EXERCISE 5

1. Examine some of the problems involved in integrating individuals with organisations, illustrating by reference to any studies with which you are familiar. (*A.E.B.*)

2. Assess the relative importance of heredity and environment in the development of personality.

3. Distinguish between *prescribed status* and *achieved status,* and explain the significance of status within the social system.

4. "One of the major problems facing our society at the present time is that of the speed with which roles change." Explain and discuss.

5. What does the sociologist mean by "norms"? To what extent is the internalisation of norms an important factor in the process of group integration?

6. Examine the premise that leadership is essentially a group function.

7. Why are secondary groups generally more formal than primary groups?

8. "The concept of deviance implies the concept of order" (W. J. H. Sprott). Explain and comment upon this statement.

9. Explain the meaning of the following:
   (*a*) Inter-personal perception.
   (*b*) Mechanical integration.
   (*c*) Isolate.
   (*d*) Deviate.

10. "Normality, within a very wide range, is culturally defined" (Ruth Benedict). Explain and discuss.

11. Describe and illustrate the way in which the concept "status" is used. (*Oxford*)

12. Discuss and illustrate the use of the concept of "role" in sociology. (*Oxford*)

13. Discuss the relationship between role and personality. (*London*)

14. "It is not the child but the group which is father to the man." Discuss. (*London*)

FOR FURTHER READING

W. J. H. Sprott. *Social Psychology*. Methuen, 1963.
C. O. Carter. *Human Heredity*. Penguin Books, 1963.
H. J. Eysenck. *The Structure of Human Personality*. Methuen, 1960.
S. S. Sargent and K. R. Stafford. *Basic Teachings of the Great Psychologists*. Dolphin Books, 1965.
T. H. Pear. *The Moulding of Modern Man*. Allen and Unwin, 1961.
Michael Argyle. *Psychology and Social Problems*. Social Science Paperbacks, 1967.
J. E. McGrath. *Social Psychology*. Holt, Rinehart and Winston, 1964.
W. J. H. Sprott. *Human Groups*. Penguin Books, 1967.

CHAPTER VI

SOCIAL CLASSES

A SYSTEM of social ranks and hierarchies is not a natural or inevitable phenomenon of society, but something which man has contrived for himself and which it is possible for him to change. Although inequalities of a natural or biological nature exist between individuals in all societies, these are of a distinctly different kind from the inequalities resulting from the social rankings which man has himself introduced, and which are, for this reason, of much greater interest to the sociologist. Rousseau, in a well-known passage, demonstrated the two kinds of inequality very clearly:

> "I conceive that there are two kinds of inequality among the human species; one, which I call natural or physical, because it is established by nature, and consists in a difference of age, health, bodily strength, and the qualities of the mind or of the soul; and another, which may be called moral or political inequality, because it depends on a kind of convention, and is established, or at least authorised, by the consent of men. This latter consists of the different privileges, which some men enjoy to the prejudice of others; such as that of being more rich, more honoured, more powerful, or even in a position to exact obedience." (*A Dissertation on the Origin and Foundation of the Inequality of Mankind.*)

Some systems of social ranking, such as castes and feudal estates, have strong religious or legal backing, and are therefore very rigid, with their boundaries clearly defined. On the other hand, classes, which most modern sociologists agree originated from economic differences, have no legal or religious support, nor does membership of any one of them confer upon the individual any special political or civil rights. Consequently, the boundaries of social classes are generally less precise. In most societies it is possible to distinguish the aristocracy from the working class or peasantry, but between these two extremes are many more intermediate classes, which, for the sake of convenience, are somewhat loosely referred to as the "middle classes." These are much more difficult to ascertain or enumerate, since there is no simple criterion by which membership of them can be determined.

In a caste or feudal society, the individual will remain in the caste or estate into which he is born, but, although an individual in a class society is born into the social class to which his parents belong, he will not necessarily remain in it, since modern social classes are not at all stable, and during his lifetime an individual may quite well rise or fall on the social scale.

The Concept of Class

Class is a concept which we still do not fully understand. This is because it is a very subjective concept, and consequently numerous definitions have been put forward, although none of them are entirely satisfactory.

The concept of *social stratification* is much simpler to comprehend since it involves an objective approach. It is possible, for purposes of analysis, to seek out the bases upon which differentiation occurs —economic, political and occupational—and examine the hierarchies which are developed from them within society. We must not, however, confuse classes with strata of this kind, since a single person may be a member of several different strata simultaneously, but he can only belong to one class. It is a relatively easy matter to divide the population into categories according to income, education, occupation and so on, but it is highly unlikely that the people placed into these categories will have many common interests or shared attitudes; they will not be conscious of belonging together. If we group people according to income, we have only to consider all the different ways in which, say, £1500 a year can be earned to realise that people earning this amount will make an exceedingly rich mixture. Again, the elderly "ladies" sitting in the lounge of the Eventide Home for Distressed Gentlefolk will not regard themselves as similar to the elderly "women" sitting in the lounge of the local authority's old people's home.

We all know that money alone cannot buy a position in an upper social class, and that possessing "good taste" is as important as possessing the means of buying expensive houses, furniture and clothes. As far as class is concerned, the impoverished earl still has an advantage over the *nouveau-riche* bookmaker.

At the root of class, then, is a consciousness of belonging, and an awareness of its inclusion–exclusion nature. Bound up with this are feelings of inferiority and superiority about which psychologists have so far been unable to tell us very much, although one of the greatest barriers to success in climbing the class ladder is to have an inferiority complex. Manner of dress, speech and general demeanour

E

are no doubt connected with attitudes of superiority and inferiority, but they alone are not necessarily responsible for the unconscious reactions which are experienced, for example, when strangers are first encountered. T. H. Pear suggests in *English Social Differences* that:

> "If we feel deferential towards a stranger, his appearance or his voice may have reminded us vaguely of someone—prefect, clergyman, officer —whose rank is superior to ours. To an adult, a tendency to obey or to agree when addressed in a 'prefect-manner' may be an embarrassment; so might the temptation to reply with truculence or frigid politeness, because the speech of the *vis à vis* stirs up vague memories of early slights or snubbings."

Past experiences and semi-conscious memories may have something to do with our feelings towards the people we meet for the first time, but, again, they do not provide us with the whole answer to the intriguing question of what makes us feel superior in one situation and inferior in another. How we behave towards other people and how they behave towards us is almost certainly determined by attitudes. These attitudes may be developed as a result of what might well be described as "cultural indoctrination," or they might be formed very rapidly on first impressions of other people, and these could change on longer acquaintance.

Another concept to be examined when dealing with social divisions and groupings is that of *élites*. Sociologists now frequently use this term to denote the groups of people who perform the functions of influencing others either directly or indirectly. We sometimes use the word "élite" to refer to those who are the best and the most brilliant or able. For the sociologist, however, the word has no ethical or moral connotations, and it is used simply to convey the functional roles within the society of those individuals who direct or lead the behaviour and attitudes of others. The members of élites may be experts in their own particular field, but their real power is derived from their ability to affect the lives and thoughts of other people.

An élite may be elected by the society or by groups within the society. Members of Parliament provide possibly the best example of an elected élite, although local councillors, trade-union leaders and other elected bodies who have the responsibility for formulating policy and seeing that it is carried through are of a similar nature.

Other élites, such as some government-sponsored boards and committees, are not elected but appointed, and, in this case, members of the élites will be selected because they possess special knowledge and have considerable experience in the sphere in which they operate. Judges, leading civil servants and those in positions of responsibility within the Established Church form élites of this second type.

A third form of élite may be self-elected. For instance, members of the Headmasters' Conference or members of the Institute of Directors are neither elected nor appointed but attain membership of these organisations by virtue of their occupational status.

Many élites function overtly; their existence is known and their activities are publicised. There are others, however, which operate either semi-covertly or completely covertly, and, although their influence is often considerable, decisions may be made and plans set in motion before outsiders have any indication that they even exist. There are sometimes sound practical reasons why this should be the case. Military élites, for example, usually plan their tactics and act covertly, because their success depends on complete secrecy. Similarly, since economic affairs are extremely complex, and the economy of any particular society is very sensitive to external as well as internal changes, members of financial élites may also have to operate covertly.

In democratic capitalist countries the plurality of élites reflects the numerous interests and opinions of the people, and even the ruling groups are divided. Raymond Aron, in his article "Social Structure and the Ruling Class," contrasts this situation with that in the communist countries, where the political rulers have:

"... infinitely more power than the political rulers in a democratic society, because both political and economic power are concentrated in their hands ... Politicians, trade union leaders, public officials, generals and managers all belong to one party and are part of an authoritarian organisation. The unified élite has absolute and unbounded power."

Many observers of communist society have noted the profound division between the ruling élite, which is made up of those who obtain special privileges and economic preference by virtue of the administrative monopoly which they possess, and the rest of the population. The economic activities of the people themselves no longer cause classes to develop spontaneously, but, instead, stratification is imposed on the society by the political élite, and a type of bureaucratic hierarchy is created. The unified élite is self-elected, and its activities are justified by the Marxist ideology which it claims to interpret and practise. Although Marx envisaged a genuinely classless society, it could be said that a new class system has been created in the Soviet Union since the revolution, and it is very closely related to the existence of the political élite.

In the major capitalist societies a similar division has been developing between the governing élite and the people, as political parties have become larger and more powerful. Successive governments have extended their scope, and increased their activities in the fields of economic development and the provision of social services. Much of this has been due in no small way to the rapid growth of all forms of communication, but in particular that of the mass media by which governmental influence is speedily exerted.

The chief difference between communist and capitalist societies is that in the former case changes in the governing élite have been reflected by changes in the class structure, and in the latter case changes in the system of government have taken place largely independently of social classes.

Social Classes in Britain

The class system in Britain is one of the most intriguing and controversial institutions—for an institution it most surely is—of contemporary society. Foreigners regard the system with varying degrees of respect, disgust, amusement or amazement, and all are provided by our society with a rich source of material from which to draw examples of all that is good, bad, curious or ridiculous in a modern society. We provide much useful ammunition for the propagandist, whether he be a politician, a satirist, a cartoonist or, of course, a sociologist.

The existence of a class system in Britain is not unique, because the so-called "classless" society does not exist, but the British system is certainly unusual. While everyone is aware of its existence—the British are probably the most class-conscious people in the world—they also have difficulty in explaining the basis on which the population is divided into these different categories, because the system cuts across all the factors which create such divisions in other countries.

The modern class system in Britain started to develop as a result of the Industrial Revolution during the last century. Before the social upheavals occasioned by the great advances in technology really became apparent, the people of this country were divided into three fairly well-defined groups: the upper class, which comprised the aristocrats or "landed gentry," the middle class, which included the professional people such as clergymen, lawyers and doctors, and the lower class, whose members kept themselves alive by selling their skill and labour to others.

At various times during Britain's long history, discrimination has been practised on grounds of religion against Roman Catholics and, more notably, against Jews, who were not granted full citizenship rights until 1866, but religion has at no point provided the basis of class distinction as it has in some other countries, such as Spain, where Protestants still suffer a social disadvantage.

As a nation we have always pointed an accusing finger at those societies where the colour of a person's skin largely determines his position in the social hierarchy, and we have taken pride in the fact that we did not discriminate against anyone on these grounds. We are now having to take a more subjective view of this whole matter owing to the increasing number of coloured immigrants coming into Britain, but it could not be claimed, by any stretch of the imagination, that our class system is based on colour as it is in South Africa or in the West Indies, for example.

In the following paragraphs we shall make some attempt to determine on what factors, or combination of factors, social class in Britain is based.

INCOME

There is obviously a close link between income and social status, and until well into the present century the link was very apparent. This gave rise to the stereotyped caricatures of the wealthy, tweedy, "huntin', shootin' and fishin'" upper classes, the bowler-hatted, rolled-umbrella-carrying middle classes and the shabby, cloth-capped working classes—caricatures which still persist today, despite the fact that dress alone no longer "places" the wearer.

However, income is by no means the sole determinant of class today, and many in the middle classes are wealthier than some of the aristocracy who are often forced by economic circumstances to sell their inherited possessions to rich businessmen in order to make ends meet, or to act as caretakers in their ancestral homes which they have donated to the nation so that they are relieved of the burden of maintaining them out of inadequate personal funds. At the other end of the social scale, many manual workers earn considerably more than some of the members of the middle classes.

This situation has been produced as the result of a combination of factors. The deliberate attempts by successive governments since the Second World War to bring about greater equality in the distribution of wealth, the introduction of new social services and the exploitation of full employment for their own ends by the trade unions have had the effect of reducing and, in some cases, abolishing the traditional differentials which existed between wages and salaries. Estate duty, surtax, capital gains tax and social security schemes may have been responsible for disrupting the old income structure within the society, and causing a considerable amount of either heartache or delight (according to whether those affected feel that they have lost or gained), but they have done very little or nothing towards reducing the class-consciousness of the society. These measures may, however, have been responsible for taking a little of the erstwhile envy and bitterness out of the class system. The great strides which have been made in abolishing abject poverty amongst the lower classes have doubtless contributed to this, and the feelings of hopelessness and futility have largely been replaced by a sense of security. To some extent this has been brought about by a rapid growth in the total national income, which has caused a general rise in the standard of living, as much as by a deliberate attempt to redistribute the nation's wealth on a more egalitarian basis.

OCCUPATION

In 1911 the Census authorities began dividing the population into occupational groups, which have since come to be regarded as social classes, and it may well be that a person's occupation is one determinant of his status in the social hierarchy. The income derived by the individual from his occupation will provide him with a certain standard of living, and this may influence his social position. However, it does not follow that all people following the same occupation will necessarily comprise a unified group or class, and there are also a large number of occupations which carry degrees of prestige which are quite independent of the incomes to be derived from them.

The Census authorities group occupations into five classes, and in the 1951 Census they were: Class 1—professional and similar occupations such as civil-service administrative officers, lawyers, doctors and professional engineers; Class 2—intermediate occupations such as farmers, retailers, local-authority officers and teachers; Class 3—skilled occupations such as coal-miners, many factory workers, actors and clerical workers; Class 4—partly skilled occupations such as bus conductors, domestic servants and window cleaners;

Class 5—unskilled occupations such as labourers, costermongers and watchmen. According to the General Register Office's *Classification of Occupations, 1950*:

". . . social class grouping provides a convenient arrangement of the unit groups of the Occupational Classification into five social classes based on general standing in the community, economic circumstances not being taken into account except so far as they are reflected in the Occupational Classifications."

In 1961 the five classes were still retained for the purpose of the Census, but a number of important changes were made in that many occupational groups were reallocated to different classes; some being moved up (*e.g.* university teachers from Class 2 to Class 1),

Table III—Social-class Distribution of Occupied and Retired Males in England and Wales—Censuses of 1931, 1951 and 1961

Class	1931		1951		1961*	
	No. (000s)	%	No. (000s)	%	No. (000s)	%
1	336	2	494	3	591	4
2	1,855	13	2,146	14	2,368	15
3	6,848	49	8,041	52	7,933	51
4	2,552	18	2,433	16	3,237	21
5	2,459	18	2,258	15	1,422	9
	14,050	100	15,374	100	15,551	100

* 1971 Census figures not available at the time of writing.

and others being relegated to a lower class (*e.g.* postmen from Class 3 to Class 4). Changes such as this mean, of course, that it is not possible to make a strict comparison of the class and occupational distribution of the population over a lengthy period, but Table III provides a broad indication of changes which have taken place.

From this table it can be seen that over forty years there has been a considerable reduction in the percentage of the population in Class 5 and a slight increase in the size of Classes 1 and 2. This kind of redistribution can largely be accounted for by changes in the educational system, which have provided greater opportunities for the children of parents in the lower classes to obtain the educational qualifications that enable them to take up occupations in a higher class on this particular scale.

For anyone who is familiar with the subtleties of the British class system, the division of the population into only five classes will be seen as an over-simplification, and this fact was recognised by the Census authorities, who in 1951 introduced the concept of socio-economic sub-groupings within the broader categories. They devised thirteen such socio-economic groups in that year, but in 1961 they found it advisable to increase the number to seventeen, and to change somewhat the method of deriving them. For the purposes of the 1971 Census the Registrar-General retained the number of socio-economic groups, and described them as comprising "people whose social, cultural and recreational standards and behaviour are similar."

These socio-economic groups are obviously not intended to correspond with social classes, and it is not always easy to decide to which class a particular socio-economic group should be allocated, but they are probably the most satisfactory means available at present for analysing status associated with employment.

It will be some time before socio-economic groupings can properly be used for the purpose of making a comparative analysis, particularly as they have not yet been stabilised and the groups have increased in number and been amended at each Census since they were introduced. Provided the subdivisions are not substantially revised in future, they should eventually provide a helpful basis for this type of study.

So far we have discussed income and occupation as determinants of social class, but other criteria may also be considered, although they are no more precise or satisfactory, and, whichever of them is selected, problems of definition and assessment are immediately presented.

PROPERTY

The possession of property in the form of land, capital, houses, furniture or cars may sometimes indicate the social class of the owner, but such a criterion is not at all an easy one to apply. At the present time there are many "pop" stars who have set up fabulous establishments for themselves out of their disproportionately large earnings, but, despite their possessions, no one would suggest in all seriousness that these entertainers enjoy a superior social status to that of members of the aristocracy or upper classes.

DRESS

With the increasing affluence of the society as a whole, the manner of dress is no longer an immediate indication of the wearer's class. It is still true that in many cases a person's clothes may provide a useful clue, but it is by no means an infallible guide. Members of the royal family have bought garments from Marks & Spencer, which is also patronised by millions of people from every sector of the population. It is probably very galling at times for owners of "the real thing" to realise that frequently a very close or expert examination is needed to distinguish it from some quite cheap imitation—a fact which has not gone unheeded by the many criminals who have been able to take advantage of it.

SPEECH

Speech—accent, intonation, vocabulary and phraseology—has also been suggested as an important criterion for determining social class, but this immediately produces a very complex set of problems. The way in which an individual speaks is the product of many influences, and not the least amongst these today is that of the B.B.C., which broadcasts to millions a stereotyped form of standard English that has the effect of reducing the very wide regional variations that once existed. We have now reached the somewhat ironical state of affairs where students of dialect are hastily combing the countryside in search of people who still retain the local manner of speech so that their accents and phraseology may be recorded and preserved for posterity. This search becomes increasingly difficult from one year to the next as speech becomes more uniform.

There are, of course, many broad variations which still exist and may be instantly recognised, but there seems to be a common desire amongst all but the lowest social classes to move away from a form of speech which enables the speaker's place of birth to be pinpointed. The much greater geographical mobility of the population, together with the potential we all seem to possess to adjust the way we speak, either wittingly or unwittingly, to that of those with whom we are in frequent contact, has no doubt contributed in no small measure to the great changes which have occurred in speech patterns during the present century.

T. H. Pear, in *English Social Differences*, remarks that:

"Euphemisms are natural class-labels, often used, unwisely, by social climbers. References to parts of the body, excretory functions, sex, preg-

nancy and childbirth are apt to be simpler and more direct in the upper
and lower classes, though this statement requires some qualification, as
doctors who work in the slums remind us. . . . As soon as members of the
lower classes rise socially, they tend to adopt, and when 'middle-classes'
become 'upper-middles' they, in their turn, to drop, middle-class
euphemisms; for unless they do, they may find their ascent of the social
ladder hindered by people at both ends of it. But the mixing of classes
and of sexes in the Forces and Civil Defence in World War II, as well as
the present popularity of scientific terms, has decreased the frequency
of certain taboos."

BEHAVIOUR

The way in which people *behave*—"behaviour" in this sense
meaning manners, etiquette and general demeanour—may also
serve as an indication of their social class. It has been said that a
gentleman is "one who uses a butter-knife even when nobody else
is there to see him." Once again, however, there are no hard and
fast rules by which these criteria may be applied, and courtesy and
kind consideration for others are as frequently displayed by members of the lower classes as they are by those in the upper strata. In
fact, it is interesting to note that members of the upper classes quite
often adopt a somewhat haughty and peremptory manner towards
people whom they consider to be socially inferior, and reserve their
charm for the benefit of their immediate circle of friends and
acquaintances.

It would perhaps be possible to look at this particular aspect of
class from the point of view of what is considered "correct" behaviour. To some extent, sophistication is associated with class,
and this implies possession of what is considered to be "good taste"
—whether in food, drink, art, literature or music—and the inhibition
of certain types of behaviour. For example, while it is quite acceptable for a lower-class woman to go shopping with her hair in
curlers, it would not be considered fitting for a member of the upper
classes to do so. But any sociologist who attempted to analyse class
with any degree of accuracy using behaviour as the basis for study
would be faced with an endless task, since the number of aspects of
behaviour he would need to investigate is so great, and there is a
considerable amount of confusion over the rules of etiquette which
are liable to change.

The influence of the mass media of communications and the
general increase in affluence have made their mark in this sphere
as well. People can no longer plead ignorance of "how the other

half lives," and, with more money to spend, they are able to imitate what they read about and see on television. The boom in the sale of wine during the last few years is just one sign that what was formerly the prerogative of the upper classes is now enjoyed by the many. In order to remain in a superior position as regards wine drinking today, it is necessary to display a very extensive knowledge of vintages and châteaux and to be able to discuss and compare them as an expert.

Probably the rather nebulous "middles" are the most conscious of class where behaviour is concerned—particularly the "lower-middles" who aspire to a higher social status. These are the people who are most likely to try to impress their friends by offering them meals with a continental flavour when they return from a holiday abroad, and the growing number of "delicatessen" shops and departments in large stores bears evidence of this. The upper classes have traditionally travelled extensively on the continent, and to them "*haute cuisine*" is not a novelty. At the other end of the scale, the lower-class holiday-makers who can now afford to go abroad in increasing numbers are less likely to make use of their experiences to help them to climb socially, and instead they are creating a new demand in foreign seaside resorts for such British fare as fish and chips and pots of tea.

CONCLUSION

Various organisations, such as the British Market Research Bureau, have devised methods for determining social class by using a combination of factors such as manner of speech, appearance, occupation, type of house and district lived in. Surveys based on these methods have really been more useful in demonstrating the rapidity with which income levels have changed and the way in which the ownership of material possessions has increased than in showing how the class structure has altered.

This leads us to the conclusion that the class system in our society really is too subjective a concept to be analysed systematically with any of the techniques available at present. The only criteria by which class membership might be indicated are too imprecise and complex to provide any kind of standard for objective, arbitrary decisions to be taken in segregating individuals into different categories, and there is nothing of any value to be gained from asking people to assign themselves. Respondents to questions about class tend to have different ideas about what the term really means, and attach widely varying degrees of importance to their class identity. Most people questioned about class take for granted the fact that the society is divided in this way, but become very confused when asked to suggest on what basis the division occurs.

Vance Packard, writing of class in the United States in *The Status Seekers*, might also be describing the situation in Britain when he says:

> "As I see it, the boundaries of class are best perceived not as fixed lines or ceilings but rather as sieves or bottlenecks. Few investigators now believe that everyone falls neatly into one of four or six or fourteen classes. We are probably closer to the truth when we view the American populace as being arranged along a continuum with an infinite number of possible divisions. . . . One way to picture the situation graphically is to imagine a host of people strung along a trail up a mountainside. Some have given up the idea of climbing higher and have pitched their tents. But many would like to climb still higher. At several points the trail becomes precipitously steep, and so narrow that only a few people can pass at a time. Between these difficult passages are broad, gentle inclines where large numbers of people can spread out as they climb or rest. Some few will be finding the climbing beyond their capacity, and will be retreating down the mountainside. Going downward can be even more painfully difficult than going upward."

Social Mobility

The term "social mobility" is used by sociologists to refer to the fluidity of the class structure, and it has been the subject of fairly intensive study since the Second World War. From the findings produced by recent investigations at least two important facts have emerged.

The first of these is that there has been some increase in the amount of mobility, which can be attributed largely to changes in the occupational structure of the population. Since the end of the war we have seen a contraction in the manual occupations and an expansion of the "white-collar" and professional occupations. This is due not only to the growth of many of the well-established organisations but also to the emergence of new ones; both these developments have resulted from rapid economic advances and the progress made in the fields of science and technology during this period. The rate of economic growth has accelerated while the rate of population growth has slackened, which means that the number and range of industries and professions open to the individual taking up an occupation for the first time is now greater than ever before.

A second important fact, which might reasonably have been suspected and which investigations have shown conclusively to be true, is that most social mobility occurs between classes which are close together. If we use Vance Packard's analogy, it could be said that there is no chair-lift from the bottom to the peak of the social mountain which enables individuals to get from one to the other rapidly and easily. In fact the climb is fraught with so many obstacles that it is virtually impossible for anyone starting at the foot to reach the summit.

A simple way to test this is to investigate the backgrounds of members of the élite occupations such as the higher civil service, directors of large public companies, or the older professions. Studies of this kind have demonstrated very clearly how difficult it is for someone belonging to a semi-skilled or unskilled manual worker's family to gain an entry to these occupations. G. H. Copeman revealed in his study of the directors of large public companies (*Leaders of British Industry*) that more than half began their careers having business connections in the family, and a further 40 per cent came from land-owning or professional families or families in a similar social position. A study of higher civil servants in the administrative class showed that only 3 per cent were recruited from working-class families despite the fact that the area of recruitment during the last thirty years or so has been extended.

Changes in social mobility due to changes in the occupational structure of the population are generally attributed to the extension of educational opportunities, but such changes have had very little effect on the class system itself except perhaps to cause the boundaries of class to be more blurred and indistinct. Egalitarian ideologists, whilst applauding the fact that mobility exists, cannot believe that we in Britain have moved a single step nearer to becoming a classless society. We may be witnessing the very beginnings of a new kind of system based on ability and merit in which the possession of paper qualifications is all-important, but we are not watching the downfall of any type of class system.

It has been suggested that, with the rise of a *meritocracy* or a *diploma élite*, class differences might become even more pronounced than at present, since in a qualification-based system there would certainly be a large group of people who would be either unable or unwilling to make the effort required to rise in the social hierarchy, and others who would descend because they failed to retain their position for some personal reason. The lower classes in this case would comprise particularly frustrated individuals who would, quite naturally, display all the normal symptoms of their bitterness and disillusionment. This would mean that such classes would be not only very distinctly different from the rest of society but also, in all probability, in direct conflict with it. The seeds of such a situation have already been sown in Britain and many other comparable industrial societies, and the anti-social behaviour which is indulged in by some members of the younger generation should at least be regarded as a warning for the future.

British people are probably no more ostrich-like than any others, but we do tend to close our eyes to reality. Overtly, we claim that our society provides rich opportunities for the individual to select and make what he wants to of his life, and we make symbolic gestures to that effect. We no longer include the verse

> "The rich man in his castle,
> The poor man at his gate,
> God made them high and lowly
> And ordered their estate."

when we sing "All things bright and beautiful" in church, but we still retain many of the traditional class buttresses, such as Oxbridge, public schools and the "old-boy" network, which serve to inhibit any great degree of social mobility. This may perhaps be because covertly we recognise that the institution of class fulfils some functions in the society which might not be performed by anything we could substitute for it.

The Functions of Class

KARL MARX'S THEORY OF CLASS

Karl Marx was the first social theorist to employ the notion of class as a means of analysing the processes of social change. He made a detailed study of the rise of capitalism in Britain, which was the most advanced industrial country in his day, and, although he disclaimed any responsibility for discovering the existence of classes in a modern society, he attempted to show that their existence is associated with different stages in the development of production. As he wrote in the preface to his *Contribution to the Critique of Political Economy*:

"In the social production which men carry on, they enter into definite relations that are indispensable and independent of their will; these relations of production correspond to a definite stage of development of their material powers of production. The totality of these relations of production constitutes the economic structure of society—the real foundation upon which legal and political superstructures arise and to which definite forms of social consciousness correspond. The mode of production of material life determines the general character of the social, political and spiritual processes of life."

He stated further that:

"No social order ever disappears before all the productive forces for which there is room in it have been developed; and new, higher relations of production never appear before the material conditions of their existence have matured in the womb of the old society."

The concept underlying Marx's theory of social change was that the development of one type of society to another is caused by the conflict which exists between the classes and depends upon one of the classes overcoming the others. He envisaged that, in a capitalist system, the working class would eventually be triumphant, and that a socialist, classless society would ultimately emerge.

He contended that when the productive forces expanded beyond the point at which the family was a self-sufficient unit, and, as a result, division of labour was extended outside it, social classes began to emerge on the basis of accumulated surplus wealth and the private ownership of the available economic resources. Once classes had come into existence, there would inevitably be conflict between them, and for a rising class to achieve a victory over the others it would have to be well aware of its situation and its aims. It would, however, need to develop an effective political organisation in order to exploit its actual economic position to the full. Marx considered that the working class would achieve victory in the end because the rapid expansion of mass-production techniques in modern industrial societies favoured the growth of class-consciousness and solidarity and the development of a working-class political movement.

Evidence which appeared to provide support for Marx's theory was abundant in nineteenth-century England. The process of industrialisation seemed to divide the society into two main classes —the wealthy capitalists on one side and a rapidly growing class of propertyless wage-earners on the other—and the social gap between them was widening all the time. Class-consciousness and solidarity within the working class were strengthening and fostering the growth of such movements as the co-operatives, trade unions and political organisations founded on the new socialist ideas which were then beginning to find expression for the first time.

One of the principal arguments which Marx put forward in his theory was that the middle classes, or "intermediate strata," as he called them, would gradually disappear, and that a simplified two-class system would develop in modern societies: "Society as a whole is more and more splitting up into two great hostile camps, into two great classes directly facing each other—bourgeoisie and proletariat."

Marx was referring to small producers, craftsmen, artisans, self-employed professional men, small farmers and people of a similar type when he wrote of the people who comprised the intermediate strata of society, and he was quite correct in assuming that most of these would eventually become absorbed as paid employees in the vast capitalist enterprises which were coming into existence. He failed to consider, however, that the intermediate strata as he knew them might be replaced by another type of middle class, although this has actually happened, and the new middle classes—comprising managers, supervisors, scientists, technologists and the people engaged in providing services of one kind or another—have assumed an even greater importance than their predecessors.

In Britain it has been suggested that increasing affluence and social mobility have undermined the strength of the working class and its support for class organisations such as the Labour Party, trade unions and co-operatives. It has even been said that we are all middle class now, although Goldthorpe and Lockwood, who have investigated the so-called *embourgeoisement* of the working class did not find any convincing evidence of a large-scale assimilation of the working class by the middle classes. Although many of the income differentials have now been eroded, the fact that members of the working class may aspire to middle-class patterns of life does not necessarily guarantee their acceptance by middle-class neighbours. This underlines the complexities and subtleties of a modern class system, which has no obvious determining factor as a basis. Further evidence of this has been supplied by Willmott and Young, who discovered very distinct status segregation in a middle-class suburb of London to which some of the more affluent members of the working class have been moving.

Marx's theory of class has been the subject of unremitting controversy for more than three-quarters of a century. It has been both widely criticised and strongly defended, and it has, of course, provided the justification for revolutionary reorganisation in the communist countries, although Marx did not anticipate the personality cults and acts of repression which have since been associated with modern communism.

DAVIS AND MOORE

More recently, a theory of class was put forward by Davis and Moore in a paper entitled "Some Principles of Stratification" which triggered off a new debate about the nature of class and its functions. The argument that they advanced was that social stratification is universal owing to its functional importance in any society; it provides the motivational force which is necessary if individuals are to fill the various positions required by the division of labour and to shoulder the responsibilities of those positions. If this is correct, then the nature of a modern industrial society would itself impose limits on the extension of any egalitarian movement. As Davis and Moore regarded it, social inequality is the means:

> ". . . by which societies ensure that the most important positions are filled by the most qualified persons. Hence every society, no matter how simple or complex, must differentiate persons in terms of both prestige and esteem, and must therefore possess a certain amount of institutionalized inequality."

Davis and Moore have been accused of failing to distinguish between objective stratification and a class system, although their functional theory should really make the distinction more obvious. The system they describe is fundamentally that of a "meritocracy" in which an individual's social status depends upon his personal ability and achievements, but it does not take into account the obstacles he may encounter which make it difficult or impossible for him to develop his potential to the fullest extent. Frequently these obstacles are placed in his way by the class system, which can be regarded as existing independently of all other forms of stratification, and which, unlike most of them, is largely self-selective and self-perpetuating. We are all well aware that "string-pulling" and influence "in the right quarters" often open doors which would remain closed if personal ability alone were the key.

The functional theory of Davis and Moore also fails to take into account the activities of pressure groups and other organisations, which create "closed shops" in certain occupations or indulge in some other form of restrictive practices. The most important positions are not always the most highly rewarded, nor are they necessarily filled by the most qualified people. In fact the theory is somewhat naive in this respect, and the sociologist who tries to analyse class in terms of ability is rather like the economist who explains economic theory in terms of Robinson Crusoe and a desert island. In reality, people do not exist in isolation, and how they live and what they achieve will depend upon their relationships with others and the activities of those others as much as upon their individual ability and personality.

CLASS AND CULTURE

T. S. Eliot, writing in 1948, argued in his *Notes Towards the Definition of Culture* that the persistence of social classes was necessary for the transmission of culture. He defined culture in the following senses:

1. The conscious self-cultivation of the individual, his attempt to raise himself out of the average mass to the level of the élite.
2. The ways of believing, thinking and feeling of the particular group within society to which an individual belongs.
3. The still less conscious way of life of society as a whole.

The sense which Eliot seems to favour is the first of these, and he deplores "the chaos of ideals and confusion of thought in our large-scale mass education" and "the disappearance of any class of people who recognise public and private responsibility for the patronage of the best that is made and written." Unfortunately, he fails to explain what he includes under "made," although we are probably safe in assuming that he is referring to paintings, sculpture, music and drama. The general tenor of his argument is that culture is what makes life worth living, but since he strongly approves of hereditary classes, and regards the upper classes as the custodians of this culture, he seems willing to deny a great deal of enjoyment to the majority of the people.

This argument runs counter to that of the *embourgeoisement* of the working classes, because Eliot fears a "levelling down" rather than a "levelling up," and if we consider the ways in which people, particularly young people, spend their leisure time, which is after all the time during which "cultural" activities are most likely to be pursued, a superficial merger between the classes does appear to have taken place. As Richard Mabey writes in *Class*:

"In bowling alleys and beat clubs the Knightsbridge deb and Stepney mod rub identical suede-clad shoulders. The Mediterranean, which only ten years ago was an almost exclusively middle-class sporting ground, is now a routine resort for working-class couples, who follow in coaches the paths (and attitudes) blazed by their scooterised offspring. And saloon and public bars, once reliable class pigeon-holes, are distinguishable now more by their atmosphere and beer prices than the status of their clientele."

In a materialist society, where so many things are expected to become obsolete very quickly, and changes occur rapidly in taste and fashion, a great deal of popular music, art and drama is commercially orientated and intended to have a very wide appeal; these ephemeral art-forms cannot be judged by the same standards as their classical counterparts. Probably what T. S. Eliot fears most of all is that for a more discriminating minority the opportunity for the enjoyment of "culture" might be severely restricted or entirely denied owing to the wishes of the majority attaining pre-eminence.

If we use the sociologist's definition of culture, then a class system is a part of a society's culture, and one of the institutions by which it is maintained. It is, in fact, a stabilising factor, and it is worth noting that, in those societies where a fairly rigid class structure exists which allows mobility within it, there is generally a greater resistance to radical innovations, and when changes occur they take place more slowly. This means that they are more easily assimilated, and conditions of *anomie* are less likely to be produced. Only when class systems contain a strong element of oppression are they likely to produce conditions favouring revolution, and, although this has occurred in some societies in the past, modern social classes are more likely to be of a *laissez-faire* nature.

EXERCISE 6

1. How far might behaviour be considered as an indication of social class?
2. "The British class system is by no means unique, but it is certainly unusual." Explain and discuss.
3. "We are all middle-class now." Are we? (*A.E.B.*)
4. "Social inequality is the device by which societies ensure that the most important positions are filled by the most qualified persons" (K. Davis and W. Moore). Explain and discuss. (*A.E.B.*)
5. What does a sociologist mean by an "élite"? How does the élitist system differ in a democracy from that in a totalitarian society?
6. "Increasing affluence and social mobility have undermined the strength of the working class in Britain." Discuss.

7. What contribution has been made to our understanding of social mobility by recent sociological investigations?

8. What factors in our society tend to inhibit any great degree of social mobility?

9. Examine the suggestion that the existence of a social class system is essential to the preservation of culture.

10. Comment upon the trends in Britain at the present time which might indicate that a new type of class system based on ability and merit is being evolved.

11. Is there a distinct working-class culture in contemporary Britain? (*Oxford*)

12. Define "social mobility." What factors determine the level of social mobility? (*Oxford*)

13. "Social class is really determined by income." Discuss. (*Oxford*)

14. How far is social mobility determined by education? (*Oxford*)

15. Outline the changes in the occupational structure of Britain since 1900, and assess their implications for the study of social class. (*Oxford*)

16. What criteria may be used to allocate a person to a social class? How important are subjective criteria? (*London*)

17. Discuss the view that the avenues rather than the rate of social mobility have changed in recent generations. (*London*)

FOR FURTHER READING

David C. Marsh. *The Changing Social Structure of England and Wales, 1871–1961.* Routledge and Kegan Paul, 1965.

T. B. Bottomore. *Classes in Modern Society.* Allen and Unwin, 1965.

R. Mabey (ed.). *Class—A Symposium.* Anthony Blond, 1967.

R. Centers. *The Psychology of Social Classes.* Princeton University Press, 1949.

R. Millar. *The New Classes.* Longmans, 1966.

T. H. Pear. *English Social Differences.* Allen and Unwin, 1955.

Vance Packard. *The Status Seekers.* Penguin Books, 1960.

T. B. Bottomore. *Élites and Society.* London, 1964.

Michael Young. *The Rise of the Meritocracy.* Penguin Books, 1967.

James Tucker. *Honourable Estates.* Gollancz, 1966.

André Béteille (ed.). *Social Inequality.* Penguin Books, 1969.

J. A. Jackson (ed.). *Social Stratification.* Cambridge University Press, 1968.

Melvin M. Turnin (ed.). *Readings in Social Stratification.* Prentice-Hall, 1971.

Melvin M. Turnin. *Social Stratification.* Prentice-Hall, 1967.

CHAPTER VII

THE INSTITUTIONS OF MARRIAGE AND THE FAMILY

THE family is the smallest and most personal of all social groups; it is also one of the most important, since the regulation of sexual and parental functions, which have their roots in the biological nature of human beings, is a prerequisite of social order. Some kind of family organisation exists in all known societies, although its actual form may vary from one society to another.

The sexual urge is purely instinctive, and, as such, there is nothing whatever wrong with it. A very young baby will normally indulge in some form of self-stimulation, because he quickly learns that the satisfaction of sexual impulses brings pleasurable sensations. As he grows older, he will become increasingly aware of differences which will lead him to seek relationships with members of the opposite sex, and, once puberty has been reached, gratification can ultimately be found only in the enjoyment of sexual intercourse of which the normal outcome is the procreation of children.

Human babies are completely helpless when they are born, and for a very long time they are dependent on others to nurture and care for them. It is for this reason that sexual intercourse and the begetting of children cannot be allowed to happen in a haphazard and irresponsible manner, and its regulation through the institutions of marriage and the family is of such importance.

There is, however, much more involved in these institutions than the mere social regulation of sexual intercourse. Within the family many functions are performed which are quite unrelated to those of a sexual nature. Each member of the family group has his or her own part to play, and will have particular rights, responsibilities and duties to fulfil, which may be economic, legal, moral, educational and, in some cases, religious.

When we think of a family, we think first of a man and a woman and their children, which is a natural group. In our own society, such a group is a conjugal unit, since it develops as a result of a couple entering into a marriage partnership, and it is a debatable point whether or not two people who marry and afterwards live together without having children can be regarded as a family in the accepted sense of the word. A married couple without children may be very strongly bound to each other by personal ties, but these are ties which could obviously exist between people who are not married, and it is perhaps more realistic to apply the term "family" only to a husband and wife who have produced offspring. The primary function of the family is, after all, that of rearing and caring for the children.

Marriage

As a basis for the establishment of a family, marriage is found amongst all societies, primitive and civilised alike, although the forms it takes are extremely varied. In some instances, relatives may arrange the marriage, in others a man may claim a bride by eloping with her and carrying her away from her people, but the most common form of marriage is that in which a "bride-price" is paid. Our own word "wedding" comes from the old "*wad*" or "*wed*," which meant a pledge, and so signifies the giving of money or goods in exchange for a wife.

Taking the world as a whole, marriage by consent has no great significance, and those societies such as our own, which require the consent of the bride as well as the bridegroom, are few in number. This indicates that amongst most people, but particularly in primitive societies, the status of women is relatively low, and it should be remembered that in this country women have only acquired legal and social equality with men during the present century, and, even now, the battle for emancipation in some spheres has not been won completely.

Surrounded as we are by advertisements, literature and films all extolling the delights of romantic love, we tend to think of "falling in love" as the only basis for marriage, but, while it is generally held to be desirable for husbands and wives to feel some affection for each other, this is by no means the most important consideration in many societies. It comes as something of a shock, perhaps, to realise that only since the end of the nineteenth century, and then mainly in Britain and the United States, has the romantic notion of love been regarded as the preliminary to a marriage which will enable the couple concerned to "live happily ever after."

Amongst the simpler peoples whose lives are centred entirely round the activities connected with procuring food and shelter, a man wants a wife who is capable and well trained in the domestic skills, while a woman hopes to marry a man who will be a good provider for herself and any children she may bear. A clear description of the ideal woman of Old Testament times is to be found in the Book of Proverbs:

"She seeketh wool, and flax, and worketh willingly with her hands. She is like the merchants' ships; she bringeth her food from afar. She riseth also while it is yet night, and giveth meat to her household, and a portion to her maidens. She considereth a field, and buyeth it: with the fruit of her hands she planteth a vineyard. . . . She perceiveth that her merchandise is good: her candle goeth not out by night. She layeth her hands to the spindle, and her hands hold the distaff. . . . She is not afraid of the snow for her household: for all her household are clothed with scarlet. She maketh herself coverings of tapestry; her clothing is silk and purple. . . . She maketh fine linen, and selleth it; and delivereth girdles unto the merchant. . . . She looketh well to the ways of her household, and eateth not the bread of idleness." (Proverbs 31: 13-27.)

Such a woman was thought by the writer to be worth "far above rubies," and the findings of modern anthropologists show that similar virtues are still held to be the most important in a wife in many primitive agricultural and pastoral societies at the present time.

In medieval England it was thought to be highly undesirable to marry the person with whom one was romantically in love. Both husband and wife frequently indulged quite openly in affairs with others, but the marriages did not break down on account of these adulterous associations, because they were established on the more prosaic premises that a wife's chief duties were to be housekeeper and mother, while a husband's were to provide his spouse with a home, food and clothing. So long as those duties were carried out, extra-marital sexual relationships were tolerated. As John of Salisbury wrote:

"A gentyle man hath a wife and a hore;
And wyves have now comunly
Here husbandys and a ludby."

Marriage is a secular contract between two individuals, although, in Christian countries, its secular nature has been overshadowed to a very great extent by the insistence of the Church on the religious and sacramental aspects of the actual ceremony. In our society today, we hardly remember that there was once a time when the Church did not claim the power of making marriages. It has always been considered advantageous to have witnesses to a marriage in case any disputes should arise afterwards. For the same reason, some visible sign of having given a pledge has generally been required of the bridal couple by society, which caused the making of the contract to be surrounded by all manner of ceremonies and rituals, which are rendered quite unnecessary once a society has reached a stage where such contracts are recorded in writing.

In our own society, marriage is an uncomplicated, legal contract, which is completely valid without any trappings and rigmarole, all of which could be dispensed with. It is really only our delight in the traditional and picturesque customs associated with weddings —bridal clothes, flowers, confetti, church bells, feastings and so on —which causes us to retain them. For many couples who arrange a church wedding the religious nature of marriage is not of any significance.

DIVORCE

Where marriage is a secular contract, it is terminated quite simply by divorce, and provisions for bringing a marriage to an end are, in many societies, included in the marriage contract. Amongst peoples where a bride-price has been paid, a man can often rid himself of his wife by returning her to her family and claiming repayment, but in some societies, where the husband resides with his wife's family after marriage, the procedure is even simpler; he just removes his personal belongings and goes away. The wife can also divorce her husband if he displeases her by placing his goods outside the door of the house, so that he sees them when he returns from his work, understands his wife's intentions and returns to the settlement of his own parents.

Amongst primitive peoples, divorce is probably more common than it is in modern societies, but it is not generally encouraged even where it is made easy, as it will always tend to disrupt the functions of the family. However, the effects of divorce on children are less serious in societies of this type, since the extension of the family group enables them to remain under the care and influence of other adults of both sexes, as will be explained later.

In Chapter XII we shall consider at some length the subject of divorce in our own society, so it is only necessary to remark at this stage that the whole matter is complicated because the society itself is so complex. The juxtaposition of religious and secular attitudes, combined with the changes that have occurred in the institution of the family, have caused it to become so.

POLYGAMY

Polygyny, one man having several wives, is a common arrangement in primitive societies, although it is found most frequently in those societies which have advanced from a purely hunting and food-gathering economy towards a better-developed agricultural and pastoral way of life. Even in these societies, however, monogamy also exists along with the more general polygyny either by choice or for economic reasons if a man cannot afford more than one wife. The Koran permits a Mohammedan to have four wives, but only a few can nowadays afford to take advantage of this right.

It has often been thought that the ratio of the sexes—the number of men in relation to the number of women—influences the marriage pattern, and certainly an excess of women would make polygyny much easier, but this system also exists in communities where there is a scarcity of females. This seems to indicate that wives are regarded as status symbols by these peoples, rather like cars and television sets in our own society, and that the husband gains prestige as additional wives are taken.

Only in a very few instances is the rarer system of *polyandry*—one woman having a number of husbands—still found. It used to be a regular practice in Tibet, and it is still prevalent amongst the Todas of southern India, where it is mainly of a fraternal form: that is, a woman marries a group of brothers. Where the polyandry is non-fraternal, the wife visits the settlements where her different husbands live, and stays with each of them in turn for a certain period.

This non-fraternal type of polyandry might be compared with the practice of wife-lending, which is customary amongst some Eskimo tribes. In this case, a man may lend his wife to a friend as a normal part of extending hospitality to a visitor who has travelled a long way perhaps to join a hunting or fishing expedition.

Both amongst the Eskimos and the Todas, the biological paternity of a child is unimportant. The Eskimo man treats all the children born to his wife as his own, and they are recognised as such by the rest of the community, while the Todas have a special ceremony during which one husband is selected to be the newly born child's legal father. It is interesting to note that, whereas biological paternity is of no great importance, both peoples require one man to accept legal and social responsibility for the child.

MONOGAMY

We tend to associate monogamous systems with the more advanced societies of the world, as though such a system were necessarily superior. This is because our attitudes about the "rightness" of a man having only one wife are based on what is acceptable in the society of which we are a part. There are monogamous systems found also amongst a number of primitive societies, as in the pygmy tribes of Central Africa, and they would disapprove as strongly as we do of any other arrangement. The Greeks and Romans objected to polygamy, but the early Christians did not regard it as sinful. The Jews were, after all, polygamous, and Christ was a Jew.

While monogamy is acceptable within societies that prefer a polygamous system, monogamous societies will not tolerate polygamy. This has recently raised a number of problems for immigrants coming to this country, for, while we are prepared to entertain the retinue of wives accompanying a Mohammedan ruler on a visit, we do not permit a permanent resident to practise what we do not preach to ourselves, and a Pakistani man, who is allowed more than one wife in his native land, may have only one legally recognised here.

Although monogamy is the established system of marriage in this country, and polygamy has been prohibited for two thousand years, the permanency of a union—"till death us do part"—is based on the doctrine of the Church rather than on secular requirements. At no time have pre-marital or extra-marital sexual relationships been legal offences, although adultery constitutes a ground for divorce, and secular opinion has always acknowledged the right to terminate a marriage.

INCEST

In every society there exists a prescription against incest, but what constitutes an incestuous relationship varies greatly from one society to another, although a marriage between mother and son is everywhere prohibited, giving rise to the "Oedipus" stories found in the folklore of many different cultures. With very few exceptions, the marriage of father and daughter is also prohibited, but in some societies, notably in the ruling classes of ancient Egypt and Peru, the union of brother with sister has at one time been allowed. The explanation for this has been sought in the fact that the rulers were gods, and therefore could not marry mere mortals, which considerably reduced their choice of marriage partners, or else it was that only by such marriages could family property be kept intact.

Although all societies prohibit incest, the reasons why they do this are not yet properly understood. Certainly such prohibition has its roots in human psychology, and serves as an important factor in the maintenance of social order. Where relationships between kindred are carefully defined, and the place of an individual within the group is clearly understood, a pattern is established which is accepted by all members of the society. This ensures a degree of stability which it would be impossible to achieve in a state of sexual anarchy.

In Britain, the law obviously prohibits incest, but the definition of an incestuous relationship is quite chaotic. It is commonly thought that the purpose of such laws was to prevent in-breeding, but this is not so, as several relationships are, in fact, excluded which would not involve the admixture of blood in this way. In principle, the Table of Prohibited Degrees as displayed in the Book of Common Prayer is adopted in law, although the Church itself has abandoned it. This list was originally drawn up in 1563 by the Church of England, and was seemingly based on religious considerations, although it has been applied regardless of a person's faith or denomination. Recent legislation has altered the list so that a man or woman is now permitted to marry certain relatives of a deceased wife or husband, but this right has not been extended to include the same relatives of a partner who is not dead but only divorced—an alteration which serves to confuse the whole issue rather than to clarify it.

EXOGAMY AND ENDOGAMY

Amongst some peoples there is a ruling that marriage partners must be found outside the group—a practice which is called *exogamy*, and this is associated with the regulations against incest. Where the culture is still very simple, groups are generally quite small, and members are related to each other in such a way that marriage within the group would contravene the incest regulations, so individuals are forced to marry outside it.

Endogamy, or the prescription of marriage within a particular group, is a much more widespread phenomenon in larger and more complex societies. In Britain at the present time, although marriage is increasingly becoming a matter of individual choice, there is still a great deal of pressure brought to bear on a person to choose a partner from within his own ethnic, economic and religious group.

There are no laws to prevent couples from different strata of society marrying, or to prohibit the marriage of people from different ethnic or religious groups, but only a small minority have the strength of will which is necessary to cross the barriers of what is most acceptable socially. We speak disparagingly of people "marrying beneath them," and feel that mixed-race marriages are in some way "unnatural," while the doctrine of the Roman Catholic Church, in particular, is very clear on the matter of mixed-religion marriages.

Gradually, however, the social pressures which make for endogamy are becoming less rigid in this country, and as a society we are coming to accept that the sharing of interests is the dominant influence on the determination of relationships. While it is more likely that a person will share the interests of another within his own group, the possibility of affinities with someone outside it cannot be disregarded.

The Family

We cannot know exactly what the family life of the earliest pre-literate societies was like for the obvious reason that no records exist, but anthropologists have provided us with a great deal of descriptive material about primitive societies which exist at the present time, and this seems to agree with archaeological findings relating to life in the past. When considering the broad outlines of the history of the family, the evidence suggests that the earliest family group was very similar to the contemporary family in our own society, both being small units with specific social and economic functions, and having a certain amount of division of labour within them.

In the simple hunting and food-gathering societies, the men go out after wild animals, while the women prepare the food, and collect fruits and berries or dig for edible roots with the help of the children. In much the same way in our own society, the man is the chief bread-winner, and his wife keeps house, does the cooking and looks after the children.

Even where the group is enlarged to include a dependent relative or relatives, the biological nature of the family remains unaltered, and the principal members are the parents and their children.

Each family is a separate economic unit, but its limited size makes it vulnerable, and it has only a comparatively short existence, since it comes into being at marriage and is immediately dissolved at death. A certain continuity may be achieved by laws of inheritance and succession, but the economic and social functions of such a small group will, of necessity, be disrupted owing to the passage of time. The institution will have to begin all over again with the marriage of the offspring. This process is a continuing one as generation succeeds generation, and it is through this process that changes in the institution will occur.

THE EXTENDED FAMILY

The primary group of parents and their children is only part of a much larger kinship organisation. Each marriage provides the foundation for a new family, but the husband and wife are both members of other families. Although their loyalty to each other will generally be of first importance, they still retain their connections with their own parents, brothers and sisters, and a whole network of relationships—grandparents and grandchildren, uncles and aunts, nephews, nieces and cousins—exists. Because these relationships are blood-ties, the extended family group is known as the *consanguine family* when it is necessary to distinguish it from the primary family.

The consanguine family was of much greater importance in ancient societies than it is in our own country today, and in the surviving primitive cultures which have been studied by anthropologists it has been found that members of this wider type of family are still closely bound to each other in very comprehensive kinship systems, which have clearly defined patterns of duties and responsibilities, affection and loyalties. A primitive family seldom has a distinctive surname, and the words "father," "mother," "brother," "sister," to which we give a precise meaning, are used in a much more general way by these peoples. A child will call all his male elders "father," and all the children within his own age-group "brothers" and "sisters," even though they may be not proper brothers and sisters but cousins in our nomenclature.

The somewhat amorphous family system of the very simple hunting and food-gathering societies is found in a more organised form —the *clan system*—amongst pastoral and agricultural peoples. In the first instance, membership of a clan was based on a well-defined blood relationship, but this could have been an actuality only for a few generations, and the blood-ties thereafter became largely fictitious, although a person still belongs to a particular clan as a right of birth. Amongst primitive peoples, however, there is still an implicit belief in the actuality of the blood relationship, and this encourages blood-feuds and vendettas, which permit the members of a clan to avenge a wrong done to them on any member or members of the offender's clan. In the same way, a whole clan must carry the responsibility for any act which is committed by one of its own members.

Whereas the consanguine family of the most primitive societies does not bear a distinctive name, an essential feature of clan life is the possession by each clan of a name by which all its members can be easily recognised.

In Britain, the clan system of the Highland Scots survived in its "primitive" form until as recently as the mid eighteenth century, when it was deliberately disrupted by parliamentary action in a final attempt to overthrow the Jacobite movement which undermined the authority of the state. The notorious massacre of 1692 which took place in Glencoe has always been looked upon by the Scots primarily as part of a long-standing feud between two clans, the Campbells and the Macdonalds, although outsiders were involved, and the defeat of the Highlanders at Culloden (1746) was partly due to the fact that their armies were not completely united in a common cause, but were fighting on opposing sides, as clans took the opportunity to settle old quarrels.

Originally, like all others, the Scottish clans were based on a blood relationship, as many of the clan names show—"Mac" meaning "son of"—but gradually they came to be more closely associated with territorial claims, and a person settling in a particular area adopted the name of the resident clan's chief or chieftain. In return for his allegiance to the chief, and the understanding that he would fight for him whenever he was required to do so, he was given the protection of the clan. The authority of the chief was "paternal," and he regarded all those who bore his name as his children—the word "clan" does, in fact, mean children. Apart from its name, each clan had its own symbol, usually a tree or a flower, and it also had its own cry, which, when called by the clansmen in battle, was intended to demoralise the enemy as much as to unite the warriors.

Even today, although chiefs are no longer responsible for the behaviour of their clansmen, and they have lost their rights to complete jurisdiction over them, a great deal of clan loyalty still exists, although the *raisons d'être* of the clan have gone. This is evidenced by the popular clan gatherings to which come clansmen from all over the world, and present-day chiefs still take a considerable personal interest in the doings of people who bear their name.

A characteristic feature of the primitive clan system, and one to which there are virtually no exceptions, is the ruling that marriage partners must be sought outside the clan, and it is this insistence on exogamy which probably originated the idea that incest regulations came into being to prevent the marriage of blood relations. Clans are endogamous to the extent that, while members have to marry outside their particular clan, they are prohibited from marrying outside their own community.

The members of one of these extended families are in close contact with each other at all times, and know each other intimately, which makes for a greater feeling of security than is the case where the primary, or conjugal, family is isolated from the wider family group. Although a child may be aware of his biological parents, he also knows that he can turn to any of his numerous "fathers" and "mothers" for help or guidance whenever he wishes. It is for this reason that the separation of husband and wife as a result of death or divorce causes less disruption in the performance of family functions, and will have a less serious effect on any children there may be, in a society where the extended family is an essential part of the organisation than is the case where the family is limited in size to include only a married couple and their children.

The decline of the importance of the extended family has been associated with the growth of industrialism. The social changes occasioned by the Industrial Revolution have gradually caused relatives to become separated from each other to such an extent that in modern societies the primary family group is much more significant. In many families, particularly in the urban areas, children may come into contact with grandparents, uncles, aunts or cousins only on rare occasions, perhaps not at all.

THE FAMILY IN BRITAIN

In our own society the family is *patrilineal*, which means that the children take the family name of their father. At first sight, this may appear to be merely for the sake of convenience, but it is far more than this, because it is also the sign of legitimacy. Unlike many primitive peoples, we attach a great deal of social and legal importance to the biological paternity of a child, although the legal difficulties suffered by an illegitimate child are rapidly being abolished. Strenuous efforts have been, and still are being, made to overcome the social difficulties about which the law can do nothing, but it is a fact that illegitimacy bears a stigma which can cause serious problems for the child conceived out of wedlock.

As well as the social and legal disabilities experienced by illegitimate children, psychologists have shown that these children are also likely to suffer setbacks in personality growth. A male child, particularly, needs a father figure with whom he can identify himself at certain stages in his development, and if such a figure is missing there is a risk that the child may have difficulty in growing up with a well-adjusted and integrated personality. Amongst peoples where the extended family is still of major importance in the social order, father substitutes will be numerous, but in this country, in the majority of cases, no such substitute is readily available, and the presence of the actual father is essential if the family is to fulfil its functions adequately.

Until quite recently, the family was also *patriarchal*, which meant that the authority of the father was unquestioned. It was considered that "a woman's place was in the home," where her responsibilities were confined to child-bearing and looking after domestic affairs; although she might have enjoyed a certain social standing, she had very little legal status. Nowadays, the role of the wife is changing, and, just as marriage is based on the mutual choice and consent of the couple concerned, decisions which have to be made within the family are generally made after joint consultation. The Royal Commission on Population (1949) considered that the emancipation of women and the movement towards equality of the sexes combined to:

"... weaken the traditional dominance of the husband, to raise the woman's status in marriage, with interests outside the home as well as inside, and to emphasise the wife's role as a companion to her husband as well as a producer of children. Unrestricted child-bearing, which involved hardship and danger to women, became increasingly incompatible with the rising status of women and the development of a more considerate attitude of husbands to wives."

However, it takes a very long time for attitudes to change completely and the patriarchal structure of the family has not been absolutely removed. For most purposes the man is still regarded as the "head of the household," and many men, who may well discuss everything else with their wives, continue to keep them ignorant of one very important matter which concerns the whole family—that is how much they earn. This fact has been noted by many people who have been engaged in surveys into such problems as poverty. Young and Willmott in their book *The Family and Kinship in East London* reported that:

> "It soon became clear that many wives still do not know what their husbands' wages are ... if, in our search for reliable facts, we asked the husbands in the presence of their wives (in practice it is impossible in this kind of research to see all husbands alone, since when he is in, in the evening, so is she) for the figure of their earnings, some of them either mentioned a sum suspiciously round and general or became obviously embarrassed. Even when we asked wives, when themselves seen alone in the daytime, they were sometimes taken aback. 'Oh no, he wouldn't want me to say anything about his wages. That's his business.' ... Our only finding is a negative one—we have no reason to believe that the ignorance mentioned so often by Rowntree and the other authors of the poverty surveys is markedly less than it was in the past."

The Functions of the Family

We have already established that the family has distinctive sexual and parental functions, which are the primary reasons for its existence, but we must remember that the family group is really a small community, and, as such, it will have many other functions to perform for its members. Ronald Fletcher, writing about the institution of the family in *The Family and Marriage in Britain,* shows clearly that much more than the regulation of sexual and parental behaviour is involved:

> "The family is, in fact, a community in itself: a small, relatively permanent group of people, related to each other in the most intimate way, bound together by the most personal aspects of life; who experience amongst themselves the whole range of human emotions; who have to strive continually to resolve those claims and counter-claims which stem from mutual but conflicting needs; who experience continual responsibilities and obligations towards each other; who experience the sense of 'belonging' to each other in the most intimately felt sense of that word. The members of a family share the same name, the same collective reputation, the same home, the same intricate, peculiar tradition of their own making, the same neighbourhood. They share the same sources of pleasure, the same joys, the same sources of profound conflict. The same vagaries of fortune are encountered and overcome together. Degrees of agreement and degrees of violent disagreement are worked out amongst them. The same losses and the same griefs are shared. Hence the family is that group within which the most fundamental appreciation of human

F

qualities and values takes place—'for better for worse': the qualities of truth and honesty, of falsehood and deceit; of kindliness and sympathy, of indifference and cruelty; of co-operation and forbearance, of egotism and antagonism; of tolerance, justice, and impartiality, of bias, dogmatism, and obstinacy; of generous concern for the freedom and fulfilment of others, of the mean desire to dominate—whether in overt bullying or in psychologically more subtle ways."

THE ECONOMIC FUNCTIONS

In the days before the Industrial Revolution, the family was an economic unit, because it was largely self-supporting—it was, in fact, a *productive* unit. Almost everything that was required by any of its members, from food and clothing to cooking utensils and medicine, was produced within the household, which was rather like a business organisation, and, like any business organisation, it was efficient because there was a certain amount of division of labour within it. Some jobs were considered to be "men's work," while others were left to the women-folk, and even the young children were expected to carry out their own little tasks or to assist their parents. Each member of the household knew what he or she was required to do, and if it was done well the family as a whole prospered.

Our society is no longer based on a domestic economy, but that does not mean that the economic functions of the family have declined in importance. Although the family is not now a productive unit, it still requires the same commodities as it has always done in order for its members to survive. Furthermore, industrialisation has made it possible for us to obtain a great variety of goods which, although by no means essential for survival, are highly desirable and add much to our enjoyment of life. How much or how little we can have of all that is available depends entirely upon the amount of money we have to spend. The family has therefore changed from being a productive unit to being a *spending* unit, but spending is as much an economic function as is producing.

The way in which the money is allocated will affect both the parents and the children, and it is likely that there will be much discussion within the group about what to have once the necessities have been obtained. Holidays, hobbies and entertainment are all matters in which interests are shared, and joint plans are made for spending money left over after housing, fuel, food and clothing have been provided.

There is still a certain amount of division of labour within the family. A man is expected to be the "bread-winner" for his wife and children, while the tasks of looking after the children, cooking and doing the housework are primarily the concern of the woman, but today these responsibilities are not nearly so clearly defined as once they were. A large number of wives now go out to work, making a significant contribution to the family's income, and, in their turn, many husbands lend a hand with the routine domestic chores, and devote a great deal of their leisure time to their children.

The well-being of the family is still largely dependent upon the efficiency of the various members. A husband who does not fulfil his obligations to support his wife and children, or a wife who cannot manage the housekeeping money, will disrupt the smooth functioning of the family as an economic unit.

THE EDUCATIONAL FUNCTIONS

All the time the family was a self-supporting productive unit, children received their education within the household, and learned all that they needed to know from their parents or older brothers and sisters. Gradually, however, economic production passed from the home to the factory, and it became necessary to earn money so that goods could be bought. The parents' ability to pass on to their children all the knowledge and skills which they required to enable them to earn their own living steadily declined, and now, of course, the education of children has largely been transferred from the family to the school and other educational institutions.

However, the educational functions of the family have not been entirely lost. Children do not begin their formal education in this country until they reach the age of 5, but this does not mean that they learn nothing before they start going to school. From the very moment of birth, babies are learning continuously, and by the time they are old enough to enter their first school they have already acquired a considerable amount of knowledge. The first five years of life are extremely important, and psychologists have devoted a great deal of attention to studying this period in the development of the child. Within these five years, not only does the child grow physically at a very fast rate, but his personality is shaped, and parents are responsible for his emotional and social development.

From parents, too, a child will absorb much of the culture of the society to which he belongs. When he is born, he does not know instinctively how to behave, but he gradually learns the rules and regulations and what is expected of him through the situations he meets in day-to-day life. Customs, morals, manners are all part of this culture, and learning them is an essential part of a child's education. The display of affection from parents, praise and a feeling of pleasure are the rewards earned by children for good behaviour, and they soon learn what they must do to gain these rewards. "Being good" can mean many things, from having nice manners at the table to being willing to let other children play with treasured toys, but, basically, all these things are concerned with the child's ability to live happily with other people—in other words, with his being a well-integrated member of the community which is his family, or the larger community to which he will be introduced as he grows older. The child's earliest, and very important, lessons on living with others will be taught by his parents.

No child is good all the time; in fact, he would be rather abnormal if he were. When he is naughty, either deliberately or because he has not had a chance to find out before that this particular escapade is "bad," he is likely to incur scolding and punishment for his misdeeds, but he does not feel that he has been permanently rejected by his parents. Corporal punishment is unpleasant, and the loss of little privileges, such as sweets or watching a favourite programme on television, is annoying, but the child learns what he must or must not do if he is to avoid these unpleasant consequences, and his necessary adjustments are made within an atmosphere of mutual affection and concern.

The educational functions of the family will still continue even after a child starts going to school, and, ideally, home and school should complement each other in the development of the individual. The child whose parents take an active interest in what he is doing at school, and encourage his reading and hobbies, will have an obvious advantage over the child who has to do his homework in a room with the rest of the family around him, where the television is always on, and where there are few books other than those he has brought home from school in his satchel.

It is interesting to note here that, despite the fact that a child's formal education is now largely the responsibility of the state, the use the child makes of his education is very much influenced by his family and social background. Many children eventually take up the same occupation as their parents—a very large proportion of doctors, for example, being the children of doctors—and, even now that the educational system in this country is such that all children are theoretically given an equal opportunity regardless of family income or social status, it has nevertheless been found that only 25 per cent of all university undergraduates come from homes where the father is in a manual occupation (Report of the Committee on Higher Education (Robbins Report), 1963. Appendix II B).

During adolescence the way in which a young person asserts his increasing independence, and his attitudes and the decisions he makes when faced with conflicting ideas, will be governed to a large extent by whether or not he accepts or rejects what he has learned from his parents, and how strongly he has been influenced by them. This is the time when the parents' guidance or lack of guidance will probably be most in evidence.

THE PROTECTIVE FUNCTIONS

With the exception of the care and protection of the very young, the family has largely relinquished its responsibilities in this direction. The decline in importance of the consanguine family, and the development of specialist organisations to care for the aged and the physically and the mentally handicapped, have contributed to a very marked decline in the dependence upon the family group of those in any way unable to lead a normal life.

The knowledge that has been gained about the nature and treatment of both the physically and mentally handicapped has meant that since the mid 1950s, in particular, many more of these people have been given an increased expectation of life, and there are now a greater number than ever before who need to be looked after. Except in the case of children, more often than not these unfortunate individuals have no relatives willing or able to care for them within the family. In more and more homes, all the occupants are out during the day, as both husband and wife go out to work and the children are at school, so that these families are not in a position to minister to the needs of relatives who are unable to look after themselves. Nor are our houses generally designed to provide accommodation for more than a primary family. There is a steadily increasing demand for two- and three-bedroomed dwellings—the type of accommodation which is practical and adequate for the small, modern family. Although the acute shortage of housing at the present time means that many families have to share accommodation, and there is a great deal of overcrowding, particularly in the vast industrial conurbations, legislation concerned with housing is mainly directed towards providing homes for single-family units, which is the accepted norm today.

Probably the most revealing feature in the evolution of house design has been the development in post-war houses of the living/dining room or the kitchen/diner and single living room. The organisation of space in this way to a large extent precludes the sharing of accommodation by a primary family with dependent relatives, since it allows very little privacy, and is not conducive to satisfactory relationships between different generations. The compromise which would have to be reached where the elderly and the young were constantly thrown together would generally not be entirely happy.

If we consider the relevant statistics, it becomes noticeable to what extent the number of people living alone has increased. In 1911 the number of "one-person" households accounted for 5.3 per cent of all private families, and in 1971 this number had risen to 18 per cent. The "one-person" household does not necessarily imply that that person lives entirely alone in a house, since the numbers include people who live in flats, apartments and "bed-sitters"; nor does it imply that these people all require the protection and care of a family, as it includes many unmarried men and women working away from their original homes. However, it gives some indication of the way in which the proportion of the population who do not live as part of a family has increased, and the fact that many of these people are frail and elderly cannot be disregarded. It should also be remembered that these statistics do not include the handicapped and old people who are cared for in special institutions.

The manner in which protection by the family has been replaced by protection by society is nowhere more clearly illustrated than in the history of the Poor Law. Even once legislation had been introduced to provide assistance to individuals in case of need, the amount of financial help to be given was very largely based on the resources of his family, and it was not until the 1948 *National Assistance Act* was passed that the assessment of an individual's need became divorced from the means of his family. Now the disabled and elderly may be cared for by the state even though they may have wealthy parents or children, which shows clearly the extent to which social policy has changed towards matters which in the past were always regarded as purely family obligations.

In our society, ties between parents and their unmarried children take precedence over all other relationships, but this does not mean that there are no bonds with parents after marriage. It has been found that only about 18 per cent of old people with children live by themselves, and, of those who do so, many remain in regular or fairly regular contact with their children and grandchildren. However, for these contacts to be retained, the units within the extended family must live within easy reach of each other, and it is becoming increasingly common for children, when they marry, to move away from the locality in which they were born so that in future the isolation of old people is likely to become an even more important social problem.

Under our system of kinship and marriage, there is inevitably a potential conflict between the interests of the primary family and the extended family. We are able to contain the situation simply because the extended family of our society is not really very extensive. Married couples are very unlikely to recognise demands made upon them by anyone other than their children and, probably, their parents, and they are even less likely to know the names of more distant relatives than uncles, aunts and cousins. Families within the extended group are independent of each other, with nothing more than the loosest of ties, and they rarely show any sign of corporate behaviour except when there is a christening, a wedding or a funeral, which, more often than not, are occasions for family "get-togethers."

The claims for aid made within the extended family today are usually only very marginal and limited, and such aid may well be provided when total aid would certainly be withheld. This is because the giving of total aid would be regarded as a threat to the well-being of the immediate family group. The decline in the economic and general welfare of the primary group which would result from the giving of total aid to dependent relatives would not be generally acceptable to most families today.

THE LEGAL FUNCTIONS

If any society is to be successful, its continuity has to be safeguarded, and in many ways the stability of the family will help to ensure this continuity. A child becomes a member of society through *descent*, and immediately he is born there will be people in the society who are legally responsible for him until he is old enough to assume responsibility for himself. In our society, the responsibilities of parents for their children do not cease until the children reach the age of 18, and we refer to those under this age as "minors."

Since our society has a patrilineal system of descent, responsibility for minors is vested in the father, and there are strong legal sanctions which can be invoked to ensure that he carries out his obligations to support and care for his offspring.

There are many anomalies in our system, because for some purposes minors are regarded as adults and expected to behave as adults before they attain their majority, and the wide gap between physical maturity and legal maturity frequently produces conflict. Parental responsibility does not finally end until a child is 18, at which age he gains the right to vote, to marry without parental consent and to administer his own financial affairs.

The laws governing *inheritance* ensure that property rights are upheld, and both inheritance and succession are determined by means of the family, so that continuity is assured in the event of death. Inheritance and succession, like descent, are normally patrilineal in our society, although, because married women are now allowed to own property in their own right, the position is somewhat less clearly defined than before.

By the right of *succession* a person may acquire a certain rank or status within the society. In Britain today succession, while still to some extent influential, is by no means as important as it used to be in the past, because the educational opportunities which are more generally available make it possible for people to achieve greater mobility within the social hierarchy.

THE RECREATIONAL FUNCTIONS

We have a somewhat idyllic notion that, before the days of cinema, television, professional football, motor racing and other forms of public entertainment, once the day's work was ended, families gathered together around the fireside and shared the delights of making music and similar pleasurable home-spun activities. While this may possibly have been true of some fortunate families in the wealthy classes, it can hardly have been the case for the majority of the population, who had very little time to spare from the task of struggling to survive. Recreation depends on leisure, and this is something which was not abundantly available for the masses in days gone by.

Nowadays, we take the forty-hour working week and a paid annual holiday for granted, but this increased amount of time which we can use as we like has made the family far more important than ever before as a recreational unit. The advent of the car has also had many far-reaching effects on the society, and not the least of these has been to provide us with the means to "get away from it all." On any fine Saturday or Sunday, parents and children are to be seen by the sea, on the Downs, and in all the well-known beauty spots, enjoying a carefree day together.

Owing to the tremendous rise in the standard of living, our houses are now much more comfortable than they were in the past, and we are tending to become more reluctant to leave them to venture out during the evenings, and when the weather is bad. This tendency to stay at home is further increased by the "do-it-yourself" attitude which has been fostered by the steadily rising cost of employing professional builders and decorators to do all the numerous jobs which need to be done about the house. There has been a boom in the sales of magazines and booklets containing information for the home handyman, and shops supplying the necessary tools and materials have been springing up all over the country. People derive a great deal of satisfaction from their own achievements, and it is only natural that, having devoted so much time and energy to making their homes more pleasant, they should want to spend time relaxing in them and enjoying the fruits of their labour.

During the daytime, women have always spent more time in their homes than their men-folk, but whereas they also used to be left in them quite frequently during the evening as well, while their husbands went out to meet their friends, nowadays husbands and wives are companions for each other in a way that is quite unprecedented, and they are therefore much more likely to spend their leisure time together than apart. Not only do husbands and wives regard each other as chums, but parents and children enjoy a friendship with each other which has not by any means always been an expected part of family life. Until well into the present century the children of upper and middle-class parents spent most of their time in the care of nursemaids, governesses or tutors, and even took most of their meals in their own rooms, while children in the lower classes were put to work at the earliest opportunity, and they were frequently subjected to all manner of cruel punishments if their parents thought they were being lazy or wasting time.

The *Factory Acts* and *Education Acts* passed during the later part of the last century had the effect of making children a financial liability rather than an asset as far as the majority of parents were concerned, and this gradually caused them to consider seriously how many children they could afford to bring up. Better nutritional standards and medical facilities made it more likely that any babies they had would survive, and for all these reasons parents began to limit deliberately the size of their families, and there was a dramatic decline in the birth-rate. As birth-control techniques improved, and parents had children because they really wanted them for their own sake, so the relationship between them became increasingly friendly, and child neglect and cruelty declined.

Friendship and pleasure in each other's company is an essential part of nearly all recreational activities, and the family is therefore well placed at the present time, since many of its more arduous responsibilities have been taken away or made easier, to provide the background for the mutual enjoyment of a great variety of leisure-time pursuits.

THE RELIGIOUS FUNCTIONS

In some societies, the family is a very important feature of the religious system. Judaism places great emphasis on domestic life, the home and the family; the prayers and blessings which are read by the master of the house form an integral part of the Orthodox Jew's practice of his religion, and many of the most significant rites, such as the celebration of the Passover, take place mainly within the home. In Japan, a god-shelf can be found in many houses; this holds a small model of a shrine in which dwell the spirits of the family's ancestors. These spirits are believed to watch over the family, and each day reverence is paid to them and the women-folk place offerings of food in front of the shrine. The belief in the existence of these ancestral spirits provides a very powerful means of maintaining the unity of the family by upholding its traditional authority over the individual.

Christianity has at all times emphasised the personal nature of man's association with God—"the very hairs of your head are all numbered"—and the family has not been called upon to fulfil any specific functions in the religious life of our society. As Rowntree and Lavers remarked, when reporting on their survey *English Life and Leisure*:

"It is usual nowadays to decry the home as a place where no religious influence is exercised and to draw a picture of the 'good old days' when in every home the family and servants are assumed to have gathered together daily for family prayers. In fact, the proportion of homes where that was the case was never more than a small minority of the whole. Even where family prayers were the custom, it seems legitimate to doubt whether, in many cases, they were of much real value. Certainly they did not stop most of the families concerned from grossly exploiting the maids who prayed with them, but whose lives otherwise alternated between basement and attic."

At no time has it been incumbent upon parents to give their children religious instruction, although, since the passing of the 1944 *Education Act,* all schools have been compelled to do so. While there are still many parents who take their children to church with them quite regularly, and set them an example in Christian living, most of what these children learn about the tenets of Christianity will be gained in classes organised by the churches themselves or at school.

The practice of Christianity may well be beneficial to family life, making both parents and children less selfish and more tolerant towards each other, but it can by no means be claimed as an important function of the family today, if indeed it has ever been.

The Roman Catholic Church is the only Church of importance in our society at the present time which attempts to control and influence the family to any extent. Through its teaching and through the regular visiting of families by priests, members of the Church are kept aware of their Christian responsibilities and risk retribution if they default. The Roman Catholic Church will not countenance divorce, nor will it allow any form of birth control to be used other than the rather unreliable "safe-period" method. It is a well-known fact that many Catholic couples, do, however, make use of both mechanical and oral contraceptives, and the Pope's encyclical relating to the use of "the pill" has caused a great deal of controversy within the Church. Many people who are devout Catholics nevertheless regard the dogmatic attitude of the Church to be out of touch with the realities of married life today, and also inappropriate to a world in which over-population and poverty are major social problems. Consequently, the Church is now being pressed by many of its adherents to revise its doctrine on family matters, which they feel have largely passed beyond its jurisdiction.

EXERCISE 7

1. The institutions of marriage and the family exist in all societies to perform certain important functions. What are these functions, and how are they performed in our own society?

2. What picture emerges of changes in the modern family from recent studies of family and kinship? How would you account for these changes? (*A.E.B.*)

3. "In Britain at the present time we claim that the selection of a marriage partner is a matter of individual choice, and yet we are largely an endogamous society." Explain and discuss.

4. In what ways might the emergence of the primary family group as the most important unit within the society have weakened the stability of the social system?

5. A boy from a middle-class background is contemplating marrying a girl from a working-class home. How far do sociological studies indicate the kinds of differences and problems which they may face in achieving marital adjustment? (*A.E.B.*)

6. "In our society conflict between the interests of the primary family and the extended family is inevitable." Discuss.

7. Write notes on the following:
   (*a*) Patriarchal family.
   (*b*) Descent.
   (*c*) Incest.
   (*d*) Polygamy.

8. Explain how new problems have emerged within the society as a result of changes in the functions of the family.

9. "It is usual nowadays to decry the home as a place where no religious influence is exercised and to draw a picture of the 'good old days' when in every home the family and servants are assumed to have gathered together daily for family prayers" (Rowntree and Lavers). Explain why these authors criticised the notion of the family as a religious unit.

10. "The family still remains one of the most important socialising agencies in industrial societies." Discuss and examine the contribution of sociology to an understanding of the process of socialisation. (*A.E.B.*)

11. Distinguish between the "extended" and the "nuclear" family. Is the extended family of importance in contemporary Britain? (*Oxford*)

12. *Either:* (*a*) "The ability of the family to adapt to changed circumstances in modern Britain has been the success story of sociology." Discuss.

   Or: (*b*) What evidence is there for the view that the nuclear family has replaced the extended family in contemporary Britain? (*London*)

FOR FURTHER READING

R. Fletcher. *The Family and Marriage in Britain.* Penguin Books, 1966.

G. Rattray Taylor. *Sex in History.* Thames and Hudson, 1959 edition.

Robin Fox. *Kinship and Marriage.* Penguin Books, 1967.

E. E. Evans-Pritchard. *Essays in Social Anthropology.* Faber and Faber, 1962.

Jeremy Tunstall. *Old and Alone.* Routledge and Kegan Paul, 1966.

Peter Townsend. *The Family Life of Old People.* Penguin Books, 1963.

M. Anderson. *Sociology of the Family.* Penguin Books, 1971.

E. Bott. *Family and Social Network.* Tavistock, 1971.

C. Turner. *The Family and Kinship in Modern Britain.* Routledge and Kegan Paul, 1969.

M. Young and P. Wilmott. *The Family and Kinship in East London.* Penguin Books, 1969.

M. Young and P. Wilmott. *Symmetrical Family: A Study of Work and Leisure in the London Region.* Routledge and Kegan Paul, 1973.

CHAPTER VIII

THE POLITICAL SYSTEM

The Evolution of the Modern State

IT is always difficult to trace the origins of social phenomena, and to locate exactly where an idea originated, but the origins of the state are particularly obscure. All we do know is that societies existed, and still exist amongst the most primitive peoples, without the state, and the state emerged very gradually comparatively recently on the time-scale of man's existence.

Politics is concerned with the organisation and control of human beings in groups. While these groups are small, rules and regulations are simple and easy to enforce, but, as the groups become larger and communications become more difficult, political systems inevitably become increasingly more complex, so that the tasks of policy making and enforcing rules become more specialised.

Amongst primitive peoples in those parts of the world which are still remote from civilisation there are tribes which have no central government, and from observing these peoples we can learn a great deal about the past, because we know that at one time our own ancestors lived in a similar way. Anthropologists have provided us with a mass of detailed information about these primitive societies which enables us to understand more clearly the beginnings of our own social organisation.

Most primitive peoples live in small groups, and survive by hunting, herding cattle and cultivating areas of land which they clear in the forests. Their lives are almost entirely dominated by the natural environment, which represents a constant threat to them as they have so little ability to control it. These people are exceedingly superstitious, and religion is an important factor in the maintenance of order; a leader can deliberately exploit the fear of the supernatural in order to control his group. Many of the decisions which the group might, at first sight, have to make, and over which there could well be dissension, are in fact decided by nature, since when to plant, when to harvest, when to move cattle to new pastures and when to hunt will be largely determined by the seasons and by the weather.

When difficulties do arise, violence is threatened or decisions have to be made, it is the kinship system which enables primitive peoples to remain organised. An individual knows that his kinsmen are his allies, and everyone outside his lineage group is a potential enemy. Within a lineage group, leadership is usually vested in the elders, who are respected for their wisdom and experience, and the "council of elders" represents the source of power and authority for the group.

In a stateless society, it is often more difficult to maintain order within a whole tribe which comprises a number of lineage groups, and feuds and vendettas are a feature of tribal life, although ultimately it can be said that the strongest group will emerge as the victors and differences will be settled in battle. In many cases, however, there is a check on bloodshed of this type, because the rules governing marriage provide links between the various lineage groups. In nearly all primitive societies, the regulations against incest prohibit marriage between people of the same lineage group, so that when a quarrel develops it is likely that it will involve a man's relatives on one side and those of his wife on the other, so that there is an obvious and immediate incentive to keep the peace. Even in more advanced societies, marriage has frequently been used as a stabiliser of this kind, as when members of different royal families have been united, and relationships between nations have thereby been improved and more easily controlled.

We can say then that primitive political systems rely on kinship and religion in order to function, but they can exist only under very special conditions. When faced with the sort of changes and disruptions which occur when they are overcome by a coloniser or a conquering army, stateless societies will always disintegrate. Wars of conquest and gradual colonisation by more powerful societies have been responsible for the elimination of all but a very few primitive societies, and the emergence of nation states throughout the world.

We can define a state as a society which has recognisable territorial boundaries, and obeys a single authority, but it is necessary to make a distinction between simple states and complex states such as our own.

Members of a kinship group are linked by means of blood-relationships, but members of a state are united by shared citizenship. Individuals belong to a state because the state authority has declared them to be members or citizens, and citizenship is considered by most governments to be a birthright. It is possible for an outsider to apply for recognition as a member of a state if he satisfies certain residential and personality qualifications, and is willing to swear an oath of allegiance. This process is referred to nowadays as naturalisation.

In a simple state, all the different jobs which are involved in maintaining law and order are undertaken by one man. This person will be the leader under all conditions, during times of war as well as peace; he will be the religious leader, the chief judge, and the holder of the greatest share of the society's wealth. In all aspects of organisation and control within the state, his power will be absolute, but of necessity, if one person is to fulfil all these roles entirely alone, there will be a limit to the number of people whom he can control within the state.

A single ruler of this type can increase his territorial holdings only by conquering another state like his own and making its ruler his vassal. The vassal will retain his powers within his own state, but he will be subordinate to the victor, and will not be able to carry out any policies which conflict with his lord's ambitions. The conqueror will offer to protect the vassal and the subordinate state against a common enemy, but in return the vassal will have to give allegiance to his lord and offer him protection as well.

This system, which we refer to as a feudal system, was prevalent in Europe during medieval times, and can to some extent be paralleled today if we consider the relationships which exist between the Soviet Union and the "puppet governments" of her satellites, or the links which have been forged between Great Britain and the members of the Commonwealth.

In simple states, loyalty and subservience to the ultimate authority is assured, because an individual is completely vulnerable and helpless unless he has the protection of a ruler; personal survival depends on obedience, so it is obviously expedient to obey.

Just as in the very primitive, stateless societies, so rulers of simple states have, in the past, claimed their authority to be a divine right, so that to antagonise the ruler was also believed to antagonise the god or gods. This proved to be a very powerful deterrent to those unsophisticated peoples who were fearful of incurring the retribution of supernatural powers if they challenged the authority of their ruler, and thus in these societies, too, religion was an important cohesive element.

Modern states usually have very large populations, but this is not the only factor which marks them off as being different from the simple states. The actual size of the population is less important than its diversity. Within a nation there will be found not only old and young, rich and poor, clever and dull, sick and healthy, as in any society, but also a tremendous variety of occupations, religious beliefs, class distinctions, dialects and even languages. When the population is so diverse, the people will have many different, often conflicting, needs to be satisfied, and this means that organisation and control will be much more complex than the government of simple states.

Before we examine in greater detail the development of our own political system, we can generalise about all complex states, because they share certain features which may be divided into three major categories—policy making, administration and interpretation of the law—although each of these categories will be subdivided into increasingly numerous parts as social complexity increases. The manner in which the authority to perform these functions of government is derived is responsible for the different political ideologies which are given expression in the world at the present time.

THE LEGISLATURE—POLICY MAKERS

The job of the policy makers is to decide what is to be done, both for the good of the whole society and for its individual members. External policy, which is concerned with the relationships between the state and foreign powers, is often less difficult to formulate than internal policy. If a state seeks to increase its territorial claims, it will adopt a warlike and hostile policy; if it is threatened by invasion it will pursue a defensive policy; if it wants to obtain goods which it cannot provide for itself, it will seek to establish satisfactory trading arrangements with those states which are in a position to supply what is required.

Internal or domestic policy is rather a different matter, however, since in this case all the varying needs of the individual members of the state have to be considered, and often the satisfaction of the needs of one sector of the society can only be achieved at the expense of another sector. Which sectors are to be given the most consideration, and which sectors will be called upon to make sacrifices, will largely depend upon the sectors from which the legislators are themselves drawn. Divisions within a society may be based on wealth, birth, religion, colour or even on sex, and these divisions will have their own particular ambitions and interests to pursue. These interests will be reflected in different attitudes towards internal social policy, and will provide the basis from which different political parties will develop.

Laws will be made to organise individuals in such a way that the well-being of the state as a whole is secured, and these will be concerned with the external policies. For example, military service may be made compulsory, the removal of wealth from the state may be controlled, and emigration and international trade may be regulated.

Other laws will be passed to make domestic policies effective, and these will be designed to organise and control the behaviour of individual members of the state in their relationships with each other in the course of everyday life. Such laws will have to do with the prevention of crime and violence, upholding property rights, regulating the distribution of wealth within the society, providing essential services, controlling traffic and so on.

However, the legislature is only concerned with making laws which control the behaviour of individuals where this behaviour, if not controlled, might constitute a threat to the stability of the state. To infringe these laws is an offence against the state.

THE EXECUTIVE—ADMINISTRATORS OF THE LAW

Acting as advisers to the legislators, and supervising the execution of the policies which have been made, are the administrators who form the executive. The executive is divided into departments, each of which has the task of looking after a different state interest — foreign policy, defence, education, transport and so on.

As the state becomes more complex, the number of administrative departments, and therefore of staff, will increase, so that the system becomes steadily more bureaucratic. Senior members of the executive have considerable responsibilities, and in order to carry out these responsibilities they also need a great deal of power, but obviously, since they are always in a subordinate position to that of the politicians, they are controlled by comprehensive and stringent regulations. Without these regulations, the administrator who finds his personal loyalties conflicting with his loyalties to the state might be liable to corruption.

For the sake of its members, the state must provide a framework of security within which all the different social systems can operate. In this sense, it must remain above politics, so that people can take for granted that it will work regularly and reliably over a very long time. Politicians may come and go within it, but the state itself will persist. For this reason, the executive cannot be allowed to become involved in the competitive arenas of policy making. Senior members of the bureaucracy who are experts in a particular field, such as technology, industry or commerce, may act as advisers to the politicians, but they can only make their knowledge available to them; they cannot help to make decisions. Once such decisions have been made, whatever their personal feelings may be, it is the duty of the executive to make them effective.

In a perfect state, all members of the executive would be completely honest and incorruptible; they would work only in the interests of the public, and would show no fear or favour. But the perfect state does not exist and the interests of the public at large often conflict with those of the administrators, who are, after all, individuals. It is therefore necessary, in order to ensure their impartiality, to make a series of general rules which are binding upon all members of the bureaucracy.

THE JUDICIARY—INTERPRETERS OF THE LAW

One of the primary and exclusive functions of the state is that of interpreting the law and administering justice. In complex states, this branch of government has become the special concern of the *judiciary*.

Wherever there are laws, there are inevitably controversies over their interpretation, and such controversies may cause disputes between individuals or between individuals and the state. Courts are established to ascertain the facts which have occasioned these disputes and to adjudicate between the parties involved.

In many societies, such as our own, the legal system is based on *common law,* and this means that many rules by which the society is governed have developed out of long-established customs and practices that are really matters of plain common sense. As a result, they have not been enacted by the legislature, and are therefore *unwritten laws,* although written laws are quite frequently based on them. If a judge is confronted with a dispute which arises out of one of these unwritten laws, he may be forced to make a decision which becomes a *precedent,* and a precedent may have the force of law in future disputes.

As well as settling disputes, the courts have to decide whether a crime has been committed in any given case, and to impose penalties when it is found that a law has been broken. Judges are, like the administrators, liable to be biased, since they are only human and may be influenced by their own attitudes and opinions as members of the society. To ensure the impartiality of the judiciary, and safeguard the rights of the individual, there are courts of appeal to which application for reappraisal of a case may be made. There is a hierarchy within the judiciary, and final authority on legal matters is vested in the supreme court against whose decisions no further appeal can be made.

Since the time of Aristotle, political philosophers have recognised the need for a separate judicial branch of the state, but the process of differentiation in this direction has been very slow and is still incomplete, so that some remnants of judicial power are still vested in the executive—for example, the power to grant pardons.

The Political System in Britain

Two of the most striking features of the British political system are its great stability, and the continuity of its development. In other countries, monarchies may fall, dictators may come and go and bureaucracy may overthrow democracy, but, rather like Tennyson's brook, the British political system seems to go on for ever.

To some extent, the insular position of Britain must be responsible for this continuity, since the English Channel acts as a very effective barrier between our society and those others which, though not far away as the crow flies, are a long way away if we measure the distance in terms of social and psychological differences. The last invasion of Britain by a major foreign power occurred as long ago as 1066; France was occupied by the Germans as recently as 1940.

Our society is unusual because, for over three hundred years, it has not been disrupted to such an extent by the violence and revolution which have occurred in other major European states right up to the present time, and the progression from an aristocracy to a modern democracy has been achieved without any considerable amount of distress and bloodshed.

FEUDALISM IN ENGLAND

Feudalism was based on the idea of the state as a pyramid, with the king at the top and below him the various strata of society, each of which was protected by, and owed allegiance to, the stratum immediately above. Theoretically the king was owner of all the land, and others were only land-holders; there was originally no hereditary claim to a holding, and it was customary for a benefice in the form of land to be given by the king to a vassal when he made his oath of allegiance.

Strong kings, such as William the Conqueror and Edward I, were able to maintain this system, but the theory was not capable of being made effective by less respected and powerful kings such as John or Richard II. During the reigns of these weak kings, there was a great deal of anarchy and civil unrest.

By the twelfth century, feudalism had become established as the basis of local government; all justice was administered at this level, and the king's tenants-in-chief assumed all legislative and administrative power except in major matters affecting the state as a whole. When such a matter had to be considered, and it was usually connected with waging war against the king's enemies, the vassals would be convened by the monarch to form a council.

The signing of Magna Carta in 1215 marked a turning-point in the relationships between the king and his vassals, but it was Edward I (1272–1307) who conceived a "popular" kingship, and paved the way for a constitutional monarchy in this country, although this was not finally established until more than four and a half centuries had passed.

CONSTITUTIONAL MONARCHY

On 30th January, 1649, as the executioner's axe fell on the neck of Charles I, a myth which for centuries had been evoked by monarchs when their authority was disputed was finally dispelled. This myth was the claim by kings that their right to rule was not a secular but a divine right—the *Divine Right of Kings,* by which they defied their parliaments and established personal autocracies.

The execution of Charles I can, in retrospect, be seen as a natural outcome of the Reformation—the period during which, for the first time, philosophers and theologians dared to raise doubts in the minds of the people who for so long had been subjugated by a combination of physical force and more subtle threats that God would punish those who disobeyed the kings who were his agents on earth. The threat was the more terrible because the people believed that God would take his revenge, not during their lifetime, but after death, and, fear of the unknown being greater than that of the known, the thought of going to hell was a terrifying prospect for the superstitious and uneducated.

A further step towards a modern, constitutional monarchy was taken when William and Mary had the Declaration of Rights imposed on them in 1689. Before they assumed the monarchy they had to pledge themselves not to levy any taxes without parliamentary consent, not to keep a permanent army, not to establish their own courts, and not to issue royal decrees by which individuals or groups were given immunity against Acts of Parliament or by which the operation of the law might be suspended. This declaration went a long way towards reducing the power of the monarch and increasing that of Parliament.

In 1701 Parliament passed the *Act of Settlement,* the main purpose of which was to ensure a line of succession to the English crown when it became apparent that Queen Anne would die without an heir. It was under the terms of this Act that the Hanoverians came to the throne and George I became king in 1714. The main purpose of the Act was to safeguard succession, but of far greater importance was the provision which established the principle of *responsible government,* and made Cabinet ministers responsible for the sovereign's actions. In return for yielding so much of the monarch's personal power to Parliament, the right of succession to the throne was limited to the descendants of the Elector of Hanover, and this remained effective until Victoria's accession in 1837 ended the connection with the Hanoverian dynasty.

It seems unlikely that the framers of the *Act of Settlement* could have foreseen all the ramifications of so far-reaching a doctrine as that of "responsibility." Not only could the king do nothing unless he first obtained the consent of his ministers, but the ministers were themselves responsible to Parliament, so that no Government could now survive unless it possessed a majority in the House of Commons. Ministers were required to be loyal to the Cabinet at all times and, in its turn, the Cabinet was obliged to support its individual members.

The idea of parliamentary responsibility was extended by consensus of public opinion to include the Opposition, as well as the Government. If any serious disputes arise, members of the Opposition are expected to behave in a responsible manner, because, if they were to succeed in their attempts to defeat the Government, they would be called upon to cope with the situation themselves.

The accession of George I had a completely unexpected influence on the political practices of Britain. The German monarch could neither speak nor understand English, and, being profoundly bored by the British way of life, he made no attempt to learn the language. He tried to communicate with his Cabinet in Latin, but this was not a notable success, and, instead of presiding over Cabinet meetings himself, as had been the custom of his predecessors, he delegated the task to the senior member of the Cabinet, who gradually came to be referred to as the "First Minister" or the "Prime Minister." In this haphazard and chance way, the office which is today the most important in the land came into being.

Virtually all the power that was originally vested in the monarch has now been assumed by the Cabinet and the House of Commons, and yet the monarchy still survives, although its popularity is based much more on sentiment than on reason.

THE MONARCHY TODAY

The Queen is the most important symbol in the political system. As head of state she is regularly called upon to carry out ceremonial functions through which she becomes involved, albeit only as a figurehead, in the processes of government, and her presence on such occasions provides them with a dignity and mystique which adds to the feeling of continuity and stability—the features of our system most envied by republicans.

As well as being the head of state, and therefore the symbol of nationalism in all its cultural and emotional aspects, the Queen is also the head of the Established Church, so that through her the two great elements of secular and religious authority are brought together. She not only represents the embodiment of law and order, but is expected to set, too, the highest example of moral rectitude.

The Queen was crowned on 2nd June 1953 amidst scenes of pageantry and great splendour, and a feature of her coronation was the strong sense of personal involvement. After months of publicity and exposure to an increasing amount of royal news and comment in newspapers, magazines and radio broadcasts, the people of Britain were emotionally aroused to an extent that was probably quite unprecedented even on royal occasions. The press generally encouraged the feeling that the lavish display of pomp and circumstance at the time of the Coronation marked the end of post-war austerity, and the idea that a new, golden, "Elizabethan Age" was dawning was popularly held and encouraged.

Apart from the crowds who lined the route of the procession on Coronation Day, many people were able to identify themselves with the ceremony and ritual by watching it on television or listening to the radio. B.B.C. Listener Research estimated that approximately one-half of the adult population of the country watched either private or public television sets, and about one-third heard the radio broadcast of the proceedings. When the new reign began, there was a general mood of excitement, of anticipation and, above all, of optimism.

This mood, however, did not last for very long. Such high-pitched emotional fervour cannot be sustained once the climax has been passed, and, as the memories of the great day began to be submerged and people became absorbed once more in the routine of everyday life, much of the excitement was dissipated. The events which followed the Coronation combined to bring about a rapid collapse of the new Elizabethan idealism within the space of a few years, and by the early 'sixties Britain had become very different from what it had been only a decade before.

Since 1953 Britain has had to face a number of serious political setbacks, and, from the time the Suez crisis occurred in 1956, her status as a major power in the world has been steadily diminishing. This has become increasingly apparent as, one by one, territories which were once her dependants have gained their independence and the Empire has crumbled away.

The political changes are not the only factors which have been at work in changing the complexion of Britain; social and economic developments have also had their effect. Average earnings have increased since 1953 and the process of social levelling has had noticeable effects. Many more people now own their own houses, possess cars, go abroad for their holidays, and buy labour-saving and luxury articles for their homes. The babies who were born just after the Second World War ended have grown up, and are now beginning to make their presence felt in society as a generation which did not experience the patriotic fervour of the war years and was too young at the time to become involved in the wave of enthusiasm which heralded the reign of Elizabeth II. This generation has, instead, seen increasing emphasis being placed on royalty as "ordinary" people, and less attention being paid to the idea of royalty as people who are dedicated, set apart and above criticism. Marriages between members of the royal family and commoners, the break with tradition when the Queen sent her children away to school instead of engaging tutors for them, and a divorce in which a close relative of the Queen was involved, have all helped to make the monarchy less remote, but also, perhaps, less important.

A survey of the attitudes and opinions of the British people concerning the monarchy was carried out in 1964 by Mass-Observation, and the most obvious fact which emerged was that the average person simply takes the monarchy for granted—so much so, that there is an apathetic attitude towards it. Leonard Harris, who based his book *Long to Reign Over Us?* on the findings of the Mass-Observation survey, writes of the average Englishman's reaction to the monarchical idea that it is "roughly equivalent to his reaction to the weather. He just accepts it. He grumbles about it, or praises it, but he does not expect to alter it. He certainly does not attempt to do anything about it." However, most people are in favour of the system (*see* Table IV).

Table IV—Assessments of Royalty

	Entirely favourable %	Largely favourable %	Mixed feelings %	Largely unfavour- able %	Entirely unfavour- able %	Don't know and un- interested %
Total poll	60	9	7	3	10	11
Men	53	8	8	3	15	13
Women	67	9	6	3	6	9
16–24	54	8	5	5	16	12
25–44	53	10	9	5	11	11
45–64	64	9	7	2	8	10
Over 65	73	6	5	1	7	8
Upper and middle class	67	12	6	3	4	8
Lower middle class	59	10	10	4	6	11
Skilled working class	58	10	5	4	11	12
Unskilled working class	60	6	9	2	13	10

Source: L. Harris. *Long to Reign Over Us?*

Harris regards the current apathy towards the monarchy as inherently dangerous, and, although he found no evidence of any significant sympathy for the movement towards republicanism (*see* Table V), this does not mean that there will be no growth in republican sentiment in the future, particularly as the greatest sympathy for it is to be found amongst the younger members of the society, the working classes, supporters of the Labour Party and non-churchgoers.

Many European monarchies have disappeared since the beginning of the century, and amongst the Commonwealth countries there is a

Table V—Reactions to the Idea of a Republic

	Entirely favourable %	Largely favourable %	Mixed feelings %	Largely unfavour- able %	Entirely unfavour- able %	Don't know and un- interested %
Total poll	13	3	3	2	68	11
Men	18	4	4	3	58	13
Women	9	2	3	2	74	10
16–24	20	5	3	4	52	16
25–44	16	4	3	2	63	12
45–64	10	2	3	2	74	9
Over 65	5	3	5	1	75	11
Upper and middle class	6	4	3	—	81	6
Lower middle class	8	3	4	4	68	13
Skilled working class	16	3	3	2	64	12
Unskilled working class	15	3	4	2	64	12

Source: L. Harris. *Long to Reign Over Us?*

very marked popularity for the republican idea. However well established a monarchy may be, it is fundamentally only as safe as its image is favourable in the minds of the people. At the present time the public image of our monarchy is satisfactory, and critics of the institution represent only a small minority of the population as a whole, but there is no guarantee that this will always be the case.

Central Government

The British parliamentary system is today one of Cabinet government. The modern Cabinet came into existence as a result of the 1832 *Reform Act,* which enormously increased the electorate and made the need for reorganisation of Parliament very obvious. Before 1832 Parliament was composed of a number of country gentlemen who had independent means and equally independent minds. They were not inclined to react favourably towards the idea of party discipline, and they had very little regard for their constituents. Fundamentally, they were all motivated by similar aims and interests, so that there were no great divisions amongst them on the basis of economic differences or social and political ideologies. Their opinions were influenced and their support enlisted almost entirely by the most eloquent orators amongst them or by the most compelling argument put forward in the course of a debate, although it was not unknown for Members of Parliament to be influenced in the way they voted by the promise of rewards and favours.

After the *Reform Act* was passed, the situation was completely changed. Members could no longer refuse to acknowledge the wishes of vastly increased numbers of their constituents if they wanted to retain their seats in the House, and the idea of "party" politics began to take on a new meaning.

THE CABINET

The Cabinet is formed from amongst members of the party which is in power, and it has three principal functions to perform. These are as follows:

1. To formulate the legislation which it wishes Parliament to approve.
2. To maintain control over the civil service.
3. To provide the necessary link between all the different departments of the Government.

At the head of the Cabinet is the Prime Minister. The Prime Minister used to be regarded as the "first among equals," but he now has so much power over his ministers that his position is the one of greatest authority and importance in the country. The Prime Minister can choose and dismiss the members of the Cabinet, and, as it is essential that the Cabinet should present a united front if the Government is to be strong, he is likely to select as ministers the people who share most closely his own views and interests.

Theoretically, the House of Commons should control the Cabinet, as its members are supposed to act independently when exercising their votes, but, in practice, the Cabinet controls the Commons. Virtually all legislation is formulated by the Cabinet, and Private Members' Bills have little chance of being introduced into, let alone being passed through, Parliament today. Once the legislation has been formulated, the strength of party discipline makes it certain of being approved. All parliamentary business is controlled by the Government Whips, and they are, in their turn, controlled by the Cabinet.

THE HOUSE OF COMMONS

There are at present 635 members of the House of Commons, and most of them are professional politicians whose chief source of income is their parliamentary salary. Party discipline is so strong that it is almost compulsory for members to attend the House every day; consequently members who represent constituencies which are any distance from Westminster are finding it difficult to visit them regularly, though it is vitally important that they should, since they form the link between the electorate and the House of Commons. Each member represents about 60,000 people.

The law requires that a parliamentary election should be held every five years, although the Prime Minister can seek a dissolution earlier than this if he wishes. Although General Elections are held at relatively infrequent intervals, they provide the only chance the electorate has to take an active part in national politics. Because a Member of Parliament is pledged to support his party colleagues in the House, the votes which are cast at an election are cast for a party rather than for a particular candidate. Since the leader of the party which has the greatest number of candidates returned at an election will become Prime Minister, and the power of the Prime Minister is now so great, the voters at a General Election are really voting, not only for one of the individuals who is standing as a candidate in their constituency, but for the party leader who they would like to see as Prime Minister.

If we accept the findings of the National Opinion Poll, and the findings of this organisation are generally reliable where political trends are concerned, the public image of a party leader is probably the most important factor in politics in Britain at the present time. According to David Butler, writing in the *Sunday Times* in February 1968:

"In fact, the poll judgments about the leaders may have a special significance.

In each of the last three General Elections the leader of the victorious party had an overwhelming ascendancy in the answers to the Gallup Poll's standard questions on the performance of the leaders. Macmillan was almost 20 per cent ahead of Gaitskell in 1959, and Wilson had a similar advantage over Home in 1964 and Heath in 1966.

It is therefore notable that today Mr Heath, after two and a half years as Conservative Leader, and aided by several months of obvious Government unpopularity, is seen as doing a good job by only 39 per cent of NOP respondents and by only 55 per cent of those intending to vote Conservative. Although confidence in Mr Wilson has slumped, he is still ahead.

Over the months to come it may be worth watching the polls' verdict on the success of the leaders and their image-makers quite as curiously as the trends in voting intention.

But it is probably the economic indicators that deserve most attention. No one, in the political game or out of it, really understands what moves voters. But it does seem in recent years that the factor most associated with switches in party loyalty has been the public's sense of the justice and efficacy of the Government's handling of the economy."

The domination of the political scene by the party leaders, and the relative lack of status accorded to the private members, has caused many of the latter to feel that they have very little contribution to make in the House at the present time, and they no longer serve any useful purpose. They argue that debates are mere formalities, since the results of a division are a foregone conclusion, that they have almost no opportunity to take part in policy making, because this is all done by the Cabinet, and that, because they are required to be in attendance at the House nearly every day, they find it exceedingly difficult to fulfil their most important role, which is to keep their constituents in touch with parliamentary proceedings.

The comment is consequently being made that, since the back-benchers find that there is so little work of any value for them to do in the Commons, people with exceptional ability and talent no longer offer themselves as candidates for election. In 1958 Lord Shawcross remarked in a speech that no new person with any outstanding ability had come into Parliament since 1950, and, although this remark met with some disagreement at the time, there is now increasing support for the argument that too much power concentrated in the hands of a party leader can have a stultifying effect on initiative and enterprise amongst the less exalted members of the House, and make the job of being a back-bencher less attractive.

THE HOUSE OF LORDS

The British parliamentary system is based on the principle of two chambers—the House of Commons and the House of Lords, which is the second, or upper, chamber.

Until the *Reform Act* of 1832 was passed, members of the House of Lords were all landed aristocrats, but after this time their ranks were swelled by the businessmen who had become rich as a result of the Industrial Revolution. Many of these industrialists received titles in reward for the handsome donations they made towards the funds of the political parties which were canvassing for their support as a result of the electoral reforms. Like the titled landowners, however, these new members of the House of Lords were very conservative in their views, since they were anxious to preserve their wealth and hand it down to their heirs.

In 1911 the Liberals, who had frequently found their policies thwarted by the existence of a Conservative majority in the Lords, passed the *Parliament Act* which severely curtailed the power of the Upper House. In order to ensure that the Bill to introduce these changes was approved, George V reluctantly agreed to the Prime Minister's request that he would, if it became necessary, create enough new peers to break the Conservative majority in the House of Lords. In the event, the king succeeded in persuading the leaders of the Conservative lords to allow the Bill to go through, but they allowed it to do so only because they feared that their continued opposition would have disastrous consequences for their House.

The effect of the *Parliament Act* was to take away the right of the House of Lords to interfere with the policy of the Government when finance was involved, and to prevent the Lords delaying a non-money Bill for more than two years.

The preamble to the Act also stated that the Government intended:

"... to substitute for the House of Lords as it at present exists a Second Chamber constituted on a popular instead of hereditary basis, but such substitution cannot immediately be brought into operation."

This intention has still not been carried out, although more than fifty years have passed since it was stated.

In 1958 some further changes were introduced in the Lords by the Conservative Government which was led by Mr Harold Macmillan. An Act was passed which enabled members of the Upper House to claim expenses incurred by them in parliamentary business, made women eligible for membership of the House and provided for the creation of life peers, who were to be called Lords of Parliament. No further move was made at the time towards abolishing the hereditary principle.

Although the House of Lords has lost many of its traditional powers, it still has certain functions. These are as follows:

1. To scrutinise and revise Bills which are brought to the Upper House from the Commons.
2. To initiate Bills which are non-controversial when requested

by the Commons, as such Bills will have an easier passage through Parliament if they have already been fully discussed and are presented in a satisfactory form as a result.

3. To hold up a controversial Bill for a period sufficient in length for public opinion to be adequately tested before it is finally approved—or rejected.

4. To devote more time to the free discussion of important issues than is possible in the Commons.

Apart from these parliamentary functions, the House of Lords is also the supreme court of appeal, although when it is in session as a court, by convention, only the Law Lords sit.

The chief recruiting-ground for new peers is the Commons, since senior members of the Lower House are generally rewarded for their services by being offered a peerage. In this way, people who have an interest in and knowledge of politics can continue to serve the country, and give the benefit of their wisdom and experience, after they have retired from the more arduous work of the Commons. Apart from these parliamentary peerages, about ten new peers are created each year from amongst men and women who are leaders in their special professions and who can make a valuable contribution by virtue of their particular knowledge and ability. These appointments do not generally meet with any great amount of criticism, since they are seldom made purely on party political grounds.

The future of the House of Lords is somewhat uncertain. The Conservatives have shown some indication that they wish to reform it, and yet they are reluctant to abandon the hereditary element, which would be the most far-reaching reform of all. Many members of the Labour Party would like to see the Lords completely abolished, but, on the other hand, they recognise the need for a second chamber of some kind, and, since they cannot reach any agreement about what form such a chamber should take, their attitude at present is somewhat negative. Labour Party members strongly disapprove of the hereditary element, and are in favour of allowing hereditary titles to die out, but they rejected the proposal made in 1961 that the leader of the Parliamentary Labour Party should in future refrain from nominating life peers. They realised that this would not bring about the reforms for which they were hoping, but would merely jeopardise any balance of power being achieved in the Upper House.

At the present time, the House of Lords gives considerable assistance to the Commons, which is heavily burdened by the pressure of work, and for this reason alone it is unlikely that those who wish to see a one-chamber system of government in this country will gain a great deal of support from either party.

THE ELECTORATE

With but very few exceptions, every British subject over the age of 18 who has been resident in the country for at least a year is included in the *electoral roll*—the list of people who have the right to vote.

This has not always been the case, and the movement towards universal suffrage began only in 1832 when the franchise, which had previously been the prerogative of a relatively few landed aristocrats, was extended to men primarily concerned with industry and commerce. Complete enfranchisement was not achieved, however, until as recently as 1928, when the right to vote was extended to women over 21 years of age. When women first became eligible to vote in 1918, the right was restricted to those over the age of 30.

Despite the fact that the British Constitution is democratic, and the British people should have popular government, two problems are apparent. In the first place, not everyone who has the right to vote exercises this right, (*see* Table VI). It is generally difficult to determine whether this is due to sheer laziness, genuine dislike of the system of government, a failure to recognise the importance of having the right to vote or dissatisfaction with the people who are candidates for election.

Table VI—Percentage of Electorate Voting in General Elections, 1945–74

1945	73·3
1950	84·0
1951	82·5
1955	76·8
1959	78·7
1964	77·1
1966	75·8
1970	72·0
1974 (Feb.)	78·7
1974 (Oct.)	72·8

Since 1945 the proportion of the electorate who vote has remained relatively high—always over 70 per cent—but it is also true to say that,

although the issues facing the Government are becoming more complex and more controversial, the apathy of the electorate is tending to
increase. Any attempt to make it compulsory to vote in an election
would meet with strong disapproval in Britain, as it would be seen as
a serious threat to the liberty of the individual, but it is nevertheless
important to recognise that democracy is by no means perfect when at
least 20 per cent of the electorate abstain from casting a vote.

In the second place, there is the system of "first past the post" single
member constituencies. This means that, although each Member of
Parliament elected has to obtain more votes than any other candidate
standing in the same constituency, it is not necessary to obtain a
majority of the votes cast. Except for the months between the February
and October elections in 1974, Britain has had majority government
since 1945—for even longer if the wartime coalition government is
excluded—and yet no party has succeeded in gaining a majority of the
popular vote during that time (*see* Table VII).

Table VII—Percentage of Votes Cast for the Winning Party in Elections, 1945–74

	Party elected	Percentage of votes obtained
1945	Labour	47·8
1950	Labour	46·1
1951	Conservative	48·8
1955	Conservative	49·7
1959	Conservative	49·4
1964	Labour	44·1
1966	Labour	47·9
1970	Conservative	46·4
1974 (Feb.)	Labour (minority government)	37·2
1974 (Oct.)	Labour	39·3

The growth of the Scottish Nationalist Party, accompanied by a
revival of the Liberals, has led to a growing awareness of the discrepancy between the number of votes cast for each party and the
number of seats obtained. Although the two major parties are unlikely to favour a change in the voting system to some form of proportional representation, because both would lose seats to the Liberals
as a result—their chances of even getting a majority of seats on their
own would thereby be greatly reduced—it is possible that some
alterations to the system will have to be introduced eventually.

Clearly the situation is absurd where a party can obtain an effective working majority in Parliament despite the fact that over 60 per cent of the votes have been cast against it.

Few people take any sustained or active interest in politics, although the party organisations in constituencies and wards provide ample opportunity for those who wish to do so. The Labour Party has a membership of about 6 million, but probably less than 15 per cent have actually joined on an individual basis, since most join indirectly through their trade unions. Both the Conservative and Liberal Parties only estimate their memberships, the Conservative Party claiming approximately 3 million members and the Liberal Party somewhat over 350,000. It should be recognised that membership of a party generally means nothing more than paying a very small subscription each year, so that the number of people who are actively involved in politics would certainly be considerably less than these figures suggest.

All parties spend a great deal of money and effort in their attempts to educate the electorate and so win their votes at an election, but perhaps these attempts are made in too concentrated and spasmodic a way—only when an election is imminent. The apathetic element in the electorate might find politics of greater interest if the local constituency parties were seen as really active organisations during the periods between General Elections.

PRESSURE GROUPS

At the periphery of the political system in Britain are a very large number of groups which, by reason of their existence, enable society to exert influence on the Government, and the Government, in its turn, to influence the society. These groups have come to be known as *pressure groups*.

It is extremely difficult to frame an exact definition of a pressure group, because, although it is easy to recognise one when it is encountered, in very many cases it will have only the most informal and vague of structures, and even people who are part of it will hardly be aware that they are members of such an organisation. W. J. M. Mackenzie, in *Pressure Groups in British Government*, has suggested that pressure groups may be defined as: "organised groups possessing both formal structure and real common interests, in so far as they influence the decisions of public bodies." He does not, however, regard this definition as entirely satisfactory, but it would include such groups as professional associations, trading

G

associations, trade unions, local-authority associations and associations which exist to promote particular interests or objects, which
are all capable of bringing influence to bear on policy makers.

Although most of the pressure groups existed before the Second
World War, their activities as part of the political system have
generally been recognised only since the war ended, and they are
now considered to be essential to efficient and democratic government. The nature of a pressure group's activities will be determined
by its size, degree of integration, type of organisation and resources,
and, of these, the extent to which its members are integrated will
be of particular importance. For example, members of the British
Medical Association have many features in common—work, educational background, class loyalties, etc.—and their association is
formally organised. In contrast, supporters of the Get Britain Out
Campaign are only loosely integrated, having little in common
with each other apart from their shared wish that Britain should
not remain a member of the E.E.C., and the structure of this group
is informal. It would be true to say, however, that a group with well-
defined interests and organised leadership will be better able to
communicate its demands and obtain recognition by the Government.

When new legislation is being formulated, the Cabinet minister
responsible usually consults, through his different departmental
officials, as many interested groups and experts as possible, and he
will use the knowledge and advice which is made available to him
to assist him in framing the necessary Bill. A minister can also
seek support for new legislation by informing interested bodies
about what is being planned and why it is necessary. So long as the
pressure groups, which after all represent minority interests, feel
that their wishes are taken into account, they are unlikely to form
themselves into political parties in an attempt to satisfy their
ambitions.

Recently, however, we have witnessed the achievements of two
such pressure groups—Plaid Cymru and the Scottish National Party
—who have succeeded in placing members of their organisation in
Parliament in their attempts to gain the recognition which they felt
they were being denied. It is much more usual, however, for
pressure groups to seek out somebody who already has a seat in
the Commons and sympathises with their ideas, and can be relied
upon to promote them at each and every opportunity.

Political Parties

Government in Britain is based on a two-party system. Although several small parties are represented in the House of Commons, Parliament is dominated by the existence of two major political parties, and this has always been the case, except for the period between the two wars when the Liberals found their supporters were deserting them and the Labour Party was rapidly gaining strength. For a time, while there were three important divisions within the system, there was a considerable amount of instability, but the further decline in Liberal support after the Second World War ended served to restore the equilibrium which is found when there are only two parties to oppose each other.

In order to function successfully, a two-party system can exist only where the society is not characterised by numerous sharply conflicting divisions of interest. Since 1966, however, there has been evidence of increasing fragmentation within the electorate, and declining support for the Labour and Conservative Parties. In the two General Elections held in 1974, 25 per cent of the votes were cast for the Liberals and other minor parties, the most prominent of which was the Scottish Nationalist Party. Thus territorial as well as socio-economic differences are beginning to emerge amongst the electorate. The major parties are finding it increasingly difficult to incorporate and cater for the interests of minority groups. If the fragmentation increases with time, it will be less easy in future to maintain a system of single-member constituencies, which is a prerequisite of a two-party system of government.

THE CONSERVATIVE PARTY

Modern electoral democracy in Britain can be said to date from 1886. The third *Reform Act* of 1884, followed by a redistribution of seats in 1885, brought Britain very nearly to the position of "one man, one vote," and since then the Conservatives have held power for three-quarters of the time which has elapsed. There are a number of factors which have enabled them to hold power successfully either alone or in coalitions which they have dominated.

To some extent the Conservatives have benefited from the lack of solidarity within the other parties. Although there have been periods during which they have had to face quite serious divisions amongst their members, these divisions have at no time produced the bitter conflicts which have split their opponents. For this reason, they have given the appearance of being a more cohesive and therefore stronger political force, despite the fact that this has been the result of negative rather than positive action on their part. Then, too, the Conservatives have always been concerned with the need to hold office, and have made rather poor showing in their periods in opposition. Their party policies have tended to be rather vague and they make provision for a wide range of alternatives, so that there is no obvious involvement in any ideological concepts. It would appear that the urge to provide the government is more pressing than the urge to support any rigid philosophy which might bring unpopularity, and this obsession with winning elections makes for greater unity and discipline within the Conservative Party.

Even more important than the image of greater strength which has, almost unwittingly, been possessed by the Conservatives has been their flexibility in the face of economic and social change. While they have always been concerned with the idea of social order, and still place great emphasis on the upholding of those institutions which maintain a sense of well-structured society—the monarchy, the family, class, religion, etc.—they have, nevertheless, been able to come to terms with the changes occasioned by industrialism, although historically they were landowners. The Conservatives believe that it is important to maintain and strengthen those institutions which make for social stability and create a firmly structured framework within which changes are acceptable although the framework itself must remain intact.

In 1872 Disraeli declared that the Conservatives' basic principles were "to maintain the institutions of the country; to uphold the empire of England, and to elevate the condition of the people." Ever since, the Conservatives have regarded themselves as being the only party which safeguards the interests of the nation as a whole and is, at the same time, concerned about the welfare of the masses. Such a claim as this is bound to have a very wide appeal to members of all strata of the society, and is certainly responsible for the support given to the Conservatives not only by the upper and middle classes but also by a number of working-class voters. Engels wrote to Marx after the General Election of 1868 that "once again the proletariat has discredited itself terribly," because so many working-class voters had obviously voted for the Tories and so given them "more than their simple percentage increase" after the 1867 *Reform Act* had considerably widened the electorate to include many more industrial workers. Over eighty years later, the Labour

Party attributed its defeat in the 1951 election to the fact that many of the people to whom it had looked for allegiance were still supporting Conservatism. In an official party publication they asked: "How is it that so large a proportion of the electorate, many of whom are neither wealthy or privileged, have been recruited for a cause which is not their own?"

The fact is that all appeals to the working-class voters to unite in the struggle to overthrow the Conservatives, who, according to the Socialists, base their policies on a minority creed founded on privilege and wealth, have met with only a limited success. To some extent this is due to the fact that the Conservatives have been fortunate, since they have not been in office during the periods when times have really been hard, and so no blame could be attached to them or their policies for what occurred. The Labour Party was in office when the Great Depression hit Britain in 1931, and, although the Conservative Government collapsed in 1940, the great wartime leader Winston Churchill emerged from the Conservative Party to lead the coalition government which took over. Although, after their crushing defeat in 1945, the Conservatives returned to power in 1951, without a very large majority, they were in control at a time when Europe was at last emerging from the devastation of the war and its aftermaths of inflation and austerity, so that they were in the fortunate position of being in office during the ensuing years of increasing prosperity and expansion.

During May and June 1958, R. T. McKenzie and A. Silver carried out some investigations into the nature of working-class Conservative allegiance in Britain, and, amongst other findings published in their chapter "The Working Class Tory" in *Studies in British Politics*, they established that:

". . . many working-class voters believe that the Conservatives have a capacity to get things done—a superior executive ability—which appears to offset their lesser concern with the class interests of manual workers.

'Concern for the interests of the common man' is almost the only criterion on which Labour is consistently ranked higher than the Conservatives. With respect to foreign policy, Commonwealth relations, national prosperity, and the sense of patriotism, the Conservatives are evaluated as far superior by Tory voters, and as almost the equal of or superior to Labour by Labour voters. In fact, Conservative voters in the working class appear to enjoy greater congruence between voting behaviour and broad perceptions of the parties than do Labour voters, who seem to be linked to Labour almost entirely in terms of class interest.

In a political culture which values so highly the Burkean themes of consensus and national community, this suggests that working-class Conservatives may be under less ideological cross-pressure than Labour voters."

The Conservatives have no doubt benefited greatly from the fact that the average standard of living has risen very appreciably since the 1940s. Compared with previous generations, more people own their own houses, have taken advantage of higher education and do work which is less physically exhausting, so that homes and families have taken on an entirely new meaning. The consequences of these changes in economic and social life have been to encourage voters away from the extremes of both the left and the right in politics in favour of more moderate ideas. In 1945 the electorate was prepared to recognise that there were very distinct and conflicting differences between the Labour and Conservative Parties, but these differences are no longer so easy to see, and this might well be responsible for the relatively small difference in the number of votes cast for each of the major parties in more recent elections, despite the fact that by sheer weight of numbers, if the working-class members of the society were solidly behind the Labour Party, the latter could expect almost complete security of tenure in office.

We have so far overlooked one very important factor, and that is the relationship between family background and party allegiance. Most people acquire their party loyalties from their parents. Although the correlation between the voting behaviour of parents and that of their children is not complete, it has been shown in the course of electoral research that most voters identify themselves with a party at a fairly early age and retain this identification for the rest of their lives. It must therefore be taken into consideration that, compared with the Conservative Party, Labour is still young, and only now is a generation growing up whose parents and grandparents have had the opportunity of voting Labour and are consequently in a position to influence their children in this direction. Now that the Labour Party is well established in the political arena, the number of "old faithfuls" giving it support may well present a challenge to the Conservatives which they have so far not encountered.

THE LABOUR PARTY

The Labour Party came into being in the early 1900s as a result of the strengthening labour movement which had its roots amongst the classes of manual workers who had grown rapidly in numbers since the Industrial Revolution. The Labour Party is only one part of the whole movement, which also includes the trade unions and co-operative societies.

The founders of the Labour Party were motivated more by their desire to create a demand for a new party to represent the working classes in political affairs than to seek office in Parliament at the first opportunity. From the very beginning there was within the party a strong socialist element which had dreams of converting the masses and bringing into existence an ideal, egalitarian society.

The uneasy relationship between the left and right wing members of the Labour Party has produced divisions within the ranks which have not yet been resolved, even though nearly seventy years have passed since the Party was established, and during that time it has become a major political force in the country. The party displays a greater semblance of unity in opposition than it does when it is called upon to form a Government. The Attlee Government which was in power after Labour's massive victory in the 1945 election failed to satisfy the Socialists in the party because it seemed more concerned with retaining the popularity of the electorate than with furthering the aims of the left wing, and today Harold Wilson, who attacked the leadership for failing to adopt a "more socialist" policy in 1951, is himself being attacked for taking too little notice of his left-wing supporters.

The Labour Party tends to be a party of factions, unlike the Conservative Party, which is a party of common interests, and these being more flexible than adherence to fixed ideals, a Conservative Prime Minister has wider scope for manœuvring his followers than has a Labour Prime Minister. The latter will usually gain the leadership of his party as the recognised spokesman for a particular faction, and he will face many difficulties as the head of a party which is largely united only for electoral purposes.

One problem facing the Labour Party has been the development of political professionalism. As Jean Blondel explains in *Voters, Parties and Leaders*, this has come about because:

"... when a party is predominantly formed of manual workers, the only middle-class groups which it is likely to attract are those who have 'ideas' rather than 'interests' in common with the manual workers; moreover when workers cease to be workers as a result of their success in trade unions or in politics, their only bond with other workers is a bond of 'ideas,' of 'attitudes,' of past recollections: it is not one of common interests. As a result, most of the non-working-class elements and some of the working-class ones are likely to become, when they are successful, full-time politicians. . . . [The Labour politicians'] main attraction in life, their real life, is the political life. Few enter politics as a matter of tradition; they enter politics because they like it."

Shared interests are a more cohesive factor than shared "ideas," and to this extent, at the present time, the Conservatives have an advantage over the Labour Party. However, professionalism is also becoming more evident amongst the newer recruits to the ranks of Conservative politicians, so that this advantage is unlikely to survive indefinitely.

While working-class voters consistently support the Labour Party, they do not do so as strongly as the middle classes support the Conservatives (*see* Table VIII).

Table VIII—(a) Working-class Voting Behaviour (percentages)

Party	1945*	1950	1951	1955	1959	1964	1966	1974 (i)	1974 (ii)
Conservative	32	36	44	41	40	33	32	33	29
Labour	57	53	52	57	54	53	61	51	55
Liberal	11	11	4	2	6	14	7	16	16

* The 1945 figures include those classed as "very poor," who were not included in the later figures.

(b) Middle-class Voting Behaviour (percentages)

Party	1945	1950	1951	1955	1959	1964	1966	1974 (i)	1974 (ii)
Conservative	61	69	73	77	76	65	68	54	47
Labour	24	17	22	21	16	22	24	28	29
Liberal	15	14	5	2	8	13	8	18	24

Source: *Social Surveys* (Gallup Poll).
Notes
    (*i*) Figures were not made available for the 1970 General Election.
    (*ii*) After 1966 the social class definitions were changed to bring them into line with those used by the Institute of Practitioners in Advertising. This means that the figures are not exactly comparable.

If the Conservatives have been "lucky" while they have been in office, Labour has been unlucky. Although Labour governments have been responsible for initiating and putting into effect much

*Table IX—Party Attitudes Towards Cultural Values, Beliefs
and Symbols*

(+ Supports; / Partially supports; — Rejects: more than one sign
indicates sharp intra-party divisions.)

	Conservatives	Labour
Liberty	+	+
Universal suffrage	+	+
Equality	—	+
Deference	+	—, /
Leadership	+	+
Trust	+	+
Privacy in politics	+	+
Collectivism	+ —	+
Consultation	+	+
Beneficent government	/	+
Defence	+	+, —
Welfare	/	+
Limits on government	+	/, —
Planning	/, —	+
Static society	+, /	—
Evolution/assimilation	+	+
Monarchy	+	+
England	+	+
Traditions	+	/
Parliament	+	+
Socialism	—	+
World power	+	/
Empire/Commonwealth	+	+

Source: Richard Rose. *Politics in England.*

legislation—notably that concerned with promoting the welfare state—which has been welcomed by the electorate and acknowledged by Conservatives and Liberals as sound domestic policy, they have had greater difficulty in carrying out their plans for bringing all the country's resources under public ownership, and they have not achieved any notable success in foreign policy. This is partly due to the fact that there is a strong sense of traditionalism in the British electorate, so there is considerable resistance to really radical changes in the economic system, which inhibits the ability of Socialists to gain support for their more revolutionary ideas, and the increasing complexity of foreign affairs almost rules out the possibility of a government in any one country being able to formulate and pursue a policy of its own. Richard Crossman remarked in a *Sunday Telegraph* interview in February 1968:

"I think you will find that ever since Governments were elected by popular vote nearly all the big decisions in foreign policy have arisen out of unforeseen crises and not from implementation of manifestos."

Labour has been in office at times when world events have taken critical turns, and they have been blamed for not taking more decisive action, even though Britain's status as a major world power has declined and this country is no longer in a position to play a dominant role.

Because the principles of social welfare, public control of the basic industries and the planned allocation of national resources have become generally accepted, and also because the standard of living of the working classes has risen so sharply, the old class struggle between Labour and Conservative has lost much of its previous bitterness, and there are now only a few areas in which there is any real conflict between the parties. Differences at the present time are more likely to be differences of degree rather than of kind, as is shown in Table IX.

THE LIBERAL PARTY

The Liberals began to lose ground rapidly during the period between the two world wars, when their place as a major political party was being challenged by Labour, and their relegation to a minor role in the parliamentary arena was completed when the Labour Party achieved a landslide victory in the 1945 election. In the ten years which followed, Liberal support continued to dwindle, and they obtained only 2·7 per cent of the votes in the 1955 election.

When Mr. Grimond addressed his first Liberal Assembly as party leader in 1957, he said: "In the next ten years, it is a question of get on or get out. Let us make it get on"; and in two subsequent elections it looked as though the Liberals were regaining a little at least of the ground which they had lost. However they slipped back once again in 1966, and it appeared very doubtful whether they could survive another election. After a particularly serious by-election defeat, a Liberal party spokesman commented:

"We need a strategy and don't have one. The party's principles aren't precise enough to tell us what to do without one, and without a strategy you're bound to get muddle. . . . Most Liberals really have no very clear idea of where the party should go from here."

The picture seemed gloomy indeed—lack of policy, lack of funds and lack of support made the future role of the Liberal Party in the political system extremely uncertain. That the Liberals managed to fight and survive the 1970 election was largely due to the windfall donation made to party funds from an undisclosed source.

The February 1974 election was notable on several counts. Neither of the two major parties managed to obtain an overall majority of seats, and, perhaps as a consequence of the disillusionment of many voters with the existing system, the Liberals made a dramatic comeback. Although they obtained only 14 seats, the fact that they had polled over 19 per cent of the votes was not obscured. For a short time they held the balance of power, and it is very likely that, had the Liberals agreed to enter a coalition with the Tories, Mr. Heath would have been obliged in return for their support to take seriously their request for a re-appraisal of the whole electoral system with a view to introducing some form of proportional representation.

The Liberals, however, did not enter a coalition when the opportunity was offered to them, and the Conservatives handed over the task of forming a minority government to Labour.

Although the Liberals obtained a substantial share of the votes in the October 1974 election, support once more began to slip away, and they may have to wait a very long time indeed before they get another chance to make any real impact in the political arena. There is a strong possibility of a backlash against the Liberals in future elections, because the implications of the intervention of minority parties are becoming more widely recognised.

There is increasing evidence of *tactical voting* being employed whereby electors consider using their votes to keep a particular party out of power rather than to ensure that a particular party is elected. Thus some people who are sympathetic to the Liberal Party might nevertheless vote Conservative, because they realise that the Liberals cannot form a government, and they want a Labour Government even less than they want a Conservative one. The Liberal Party stands to lose support as a result of tactical voting.

On the other hand, the Liberals may attract *protest votes*. Although it would be difficult to prove, it is possible that the votes polled by the Liberals in the February 1974 election were, to a large extent, votes against the Conservatives and Labour, both of which had declined in popularity.

The Liberal Party is therefore extremely vulnerable, and its popularity at any given time is more an indication of people's attitudes to the two main parties than to itself.

THE SCOTTISH NATIONAL PARTY

Before the General Election of 1966, many political scientists adhered to the theory of *British political homogeneity,* which explained party differences mainly in socio-economic terms and considered the United Kingdom as a single political community. That election, however, caused many people who had until then refused to take nationalism very seriously to change their minds.

Until Ian Macdonald assumed the role of National Organiser in 1962, the nationalist movement in Scotland was of little significance as a political force. It had attracted a number of colourful eccentrics who had led a fairly energetic pressure group, but little impact was made when it came to campaigning during elections. By 1966, it was clear that changes were occurring in Scottish political behaviour.

In that election the Scottish National Party contested 23 of the 71 Scottish seats, and although its results were not good in terms of gaining representation in Parliament—it came second in only three seats and many candidates lost their deposits—it obtained 5 per cent of the Scottish vote, and gained considerable publicity.

Macdonald had set out to establish the Scottish National Party as a "grass-roots" party, and, building on his work, many more local branches were formed after 1966. These organised numerous social activities—dances, concerts, whist drives, outings and so on—and in this way many people were attracted who had previously not been very interested in politics. In the more remote rural areas of Scotland particularly, people were brought into contact with a political party in a way that had not occurred before. In the cities and large towns the Scottish National Party was much more in evidence than were other political parties which became noticeable only during election campaigns.

This constant prominence of the Scottish National Party, combined with its firm financial basis—raising funds from social functions and membership fees and establishing a lottery (Alba Pools)—contributed towards its success. However, it was also aided by other factors. The Conservatives had lost support in Scotland, because at times when the rest of the United Kingdom had "never had it so good" and growing prosperity was loudly proclaimed, the Scots suffered still from the high unemployment, poor housing, low wages and general lack of amenities and services. They were constantly reminded of the imbalance between Scotland and other regions with the exception of Northern Ireland, and the Conservatives were blamed for neglecting them.

Labour too, although promising much in its election campaign, and gaining huge support for its policy of regional development, rapidly lost credibility when the tight economic squeeze was introduced in July 1966. Many hopes had been pinned to the Scottish Economic Planning Council and Board, and to the Highlands and Islands Development Board which the Labour Government set up, but their activities were very much reduced in scope as a result of the changed economic climate.

It was at this point that the Scottish National Party began to make very real headway, since it represented a means of registering protest at the failure of both main parties to deal with Scotland's problems. In November 1967, the Scottish National Party got its first seat in Parliament as a result of a by-election in Hamilton.

The 1970 election was something of an anti-climax. The Scottish National Party's share of the Scottish vote rose to just over 11 per cent, but only one member was returned to Parliament, and most people probably felt that its force was spent. Nationalism was nothing more than a safety-valve for disillusioned voters who found in it a useful means of indicating their feelings to the major parties *between* elections rather than *at* elections.

Since 1970, however, circumstances have changed very considerably. The overall decline in Britain's economic position, combined with the expectations of an improvement once oil from the North Sea begins to come ashore, has caused attention to be focused on Scotland. The Scottish National Party has seized upon this, and has strengthened its campaign for devolution and the right for Scots to have a much greater say in how their affairs are managed.

During the two 1974 election campaigns much was said about *Scottish* oil, and earlier arguments that Scotland was too dependent upon the rest of Britain to have any real power were dismissed. The development of North Sea oil and its key role in the economy in future are likely to change Scotland from the poor country cousin into the rich relation, and the Scottish nationalist movement has gained renewed strength from the possibility of economic independence from England. In February 1974, it returned seven candidates to Parliament and in the October election the number was increased to eleven. Scottish Nationalism is a force that will have to be reckoned with, and some plan for devolution will almost certainly be introduced before long. Plans for a Scottish National Assembly are being debated in Parliament at the time of writing.

As Kellas has written in *The British General Election of 1970*:

"The Scottish National Party has heightened Scottish national consciousness since 1966, and has committed many influential organisations and individuals to the support of devolution. . . . But it has not explained the nature of Scottish nationalism, which remains enigmatic. Compared with nationalisms throughout the world, it is essentially of a non-violent nature, and its leaders are well-adjusted to living in their existing society. Unlike Welsh nationalism, it has no lingusitic basis, and Scottish culture seems to have had little influence on the Scottish National Party's policies, which have been mainly socio-economic in character. Scots, too, base their politics on such matters, and have relied on the British parties at general elections as vehicles for their realisation."

Local Government

Traditionally, local government has always been concerned with the administration of those affairs which are of direct and immediate interest to the inhabitants of a particular area, and the provision of services and amenities that make life more comfortable and pleasurable in that area.

The three primary functions of government are still evident at the local level, since local authorities have the power to formulate policies and pass by-laws, to set up departments to administer these policies and to establish magistrates' courts to deal with minor offences committed in their areas.

The *Local Government Act*, 1972, which made provision for the fundamental reorganisation of local government in England and Wales, was brought into effect on 1st April 1974. Under this act, new administrative areas and new authorities were created outside London, which had been reorganised earlier under the *London Government Act*, 1963. The main purposes of reorganisation were to reduce the number of authorities, and thereby promote greater efficiency in administration and in the provision of services and the allocation of resources.

Under the Act, the country is divided into *counties*—six of which are "metropolitan counties"—and within the counties are *districts*. Provision is also made for *parishes* (to be known as *communities* in Wales) but as these small, local councils have virtually no powers or responsibilities, their ability to survive within the more centralised, more bureaucratic system is perhaps doubtful.

As yet it is far too early to assess the effects of adopting the new system, because it is difficult to see it in perspective at this stage. Many people regard the reorganisation as a very costly bureaucratic exercise, which has contributed much to the inflationary situation which exists at present. The new administrative units are by their very nature less "local" than the units they have replaced, and it is perhaps not surprising that the changes have not been greeted with enthusiasm.

PARTICIPATION IN LOCAL GOVERNMENT

If there is apathy on the part of the electorate towards national politics, this apathy is even more apparent in the realms of local politics. According to statistics compiled by the Registrar-General, less than half the people on the electoral roll normally vote in local elections.

However, it is not only the voters who are uninterested, because the apathy spreads further than this, and results in the very large number of seats on local councils which are uncontested when elections take place. This would indicate that there is an acute shortage of people who feel sufficiently strongly about local affairs to become actively involved by offering themselves as candidates.

One good reason for this obvious lack of interest in local matters may well be found in the fact that, increasingly, national party politics and local politics are merging, and for the man in the street there must often seem little difference between the two. Really he cannot be blamed for thinking this, because so often such matters as whether or not the local swimming-pool should be heated, or whether an extra pedestrian-crossing would make the High Street safer for shoppers, develop into fierce arguments between Labour and Conservative councillors, and are no longer debated by councillors who are completely independent.

We must also remember that in cases where very heavy expenditure is necessary—housing, education, major roadworks and hospital services—local authorities are quite unable to meet the demands made upon them unless they obtain financial assistance from central-government funds. In fact, at the present time, the amount available to local authorities in the form of grants is almost equal to their revenue from rates, and their dependence upon national resources is thus obvious. In recent years, the policy of the central government has been to direct the manner in which local authorities should deploy these grants, or to require local authorities to submit their plans for approval before such grants are made.

The reluctance of local councils to allow full press coverage of their meetings when controversial or "private" matters are being discussed might also be responsible for a lack of enthusiasm on the part of the people who learn that decisions have been taken which will considerably affect them only when it is too late to voice their opinions.

THE LOCAL COUNCILLOR

The person who offers himself for election as a councillor should, ideally, be someone who is a well-known leader of the local community. Unfortunately, however, such people are often deterred from service in local government, because they are so heavily committed in their professions, because they find the work somewhat tedious and frustrating owing to the encroachment of party politics on the preserves of local affairs, or because the central government has taken over control of most of the matters of major concern. For various reasons, it is becoming more than ever difficult to find men and women with the necessary personal qualifications who are willing to enter local government and devote a great deal of their time and energy to public work which is entirely voluntary. People who are sufficiently dedicated, and, probably even more important, disinterested, are few and far between.

The right to claim attendance allowances as well as travelling and subsistence allowances is a wholly new provision under the 1972 *Local Government Act*. It may well be that these improved financial arrangements will have the effect of encouraging more people from a wider range of backgrounds to consider serving in local government.

There is an increasing movement at the present time towards "professionalism" in local government. With the ever-growing complexity of local politics due to the expansion of the population and the development of urbanisation, there is much to be said for employing full-time local councillors. However, if democracy is to be maintained, these professionals would have to be popularly elected. If the job of local councillor were to be a full-time "career," the ever-present risk of losing one's seat at the next election would introduce an element of instability which would largely preclude all but retired people, married women and candidates representing organisations with vested interests from seeking election. This could be seriously damaging to a system which, if it is to succeed, must remain local.

EXERCISE 8

1. "The major task facing the political system in advanced industrial societies is to aggregate a wide range of interests in the formulation of policies." Explain and discuss the part played by *either* political parties *or* pressure groups in this process. (*A.E.B.*)
2. How far can the idea of a "ruling class" be applied in the study of British politics today? (*A.E.B.*)
3. Write notes on the following: (*a*) Legislature. (*b*) Executive. (*c*) Judiciary.
4. What do you understand by the concept "bureaucracy"? How useful is this concept for understanding organisations such as schools, hospitals and research laboratories? (*A.E.B.*)
5. *Either*: (*a*) Discuss briefly the view that the power of the House of Commons is being eroded.
   or: (*b*) Examine the functions of political parties in Britain today. (*A.E.B.*)
6. It has been argued that growing affluence is eroding the traditional working-class support for the Labour Party. How far do sociological studies of manual workers support this view? (*A.E.B.*)
7. Discuss the suggestion that the average Englishman's reaction to the monarchy is similar to his reaction to the weather.
8. Examine the socio-demographic factors which influence voting behaviour.
9. Examine the role of pressure groups in the political process in Britain. (*A.E.B.*)
10. Explain how the fact that shared interests are a more cohesive factor than shared ideas is apparent in Britain's major political parties at the present time.
11. How would you define "power"? Do you think that there is an "establishment" of power in Britain? (*Oxford*)
12. Can a valid distinction be made between "primitive" and "modern" societies? (*Oxford*)
13. To what extent has there been structural and ideological convergence between the two major British political parties over the past decade? (*London*)
14. If it is true that social class is the primary determinant of voting behaviour how do you account for (*a*) political apathy *and* (*b*) deviant voting? (*London*)

FOR FURTHER READING

Lucy Mair. *Primitive Government*. Penguin Books, 1964.
Leonard Harris. *Long to Reign Over Us?* Kimber, 1966.
J. Blondel. *Voters, Parties and Leaders*. Penguin Books, 1963.
R. Rose (ed.). *Studies in British Politics*. Macmillan, 1966.
R. Rose. *Influencing Voters*. Faber and Faber, 1967.
R. Rose. *The Problem of Party Government*. Macmillan, 1974.
A. Pizzarno (ed.). *Political Sociology*. Penguin Books, 1971.
R. McKenzie and A. Silver. *Angels in Marble*. Heinemann, 1968.
B. Hindess. *The Decline of Working Class Politics*. MacGibbon and Kee, 1971.
D. Butler and D. Stokes. *Political Change in Britain*. Penguin Books, 1969.

CHAPTER IX

THE ECONOMIC SYSTEM AND THE SOCIAL ASPECTS OF INDUSTRY

The Nature of Wealth

ECONOMICS is the systematic study of wealth, of the way in which it is accumulated and the way it is distributed.

Wealth may be defined as the stock of goods which exists at a particular moment in time and has the following characteristics:

1. The goods must be capable of satisfying some need.
2. They should be relatively scarce—*i.e.* the available supply should not be greater than the demand.
3. They must have a specific value.
4. The ownership of the goods must be transferable from one person to another.

The goods which constitute wealth can be divided into two categories—capital, or producers' wealth, and consumers' wealth.

CAPITAL

: This type of wealth includes everything which is desirable, not for is own sake, but for what can be produced with it. It comprises such things as factories, machinery, tools, transport systems, laboratories and so on.

One particularly important fact concerning capital is that the way in which it is owned in a society will determine the political system of that society. Where all the capital is publicly owned, there will be *communism*; where it is all privately owned there will be *capitalism*. In our own country, much of the capital is publicly owned in the form of nationalised industries and public corporations, but much is also owned privately, so we have a *mixed economy*. This is reflected in the opposing policies for the ownership of capital which are put forward by our major political parties; the Conservatives supporting private enterprise, or capitalism, and the Labour Party advocating nationalisation.

CONSUMERS' WEALTH

This includes everything that is desirable for its own sake, and most of our personal possessions such as clothes, jewellery, furniture, books, etc., come into this category.

Apart from these personal possessions, some consumer wealth is, like some capital, socially owned. By joining together, people are able to own and enjoy collectively things which they would otherwise be unable to afford. Local authorities provide such amenities as swimming-pools, museums and libraries for their ratepayers, and, on a bigger scale, there are art galleries, theatres, historical buildings and parks which belong to the whole nation.

The Accumulation of Wealth

Wealth is produced by combining the *factors of production,* land, capital, labour and enterprise.

LAND

Land, to the economist, includes not only agricultural and building land but all the natural resources such as mineral deposits, rivers, lakes and the sea which are available to man. Societies which have a good supply of these resources together with the ability to exploit them will enjoy a much higher standard of living than those societies which lack these essential ingredients of wealth.

When we refer today to countries of the world as the "haves" and "have-nots," we are, in fact, distinguishing between those which are well endowed with natural resources and those which have no such advantages.

CAPITAL

Capital, as we have already seen, is what man accumulates by his own efforts in order to further production. The simplest of tools could, in this sense, be classified as capital, but, the more time that can be devoted to making capital goods, the more sophisticated and efficient they will be. In those societies where the standard of living is so low that the whole of a man's time is taken up with the struggle to wrest a meagre living from the soil, there will be little opportunity for accumulating capital. This can only be produced out of any surplus which remains after the basic needs have been satisfied.

More efficient capital means more efficient production, and, once a start is made on accumulating capital, the greater the opportunity becomes for acquiring more in the future. Once again, those countries which are rich in natural resources, which have a favourable climate, and which can produce more than is necessary for their own consumption will have a tremendous advantage. Rich countries can hardly fail to become richer, while poor countries, without a great deal of assistance, will become increasingly poor by comparison.

Technological achievements and scientific progress make it possible to exploit natural resources to their full, but these are the advantages derived by a highly skilled, well-educated society. Educating a population to this level is only possible if the people concerned have time to spare for learning when they have satisfied their more immediate material needs.

LABOUR

Labour is, of course, the human effort needed in production, and the quality of the available manpower will depend on many factors, both physical and psychological.

The most efficient worker is one who is not only skilled at his job but also well nourished, comfortably housed and healthy. It was not until the 1920s, when the famous Hawthorne Investigations were carried out under the guidance of Dr Elton Mayo at the Western Electric Company's factory, that the importance of the emotional factors involved in working came to be realised.

Whether or not there is an adequate supply of labour in any society must be reckoned in terms of the *optimum size of the population*—that is, the number of people who can be supported, and who can achieve the maximum level of output per head, with the resources and capital available. This is a rather idealistic concept, because such a number cannot be arbitrarily fixed or varied, but it helps us to understand why some countries, such as India and Egypt, are suffering from the very serious problems associated with overpopulation and why others, such as Australia and Canada, are well below the optimum level at the present time.

Really efficient mass production relies upon division of labour and a high degree of specialisation, but this only becomes possible where there is a sufficiently large labour force of skilled people to make the best use of the resources at their disposal.

ENTERPRISE

Classical economists considered that there were only three factors of production, and they failed to include that factor which is needed to combine land, capital and labour in such a way that production becomes possible. No matter how abundant the available resources are, they cannot be utilised to their full advantage unless they are organised. The entrepreneur, either an individual or a group which we can call management, has the task of organising the other factors of production in order to achieve the level of output which is required.

Enterprise is also necessary to ensure that consumers are made aware of what is available, and to assess the potential market for the goods. In a modern industrial society there are considerable risks involved in production, because there is no direct link between manufacturers and consumers, and a very important function of the entrepreneur is to estimate these risks and to bear them by undertaking the responsibility for making decisions.

The Distribution of Wealth

In all but the most primitive of societies where each family group is a self-supporting economic unit, goods and services will be exchanged. As division of labour is developed and individuals or groups begin to specialise in the occupations at which they are most able, this exchange will become a necessity. People will become increasingly dependent upon each other, but they will enjoy a higher standard of living as a result.

The simplest form of exchange is the *barter system* in which goods are exchanged directly for goods, but the disadvantages of barter make it far too unwieldy and inconvenient for a modern society to practise. Barter depends in the first place on the "double coincidence of want"—each party in the exchange must have what the other wants and must want in return what the other has to offer. The problems encountered in bringing two such parties together as groups became larger and more scattered led to the development of an intermediate stage by means of which goods could be exchanged for money and that money could then be exchanged for other goods either immediately or at some time in the future.

Once a monetary system exists it becomes possible to assign a price to commodities and services and to calculate the value of wealth in terms of money. The distribution of wealth will be made possible by the *price mechanism*, which enables goods and services to be purchased by the people who want them and have the money to pay for them. The price mechanism makes it possible for goods and services to be distributed amongst consumers and also for the factors of production to be distributed amongst manufacturers.

The factors of production will be paid for in money, and the payments, which are called variously rent, interest, wages and profit, represent their *income*. Two of the factors, labour and enterprise, involve individuals to whom payment can be made directly for their personal services, but land and capital are inanimate and payment will, in these instances, be made to the people who own them. Thus income may be obtained in two ways:

1. By performing a personal service—*i.e.* by working, or carrying out the functions of the entrepreneur.
2. By owning land or capital.

Because there are considerable differences in the amount that people are paid for their services, and also because there are considerable differences in the amount of property which people possess, incomes, and therefore wealth, tend to be distributed unevenly (*see* Table X).

Table X—Distribution of Personal Incomes (Before Tax), 1971–72

Lower limit of range of income £	Number of incomes (thousands)
420	699
500	891
600	1,041
700	1,019
800	2,183
1,000	4,961
1,500	4,492
2,000	4,106
3,000	1,187
5,000	323
10,000	58
20,000	10

Property can be acquired as a result of saving or of inheritance or a combination of both. It is made up of land, buildings and all types of investments such as company shares, government securities and so on. In our society, the system by which all property and personal possessions were customarily left to the eldest son on the death of the owner tended to concentrate the wealth of the population in the hands of a comparatively small number of people and to increase the inequality in its distribution. In those societies where property has traditionally been shared amongst all the children when a father dies, there is, as a result, much less inequality because great quantities of wealth are less easy to accumulate when property is constantly being divided and subdivided.

It has been the policy of successive governments in this country, particularly since the Second World War ended, to introduce measures to bring about a more egalitarian distribution of incomes. But despite progressive income tax, estate duties, rent control, capital gains tax and all fiscal methods designed to reduce inequality, there is still a very wide gap between the income of those individuals who are in the lowest income groups and those who are in the highest. This is largely because, at the present time, wages and salaries provide the major source of personal incomes (*see* Table XI). Government policy could possibly have very marked effects on the amount of income derived from the ownership of property, but it is less easy for it to influence the distribution of incomes derived from working.

Table XI—Composition of Total Personal Income, 1951–73 (percentages)

	1951	1961	1971	1973
Source of income				
Employment	71·4	71·9	70·3	69·2
Self-employment	12·1	9·3	8·9	10·1
Rent, dividends and net interest	10·5	11·3	10·7	10·2
National insurance benefits and other public authority grants	6·0	7·5	10·0	10·4

Source: *Social Trends, 1974.*

Wages and *salaries* differ considerably, because they represent the price paid for labour, both physical and mental, and labour is not a homogeneous commodity. There is an abundant supply of unskilled and semi-skilled labour available upon which employers can draw, but many occupations require a very high degree of skill and special aptitudes which are less easy to obtain. For obvious reasons, it is not possible to substitute one type of labour for the other, and the more highly skilled and better-qualified individuals will be able to command a higher price for their services in consequence. This precludes the possibility of obtaining an equal distribution of incomes in a competitive economic system.

If there were no differentials in the payment of incomes, people would be reluctant to undertake long periods of training or to take jobs in which they had to carry considerable responsibility, because they would not have any inducement to do so. In a society such as ours, the standard of living we are able to achieve depends entirely upon the amount of money we have to spend, and very few people have a sufficiently strong sense of vocation to make them heedless of how much or how little they are paid for doing their particular jobs.

If the distribution of *money incomes* were to be made more even, people would have to be offered some other benefits to attract them to certain types of work. Their incomes would most likely be supplemented by perquisites such as free accommodation, free or subsidised meals, travel allowances and so on. Such "fringe" bene-fits are already provided by some employers in order to attract employees, and in certain cases we find that people who earn seemingly low money wages have their *real incomes* increased because their work carries perquisites which people in other jobs have to provide for themselves out of their wages. For example, it has been estimated that the average wage earner spends nearly fourteen per cent of his income on housing, and therefore a person doing a job where he is provided with free accommodation can consider his real wages to be worth about fourteen per cent more than his actual money wages.

Trade Unions

THE HISTORICAL BACKGROUND

One of the most important developments resulting from the Indus-trial Revolution has been the growth of trade unions. As the number of people moving into the rapidly expanding industrial towns increased, and as these people had nothing to sell but their labour, they started to join together to bargain for better wages and working conditions. This was hardly surprising since at that time individual employers were able to decide for themselves how much they would pay their own employees. However, the employers regarded these associations as conspiracies against the expansion of trade, and the wealthy aristocracy feared that such unions formed by the labouring classes would lead to the spread of revolutionary ideas from France to this country. As a result, the *Combination Acts* of 1799 and 1801 were passed which made trade unions illegal. In 1824, owing mainly to the efforts of Francis Place, these Acts were repealed only to be reintroduced a year later in a modified form. Trade unions as such were no longer illegal, but their leaders could be charged with conspiracy, and members were not allowed to take any form of oath of allegiance. Employees had only the right to hold meetings and to strike, but the unions at this time did not, in any case, gain a great deal of support, largely on account of their reputation for violence.

After 1848 the "New Unionism" movement, which was characterised by a more peaceful and reasonable attitude on the part of members, and the admission of unskilled as well as skilled labour to unions, gained in popularity fairly rapidly. Eventually, between 1871 and 1876, the *Trade Union Acts* were passed which finally freed members from the liability of being prosecuted on conspiracy charges and regularised their legal status. Not until 1913, however, were trade unions legally permitted to allocate any of their financial resources for political purposes.

The first trade unions were inevitably fairly small local associations. Obstacles in the way of travel and communications, differences in the demand for labour, and customs and habits varying between one area and another, all combined to limit the size and scope of the early unions. The original craft associations were also reluctant to open their ranks to the new classes of general labourers who possessed no apprentice-trained skills, and were rapidly increasing in number. As a result, the unskilled workers began forming their own unions on an industry-centred basis rather than on the basis of particular occupations or crafts.

TRADE UNIONISM IN THE TWENTIETH CENTURY

The typical trade union today is a very large-scale organisation. The same complex factors which were responsible for the development of big business also produced big unions, and since the beginning of the present century the trade-union movement has been marked by certain outstanding features:

Growth in scale

The early labourers' unions have developed into the great general unions of today. Unions such as the Transport and General Workers Union with a membership at the end of 1973 of 1,785,496 the Amalgamated Union of Engineering and Foundry Workers with 1,172,512 members and the General and Municipal Workers Union with 863,904 do not restrict their membership either by occupation or by industry.

Admission of unskilled workers

The original craft unions no longer limit their membership only to those who have apprenticeship qualifications, but are nowadays willing to admit the semi-skilled and unskilled workers who are employed in the same occupations.

Amalgamation of unions

Many unions are now grouped together in federations for the purpose of collective bargaining, and most are affiliated either directly or indirectly to the *Trades Union Congress*, which represents them at the national level. Owing to a continuing process of amalgamation the number of unions has been declining over the years although their total membership has increased steadily, and there are now approximately 465 unions with a combined membership of over 11 millions. Out of this number, 10,001,419 members belonged to unions affiliated to the Trades Union Congress in 1973–74.

"White-collar unions"

Possibly the most interesting feature of trade unionism over the last fifty years has been the formation and development of unions representing non-manual workers—the "white-collar" unions. People employed as civil servants, teachers, supervisory and managerial staff, clerks and so on now have their own national organisations, and membership of them is still growing rapidly.

This may be explained by the fact that, with the expansion of firms and commerce and the increasing bureaucratic trends in both central and local government, the relationship between the "white-collar" worker and his employer is becoming steadily more remote. These employees are, like the manual workers, coming to regard themselves as only very small cogs in a vast piece of machinery, and, in growing numbers, now look upon their unions as providing their only means of influencing their pay and work conditions.

We must also take into consideration the fact that the considerable pay and educational differentials which existed until quite recently between manual and non-manual workers are declining steadily, and the non-manual workers' previous claim to superior status is consequently being threatened. University graduates are being recruited directly into managerial and executive positions, and this means that people already employed who have a great deal of experience but lack these particular qualifications see their chances of gaining promotion being jeopardised.

Decline in members' interest

As the trade unions have increased in size, there has been a notable falling-off in the active participation of the rank-and-file members. Unions were originally small, local organisations, and bargaining was carried out at the local level, but since 1909, when *Wages Boards* (now called wages councils) were first established to fix the minimum level of wages in certain industries, bargaining has gradually become a national rather than a local concern. Leadership of the very large unions has become remote from the local members, and the members themselves are often scattered throughout the country, which has caused the unions to develop bureaucratic tendencies. Bureaucracy may well be a more efficient system than democracy in a large-scale organisation, but it also creates problems as a result of the apathy which it usually produces, and there is ample evidence of apathy existing amongst trade-union members at present. The average attendance at branch meetings of the larger unions today is usually only between 4 and 7 per cent of the total branch membership. One particular outcome of this lack of interest in union matters has been the ease with which determined minority groups have taken advantage of the situation to gain an influence in branch affairs which is out of all proportion to their numbers.

In the very large unions, too, the local loyalties and interests of the members are often at variance with the national union's policy, with the interests of the society as a whole, and with the ambitions of other unions for their members. Where there is very marked conflict between local units and the formal organisation, there is always the risk of unofficial strike action being taken or *break-away unions* being formed, and this not only seriously undermines the strength of the union itself but also presents a threat to the whole economy.

THE FUNCTIONS OF TRADE UNIONS
Collective bargaining

First and foremost, trade unions exist to bring pressure to bear on employers to increase wages, to reduce working hours and to provide improved working conditions. They are also anxious to safeguard the jobs and status of their members. How far they are able to achieve these aims will depend upon a number of factors, the most important being the level of employment prevailing at the time a claim is put forward.

Since the Second World War, government policy has been directed towards maintaining full employment. This does not mean that no one is ever out of a job, because this would clearly be an impossibility since a certain amount of unemployment is unavoidable. Lord Beveridge held that an average unemployment rate of three per cent would, however, provide for this contingency, allowing one per cent each for the people affected by seasonal fluctuations in the demand for labour, for those temporarily made redundant by reorganisation within industries "incidental to progress" and for those out of work owing to changes in the overseas market.

Full employment places the trade unions in a very strong bargaining position, since it creates a seller's market for labour, and makes the maintenance of discipline extremely difficult. If wages, as a result, rise more rapidly than output, prices will be forced up and the way will be paved for general inflation. We are, unfortunately, only too aware of the effects of a continuing inflationary situation.

Having assumed responsibility for maintaining full employment, the Government is placed in the position of having to keep the resulting inflation in check, because the unions have taken advantage of their much strengthened position to push wages up much more rapidly than the increase in the output of goods and services has warranted.

There have been several attempts made by governments to replace a free collective bargaining system with a statutory incomes policy in order to control the economy. This has not proved very successful because such policies create a great deal of resentment. This is largely due to the fact that governments are better able to enforce such policies in the public sectors of employment than in the private sector, so that the effects appear to be unfair. However, unless all the unions co-operate in keeping wage demands down to a level which can be achieved within the rate of economic growth, the possibility of the government introducing compulsory measures in the national interest becomes greater.

Quite apart from intervention by the Government, there are certain other limitations on the bargaining power of the unions. If their claims for higher pay and shorter hours in a particular industry are unreasonable, employers may resist these claims and attempt to economise on labour by adopting different techniques of production, such as substituting machinery for men or introducing automation, which they might not have considered worth while all the time labour was fairly cheap.

If wage increases force prices up unduly, consumers, like employers, may practise their own type of substitution and switch their demand from the more expensive goods to others which are cheaper and serve virtually the same purpose. This is quite possible in very many cases, except where the goods in question are essential and produced by a monopolist. This means that if wages rise too steeply there may well be unemployment as a result of the subsequent fall in demand.

Safeguarding the status of workers

Trade unions based on crafts or occupations are also concerned with trying to ensure that their members are protected against the possibility of large numbers of new entrants in an industry robbing existing employees of their status. Many unions attach considerable importance to the idea of the *closed shop*—employing only union members—and make the serving of an apprenticeship a condition of membership.

Some unions also insist on strict demarcation rules being observed. They state that certain work must be undertaken only by certain workers, and will threaten to strike if these rulings are contravened even though it may cause considerable inconvenience.

The political functions

For the last fifty years there has been a very close association between the trade unions and the Labour Party, for the creation of which they were largely responsible, and the trade unions attempt to gain their political objectives through the party.

The early trade unions, however, were not regarded by their members as political associations, and it was not until the period of the Great Depression—about 1873 to 1895—that massive unemployment and distress caused the workers to take steps towards obtaining political power. Even then, the leaders of the groups which were formed during this period in order to secure political influence were not generally members of the working classes but were instead radical young intellectuals like Henry Hyndman, who, with William Morris, founded the Social Democratic Federation in 1881, or the Webbs, who were amongst the founder members of the Fabian Society formed in 1884.

The history of the socialist movement in Britain is somewhat confusing, because the first socialists had rather different ideas about the best way of achieving their political ambitions. Hyndman was strongly influenced by the writings of the German revolutionary Karl Marx, and the Social Democratic Federation was accordingly against the parliamentary system, which it wished to overthrow. The Fabians, on the other hand, were less militant, believing in the slow "inevitability of gradualness" rather than revolution- ary methods, and they wanted their members to infiltrate their ideas within the existing political organisations. Certainly the Webbs did not consider it a function of the trade unions to form an inde- pendent party. They wrote in their *Industrial Democracy* (1897) that if the Trades Union Congress:

> "... diverges from its narrow trade union function, and expresses any opinion, either on general social reforms or party politics, it is bound to alienate whole sections of its constituents. The trade unions join the Congress for the promotion of a Parliamentary policy desired, not merely by a majority, but by all of them; and it is a violation of the implied contract between them to use the political force, towards the creation of which all are contributing, for the purposes of any particular political party. The trade unionists of Northumberland and Durham are predominantly Liberal. Those of Lancashire are largely Conserva- tive. Those of Yorkshire and London, again, are deeply impregnated with Socialism."

However, in 1899, the Trades Union Congress passed a resolution which resulted in the formation of the Labour Representation Com- mittee—renamed the Labour Party in 1906. This committee was made up of co-operative, socialist and trade-union organisations, which combined for the express purpose of increasing working- class representation in Parliament. The first trade-union M.P.s formed a left-wing element within the Liberal Party, but the so- called Lib-Labs soon found that their influence within this party was too weak to achieve very much.

After the Taff Vale and Osborne judgments, when it was ruled that companies could sue trade unions for loss and damages sus- tained as a result of strike action, there was renewed agitation within the unions for better representation. In the 1906 election the Labour Representation Committee gained thirty seats and the Lib-Labs twenty-four.

Under pressure from this large group of Labour members, the Liberal Government was persuaded to pass the *Trade Union Act* of 1913, which allowed trade unions to spend part of their funds on political objectives, and to collect a levy for this purpose provided that they obtained the consent of their members. The way was now clear for a much closer relationship to be established between the trade unions and the Labour Party. In 1918 the Labour Party was reorganised and it became a true political party in its own right with local organisations of its own in every constituency. The party, for the first time, acknowledged a distinctive policy, which was:

"To secure for the producers by hand or by brain the full fruits of their industry, and the most equitable distribution thereof that may be possible, upon the basis of the common ownership of the means of production and the best obtainable system of popular administration and control of each industry and service."

The present relationship between the Labour Party and the trade unions is extremely complex. Some trade unions admittedly support the party wholeheartedly, but this does not mean that by so doing they have lost any of their independence nor does it mean that they have forfeited any of their functions as trade unions. The Labour Party does not control the unions nor do the unions control the party.

As far as politics is concerned, the trades unions act as large well-organised pressure groups, but traditionally there were limitations on their ability to take direct political action. As was pointed out in a statement issued by the General Council of the Trades Union Congress in 1952:

"It is our long-standing practice to seek to work amicably with whatever Government is in power and through consultation jointly with Ministers and the other side of industry to find practical solutions to the social and economic problems facing this country."

The unions have frequently demanded political action. In the early days of unionism there was pressure for legislation to protect women and children who were employed in factories; later on there was the need to protect union funds, and also the fight to improve working conditions and to provide better standards of safety as well as the continuing determination to obtain better wages.

As a consequence of nationalisation and the increasing amount of government intervention in industry, the relationship between unions and government has become more direct, but there were until quite recently strong sanctions against industrial action being taken to achieve political objectives. Such action threatens the whole concept of parliamentary democracy, and challenges the authority of elected governments.

During the 1960s the weaknesses of the system of collective bargaining became increasingly apparent. Public uneasiness grew as unofficial strikes frequently brought many industries to a standstill, and the country's disappointing economic performance was largely blamed on the lack of any formal control over the activities of union members.

In 1965, the *Royal Commission on Trades Unions and Employers' Associations* was set up by the Labour Government to examine the problem of industrial relations and the whole system of collective bargaining. When the Commission published its findings in 1968 there was considerable dissatisfaction with its somewhat bland analysis of the situation, particularly as the unions could be regarded as having emerged comparatively unscathed from the investigation. Although the Commission made certain recommendations for reforming the system of collective bargaining, it rejected any form of legal enforcement of agreements as a means of settling unofficial strikes. This

". . . would divert attention from the underlying causes to the symptoms of the disease and might indeed delay or even frustrate the cure we recommend."

As members of the Commission saw it,

"By far the most important part in remedying the problem of unofficial strikes and other forms of unofficial action will be played in reforming the institutions of whose defects they are a symptom."

In January 1969, the Labour Government published its proposals for new legislation in the form of a White Paper, *In Place of Strife*. Although it was intended to implement many of the recommendations of the Donovan Commission, the Government also wanted the right to intervene in certain disputes in order to safeguard the interests of individuals and of society against the consequences of unofficial action and inter-union disputes. The Government proposed to introduce penal sanctions against defaulting unions or union members.

In Place of Strife was greeted by fierce opposition, and the Labour movement in the country was split, as was the Cabinet, when it was recognised that the Government intended to introduce compulsory measures into the collective bargaining system. Some of the more powerful unions threatened industrial action to resist the introduction of the new legislation, and the Government was eventually forced to abandon its proposals and enter instead into "a solemn and binding agreement" with the Trades Union Congress that the latter would take a more active role in settling disputes and gaining voluntary union support for the Government's economic and financial policies. The efforts of the Trades Union Congress were, however, largely unsuccessful, as many people outside the union movement had predicted they would be, and in the face of increasing industrial unrest and falling productivity, the Government was eventually obliged to call a General Election.

Following their defeat of the Labour Government's proposed legislation, the unions were determined to resist any further attempts to introduce compulsory elements into collective bargaining and it was evident that a new stage had been entered in the relationship between Government and organised labour. The traditional sanctions that had formerly prevented unions from taking direct political action no longer carried very much weight, and the Conservative Government elected in 1970 was, like its Labour predecessor, defeated after a major confrontation with the unions.

This confrontation, which culminated in the three-day working week and a General Election, resulted from the determination of several very powerful unions to have the Conservatives' 1972 *Industrial Relations Act* repealed. During the election campaign, the question "Who governs Britain?" was frequently raised.

The minority Labour Government that took office in March 1974 abolished the Act and in its place pinned all its hopes on the *Social Compact* or *Social Contract* made with the Trades Union Congress, which once again relied upon the voluntary co-operation of unions in effecting the Government's economic and financial policies.

So far, there has been little evidence of the "Social Contract" being any more successful than previous attempts to gain the voluntary co-operation of unions in controlling the demands of their members, despite the fact that the country is facing its most serious economic crisis since the 1930s. There is, however, evidence of the growing power of the unions, and of the new willingness of unions to use this power to achieve political objectives. Union action is no longer confined to attempts to improve wages and working conditions or to

H

safeguard the jobs and status of their members, but is increasingly used to put pressure on the Government to adopt policies which the more militant union members want to see introduced. There has been a very noticeable shift of power away from the elected government into the hands of the unions, and the question that was asked during the final stormy months of the Conservative regime in 1973–74, "Who governs Britain?", urgently requires an answer.

Professional Associations

There is considerable confusion over what is meant by a profession, since there is no specific set of characteristics which mark off particular occupations as professions. Broadly speaking, however, a profession might be defined as an occupation which is carried out by people who have acquired some special knowledge, and proved, by formally recognised examinations, their ability to apply this knowledge for a practical purpose. Into this category would come occupations concerned with law, medicine, teaching, accountancy and so on.

People in these occupations have nearly all formed their own associations, the main functions of which have been to devise systems for examining the ability of those who wish to practise, and to award appropriate certificates or diplomas. Some professions, such as those connected with the law and medicine, have also gone so far as to establish ethical codes to control the behaviour of their practitioners. Careful selection by examination and compliance with a professional code of behaviour not only help to safeguard the status of members of a profession, but also enhance the economic value of their services, and justify their claims for high pay.

In some cases professional people charge their clients a fee for their services, and these fees are fixed according to a scale agreed by the association to which they belong. This means that the profession enjoys a monopolistic position, controlling completely both the supply and quality of its services.

Members of professions where it is customary for payment to be made in the form of salaries are in a somewhat weaker position than those which charge clients a fee. A professional person who enters into a contract with an employer and receives a salary in payment for his services is in virtually the same position as any other employee who has to negotiate for better conditions. Professional associations therefore frequently assume the functions of a trade union for the purpose of collective bargaining, although they generally do not regard themselves as trade unions and very few are affiliated to the Trades Union Congress. To some extent this reflects the traditional claim to superior status of the professional worker, and the exclusive nature of professional associations.

While some professional associations undertake the trade-union functions of collective bargaining, there still remain a number which refuse to do this, and, consequently, within some professions there exist two separate organisations—one concerned with examinations and qualifications, and the other providing the machinery for collective bargaining. Within banking, for example, there is the Institute of Bankers, which is concerned only with the qualifications of members of the profession, and the National Union of Bank Employees, which exists for the purposes of collective bargaining.

Employers' Associations

The growth of trade-unionism produced a situation in which employers were no longer able to act alone when pressure was brought to bear on them. They could no longer think in terms of reaching private agreements with their own employees, but were forced to take into consideration the conditions of workers in other firms within the same industry. Naturally enough, employers began to join together for many of the reasons that had originally caused employees to form unions for purposes of collective bargaining. In association with each other they were in a much stronger position to resist pressure for higher wages and changes in working conditions.

There are at present about 1400 employers' associations in Britain. The large numbers are accounted for by the fact that, although they are generally organised on an industrial basis rather than a product basis, most of the groups are purely local or regional bodies. They have, however, formed federations for negotiating with the unions, and approximately eighty national federations are now involved in the general discussion of problems relating to wages and the safety, health and welfare of the workers.

Rather different are the *trade associations*, which are concerned with the actual state of trade, and are formed to make representations to the Government, to ensure the provision of common services and to undertake the regulation of trading practices.

Employers' federations and trade associations are eligible for membership of the *Confederation of British Industry*, as are individual companies, and the total membership of this central body comprises over 200 trade associations and employers' federations and about 13,000 companies. The Confederation of British Industry is recognised by the Government as the official channel for consultation between government departments and representatives of private employers as a whole. It also acts as an advisory organisation, and is responsible for representing its members not only in Britain but internationally as well. For example, it sends delegates to conferences held by the Council of European Industrial Federations.

The Socio-Economic Aspects of Industry

Collective bargaining over wages and working conditions is, however, only one aspect of industrial relations, which are of vital importance to the economic well-being of the whole community. Elton Mayo successfully demonstrated in the experiments that he conducted at one of the Western Electric Company's factories at Hawthorne near Chicago between 1924 and 1932 that satisfactory relationships between workers and their colleagues and supervisors are as important as wages and physical working conditions in promoting greater efficiency and higher levels of output. He also showed that the lack of a sense of purpose will cause dissatisfaction and frustration.

In a modern industrial society there is a fundamental difference between the jobs which people do; some work is enjoyable and a great deal of satisfaction may be derived from it, but much work is tedious or even unpleasant and is only undertaken by people who hope to gain some other end by doing it. One of the drawbacks to industrialisation is that, as people cease to be self-supporting and division of labour increases, the gap between what individuals need or want and what they have to do to obtain it becomes steadily wider.

INCENTIVES

The term "incentive" may be used with reference to anything which encourages anyone to work. There is a great deal of disagreement as to the real nature of incentives, and it is interesting to note that a person is generally far more willing to discuss other people's incentives than his own. This is perhaps because it is very difficult for someone to analyse and describe his own incentives, and what an individual thinks and feels about his job will vary according to the mood he is in at a particular time. Incentives cannot be listed in order of importance, because even those of a single individual will tend to change in degrees of urgency from one time to another. However, since monetary incentives in some form are important for the majority of people today, it is useful to consider them first.

Financial incentives are associated with the search for material security, because nowadays we have to use money to buy what we want to satisfy our basic needs. Social security benefits have largely made gross material deprivation unknown, and people are protected from the desperate need to take work of any kind in order to survive. However, in a society such as our own, with a high standard of living, few people would be happy if they had to live at, or only just above, mere subsistence level. We nearly all want more than we actually possess, and money is our means of obtaining all these extra desirable things, so that we are likely to respond to the "carrot" of more money if it is dangled before us to make us work harder.

There is a point beyond which the value of money as an incentive will eventually decline. The exact point will vary from one individual to another because people's circumstances will all be different. A married man with a large family will have to provide for his dependants as well as himself, so he will require more money than a single man who has fewer responsibilities, but, so long as the basic needs are satisfied, people are unlikely to think about money all the time. After a certain stage the primary financial incentive, which might cause a person to work harder in order to earn enough money to live on, will begin to decline in importance, and the higher up the income scale he goes the less attention he will pay to the prospect of receiving more, since taxation and other compulsory deductions will act as disincentives to work harder simply to gain more money.

The opportunity to exercise—and take a pride in—*a particular skill* may also make work attractive. Such an opportunity can provide satisfaction and a sense of purpose which is not necessarily concerned with demonstrating superiority. The society as a whole attaches different levels of prestige to different kinds of work, and we come to accept the idea that a surgeon, for example, takes a pride in his work and is proud to be what he is, while we deny the idea that a dustman or factory floor-sweeper can also be proud and derive satisfaction from his job as a result. However, it would be unrealistic to limit satisfaction in the prestige of a job to work which is approved according to a social scale, because it should be recognised that a person with lesser ability and skill can derive proportionate amounts of satisfaction even though his level of achievement is lower.

Sheer *acquisitiveness* or the non-materialistic acquisition of possessions can act as an incentive to many people. We may be encouraged to work harder, if, by so doing, we are enabled to obtain things which are a delight in themselves. In this context, this does not mean the acquisition of articles which bring enhanced social prestige for their owners, but rather the obtaining of all those different things which people enjoy possessing for their own sake. They are more likely to be connected with hobbies and leisure-time pursuits and interests than with the routine of day-to-day life.

A sense of responsibility and obligation to the rest of society will cause people to work where the gap between the person who is doing the job and those for whom he is doing it is not very wide. Most people in such positions will be helping other individuals directly, and they will feel a certain involvement with them. Doctors, nurses, schoolteachers and other public servants such as firemen and policemen will need a strong sense of vocation in order even to consider taking on the jobs that they do. Generally speaking, this type of incentive is unlikely to have any particular importance for industrial workers, because the gap between them and the consumers of their products is too great for the relationship to be meaningful. The social obligations of a job will provide an incentive to the more responsible workers.

Some jobs provide people with *the chance to express their personality*. This can prove a very big incentive, since the desire to feel that we are "somebody" is inherent in all of us, and we usually refer to work which denies us any opportunity of this kind as "soul destroying." Many people are handicapped in the ability to express themselves owing to lack of intelligence or lack of education, but many more are entirely prevented from showing any individualism by the very nature of their jobs. If there are to be any incentives, other than financial incentives, for such people, they will need to be provided by the social environment in which they are working in order to compensate for the lack of such incentives directly associated with the job. The worker who cannot express his personality through what he is employed to do may instead derive a great deal of satisfaction from his individual role in the group of workers with whom he comes into regular contact.

Frustration

It is unfortunately true that the factory environment is rarely conducive to the satisfaction of any needs other than that of money, and yet many people spend the greater proportion of their time in just such conditions. Employees in factories are seldom in a position where they can influence their working environment, gain any personal satisfaction from their jobs or be able to enjoy the security that comes from knowing that the ordered routine will continue well into the future. Dr Graham Wootton, in *Workers, Unions and the State*, observes that, in the factory: "The very terminology is significant: 'hands' (one's face and brain not counting), 'operatives' (extensions of machines), 'personnel' (neutral, grey protoplasm, which, however, reacts to stimuli)."

Although it is most likely to develop as a result of mass-production techniques used in a factory, conflict between individual needs and the working environment may be experienced by people in all walks of life, and it inevitably leads to frustration. We all know what it feels like when we very much want something, but somebody or something prevents us from having it. If we are fortunate such frustration is only transitory, and we are not subject to it for long periods at a time. Psychologists have produced considerable evidence that the most usual response to frustration is constructive, and people who are thwarted in their desire to achieve their goals and satisfy their needs will attempt to do something about it, or "take it out" on whomsoever or whatever is obstructing them. If there is no chance of responding to frustration constructively, tension will increase all the time that satisfaction is denied.

People who are frustrated become aggressive, and, if they cannot discharge their aggression on the object that has caused the trouble, they may *displace* it by passing on the blame for whatever is annoying them to somebody else who is not likely to retaliate. There are numerous examples of "scapegoats" who have been used in this way: the man who has an argument with his wife over breakfast, and has to admit she is right, may find a pretext to "let off steam" by telling off the first person he meets at work who is in a subordinate position to himself; social workers who have to deal with "problem" families remark upon the frequency with which one of the children is blamed for all their misfortunes; coloured immigrants are often held responsible for causing all the unemployment, housing shortages and overstretched medical services in the country. Displacement of aggression in this manner is closely associated with attempts to *rationalise* such behaviour, and the individual who finds an unfortunate victim on whom to vent his wrath will usually also be able to explain why he deserved "all he got."

Some people respond to frustration not by blaming others but by blaming themselves. They become resigned to the idea that, because of some fault of their own, there is nothing they can do to surmount the obstacle that stands between them and what they are trying to achieve. As a result, they become depressed and apathetic, and may be able to relieve the tension only by indulging in flights of fancy as a form of escapism. People who live a "Walter Mitty" type of existence are those who are frustrated in reality.

In whichever way aggression is discharged the subsequent relief of tension is purely temporary, because it does nothing to solve the problem which is causing the frustration.

Regression is also characteristic of frustrated behaviour, and people who are faced with a problem to which no solution can be found tend to behave in a childish way. Temper tantrums and senseless destructiveness are typical symptoms of regression, and in industry lack of satisfaction is often evidenced by a lack of emotional control, which leads to poor relationships within the organisation, the spreading of rumours, irrational loyalties and even, sometimes, to deliberate acts of sabotage.

Yet another symptom of frustration is *fixation*. This is a compulsion on the part of the individual that he has to go on behaving in a certain way although experience should have taught him that he will achieve nothing by his actions. A fixation may seem very similar to a habit, but, whereas habits will usually be abandoned when they cease to bring satisfaction, fixations are much more rigid, and will usually become more strongly implanted under the circumstances which could be expected to break a habit. Fixations, because of their rigidity, make people resist any changes or new ideas that are introduced into the system with which they are familiar, even where there are obvious benefits to be derived from them. Managers who persist in the belief that the only real incentive for their workers is money—a belief that seems to be only too prevalent amongst people in managerial positions despite all the evidence which has been produced to the contrary—are themselves suffering from fixations.

Dr J. A. C. Brown, in his book *The Social Psychology of Industry,* provides a list of the types of situation which experiments have shown are likely to produce extreme frustration. He includes: the arbitrary withdrawal of desirable objects; preventing subjects from completing a task; inducing in subjects a sense of failure and a distrust of their own abilities; curbing an individual's drives towards self-expression and self-assertion through interference from outside; frustration due to satiation; frustration due to a discrepancy between desire and ability to solve a task; unsatisfactory leadership. Dr Brown adds this comment to his list: "It will be noted how many of these conditions may readily be found in the average factory."

The existence of frustration in a predominantly industrial society is not a problem that can easily be overcome, but its effects on the morale and, consequently, on the output and efficiency of everybody concerned are seriously damaging to the whole economy.

We have already noted that people who are in a state of tension may "withdraw from the field" mentally by indulging in such forms of escapism as day-dreaming and other flights of fancy, but it is possible in some circumstances to withdraw physically. The most obvious way in which an employee can withdraw from a frustrating situation is by leaving his job, and for a considerable time now *the rate of labour turnover* has been regarded as a possible gauge of morale. It has been found that the turnover of unskilled workers is considerably higher than that of skilled workers, but there seems to be little relationship between rate of turnover and earnings. This, of course, adds support to the evidence that financial incentives are by no means the only factor of importance to the employee.

Absenteeism, like leaving, is also a form of withdrawal, but, as Trist and Hill have observed in *Industrial Accidents, Sickness and Other Absences*:

"Though leavings and absences may both provide means of withdrawal from the work situation, absences are nevertheless the obverse of labour turnover. In contrast to leaving one place of work for another, they represent being away from the job while still remaining with the same employing institution. In terms of the relationship between the individual and his work organisation, they indicate disturbances in a continuing relationship, whereas leavings are a sign that the relationship has been broken."

It has been estimated that approximately 7 per cent of the working population is absent for reasons other than holidays every day in Britain. A reduction in the level of absenteeism would not necessarily be matched by a proportional increase in output, but, nevertheless, it is apparent that the cost of absence to firms and to the economy as a whole is very great.

Different investigations of absenteeism have shown that there are substantial differences between the absence rates of the two sexes—the rates for women invariably being higher than those for men. Absence tends to increase with the length of the working week, and there is a correlation between absence rates and the size of firm or unit within a large organisation. The *General Household Survey* (1973) also found that very young workers and elderly workers are less likely to be absent than others. This suggests that, while a certain amount of absenteeism is bound to occur, a great deal of it is "voluntary" rather than "involuntary."

Voluntary absenteeism—that is, absenteeism which is not the result of illness, accidents or domestic crises—is quite consistent with the concept of "withdrawal from the field," and may be as undesirable for the worker as for his employer, since it is almost certainly a symptom of discontentment. Voluntary absence sometimes reaches considerable proportions. For example, Lord Robens stated in 1964 that in coal-mining the number of absentees was so great on Fridays and Mondays that frequently the collieries were functioning with only three-quarters or even half of their total workers.

There is, too, a close link between accident-proneness and absenteeism. As Trist and Hill remarked:

". . . the occurrence of accidents may be frequently (though not necessarily always) related to the personal characteristics of those sustaining them, and as a result accidents may be consciously or unconsciously motivated by the individuals concerned. Characteristically, industrial accidents cause both injury and absence from work, and, so far as they are motivated events, the motivation (however unconscious) may be directed towards either of these ends. . . . [Accidents may] be considered as a means of withdrawal from the work situation through which the individual may take up the role of absentee in a way acceptable both to himself and to his employing organisation."

Until quite recently accident-proneness was generally held to be some quirk of personality that was well established before the individual started work, but we now know that differences in morale, which is associated with frustration, can be equated with variations in the accident rate. Dr Paterson of Glasgow University discovered that coal-miners from the same village who worked the same seam in two different collieries had an accident rate which was three times greater in one colliery than the other. Dr Paterson also showed that the number of crashes in an R.A.F. squadron increased as collective frustration increased, but was reduced as the factors causing the frustration were removed.

Like accidents, industrial illness may be regarded as a form of withdrawal. All emotional disturbances are accompanied by physical symptoms, but where such disturbances are only temporary the physical symptoms will disappear as soon as the cause of the upset has been taken away. In those cases where the individual is continuously under tension the physical reactions are likely to become chronic and produce psychosomatic ailments. Some people have a greater capacity to tolerate emotional stress than others, but it is unfortunately the case that psychosomatic disorders are increasing in frequency, and this would seem to indicate that more people nowadays are finding themselves in the kind of situation which tries them beyond their endurance.

The diseases associated with stress are relatively unknown in non-industrialised countries, and even in the more remote rural areas of Britain, the United States and other predominantly industrial countries of Western Europe. However, it is unfortunately the case that as industrialisation spreads so does the incidence of psychological and psychosomatic illnesses. In Britain, coronary heart disease accounts for about 100,000 deaths each year, approximately 800,000 people receive treatment for peptic ulcers, of whom 250,000 are new cases, and up to 15 per cent of all the work done in general practice is with people suffering from emotional disorders. A great deal of what we have gained on the swings, as advances in medical knowledge and techniques have brought a decline in the general death-rate, the infant mortality rate and better control of the major "old" diseases such as tuberculosis, malnutrition and serious infections, we have unfortunately lost on the roundabouts, as the prevalence of stress diseases is now a matter of increasing concern.

We have so far discussed the unconscious responses to frustration which give rise to behaviour that affects both industry and the individuals concerned, but does not generally attract the attention of outsiders. Sometimes, however, simmering discontent makes itself apparent in a more dramatic form, and results in the externally observable *strikes* which are so commonplace today. Although the number of working days lost—7,173,000 in 1973—is seriously damaging to the economy, as a measure of frustration the actual number of strikes is more important in our context, since these will correspond with the number of centres of grievance. Although a relatively few big stoppages can entail the loss of millions of working days, in this country the big stoppage has virtually disappeared, and it has been estimated that about 95 per cent of all strikes at the present time are the result of unofficial action involving comparatively few workers. It is the unofficial strikes which are responsible for 60 to 70 per cent of all the days lost in this way, and most unofficial strikes are very short and sharp, lasting from a few hours to a few days only. There were 2854 such stoppages in 1973.

When using the number of strikes as a measure of frustration in industry it is really necessary that the causes of strikes should be known precisely. This is clearly impossible because the statistics available do not provide us with this information, and, in any case, so much motivation is unconscious that even the workers involved may not be aware of all their reasons for taking such action. The information that *is* available suggests that of all the strikes which take place, approximately half are concerned with wage claims and disputes (*see* Fig. 4). However, Knowles, in his authoritative study, *Strikes—A Study in Industrial Conflict,* has suggested that the number of disputes officially recorded as attributable to wages disputes exaggerates the strictly financial motives. He considers that money matters are frequently only the excuse to express more vague dissatisfaction. Certainly the number of strikes which seem to be called on the flimsiest of pretexts, but nevertheless gain considerable support, bears out the idea that such behaviour is at times completely irrational, and likely to be the overt response to some unrecognised frustration.

It is also interesting to note that the two worst years for working days lost by strikes in modern times—1972 with nearly 24 million days lost and 1974 with over 14 million—were years in which the new phenomenon of politically motivated industrial action became part of the social scene.

Work and Non-Work

The kind of work a man does clearly influences his whole way of life, but, unfortunately, sociologists have so far done little detailed work in the field of occupational influence on non-work behaviour, and our picture of its exact nature is far from complete.

Dennis, Henriques and Slaughter made a study of a mining community (*Coal is Our Life*) and found that the dangerous and

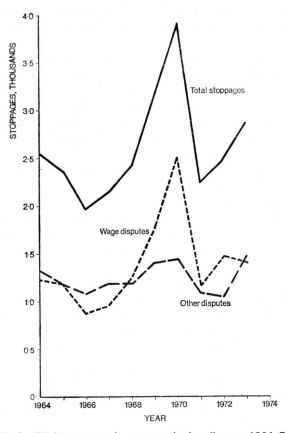

Fig. 4.—Work stoppages by wage and other disputes 1964–74

demanding work of the face-worker leads him to spend his free time seeking oblivion in public houses and causes him to dislike any further demands being made upon him at home, even by his wife. Similarly, Jeremy Tunstall found that distant-water fishermen pass their time ashore with their ship-mates, spending money lavishly and treating their wives like slaves (*The Fishermen*). By way of contrast, we know that many people who are ambitious for promotion will give up a great deal of their time to furthering their education and training, and may have little social life in consequence, while others who are deeply involved in their occupations may attempt to "combine business with pleasure" as much as they possibly can. Their wives will be expected to act as hostesses to their business friends, and they themselves will not be able to make any definite distinction between what is work and what is not.

Occupation has a direct influence on leisure, because it determines firstly how much free time a person has, and secondly how much money he has to spend once the necessities of life have been provided. Workers whose occupation does not provide them with any opportunity for status recognition may attempt to compensate for this by choosing out-of-work activities which give them the status otherwise denied to them.

The relationship between work and leisure is of three different types—either opposing or supporting it, or else, between these points, a form of neutrality.

Many workers will indulge in leisure-time pursuits which are quite distinct from activities associated with their jobs. This "opposing" type of relationship stems from the fact that the jobs are not in themselves attractive or particularly absorbing, and the workers do not carry their interest in them over to their free time. For those whose work is dangerous, unpleasant or regarded with mixed enthusiasm, leisure will provide the means of escaping from it, and drinking, gambling, watching football or dog-racing and so on are typical "escapist" activities during which work can be entirely forgotten.

For those people whose work is deeply satisfying and interesting, leisure may play a supporting or extending role. The working day is not very rigidly defined, and it is not easy to determine at what point work ends and leisure begins. Most social workers, for example, are often considered to "live for their work," and lecturers and teachers devote a great deal of time to reading, which they obviously enjoy but which also will almost certainly be an advantage in their particular occupation.

The rather neutral attitude many people have towards their jobs is frequently reflected in their similarly neutral attitude towards leisure. The work of those engaged in clerical jobs, for example, is seldom particularly demanding or of absorbing interest, and it is certainly not dangerous; it is not the sort of work that is likely to engender feelings of hostility, but neither is it likely to be carried over into non-work activities. For this reason the leisure pursuits of clerical workers tend to be less positive, and much of their free time may be spent in dozing, sitting passively for long periods in front of the television or pottering about rather aimlessly.

Most of what we know about the use of leisure in this country is based on studies of different social classes rather than on studies of different occupational groups. However, the process of modern civilisation has made leisure no longer the preserve of a privileged minority but something which is shared by the masses, and this means that however the leisure is used, or perhaps even abused, it is of significance both economically and commercially.

It is estimated that about six million people go dancing each week, and, although audiences have been declining steadily, over two and three quarter million still go to the cinema. Sporting activities of many types attract enthusiasts not only to watch but also to participate, as is evidenced by the steadily rising sales of sports goods. According to the Stationery Office publication *Britain: An Official Handbook,* 1974, on any weekday evening roughly seven families out of eight stay at home, and entertaining friends is a popular leisure-time pursuit. The scale and standard of home entertaining has been rising, and this is indicated by the increasing sales of table wines—now more than double those of the 1930s—and of the more expensive foods, as well as by the standard of the recipes which are featured in newspapers and in magazine articles devoted to cookery.

There are probably over 20 million spare-time gardeners, and the boom in nursery sales and the spread of shops specialising in garden implements bear witness to the interest taken in this pastime. There are now over 3,000 local horticultural societies affiliated to the National Allotments and Garden Society; local flower shows and horticultural competitions are popular events, attracting a wide following.

The boom in sales of magazines and periodicals dealing with a very wide range of interests is an important development of recent years, but reading of all kinds is enjoyed by many—nearly one third of the population are registered members of public libraries at the present time.

In terms of money spent, probably the most popular home hobby is photography, with an estimated one and a half million amateur photographers entering competitions, but a great deal of money is also spent on "hi-fi" equipment and records—48 million were pressed in 1971—and on television. It is thought that over 90 per cent of the families in Britain have a television set today.

Holidays are now a prominent event in the year for most people, and, out of the estimated 40.5 million who spend their annual holiday away from home, at least 8.5 million go abroad. Caravans are increasing in popularity, and in 1972 nearly 20 per cent of main holidays were taken in caravans.

Many industries cater almost exclusively for leisure-time activities and interests, so that what is available to entertain, relax and enrich the lives of people during their spare time also makes for big business, actuated by all the usual business motives, and providing employment for a large number of people.

EXERCISE 9

1. "Rich countries can hardly fail to become richer, while poor countries, without a great deal of assistance, will become increasingly poor by comparison." Explain and discuss.

2. Explain how incomes are derived and why Britain's wealth is unevenly distributed.

3. *Either*: (a) Compare professional associations with skilled craft unions. *or* (b) "All occupations seek to devise methods for regulating and controlling their market, work and status situations." Explain and discuss. (*A.E.B.*)

4. Examine some of the main ways in which technical changes may affect the manual worker. (*A.E.B.*)

5. Discuss the contribution made by sociological studies to our understanding of the conflict between individual needs and the working environment.

6. Write notes on the following:
   (a) Displaced aggression.
   (b) Regression.
   (c) Fixation.

7. "Many plays and novels are woven around occupational roles and provide us with insights into the significance of occupation in the lives of people like scientists, teachers, nurses, policemen, factory workers and miners." Discuss and explain the ways in which the approach of the sociologist differs from that of the novelist. (*A.E.B.*)

8. "Stultifying work stultifies leisure." Does it? (*A.E.B.*)

9. What part do trade unions play in industrial relations in Britain? (*Oxford*)

10. Illustrate the distinction between professional associations and trade unions. (*Oxford*)

11. Describe recent changes in the distribution in Britain of wealth and income. (*Oxford*)

12. Why have white collar unions and manual workers' unions experienced different rates of growth since World War II? (*London*)

13. To what extent is the nature of British trade unionism incompatible with central economic planning? (*London*)

FOR FURTHER READING

N. J. Smelser. *The Sociology of Economic Life*. Prentice–Hall, 1964.
G. Wootton. *Workers, Unions and the State*. Routledge and Kegan Paul, 1966.
G. Millerson. *The Qualifying Associations*. Routledge and Kegan Paul, 1964.
J. A. C. Brown. *The Social Psychology of Industry*. Penguin Books, 1954.
British Institute of Management. *Absence from Work*. 1961.
K. G. J. C. Knowles. **Strikes—A Study in Industrial Conflict**. Blackwell, 1952.

J. M. M. Hill and E. L. Trist. *Industrial Accidents, Sickness and Other Absences*. Tavistock Pamphlet No. 4.
Council of Europe. *Leisure in Our Life*. 1966.
Nels Anderson. *Work and Leisure*. Routledge and Kegan Paul, 1966.
Jeremy Tunstall. *The Fishermen*. London, 1962.
N. Dennis, C. Slaughter and F. Henriques. *Coal is Our Life*. London, 1956.
E. R. F. W. Crossman. *Automation and Skill*. H.M.S.O., 1965.
P. Hollowell. *The Lorry Driver*. Routledge and Kegan Paul, 1968.
S. Parker. *The Future of Work and Leisure*. MacGibbon and Kee, 1971.
S. Parker *et al. The Sociology of Industry*. Allen and Unwin, 1971.
Malcolm Warner (ed.). *The Sociology of the Workplace*. Allen and Unwin, 1973.

CHAPTER X

THE EDUCATIONAL SYSTEM

EDUCATION is a word which may be defined in a number of ways. The term can be used in a very broad sense to include every agency which enables an individual to master his physical and social environment, and adapt himself to the demands made upon him by the society of which he is a member. It can also be used in a much more limited sense to include only the deliberate and formal instruction which is given in educational establishments, such as schools, colleges and universities. For the purposes of this chapter, we shall use the word "education" in the second, narrower, sense, and examine the nature of the educational system in our own society with reference only to its institutionalised aspects.

All social institutions come into existence because they are the means by which a social system is maintained, and, as a society becomes more complex, so its institutions will become more complex and more numerous. Each of these institutions develops to perform certain functions, although the way in which the functions are actually carried out may change in the course of time, and reflect the changes which take place in the society as a whole.

The Social Functions of Education

THE ECONOMIC FUNCTIONS

To put it very simply, the most important economic function of education is that of ensuring that the society's need for a labour force is satisfied. A modern industrial society requires not only a great deal of manpower but also a certain quality of manpower, and both the quantity and quality available are controlled by the educational system. The relationship between the economy and the educational system is, however, fairly complicated, and it is not easy to ascertain the extent to which economic pressures influence the nature of education or, conversely, the extent to which attitudes and ideas transmitted through the educational system determine the development of the society economically.

Within the society at the present time, two rather conflicting tendencies are found to exist which have caused something of a gulf to appear within the educational system. Middle-class attitudes are beginning to be adopted by larger numbers of the population and this has produced a demand on the one hand for a more prolonged education of a general nature for everyone. On the other hand, much of this more general education appears to be irrelevant in a society in which technical expertise and specialised knowledge are at a premium, so that even more importance is being placed on purely vocational training. Protagonists ranged on the two sides are equally justified in the arguments which they put forward to support their case within the present system. Too narrow an education will deny many individuals the chance of learning about those aspects of life which might be regarded as purely pleasurable but are nevertheless desirable for the enjoyment and satisfaction which may be derived from them. However, the old saw that "the best things in life are free" is not a truism in an affluent, materialist society, and occupational training is a very important factor in education if a person's standard of living is almost entirely dependent upon his earnings.

Although occupation and education are so closely related, the actual objectives of each can be seen to differ. In the words of the Central Advisory Committee on Education's report *School and Life* (1946):

> "Even if the practical difficulties could be overcome, the principle of basing school-education primarily on the needs of industry is bad. The objects of education and employment are not the same. The object of education is men and women; industry aims at producing coal and textiles, breakfast cereals and cinema films, newspapers and cosmetics, and other economic goods. The object of employment is the product; in education it is the process that matters. In industry the worker is part of a process ending in goods; in education he is an end in himself. This means that the industrial organisation of which a worker forms a part will not be concerned with the claims of the whole man, which education develops, and it would be surprising if industry could ever supply a full education."

This is all quite true, but, in a period when young people are not only physically but also socially more mature than their parents or teachers were at the same age, influences and attitudes held by the community outside the school are not likely to go unheeded. The realistic incentives which are offered by vocational training are frequently much more attractive than those offered by more academic or cultural studies, and it would be nonsensical to pretend otherwise. The author has questioned many young people on this matter and has found that, in the vast majority of cases, they regard anything but purely vocational training as a "complete waste of time."

Something of the conflicting elements and aims of the educational system in this country at the present time are perhaps more easily understood if we recognise that there are also considerable differences in the attitudes towards the rewards to be gained from work. In the United States, children are brought up to measure success in terms of the ability to make money, and it is assumed that for the majority of them earning money will begin very early in life. Schoolchildren find spare-time jobs, and many Americans work their way through college or university, so that by the time they have completed their formal education they are thoroughly used to the idea of competition in which the winners are those who gain the highest financial rewards. It is perhaps significant that in Britain grants and scholarships, at one of the highest rates in the world, are available, and enable schoolchildren and students to complete their education as far as possible before they are brought into contact with the harsh reality of having to earn a living.

The traditional ideal, particularly prevalent in the middle classes and fostered by the grammar schools, is that money-making is something of an unfortunate necessity which ought not to be allowed to take precedence over the rewards to be gained from dedication and service to the community. This means that, whether it is true or not, most of us are brought up to believe that the satisfaction to be derived from the job itself is more important than the money that can be earned from it. This attitude becomes apparent when people are questioned. Industrial psychologists have found that many people will quickly assert in rather derogatory tones that others working with them "are only interested in the money" but they will be unwilling to admit that money is their own principal concern.

Middle-class attitudes towards other things as well as towards money will tend to be transmitted and perpetuated through the educational system, since the majority of teachers are the products of middle-class backgrounds. For the children whom they teach these attitudes will not be greatly at variance with those they encounter outside school if they come from middle-class homes themselves, but for the very large numbers who belong to working-class families and who eventually take up working-class occupations, the difference between what they are taught in school and attitudes they encounter outside it may well cause frustration and tension.

It could be said that, in the days before economic pressures had any great amount of influence on the educational system, the hallmark of a "good" education was its apparent irrelevance to the practicalities of life. Its real object was that of providing the sons of gentlemen with a cultured veneer and panache which made them more self-confident and assured than the less privileged ordinary people. Positions of authority and power were filled by members of the upper class, and the public schools provided the education designed to fit individuals from this class to fulfil these roles. Traditionally, public-school and Oxbridge entrance depended upon parentage rather than upon innate ability or intelligence, since only the wealthy could afford the fees, and a strong element of this tradition still exists in this area of the educational system today. However, the old aristocracy no longer have a monopoly as far as wealth is concerned, and the exclusiveness of the public schools has been challenged strongly since the Industrial Revolution first began to disturb the distribution of wealth within the society. The newly rich industrialists of the nineteenth century became able to afford, and demand, public-school education for their children.

The professional classes were catered for by the grammar schools, which were strongly biased towards providing the education required by those who intended, or, more likely, were intended by their parents, to become doctors, lawyers, ministers of religion or schoolmasters. Considered in this light, it is easy to recognise why these schools developed their sense of service and dedication to the community. Most of these schools were for fee-paying scholars, although there were a number of endowed places for the children of suitable and deserving parents unable to afford the expense of education themselves.

The demands made upon the lower classes by the emerging industrialism of the nineteenth century were not very great as far as education was concerned. General labourers and factory workers in those days really did not need anything more than a fairly rudimentary knowledge of the "three R's" in order to get by, and this was all that the first elementary schools, publicly provided after 1870, were able to give their pupils. Before that date, most schools for lower-class children were organised either by the Church or by individual philanthropists who wished to offer a Christian upbringing to a section of the population which was becoming increasingly apathetic towards religious matters. The teaching in these schools was largely centred round teaching children to read the Bible, and to answer questions or recite long quotations from it. Attendance at school was not made compulsory until 1902, when the leaving age was set at 13, although it was possible for children to leave before this provided that they passed an examination to prove that they had learned all that the schools were expected to teach them. The idea of providing educational facilities for all, whether rich or poor, is therefore of comparatively recent origin in this country, and only since 1944 have all children been entitled to some form of secondary education as well as an elementary schooling.

During the present century, the rapid growth of knowledge and increasing division of labour have produced a situation in which vocational training is of extreme importance, since in all spheres of economic activity the key to occupational advancement rests largely with the possession of educational qualifications. According to Millerson, *The Qualifying Associations* (1964), there are now nearly two hundred occupations for which qualifications may be gained by passing written examinations, and, over and above these, there are many more occupations in which promotion prospects depend upon obtaining the certificates and diplomas awarded by engineering institutes or the City and Guilds of the London Institute. In response to these developments, the educational system has been called upon to provide vocational classes in the technical colleges which have mushroomed all over the country. It is estimated that there are now approximately 1·5 million students attending courses leading to recognised qualifications in colleges of further education.

Despite the quantity and variety of classes available, the demand for qualified manpower still exceeds the supply in many fields, and the methods of training which have been acceptable for some time are now proving inadequate. The *Industrial Training Act* of 1964 laid down that in each industry boards responsible for vocational education should be set up. This represents a definite movement towards keeping technical education in step with the needs of the economy, but, on the other hand, it also represents a movement away from the idea of a more prolonged general education for everyone, which has been advocated by many educationalists as has already been mentioned.

So far we have discussed the relationship between the economy and education mainly from the point of view of production, either of goods or of services, and the availability of manpower. We must remember, however, that economics is as much concerned with demand as with supply, and producers are also consumers. In any capitalist society, individuals have considerable freedom of choice in the matter of what they buy, and the curriculum in many secondary schools at the present time includes courses which aim to teach children to discriminate between the many choices open to them. Advertising, hire purchase, consumer protection and other aspects of trade and commerce are all subjects which are likely to be discussed at length in a modern school, and should help the children to become more discerning consumers. The most efficient allocation and usage of scarce resources in a competitive economy becomes possible only if consumption is based upon knowledgeable and rational choice.

THE POLITICAL FUNCTIONS

The stability of any autonomous political unit depends upon two criteria—consensus of opinion about the assumptions underlying the system, and the ability of the system to provide leaders from within itself. In both cases, education has an important role to play, because it is largely responsible for instilling feelings of patriotism and loyalty to the existing regime in the younger generation, and also for selecting and training future leaders.

Consensus of opinion

Much of what is done within the educational system to strengthen beliefs and attitudes is not necessarily done deliberately. In a society such as ours, which has a long history and well-established traditions and customs, many beliefs and attitudes are so much taken for granted that it is generally assumed that they are shared by everyone, and little formal teaching along these lines is undertaken in schools. Only on rare occasions—such as the last years of the First World War and the early 1930s, when there was considerable political unrest—has there been any conscious attempt to use the educational system as a means of strengthening political unity and teaching the advantages of democracy. Unconsciously, however, a great deal is done in subjects such as history, geography and literature, which can so easily be important in this respect. From the time a child starts school, he hears stories relating the exploits of the nation's great heroes and leaders, and these are likely to be told in such a way that he will come to feel proud of belonging to a society which has achieved so much and produced such men and women. What is omitted in the telling of these stories is interesting when we consider the influence they have on young people. How much, for example, are they told about the private lives of public heroes? Many children must have been thrilled by tales of Lord Nelson and his valour, and filled with admiration for him, but they are not likely to know much about his behaviour when he was ashore, because this was not above reproach, and he could not be presented to them as an example of moral rectitude.

The beliefs and attitudes which are embodied in a democratic society are highly sophisticated, because they depend entirely upon the tolerance and consideration for minority groups by the majority, which has political power, and the willingness of minorities to recognise the authority of the majority. In this country, the fact that the Leader of the Opposition in Parliament is in an official salaried position underlines our ability and desire to recognise that political minorities are important.

The American John Dewey may be considered as one of the most important modern educational philosophers, and the views he expressed have become part of the generally accepted idea of the functions of education in an industrial society. In his work *Democracy and Education* (1916), he contended that it is necessary for the educational system to provide children with knowledge about the society to which they belong, its culture and traditions, and also to instil in them the qualities which will make them desirous, and capable, of sharing in the ruling of their country as adult citizens. Only in this way, he argued, could a democracy survive.

Dewey was a theorist and since his day a considerable amount of more systematic work has been done in an attempt to assess the importance of education to a democracy. While we are generally aware that for a democratic system to work the members of the society must be capable of understanding and shouldering their electoral responsibilities, it has been shown that there is a definite connection between the length of an individual's education, his interest in politics and the regularity with which he is prepared to vote.

Not only do relationships between voting behaviour and length of education exist within our own society but they can also be observed if comparisons are made between different countries for which statistical evidence is available. S. M. Lipset in *Political Man* (1960) says he has found that, in the various countries he studied, those people with a longer education voted more frequently than those with less education. In the first place Lipset compared democracies with unstable democracies and dictatorships in Europe, and then he compared democracies and unstable dictatorships with stable dictatorships in Latin America. In each case he found that the more democratic group had a higher score on an index which he based on four criteria—the percentage of the population that was literate and the percentages receiving primary, post-primary and higher education. Although the statistics which Lipset used were not suitable for making strict comparisons, the differences which were apparent between the groups were so great that it could safely be concluded that the countries which were more educated were also more democratic. Lipset's conclusions seem, with hardly any exceptions, to be supported by trends which can be seen in countries throughout the world, and we have ample evidence to show that undemocratic regimes frequently have to resort to the use of military force in order to maintain control over people who are well enough educated to think for themselves, and want to take some part in determining the type of society in which they live.

The fact that there is a relationship between the level of education and the survival of democracy also provides the basis for arguments which are put forward against the idea of giving largely illiterate and unsophisticated societies political independence. Political scientists are more or less convinced that the members of such societies are open to exploitation by extremists, and events in the emerging African and Asian nations have done little to suggest that countries which are educationally backward can support stable democracies. This is of course causing a great deal of concern in many areas at the present time.

Although it is generally unnecessary to use the educational system deliberately to strengthen feelings of loyalty and patriotism in well-established democratic societies, schools and educational institutions are commonly used for this purpose in totalitarian countries.

M. I. Kalinin, a former President of the Soviet Union, wrote in *On Communist Education*:

> "Communist principles, taken in their elementary form, are the principles of highly educated, honest, advanced people; they are love for one's socialist motherland, friendship, humanity, honesty, love for socialist labour, and a great many other universally understood lofty qualities; the nurturing, the cultivation of these attributes, of these lofty qualities, is the most important component part of communist education."

He wrote also, in the same work:

"To learn Marxism means to know after mastering the Marxist method how to approach all the other problems connected with your work. If, let us say, the sphere of your future work is agriculture, will it be of advantage to employ the Marxist method? Of course it will. But to employ the Marxist method, you have to study agriculture too; you have to be an agricultural expert. Otherwise nothing will come of your attempt to apply Marxism to agriculture. This should not be forgotten if you wish to be men of action and not textmongers of Marxism. But what does being a Marxist mean? It means being able to adopt the correct line. But to be able to adopt the correct, Marxist line, you also need to be a first-rate expert in your particular sphere of activity."

One thing we must realise, then, is that in communist countries all education is carried on within a framework of Marxist philosophy, and there can be no deviation from the principles laid down by Marx, Engels and Lenin.

Bertrand Russell remarks in *Education and the Social Order* that:

"Under communism, nationalism is not taught, but there is a very intense propaganda for communism, combined with the information that the U.S.S.R. is its protagonist. It may be doubted whether the effect upon the minds of the children differs very greatly from the nationalism produced by education in capitalist countries."

However, Bertrand Russell does not make any mention in his book of the censorship and deliberate attempts to prevent children in communist countries from gaining knowledge about how systems other than their own really function. Those of us who have seen films of young Chinese children singing "nursery rhymes" about American imperialist murderers, or who have been appalled by the use of military force to quell the Hungarians' and Czechoslovakians' desire for a more liberal system, may question Russell's apparent belief that capitalist and communist countries differ little from each other in the use they make of their educational systems for purposes of producing consensus of opinion amongst their members.

The training of leaders

When we refer to the people who are the leaders in a democratic society, we naturally think first of our political leaders—Cabinet ministers, Members of Parliament and higher-grade civil servants—who are leaders at a national level, but we must also include their counterparts in local government—councillors and full-time officials

—as much of what is done to formulate and carry out policies is at this level. Since the educational background of the national leaders differs somewhat from that of the local leaders, it is necessary to consider them separately.

1. *National leaders*. Baldwin is reported to have said that his first thoughts when he had to form a Government in 1923 were that "it should be a Government of which Harrow should not be ashamed," and Macmillan is said to have had much the same idea thirty years later, only in his case Eton took the place of Harrow when he chose his ministers. The educational background of our leaders is changing, however. Cabinet ministers are drawn largely from the House of Commons, and, while in 1955 exactly fifty per cent of all its members had been to a public school, this percentage had fallen to thirty-three by 1974 (*see also* Table XII).

There has been a slight change in the section of the population from which the leaders have been recruited during the last hundred years. Originally, they were drawn almost entirely from the upper class, because only people who were largely independent financially were in a position to take up a career in politics. It was also considered necessary to serve a fairly lengthy apprenticeship as an ordinary Member of Parliament before becoming a suitable candidate for a ministerial post. For both these reasons, the tradition of "political families" became well established, and traces of this tradition still remain with us. Although more Members of Parliament are now drawn from the upper middle and middle classes, their educational background is broadly similar to that of their more aristocratic predecessors. It will be some time yet before the numbers of Members from the grammar schools and new universities, who have been attracted to politics as a professional career by changes in the structure of parliamentary salaries, have served their apprenticeship in the House and reached a position where their presence will significantly alter the emphasis in the educational background of Cabinet ministers.

Recruitment to the senior grades of the civil service follows very similar lines to that for senior parliamentary positions. In his contribution to *Class—A Symposium*, John Windsor reports that a rather tactless lecturer in government at Manchester University remarked to a class, "Don't worry, none of *you* will ever get to the civil service," and adds that:

"She was about right. The Civil Service is only one example of an Oxbridge-dominated profession. The sixth report from the Estimates

Table XII—Educational Background of Members of Parliament, October 1974

	Labour	Conservative	Liberal	Other
Oxford	60	80	3	1
Cambridge	24	73	2	3
Other universities	106	56	2	13
	190	209	7	17
Service colleges	—	9	—	—
Technical colleges	34	2	2	1
Eton	1	48	2	—
Harrow	—	10	—	—
Other public schools	24	116	3	2
Grammar	161	58	6	11
Secondary or technical	27	4	—	1
*Elementary and adult	7	1	—	—
Elementary	54	2	—	1

* Including Ruskin College and National Council of Labour Colleges.
Source: *The Times Guide to the House of Commons, October 1974.*

Committee on Recruitment to the Civil Service, published in 1965, showed that in the years 1957–63, the administrative class recruited 260 Oxbridge graduates, and only nine from Redbrick proper. The success rate was about 15 per cent for Oxbridge and about 6·4 per cent for Redbrick. Sir Alexander Carr-Saunders told Anthony Sampson, Britain's anatomist, that when he was invited to sit in on interviews for the Civil Service, he found that: 'Everyone on the board was prejudiced in favour of the Redbrick candidates: yet they always ended up choosing Oxbridge men. You see, they speak the *same language.*' "

The ability of public-school–Oxbridge-educated people to "speak the same language" is probably the strongest reason why, at the present time, recruitment to positions in political élites is so much influenced by a particular type of educational background. It is necessary for our political leaders to have the self-assurance and authority to mix easily with leaders in other spheres of life at both the national and international level, and this confidence and assurance may come from the knowledge that they have experienced a similar form of education. We also expect our national leaders to be people whom we can respect, and it is generally much easier to respect those whom we feel are superior to ourselves. We definitely regard the public-school–Oxbridge system to be something that is a privilege which gives favoured individuals a superior education to that obtained by the vast majority of the people, and this immediately produces a situation in which feelings of inferiority and superiority are bound to exist.

This is closely related to the vexed question of class, which we noted in Chapter VI to be largely a matter of attitudes based on feelings of inferiority and superiority. Mark Abrams, who has conducted a number of surveys amongst the people of Britain into their attitudes towards politics and political issues, has found what he refers to as "widespread complacency" about our educational system, and yet recruitment to membership of political élites is almost synonymous with the process of recruitment to the upper classes which is perpetuated through our existing educational system.

The arguments against recruiting our political leaders from a very small sector of the community are based on the obvious need for leaders to be in contact with, and to understand, the people whom they represent, which is clearly impossible if they have been kept apart from the "common herd" during the most formative years of their lives.

2. *Local leaders.* In local politics, the educational background of councillors and committee members closely reflects the educational background of the majority of the people in the area which they represent.

Conservative leaders are generally drawn from amongst the professional people, who may be businessmen or hold managerial positions but who will nearly all have attended grammar school or possibly a public school. Labour leaders, on the other hand, tend to be people in lower managerial positions and skilled manual or clerical occupations, and at present few of these have received a grammar-school education. Because of the increasing emphasis being laid upon qualifications, however, it is likely that in future, as a new generation reaches the age to take part in local politics, more recruits to the ranks of councillors on the Labour side will have been through grammar school. We must remember, too, that there is a left-wing movement in intellectual circles, which has caused a number of teachers and lecturers to participate in local government, and these people nearly all have a grammar-school background.

Full-time local-government officers, by virtue of the work they do, require a fairly lengthy formal education. In 1963 F. Musgrove found that 76.9 per cent of the senior officers in a large Midland city had attended grammar or public schools, and this is a pattern which is almost certain to be repeated elsewhere. The grammar schools also provide many recruits for the middle levels of local-government office, and many of the children who leave these schools at the age of 16 are advised to take up this type of work.

The grammar schools attach a great deal of importance to the idea of service to the community, and it is therefore hardly surprising that so many of the people who become engaged in organising and running the numerous activities which are found in an urban or rural area, such as amateur operatic or dramatic societies, youth clubs, the Citizens' Advice Bureaux and so on, have received their education at this kind of school.

THE STABILISING FUNCTIONS

Under the heading *stabilising functions* we should include all the functions performed by the educational system which, in combination, help to ensure the continued existence of the society and enable the individual to fit into the established pattern. This does not mean that the educational system has to be a static institution, but we must remember that there is a very critical balance between stability and change in all societies, and, if changes occur too rapidly, there is a danger of an insecure, anomic situation developing. New ideas need a period of time during which they can be assimilated and accepted, and it is as well to remember that, because the society is such a delicately interwoven network of relationships, changes in one area of the system are bound to have repercussions in all other areas. Therefore, because educational establishments are going to provide each new generation with its first and most vital experience of society beyond the narrow confines of the family, the system is largely responsible for preserving what is considered most worth preserving within the existing social structure while at the same time providing the environment within which new ideas are stimulated and progress can be made possible.

To change the existing educational system would mean that the existing social system would be changed in many ways as well, and it is for this reason that the society has become so sharply divided in recent years. Those members of it who answer the question "Do we want the social system changed?" in the affirmative see the educational system as the means of achieving their purpose and practising some social engineering. Those who are more cautious, those who are satisfied with the existing social system, or those who are perhaps prepared to accept the devil they know rather than risk entertaining a devil they do not know, will wish to preserve the educational system in its present form. It is rather tragic that education has now become a major political matter, and it is almost impossible to remain impartial, because the basic issues involved have become rather obscured by emotional, and often irrelevant, discussion and argument.

Not only are attitudes towards the educational system as a whole divided, but there are also important differences of opinion as to how certain matters within it, such as discipline, religious instruction, moral responsibility and so on, should be handled. Headmasters, headmistresses and the teachers who are subordinate to them are as divided in their opinions as any other members of the community, and they are given little guidance by the Department of Education and Science or the local education authorities who are their immediate employers. National policy is laid down by the Department, which has the guidance of two Central Advisory Councils for Education established under the 1944 *Education Act*, but local authorities are largely able to develop their own interpretations of this policy. The detailed administration of a particular school—curriculum, choice and supervision of staff, teaching methods used and day-to-day organisation—is the responsibility of its own head teacher. Probably head teachers in Britain have more power and freedom in this respect than the heads of schools in any other country.

There are at least two good reasons for this. Firstly, there is a widely held conviction in Britain that the most satisfactory way in which to ensure good results is to vest responsibility for a job in an individual and allow him to decide for himself the best method of tackling it, only interfering if it is obvious that he is not doing it properly. Secondly, we regard our schools, not as "learning factories," but rather as small communities or societies in their own right, free to conduct their own affairs as seems best for them, provided that they do not go beyond the limits of social convention and the very broad national policy laid down for education.

Let us compare the attitudes of two headmasters towards corporal punishment, about which there is no official regulation concerning whether it should be used or not. The first attitude is shown in this extract from Leila Berg's *Risinghill: Death of a Comprehensive School*:

"The staff meeting decided it was wrong to cane a boy who was imitating his father; and that not only was corporal punishment wrong in this specific case—it was unnecessary, always. Mr Duane [the head-master] was not present at this meeting and he knew nothing about it, but when the decision was passed to him he was pleased. The next day, he announced to the assembled children that there would be no more caning.

. . . many of the teachers had probably never thought of translating what they said into fact; they had merely been entertaining themselves with indulgent philosophy. When Michael Duane made his announce-ment, these teachers were angry, because they were frightened and because their ordeal had been decreed by themselves. They said nothing at the time, but much later they said 'We didn't mean you to tell the children,' and Michael Duane said, simply, 'But you are not doing away with corporal punishment unless you tell the children.' "

However, a totally different attitude towards corporal punish-ment is demonstrated in John Partridge's *Life in a Secondary Modern School*:

"When a culprit arrives at the Headmaster's door . . . he is invited in; the boy may then explain why he has been sent, or make excuses for a known misdemeanour; if the excuses are unacceptable, as they usually are, these will be dismissed with the briefest of words; the Headmaster will quickly move across to the door just inside of which the boy is probably standing; he reaches for his cane on top of the cupboard with one hand and pulls the boy into position with the other; he grips the boy firmly round the wrist and strikes him across the hand, twice, four times or six according to the seriousness of the crime. This cere-mony has been witnessed by individual teachers, and can always be seen by any boys on the first stairway inside the main classroom block.

No headmaster enjoys deliberately hurting boys in this way; but the Headmaster of Middle School sees it as an unpleasant but necessary duty. Bad boys must be punished both for their own sake and so as to deter similarly inclined individuals. It is something that he thinks he has to do because he is the Headmaster, and if he does not do it and establish an atmosphere of order and authority within the school, then nobody else will."

The matter of discipline is only one very small aspect of all that happens within a school, and, for this reason, many people might consider that to single out attitudes towards corporal punishment is hardly relevant. However, these attitudes are likely to reflect attitudes to many other aspects of the structure and social life of a school, and may provide a clue as to whether a headmaster upholds a rather rigid, authoritarian system, or wishes to provide a more flexible and democratic regime in which not only the staff but also the pupils are expected to contribute towards producing a system which is evolved from within rather than imposed from above.

Although their attitudes and opinions may differ, most teachers agree about the general objectives of education and consider that children not only need to learn certain skills but also have to be given some understanding of the world and of the particular society in which they are growing up. Schools therefore have an important part to play in the transmission of culture, and, on the whole, the transmission of culture is conservative, since teachers usually pass on to their pupils what they have themselves been taught, or have experienced. With few exceptions, the idea of conformity is implicit in the way they discuss such topics as marriage, sex, religion and politics, and the more practical classes, for example games, domestic science, music and handicrafts, help to preserve national characteristics. Football and cricket are part of our social inheritance in just the same way that baseball is part of that of the United States; it is considered more useful to be able to cook roast beef and Yorkshire pudding well or to produce a good shepherd's pie than it is to experiment with strange foreign dishes in domestic science classes. These are small details when considered in isolation, but, in combination, they help to stabilise and conserve the culture patterns of our own society.

THE SELECTION FUNCTIONS

There are two factors which must be considered when discussing the selective functions of education. First of all there is the society itself, which is based on a very complex division of labour and therefore requires that a seemingly endless variety of roles and responsibilities should be undertaken by its members. Secondly there are the millions of children within the society who all have different personalities and abilities, and who will undertake these roles and responsibilities when they become adults. The educational system can be regarded as an enormous sieve, through which these children pass, and by means of which they are classified, grouped and graded.

One of the biggest arguments at the present time rages around

I

whether or not the sifting and grading which takes place is done on a fair and rational basis and in such a way that each child is given an equal opportunity to develop his personality and abilities to the full, and to make the best possible use of his talents. No modern political party could afford to support overtly a system which did not aim at providing equality of opportunity, and politicians can count on the support of psychologists, economists and moralists to demonstrate the desirability of such equality. Psychologists can show that a mentally healthy adult is one who is able to make full use of his talents, and does not have a sense of frustration with its accompanying tensions. Economists argue that efficiency depends upon utilising all resources to the full, and one of any society's greatest resources is the ability of its members; expressions like "pool of ability" and "pool of talent" are bandied around in this context. Significantly, a much publicised article on the future of education which appeared in the *Observer* a few years ago was headed "Education: Our Untapped Wealth." Moralists, and those who have a "social conscience," would say that the principle of equality of opportunity is right because everyone ought to be able to develop his personality and potential to the full.

Even if it is unanimously agreed that everyone should be given this equal opportunity, a very big problem faces the society—how is this to be achieved? We are at this moment in our society's history being faced with the difficulty of trying to provide an answer to this vexed question.

Let us consider the moves which have been made in this direction since the 1944 *Education Act* was passed. This was the Act which made free secondary education available to all children over the age of 11, and charged local education authorities with the responsibility of providing for all pupils "such variety of instruction and training as may be desirable in view of their different ages, abilities, and aptitudes, and of the different periods for which they may be expected to remain at school, including practical instruction and training appropriate to their respective needs." The Act did not, however, bring all schools into the state system, and consequently the division between the private and state sectors was emphasised. It thus paved the way for one type of selection—selection on the basis of wealth.

Nor did this Act attempt to alter the structure of the university system in higher education. The universities are autonomous bodies, and they alone are responsible for deciding which students to admit and whom to appoint as professors and academic staff. They also agree upon their own curricula and make their own conditions about the awarding of degrees. Most universities exercise their rights by virtue of having been established by royal charters.

The Private Sector

At the present time about 5 per cent of all children at school are being educated independently of the state system, and these children appear to have a greater chance of proceeding to higher education than the equally able, sometimes more able, children in the state schools. This is partly due to the fact that there has always existed a special relationship between the public schools and, in particular, the older universities. Traditionally, it has been generally expected that children in public schools would proceed almost as a matter of course to a university, and therefore there is a very strong sixth-form element within the public schools. The idea that children would leave these schools at the first opportunity, whatever their academic ability, has never been a matter for consideration. As recently as January 1972, the total number of children in sixth forms throughout the country who were following "A" level courses was 265,769, and of these 34,396 (about 13 per cent) were in the sixth forms of independent schools recognised as efficient by the Department of Education and Science. If we consider boys only, the percentage increases to about 16 per cent because there are considerably more independent schools for boys than there are for girls.

The members of élites, whether political, financial, legal or industrial, are still largely recruited from the older universities, and thus indirectly from the public schools, which means that these schools have a significance within the society out of all proportion to the numerical importance of their pupils in the educational system as a whole. The prestige of the public schools is such that even their less able pupils acquire a social status that is generally denied to children educated in state schools, however outstanding their ability. *The National Survey of Health and Development of Children* published in 1966 revealed that many grammar-school pupils are dissuaded from even applying to the universities of Oxford and Cambridge because of their feelings of social and academic inferiority, and there is a form of self-selection in operation which is impossible to control.

Seemingly, therefore, parents who are able to afford it, and, equally important, are willing and prepared to afford it, can obtain for their children a greater opportunity to enter the élites within the society, and thus achieve positions of some power and authority. It must not be assumed from this that the complete cost of a public-school education is always met by the parents, because there are often scholarships available, and, in some cases, local education authorities are prepared to assist in sending children from their area to a public school. There has been a gradual downward trend in the overall number of children who have the backing of their local education authority in this way. This is probably due to the fact that the local authorities understandably prefer to use their money for the benefit of all the children for whom they are responsible, and they do not consider it justified to devote a disproportionate amount to the education of a favoured few in schools outside their own area.

Nevertheless, in a survey of the public schools undertaken by Graham Kalton—*The Public Schools: A Factual Survey*—it was found that at least 25 per cent of the boys in independent boarding schools, and 48 per cent of those in independent day schools, were receiving some financial assistance.

"The independent day schools have a considerable proportion of boys who receive assistance from the L.E.A.s, usually amounting to the full fees . . . these schools do not themselves assist many boys in the payment of fees. The L.E.A.s are also the main source of assistance for dayboys in independent mixed schools, but only one entrant in five is known by the schools to receive such assistance. School scholarships appear to be the most common source of assistance for independent boarding entrants but in fact there are possibly a greater number of L.E.A. awards, and also many boarders are assisted by some form of bursary. A high proportion of the independent boarders, however, are not known to receive any assistance, and only about one in eleven is known to receive more than £125, a figure which is less than the tuition fees of most independent schools."

We have already noted that education is now a major political issue, and politicians who feel so inclined can argue from a position of strength that, so long as there is a private sector within the educational system, some children will have a greater opportunity than others to perform certain roles within the society or to enter certain occupations. The appointment of the Public Schools Commission, charged with finding a way of *integrating* these schools into the national system, has now raised the question as to whether we should retain a private sector at all, although it would clearly be impossible to ban it without a lot of supporting legislation which would be intolerable in a free society. In just the same way that people take out private medical insurance in order to "protect" themselves against the National Health Service, and use their own cars in preference to public transport, they would seek alternatives to any state monopoly in education—even if it meant sending their children abroad to be educated. As Mr Crosland, a former Labour Minister of Education, has himself pointed out, nothing could prevent the establishment of new private schools, and "The right headmaster could set up a new high-prestige Public School in ten years."

Since education has become so much a matter of politics, and party politics particularly, there is one reason for retaining independent schools which is generally overlooked. These schools are now the only ones which have any real element of stability in them. C. Northcote Parkinson, writing in the *Illustrated London News* in July 1966, pointed out:

> "Differing from each other, and so offering a choice, the schools remain more or less the same. By contrast state schools are liable to change in character at every general election—indeed with every alteration in the party strength on the borough council. Should the far-seeing parent decide to live near Whatsit Grammar School, that institution may have ceased to exist before little Billy can even compete for a place. It can be Comprehensive next year, incomprehensible the year after, and may be turned, subsequently, into offices for the Board of Trade."

More recently, in July 1974, Mr. Lawrence Cadbury, the chairman of the Council of the Independent Schools Information Service, commented that it is uncertainty over the future of maintained schools which is leading parents to opt for independent schools for their children. A statistical survey of more than 1,000 independent schools revealed an increase of more than 3 per cent in the number of boys attending public schools in 1974 over the number in 1973, despite the fact that fees had risen sharply.

It is not yet known how the members of the Public Schools Commission will settle the problem of integrating these schools into the national system, although this can surely only be done by providing a high proportion of free places in these schools for children who would otherwise be unable to benefit from this type of education. Since all children will not be able to attend these schools, some form of selection will have to be devised, and it is not unreasonable to suppose that however it is carried out, if the alternative to an independent school is a state comprehensive, the 13-plus will produce even more problems than the present 11-plus.

The State Sector

THE TRIPARTITE SYSTEM

The report of a committee set up in 1941 (the *Norwood Report*) stated that there were three types of children needing three different kinds of education, and, accordingly, under the 1944 *Education Act,* the tripartite system was established within which children at the age of 11 proceeded to a grammar school, a modern school or a technical school. However, so few local authorities provided technical schools that we do not realy need to consider them separately. The different schools were intended to enjoy parity of esteem, but unhappily this was not to be.

For one reason, the names themselves were of significance. "Grammar" was a continuation of a word that had for generations been associated with middle-class education and entry to the professions. The new technical schools comprised the schools which had previously been known as "junior technical," "junior art" and "junior commercial," and were regarded by the public at large as very much a "second best" when compared with the grammar schools. The secondary modern was simply a new name for the "senior elementary school" of former days in which children remained until they left school if they were uninterested in, or obviously incapable of, more advanced education.

Generally in our primary schools there is no streaming, and the children of different abilities are not divided from each other. At the age of 11, however, under the tripartite system, children had to be allocated to the various secondary schools, and this allocation was generally made according to results obtained in the 11-plus examination, those who passed the examination being transferred to the grammar schools. The word "allocation" is used here advisedly, because it is a well-known fact that the number of grammar-school places available in relation to the number of children varied considerably from one area to another. A child's chances of getting such a place could, in many cases, if he were not outstandingly brilliant, depend upon where he lived, and there were childen with a higher intelligence rating in the secondary modern schools in some districts than some of the children in grammar chools in another.

It was realised that the 11-plus examination was assuming such importance that children had the prospect of it looming over them almost from the time they first entered the primary school, with the result that they were under considerable pressure, both at home and in the classroom, and this caused many of them considerable distress. Most local education authorities eventually abolished the formal examination in favour of a more "humane" procedure in which the children's work over several years was observed, and allocation to the different types of secondary school was made according to teachers' reports and interviews with the children. This type of assessment is likely to be made in those areas where selective secondary education is still available and the schools have yet to be reorganised along comprehensive lines.

Abolishing the 11-plus examination did not, however, make any difference to the feelings of success or failure which were experienced by both parents and children when it was made known in which of the secondary schools the 11-year-olds had been given a place. The status of a secondary school largely depended upon the sort of occupation that its pupils would be able to enter later in life, and it was the grammar schools which offered the kind of education which is required to gain admittance to the much-coveted professional and executive ranks in employment. These schools were therefore regarded by the public at large as vastly superior to the secondary modern schools. There are still areas in which a great deal of resistance is being encountered to plans to abolish remaining grammar schools and to establish comprehensive schools.

By the time the tripartite system had been in operation for a few years, the secondary modern schools were attempting to compensate their children for what they had seemingly lost by failing to get a grammar school place. They began to stream their own pupils according to academic ability, and enter the brightest for the same examinations that were taken by the boys and girls in the grammar schools. This was despite the fact that the secondary modern school was originally intended to provide an education in an atmosphere free from the stresses and strains associated with examinations. The growth of a "meritocracy" became increasingly felt, and the need for paper qualifications grew so rapidly that the secondary modern schools were really forced by public pressure to carry the examination business a stage further. The Certificate of Secondary Education was introduced in 1965, and 66,000 candidates sat for the first examinations held by nine of the regional boards which were set up to organise them, and by the following year, when all fourteen regional boards in England and Wales offered the examinations, the number of candidates had more than doubled to 141,000. In 1966 the Department of Education and Science, in

The Educational System in England and Wales, had this to say about the C.S.E.:

> "The examination is on a single-subject basis and can be taken by pupils completing five years of secondary education. There is no pass-or-fail verdict; pupils are awarded one of five grades, or are ungraded, in each subject they take. Grade one represents a standard equivalent to a pass at Ordinary level in the G.C.E. The information given on the Certificate is of help to employers in placing young people in jobs and as an entry qualification for the growing number of young people who seek further education in technical and other colleges."

To some extent the differences between secondary modern schools and the grammar schools became just a little blurred. The introduction of examinations meant that for many children the modern school could be seen to offer opportunities of progressing to higher education and further qualifications that were formerly regarded as accessible only to pupils from the grammar schools. However, the differences in social prestige which the schools possessed were not altered materially, and much of the reason for this can surely be found in the fact that the number of grammar-school places available were so few. Scarcity added an enhanced value to them.

COMPREHENSIVE REORGANISATION

In July 1965 the now famous Circular 10/65 was sent to all the various authorities concerned with secondary education. This stated that:

> "It is the Government's declared objective to end selection at eleven plus and to eliminate separatism in secondary education. The Government's policy has been endorsed by the House of Commons in a motion passed on 21st January, 1965: 'That this House, conscious of the need to raise educational standards at all levels, and regretting that the realisation of this objective is impeded by the separation of children into different types of secondary schools, notes with approval the efforts of local authorities to reorganise secondary education on comprehensive lines which will preserve all that is valuable in grammar school education for those children who now receive it and make it available to more children; recognises that the method and timing of such reorganisation should vary to meet local needs; and believes that the time is now ripe for a declaration of national policy.' "

The publication of this circular was greeted with a veritable uproar, particularly as it was quite obviously intended to provide the means whereby the Labour Government could indulge very effectively in some social engineering, and no effort was made to deny the fact. The following extract is from the government publication *Education in 1966*:

"At the North of England Education Conference in January the Secretary of State rehearsed the arguments underlying the move to non-selective schooling. Selection at 11 plus on a basis of measured intelligence was socially unjust, inefficient, wasteful and divisive. The environmental factors which exerted the strongest influence on measured intelligence—home and neighbourhood, size of family and parental aspirations—were all strongly linked to social class. Quite apart from any hereditary differences, the working-class boy suffered under a clear social handicap. In consequence, the stimulus that education could offer to large sections of the population was limited because of their social background at the age of eleven. Moreover the system of selection was known to produce a considerable number of wrong allocations, and once children were segregated into different schools it was hard to correct the miscalculations. In the result the country was wasting good educational talent and discouraging a large group by the label of failure. If this could be eliminated a lot of unnecessary human misery could be avoided and there might be a sharp increase in the performance of the seventy-five per cent who so often fulfilled the gloomy prophecy made about them 'at the cruelly early age of eleven.' Although educational re-organisation alone could not solve the problem of social division it could diminish instead of exacerbating it."

It is worth noting that many people were more concerned with the notion of social equality than with the provision of equality of educational opportunity, and it was indicated that if the secondary schools were reorganised along comprehensive lines differences of ability could still be extremely divisive factors within the new schools. Later in the same year that Circular 10/65 was issued the Labour Party Conference noted that "the education system could become genuinely comprehensive only if the practice of selection [*i.e.* streaming] was actively discouraged."

John Partridge, in *Life in a Secondary Modern School*, claims that:

". . . streaming is an artificial and unnatural form of selection. Nowhere else but in school are children so meticulously graded according to supposed intelligence. At home, in the factory, shop or office, in life outside school, people mix with each other regardless of intelligence; we marry, make friends, earn promotion in our jobs, all without any direct reference to our intelligence quotients; we do not decide whether to make friends with our neighbours by asking them to take an I.Q. test, yet we are imposing considerations such as these on children in our Schools. The intelligent person surely has a stimulating effect on his or her work-mates, and the most intelligent parent of a large family may make all the difference between that family getting by or not. Why, if perceived intelligence is not used to grade us as adults in our wider society, should children in the most formative years of their development be so selected within schools like Middle School?"

On first reading, this appears a fairly logical argument, but, while we do not obviously spend our lives subjecting each other to I.Q. tests, we do employ a less arbitrary form of selection. We usually make friends with people who have similar attitudes and interests to ourselves, work with those who have similar skills and qualifications, and live in a neighbourhood which is inhabited by people who are largely very much like ourselves. Even if we accept that selection at the age of 11 is absurd, we have to face the fact that the diversity of occupations and statuses demanded by the complex society of which we are members must mean that selection takes place at some stage. We may attempt to delay it for as long as possible, but it is bound to occur eventually.

The Labour Government brought a great deal of pressure to bear on local education authorities to reorganise their schools, although it was met with considerable resistance in many areas. By 1970 just over 31 per cent of the secondary school population was being catered for in comprehensive schools, compared with 8.5 per cent in 1965, although Benn and Simon in their report on comprehensive reorganisation *Half-Way There* (1970) estimated that if a "pure" definition of comprehensive schools were used—where *all* selection at 11-plus and throughout the secondary stage had been abolished—the percentage would not be greater than 10 per cent.

By 1974 approximately half the children of secondary school age were attending comprehensive schools, but it is still almost impossible to make any satisfactory assessment of the consequences of the reorganisation. In many areas, the comprehensive schools are so only in name, because the more able pupils still have the possibility of attending grammar schools, and there is not a complete mixture of academic ability within the new comprehensive schools. To be truly comprehensive, a school has to receive a complete cross-section of pupils in terms of both ability and social class.

Although at this stage there is insufficient data available relating to the effects of reorganisation in our own country, it is possible to consider the comprehensive system in the United States, where the democratic theories of John Dewey have been extremely influential.

Dewey, in his *Democracy and Education*, denied the idea of any hierarchy of values among studies undertaken at school:

> "We cannot establish a hierarchy of values among studies. It is futile to attempt to arrange them in order, beginning with one having least worth and going on to that of maximum value. In so far as any study has a unique or irreplaceable function in experience, in so far as it marks a characteristic enrichment of life, its worth is intrinsic or incomparable. Since education is not a means to living, but is identical with living a life which is fruitful and inherently significant, the only ultimate value which can be set up is just the process of living itself."

From this it is easy to see how the curriculum in American schools, under the influence of Dewey, has always been geared towards providing the less able children with incentives for learning. The American system is concerned with the needs of the majority more than it is with the special needs of the few, and, while it is true that we can learn a great deal about how to cope with our average and less able children from the Americans, they readily acknowledge that we have been considerably more successful at coping with the bright ones than they are. If this were not the case, they would have no need to import our scientists and technologists, and there would be no "brain drain" from Britain.

Many people would like to see some comparative research undertaken into the educational development of comprehensive school pupils and that of pupils in selective schools, although research of this type is clearly impracticable for a number of reasons, not the least of them being that the philosophies and objectives of the two systems are different so that it would not be possible to make valid judgements about their merits or demerits.

It is precisely because the philosophies and objectives of the systems are different that so much emotion has been aroused over the switch to comprehensive secondary education, and there will inevitably be a great deal of controversy over the matter for a long time to come.

The Environmental Factors in Education

Michael Young remarks, in *The Rise of the Meritocracy*, that "In the long run ambitious parents always brought to grief the best-laid schemes of egalitarian reformers," and Angus Maude, in

Education: Quality and Equality, has pointed out that: "If he is determined to abolish all inequality of opportunity, and if the major inequality is due to the accident of birth, then logically the egalitarian must try to abolish the differential accidents of birth."

Just what are the effects of these "differential accidents of birth," which were also mentioned by the Secretary of State in a passage quoted earlier?

THE SIZE OF FAMILY AND MEASURED INTELLIGENCE

A number of large-scale and carefully conducted surveys have produced evidence that intelligence, when measured according to rigidly devised tests, varies directly with the size of the family. Probably the best known of these surveys was the 1947 Scottish Mental Survey which covered all children born in Scotland in 1936. A representative sample containing 7380 children born on the first three days of each month of that year was chosen, and the connection between family size and measured intelligence *at all class levels* was clearly shown (*see* Table XIII).

In 1964 J. W. B. Douglas carried out a survey of children living

Table XIII—Mean Test Score by Occupational Class by Size of Family

Occupation	Size of family				
	1	2	3	4	5
Professional and large employers	52·5	52·3	53·7	51·3	43·1
Skilled manual workers	41·7	40·7	39·4	35·8	33·4
Unskilled manual workers	34·6	36·1	33·1	32·8	29·4

Maximum score possible = 76

Source: *Social Implications of the 1947 Scottish Mental Survey.* Table XXIV London, 1953.

in England, Scotland and Wales, and his sample contained 5362 children born during the first week in March 1946. He found also that family size has some influence on the measured intelligence of the children. There are a number of reasons which could account for this.

A large family is more likely to draw near the poverty line than a small one, and in many cases it is not possible to afford the facilities, such as a separate warm room or books, which are necessary if children are to be encouraged to do their homework properly. Frequently, too, children who come from poorer homes either are compelled to, or feel they should, help towards keeping themselves, and they undertake paper rounds, week-end jobs and other paid spare-time activities in order to do this. This not only serves as a distraction from school work, but also may overtax the children so that they are tired and unable to benefit fully from their lessons.

Even where there is no financial hardship in large families, the constant interruption by other children, and a reduction in the amount of individual tutoring which parents might otherwise be able to give, may prove a handicap. Certainly the verbal ability of children in large families is generally less than that of only children or children who have only one or two brothers and sisters. They spend a great deal of their time talking with each other, and do not have the same opportunities for extending their vocabularies that they would have if they were able to command more of their parents' time and attention.

THE ATTITUDE OF PARENTS TOWARDS EDUCATION

Both the Crowther and Robbins Reports showed that, if the nation's children were classed into groups on the basis of measured intelligence, about one-half of the top two ability groups would have left school by the time they were 16 years old. (In 1972 the school-leaving age was raised to 16.) Yet these are the children whom we would expect to enter our universities or higher education establishments and eventually become absorbed into the upper professional and industrial occupations. It is this wastage of ability which is causing so much concern at the present time, and yet there is no barrier within our system which denies children the opportunity to continue their education beyond the minimum age if they wish to do so. There must, however, be some factor or factors which cause many of our most able children to leave school as soon as they are officially entitled to, and recent surveys have shown that much depends upon the attitudes and expectations of parents.

The committee which, under the chairmanship of Sir Geoffrey Crowther, investigated the education of children between the ages of 15 and 18, reported that:

"Premature school-leaving at 15 years was almost non-existent amongst the children of professional and managerial fathers; and the proportion who left school at 15 is highest amongst the children of manual workers. Twenty-one per cent of the sons of skilled manual workers and twenty-five per cent in the semi or unskilled manual group left school at 15 years, as compared with fifteen per cent of sons of the clerical and other non-manual category. For daughters, the figures for those leaving school at 15 is nine per cent in the clerical and other non-manual category, as compared with fourteen per cent and nineteen per cent for the daughters of skilled and semi or unskilled manual workers respectively."

The committee also noted that:

"The proportion of parents who themselves left school above the minimum leaving age is highest amongst the children who stayed longest at school, rising from eleven per cent, in the case of the 15-year-old leavers, to around forty per cent in the 18-year-old leavers group. It is, however, perhaps equally important to note that more than half the children who stayed at school until 18 years or over had parents who had themselves left school at 14 or under."

The extension of secondary education, and also that of university education, has brought about a change in the proportion of university students coming from the different types of schools, but the report of the Robbins Committee clearly showed that there has been very little change in the social class background of students entering the universities. Between 1928 and 1947 only 23 per cent of undergraduates entering the universities were from working-class homes and between 1955 and 1961 the percentage had increased only to 25 per cent, although a much higher percentage than this is *known* to have the necessary ability.

Although, as we have seen already, a selection system which rejects three-quarters of our children at the age of 11 is extremely wasteful, there is also a considerable amount of wastage even within the grammar schools, and much of this can be attributed to parental attitudes and family background. Concern about the children who enter grammar schools in a high position on the entrance list, therefore giving some promise of good academic progress, and yet achieve a very low standard of attainment, caused Dale and Griffith to undertake a detailed study of the children in one grammar school (*Down Stream: Failure in the Grammar School* (1965)).

In a grammar school, lack of academic aptitude is not a major cause of deterioration and wastage, and Dale and Griffith found that the difference between pupils who made normal progress or improved and those who deteriorated was largely a reflection of their application and attitude to academic work. They concluded that:

> "The attitude of pupils to their studies can be affected by a great variety of influences . . . the extent to which they affect work is largely decided by the character of the boy and the nature of his home background. In a very few cases we decided that the pupil himself or herself was mainly at fault, through his or her neglect of homework. In these cases the home background in general was good, though the lack of a sufficiently firm home discipline was sometimes a minor contributory factor in the decline. . . . In most of the cases of deterioration it was the nature of the home which was the decisive force in moulding the attitude of the pupil. In a few instances the deteriorator was emotionally disturbed by some aspect of home life that could not be changed. . . .
>
> In contrast to the relatively small incidence of these 'acts of God' there were many other aspects of the home background which adversely affected the progress of most of the deteriorators. These aspects ranged from the lack of proper facilities for doing homework, through a parental *laissez-faire* attitude to discipline, to severe emotional disharmony in the home. Of all these aspects undoubtedly emotional disharmony was the most disturbing to the child, and the most harmful to satisfactory progress in school."

The authors of this work also found that there was a strong relationship between deterioration and social class, which seemed to suggest that children from lower-class homes are more likely to be subjected to emotional disturbances and disharmony than the children of parents in a higher class. Dale and Griffith suggest that the type of conduct which results from disharmony in the home may differ according to the social class of the parents, and may therefore produce more or less stress in the child. Upper- and middle-class parents may try to avoid "inflicting their more serious disputes on their children," and husbands in these groups are not likely to resort to physical assault on their wives, drunk or sober.

One of the most startling findings of this particular study was that only one parent out of more than seventy belonging to first-year entrants who deteriorated had been educated in a grammar school. This again emphasises the relationship which has been found to exist between success at school and the educational background and social class of parents.

THE AREA IN WHICH THE SCHOOL IS LOCATED

Any school is really a reflection in miniature of the wider society in which it exists. We noted in Chapter III that, while there is such a thing as a national culture, or a culture which belongs to the society as a whole, there are also regional and local cultures which are in many ways of greater significance to the individual. This variety of sub-cultures duly finds its parallel in the variations which are found in the nature and structure of our schools.

The most obvious variations are to be found in the provisions made by local education authorities in urban and rural areas, because the needs of the types of community which they serve are considerably different. But, although it is very easy to recognise that the needs of a small community in the Highlands of Scotland are not the same as those of a large industrial city, less obvious differences are also found even within the area served by a single authority. Schools built to serve "good" residential districts will draw their pupils mainly from middle-class homes, and the backgrounds and aspirations of these children will be quite unlike those of the children who attend schools serving a slum area or a large council estate in another part of the same town.

There are differences, however, in local attitudes towards education for which, as yet, there is no explanation available. For instance, if we compare the records of different counties, we find that the five counties with the highest proportion of children staying at school until they are 17 are all Welsh, as are those with the highest proportion proceeding to further education after leaving school.

It is sometimes tempting to be facetious when using statistics, and a great deal of fun can be obtained from interpreting them, as some radio and television comedians have realised. However, it would appear from the considerable amount of data available that reformers seeking to ensure that children are given equality of opportunity and that talent is not wasted will have to make certain that all children in future are born in Cardiganshire, and that they are the only children of happily married middle-class parents, both of whom have stayed at school longer than was officially necessary.

EXERCISE 10

1. Give an account of some of the main ways in which the educational and the economic systems are inter-related. (*A.E.B.*)

2. Examine the contribution of recent sociological studies to our understanding of the problems facing school-leavers in the transition from school to work. (*A.E.B.*)

3. "Company directors, high-court judges, senior bishops, and cabinet ministers are still predominantly recruited from the older universities and the public schools." Discuss. (*A.E.B.*)

4. Analyse the relationship between education and a democratic political system.

5. "Under communism, nationalism is not taught, but there is a very intense propaganda for communism combined with the information that the U.S.S.R. is its protagonist. It may be doubted whether the effect upon the minds of the children differs very greatly from the nationalism produced by education in capitalist countries."
To what extent would you agree with this statement by Bertrand Russell?

6. "We tend to think of the 'brain drain' of scientists and technologists from Britain to the United States as a phenomenon produced by economic pressures. There is some justification, however, in attributing it to differences in the educational systems of the two countries." Discuss.

7. "In the long run ambitious parents always brought to grief the best-laid schemes of egalitarian reformers" (Michael Young). Explain and discuss.

8. "Sociological studies have demonstrated the decisive influence of home and family background on the educational achievements of the child. Comprehensive reorganisation of secondary education will do little to increase equality of educational opportunity, if we mean by this the opportunity for every child to achieve the limit of his educational potential." Discuss. (*A.E.B.*)

9. Is it possible to keep politics out of education?

10. Argue the case for *or* against the retention of the private sector in the educational system.

11. Describe and discuss the position of the "Public Schools." (*Oxford*)

12. Discuss the view that the "function" of education in modern Britain is to transmit the society's values and culture. (*Oxford*)

13. "Occupational and technical changes still, as they have always done, determine both the pattern of secondary educational provision and proposals for reform." Discuss. (*London*)

14. Comment on the figures in the table below in the light of researches into the social factors which influence educational achievement.

Occupations of Parents of Pupils in Maintained and Direct-grant Schools

	Professional and managerial %	Clerical	Skilled	Semi-skilled	Unskilled	Total %
All schools	15·0	4·0	51·0	18·0	12·0	100
Grammar	25·0	10·3	43·7	15·3	5·6	100
Sixth forms	43·7	12·0	37·0	5·8	1·5	100

(Central Advisory Council, *Early Leaving.*)

(*A.E.B.*

15. "However 'unjust' it may be, streaming is essential to the achievement of the major functions of our educational system." Discuss. (*London*)

16. Are the arguments in favour of fully comprehensive secondary schools based on anything other than mere ideology? (*London*)

17. "It is necessary for us to sacrifice the freedom of choice of the consumer in order to pursue justice and efficiency in our educational system." Discuss. (*London*)

FOR FURTHER READING

K. Mannheim and W. A. C. Stewart. *An Introduction to the Sociology of Education*. Routledge and Kegan Paul, 1962.
A. K. C .Ottaway. *Education and Society*. Routledge and Kegan Paul, 1962.
E. J. King. *Education and Social Change*. Pergamon, 1966.
G. H. Bantock. *Education in an Industrial Society*. Faber and Faber, 1963.
K. Leipmann. *Apprenticeship*. Routledge and Kegan Paul, 1960.
Report of the Central Advisory Council for Education, 1947. *School and Life*.
Report of the Central Advisory Council for Education, 1963. *Half Our Future*.
C.O.I. Pamphlet 7. *Education in Britain*. H.M.S.O., 1967.
Ministry of Education Circular 10/65. *The Organisation of Secondary Education*.
G. Kalton. *The Public Schools—A Factual Survey*. Longmans, 1966.
R. R. Dale and S. Griffith. *Down Stream: Failure in the Grammar School*. Routledge and Kegan Paul, 1965.
Robin Davis. *The Grammar School*. Penguin Books, 1967.
John Partridge. *Life in a Secondary Modern School*. Penguin Books, 1968. (Originally *Middle School*, published by Gollancz.)
Leila Berg. *Risinghill—Death of a Comprehensive School*. Penguin Books, 1968.
T. Veness. *School Leavers: Their Aspirations and Expectations*. Methuen, 1962.
J. W. B. Douglas. *The Home and the School*. MacGibbon and Kee, 1964.
J. M. Ross, W. J. Bunton *et al. A Critical Appraisal of Comprehensive Education*. National Foundation for Educational Research, 1972.
B. Cosin (ed.). *School and Society*. Routledge and Open University Press, 1971.

CHAPTER XI

RELIGION AND BELIEF SYSTEMS

The Nature of Beliefs

DURING our lives we are faced with a bewildering choice of things to do. Without some guidance we should flounder helplessly amongst all these alternatives and probably end by not doing anything at all. Our beliefs provide us with the guidance we need to select a particular course of action and the sense of purpose which is necessary to carry it out. Belief in what we are doing, why we are doing it and how we are doing it is, therefore, an essential motivating factor within us.

Our beliefs also influence the way in which we perceive and interpret the various situations which we encounter in day-to-day living, and determine the attitudes which we have towards them. This means that any actions we take to deal with a situation will be based on our beliefs. A man who firmly believes that "a woman's place is in the home" will be unlikely to encourage his own wife to go out to work, and he will not be very sympathetic either towards any other married women who have careers.

Beliefs are not only important at the individual level. Shared beliefs are an essential ingredient in the integration of social groups, both large and small. People who have a common set of beliefs will tend to behave in the same way in order to achieve their purpose, and this produces a vast range of groups and sub-groups varying from an entire nation that is welded together in a great wave of patriotic fervour during a war to a very small group of individuals who share a belief in the flatness of the Earth.

Beliefs do not exist in isolation but belong to one or other of the complex *belief systems* which are part of a society's culture. Each individual will learn about the belief systems of his own society in the same way that he learns about the other aspects of its culture.

Belief systems are not all alike. Science, religion, magic and political ideologies are all examples of very different types of belief systems, and one distinction which can be made between them is the extent to which the beliefs can be verified. Whilst it can be proved that hydrogen and oxygen combined in certain proportions will form water, it cannot be proved that "God so loved the world that he gave his only begotten son that who so believeth in him should not perish but have life everlasting."

Both verifiable and non-verifiable belief systems give rise to other systems which are concerned with values, and these evaluative systems refer to the way in which people ought to behave. If a person believes that divorce is wrong because it has harmful effects on children, his belief is based on something which has been adequately demonstrated, and his behaviour is determined by *secular ethics*. If, on the other hand, a person believes that divorce is wrong because Christian doctrine about marriage is that it is a union for life, his behaviour is determined by *religious morality*. In many instances, secular ethics and religious morality support each other, because the religious system is part of the social system as a whole, and therefore cannot be isolated from it.

Even though there is a considerable amount of overlapping and merging amongst the different belief systems in any society, it is possible to make distinctions between them for the purposes of analysis.

MAGIC

Max Weber was the first theorist to discuss the sociology of religion in depth. Although Durkheim referred to religion in his analysis of the factors responsible for creating and reinforcing social solidarity, and made a detailed study of the organisation of religion amongst the primitive tribes of Central Australia, he did not focus his attention upon it or regard it as a primary dynamic force in the evolution of society as did Weber. The latter was particularly interested in the process of differentiation during the evolution of social structure. His analysis was largely based on the premise that, during this development, it is possible to recognise the dichotomies open to society at particular stages.

The first of these twofold alternatives which Weber developed in his theory was that of magic and religion, and he made a clear distinction between the functions of the magician and the priest, both of whom are mediators between man and supernatural beings. He held that the role of the magician is that of dealing with numerous and largely unrelated human problems and tensions as they arise on a fairly informal basis. The function of the priest, on the other hand, is more formal and develops into a well-organised cult system which can continue as an almost independent entity. The religious systems developing from the priestly functions can, in fact, become so independent of the rest of the social system that they can be instrumental in changing the existing order; the more spontaneous, less organised practitioners of magic could not expect to achieve such a position of influence.

A further distinction between magic and religion is that of the approach to supernatural forces. In the case of magic, such forces can be compelled to satisfy human needs if the correct formulae or spells are known; failure to achieve the desired response is nothing more than faulty magic. By contrast, religious forces cannot be controlled in the same way, since they have an independent capacity to influence man's destiny, and consequently it is necessary to worship and conciliate them in order to enlist their sympathy and aid. Failure, in this case, indicates either that the individuals concerned have not done enough to please the gods or else that the gods do not intend them to have what they want. Divine beings will determine what happens to humans, and humans can only hope that, if they please these supernatural forces, what happens will be beneficial.

Sir James Frazer, in *The Golden Bough*, likens magic to science:

"The magician does not doubt that the same causes will always produce the same effects, that the performance of the proper ceremony, accompanied by the appropriate spell, will inevitably be attended by the desired result, unless, indeed, his incantations should chance to be thwarted and foiled by the more potent charms of another sorcerer. He supplicates no higher power: he sues the favour of no fickle and wayward being: he abases himself before no awful deity. Yet his power, great as he believes it to be, is by no means arbitrary and unlimited. He can wield it only so long as he strictly conforms to the rules of his art, or to what may be called the laws of nature as conceived by him. To neglect these rules, to break these laws in the smallest particular, is to incur failure, and may even expose the unskilful practitioner himself to the utmost peril. If he claims a sovereignty over nature, it is a constitutional sovereignty rigorously limited in its scope and exercised in exact conformity with ancient usage. Thus the analogy between the magical and scientific conceptions of the world is close. In both of them the succession of events is assumed to be perfectly regular and certain, being determined by immutable laws, the operation of which can be foreseen and calculated precisely; the elements of caprice, of chance, and of accident are banished from the course of nature. . . . The fatal flaw of magic lies not in its general assumption of a sequence of events determined by law, but in its total misconception of the nature of the particular laws which govern that sequence."

Weber compared also the influence on behaviour of magic and religion, and outlined the differences between *taboo* and *religious morality*. He showed that basically taboo, which is always associated with magical practices, is concerned with the prescription and, more particularly, the proscription of certain unrelated acts. While there are numerous examples of similar prescriptions and proscriptions associated also with religion, religious morality goes much further and attempts to enforce a more generalised and integrated pattern of behaviour—a whole "way of life." What is more, the observance of religious morality places a considerable burden of responsibility on the individual, and the concept of sin is inherent in all religions. Magic does not produce similar evaluative systems, and a "mistake" can be counteracted directly by the application of corrective magic if punishment is to be avoided.

THE NATURE OF RELIGIOUS BELIEF

Religion, like magic, is a cultural phenomenon reflecting man's attempts to come to terms wtih his environment, particularly with those aspects of it which he does not understand such as death, pain and suffering. Different cultures produce very different systems of religious beliefs, but they all have one feature in common, and that is that they are centred round a fundamental belief in the supernatural—that which is above and beyond the natural world.

Man is largely incapable of thinking in other than personal terms, and, as a result, supernatural phenomena are regarded as beings with attributes that are in many ways human. Gods and spirits in the unseen world may be good or evil; they marry and beget children; they are proud and jealous; they can be offended and appeased; if they are angered, they can take their revenge either in this life or in the hereafter. Religious beliefs in the form of *creeds* and *myths* describe these supernatural beings and the unseen world, so that they become meaningful. Heaven, Hell, Hades, the Elysian Fields and so on are "places" populated by God, Satan or other gods and spirits. Creeds and myths also explain how the unseen world is related to the real world, and frequently we find that this is based on a belief in the ability of God or gods to take on human form and associate directly with mortals, or else to beget children in mortal mothers and thereby establish an indirect relationship.

In all societies, certain objects are associated with the religious beliefs and are regarded as *sacred*. A clear distinction is made between what is sacred and what is secular or profane; although there is hardly anything on Earth which has not been held sacred by some people at some time, what is sacred in one society may not be sacred in another. Christians consider the Cross as sacred, Jews the Ark of the Covenant, Mohammedans the Black Stone of the Kabah, Hindus the cow, and most preliterate societies had animal totems. The sacredness of an object is not, therefore, an intrinsic property, but results from the mental attitudes which people have towards it—mental attitudes which are supported emotionally.

In order to continue, creeds, myths and the existence of sacred objects must be kept alive in the minds of the people, and this is achieved by religious practices. *Ritual* and *ceremony* are the active and observable manifestations of religious beliefs. Sometimes ritual requires a special type of behaviour such as making sacrifices, praying, fasting or wearing particular clothes. At other times the ritual involves behaviour which would be secular in a different context. For example, eating and drinking are secular activities unless they are performed as part of a religious ritual such as Mass or the Feast of the Passover. The most important functions of ritual are to strengthen belief by bringing people together in such a way that they stimulate each other, and to provide them with a symbolic means of expressing their religious emotion.

The Social Functions of Religion
GROUP INTEGRATION

Like all beliefs which can be shared, religious beliefs provide a basis for people to unite together, and form integrated groups. If a society has a religion to which all or most of its members adhere, the religion will play a very important part in holding individuals to each other. This will probably be most apparent at those times when a group or a whole society faces a crisis or a disaster, when, without shared beliefs of this kind, the people might easily become disorganised and lose the sense of purpose which is necessary if they are to cope with a situation or take action to avert a disaster. Taking part in rain-making ceremonies during a period of drought may hold people together in their belief that their gods will come to their assistance, whereas, without such a belief, people might put their own interests above those of the community and possibly resort to violence in their attempts to find food. Praying together on the deck of a sinking ship may avert a stampede for the lifeboats and enable people to behave in the calm and orderly fashion which would increase their chances of survival. Going to church and praying for victory during wartime may strengthen the people's resolve to win the war by renewing their belief that God will help them in their struggle.

We must remember, however, that religious beliefs are also divisive factors, particularly in very large, complex societies such as our own. Believers are separated from non-believers, Jews from Gentiles and even Christians from Christians where they belong to different denominations. Some of the bloodiest wars in history have been waged between rival religious groups. In Britain, the antagonism between Catholics and Protestants was an important contributory factor leading to civil war and a long dynastic struggle for supremacy.

On major social issues such as abortion, divorce, birth control and nuclear warfare, the Christian denominations are still divided, although the attitudes of church members towards political and economic issues appear to be related to their secular roles within the community rather than to their religious beliefs. The various Churches are reluctant to put forward rigid doctrines concerned with politics and economics, since they attract members from all walks of life, and if they were to take a positive line on such matters as strikes, education, financial speculation or international relations, they would inevitably lose many of their adherents. As a result the Churches do not provide people with a standard to guide them in many spheres of everyday life, and the resulting remoteness of religion is probably a main contributing factor in its decline in this society.

THE MAINTENANCE OF BEHAVIOUR PATTERNS

Ideal behaviour patterns are provided by religious morality, and supernatural sanctions may be invoked to ensure that individuals conform to these patterns. Rules and regulations are derived either from the fundamental religious beliefs or else from the revelations made by God to man through the agency of prophets and others divinely inspired. In this way Moses was responsible for passing on the Ten Commandments and Christ for preaching to the crowds which followed him. Enforcement of religious morality is assured where people sincerely believe that contravention of the code of behaviour will incur the wrath of the divinity, and such morality is essentially personal, because the responsibility for his actions is placed on the individual.

Because it is difficult to measure the strength of religious belief it is also difficult to assess the extent to which religion influences behaviour. In our society there appears to be no significant difference in the crime rates in the religious and non-religious segments of the community. Catholics have a slightly higher fertility rate than non-Catholics, and marriages between active Christian partners are marginally less likely to end in divorce than those between partners with no firm religious beliefs. There is, however, no real evidence that in this country today the behaviour of those who claim to be religious differs to a marked extent from that of the non-religious.

THE CONTROL OF STRESS

We have already noted that religious ceremony and ritual are means of reaffirming beliefs and giving expression to religious emotion, but they can also provide outlets for other feelings as well. There is a very close relationship between the doctrines of various religious sects and the social condition of the people adhering to them. Dispossessed people, such as the Jews, are likely to pin their hopes on a Messiah who will be successful in overthrowing the established system and who will place his followers in positions where they will have the power and influence they have so far been denied. Those who are amongst the least privileged and in a state of poverty and ignorance will respond most readily to those who preach to them about the happiness which awaits them in the next life. People who have shoes to wear, and take the fact for granted, will not attach any importance to the idea that "all God's chil'en got shoes" and that shoes will be abundantly available to those who go to heaven, but people who long for a pair of shoes could find the idea attractive. Faith that, in the end, everything will be just how they would like it to be helps people to tolerate the conditions in which they actually have to live their daily lives, and the religious ceremonies in which they take part enable them, not only to confirm their faith, but also to relieve the frustrations which are inherent in the social situation and receive some amount of compensation for their troubles. In *Family and Colour in Jamaica,* Professor Fernando Henriques, comparing cult groups with orthodox churches, remarks:

"The rites of the orthodox churches are similar in detail to those of the parent bodies in Europe or elsewhere. These churches make no attempt in ritual, or in the conduct of the services, to satisfy the emotional needs of the majority of the people. . . . But on the other hand [the cult groups] do cater to the desire for emotional stimulation and excitement which is prevalent in the lower class throughout Jamaica. This desire and its partial gratification in a religious form must be seen against the background of extreme poverty and lack of social opportunity. The cult groups provide the means of temporary escape from the tedium of everyday life."

The Oxford sociologist Bryan Wilson, in his *Sects and Society* (1961), has made a detailed comparative survey of the Elim, Christadelphian and Christian Scientist sects in our own society, and has shown that the first two are more likely to appeal to the "poor, socially neglected and culturally deprived" since they preach that God will not only reward believers in heaven but also provide them with wonderful experiences during this life through the "gift of tongues." Christian Scientists, however, are more likely to be comfortably situated middle-class people, because the preachers are generally expressing an attitude of satisfaction with the existing state of society, and they accept wealth and possessions as the just deserts of the righteous. More emphasis is placed on the good things offered to people in this life, and proportionately less on what they can hope for in the next.

It is, in fact, the poor and oppressed sectors of the community who are most likely to suffer from frustration and tension. It is obviously more desirable as far as social order is concerned if they can give expression to their emotions and relieve their tension through organised religious practices than for them to resort to violence and acts of wanton destruction.

The control of stress and tension as a function of religion will inevitably become less important where the society is able to overcome successfully the conditions most likely to produce frustration and misery. Improvements in living standards, greater prosperity, the achievements of medicine in the alleviation of pain and the reduction of disease have all combined to produce a less hostile environment for the majority of people who live in Britain. Although the great evils of want, ignorance and disease have been largely destroyed, it is significant that amongst the most pressing problems today are those resulting from loneliness and boredom. These are reflected by the more widespread religious beliefs of widows and old people noted by Michael Argyle in *Religious Behaviour* (1958), although the old people may not only be displaying symptoms of loneliness and boredom but may also be continuing the more religious traditions of days gone by.

Religion as a Part of the Social System

Like all social institutions, religion performs certain functions because it is capable of satisfying some of the needs of human beings either in isolation or in groups.

Sir James Frazer, in *The Golden Bough*, defines religion as:

". . . a propitiation or conciliation of powers superior to man which are believed to direct and control the course of nature and human life. Thus defined, a religion consists of two elements, a theoretical and a practical, namely a belief in powers higher than man and an attempt to propitiate or please them."

There are very few societies which do not have a religion of this nature, and those that lack one produce ideologies of secular origin to fill the vacuum. Political ideologies such as communism, fascism and Nazism or personality cults like that which has developed around Mao Tse-tung in China, and philosophies like hedonism and humanism, will assume importance instead.

These secular ideologies will perform many of the functions of a religion. The sharing of beliefs in the secular system will bring people together and provide them with a common sense of purpose; some form of ritual or ceremony will, in many cases, be associated with the beliefs, helping to control stress and giving an outlet for the expression of emotion, and certain objects may come to symbolise the beliefs in much the same way that sacred objects symbolise religious beliefs. The Nuremberg rallies of Nazi Germany, and the May Day parades in the Soviet Union and China are examples of secular ritual and ceremony associated with political ideologies. National flags and uniforms often symbolise these beliefs, although probably the best example at the moment of such a symbolic object is the book of Mao's "Thoughts" which can be compared with the Bible in the way that it is regarded by the Chinese.

Where there is a religion, however, there is a close association between it and the other social systems, and religious organisations will exist within the structure of the society. A religion would not survive unless it were compatible with the political, economic and legal systems of the society.

In Britain, despite the marked decline in religion, there is still a very close relationship between the Church of England, which is the Established Church, and the state. This relationship is symbolised in the monarch, who is the head of the Church as well as the head of state, and the coronation of a king or queen is as much a religious occasion as a secular affirmation of national belief. Many political and civic occasions have religious ceremonies associated with them, and these activities take on an added prestige in the minds of the people as a result. The Church and its property are protected by secular laws, and, although they are the prerogative of the Church, ecclesiastical laws cannot be made or altered without parliamentary approval. The state is responsible for making appointments within the Established Church.

Even at the individual level, there is much evidence that people mark important events with religious rituals, and a large proportion of the population today might justifiably be described as "four-wheelers"—only going to church in a pram, a wedding-car and a hearse. Leslie Paul, in his report *The Deployment and Payment of the Clergy*, remarks that:

> ". . . the massive shift of the Church from the centre to the periphery of affairs simply and perhaps properly reflects the shift which has taken place in the faith of ordinary men and women. The Church is not at the heart of *their* affairs as once it was, despite popular attachment to it as an historical and picturesque institution."

Within the economic system, the Church plays an important part. It is very wealthty, owning property and acting as a landlord to numerous tenants. The income of the Church Commissioners from stock-exchange securities in 1973–74 was £14,801,016, from the Church's land and property £11,454,128 and from mortgages and loans through the Church of England Building Society £3,520,647. Charitable institutions under the auspices of the Church relieve the community of a considerable amount of the financial responsibility which it would otherwise be called upon to shoulder.

There are also close links between the Church and the educational system, since each year the Church sets aside considerable sums for the provision of schools, training colleges and university scholarships and grants.

Although the Church of England makes by far the largest contribution of all the religious organisations to the social system, most of the other denominations are related to the society in the same way and their contributions are only limited in comparison by their size.

In a complex modern society, religious attitudes and secular attitudes may at times conflict with each other. Unless some form of compromise is reached between religion and the other social activities they would not be able to achieve the type of working partnership necessary for their co-existence. While it is not possible to show conclusively whether religious or secular attitudes are the more adaptable, all the evidence that is available seems to indicate that changes in the society are gradually reflected by changes in the religious attitudes of its members. Such changes are unlikely to occur simultaneously, and religious attitudes are sometimes particularly slow in their adaptation, so that religious organisations become open to the criticism that they are old-fashioned and out of touch with modern life.

The State of Religion in Britain

There are, unfortunately, no reliable means of measuring the strength of religious belief in the society. Many people consider that empty churches, low Sunday-school attendances and the large number of religious buildings now being used for warehouses and other commercial purposes are all indications of the fact that religion is a declining force in Britain. Leslie Paul, however, in *The Deployment and Payment of the Clergy,* argues that, despite these outward signs of decay, the Established Church is still a factor to be reckoned with:

"If one takes infant baptism and church marriage as, for some residual religious reason, necessary to those participants who never go religiously beyond them, then some two-thirds of the people of England need the services of the Church in baptism and over half in marriage; possibly the greatest percentage at burial. If we take a more real figure of commitment—confirmation, 9·8 million in 1960, this is larger than the membership of the T.U.C., which in 1961 was 8·1 million. Or again if we take such a figure as the Christmas communicants, which is approximately 2·1 million in 1960, it is perhaps not ludicrous to point out that this is of a higher order than those who in 1961 were attending evening institutes in England and Wales (1·7 million)."

Church attendance figures are often taken as a guide to the strength of religious belief, because other statistical information is very difficult to obtain in this field. The three censuses of church attendance made in York by B. S. Rowntree and G. R. Lavers in 1901, 1935 and 1948 disclose a striking decline, and their findings are indicative of the situation over the country as a whole (*see* Table XIV).

The authors note that:

". . . in the thirteen years from 1935 to 1948 the Roman Catholic Church improved its position substantially relative to the other Churches, but the attendances in 1948 represented a somewhat smaller

Table XIV—Church Attendance in York

	Percentage of adult population attending places of worship	Percentage of total attendances			
		Anglican	Non-Conformist	Roman Catholic	Salvation Army (indoor services)
1901	35·5	43·7	37·8	13·8	4·7
1935	17·7	42·2	30·4	23·4	4·0
1948	13·0	33·1	34·4	30·1	2·4

Source: B. S. Rowntree and G. R. Lavers, *English Life and Leisure*.

proportion of the adult population of the city in 1948 than in 1935, and thus its real position is slightly less favourable than in 1935. The Anglican Church has lost ground sadly in the same years, both relatively and absolutely. It is indeed startling that in an archiepiscopal city the total attendances at Anglican Churches is less than at the Free Churches, and only 10% more than attendances at the Roman Catholic Churches. Nor can the relatively improved position of the Free Churches since 1935 be a source of consolation to their members, for they too have lost ground in terms of total attendances."

In 1970, the author together with a group of students undertook a survey of church attendance in the adjacent towns of Hitchin and Letchworth. The findings are set out in Table XV.

In Hitchin there is a sizeable Italian community as well as a large number of Irish, and it has been estimated that approximately 5 per cent of the population is Catholic. In Letchworth, the Catholic congregation is drawn not only from the town itself, but also from the outlying rural areas, while the other churches serve a much more local population.

In Hitchin between fifty and sixty West Indians attend their own Pentecostal meetings which are held each week in the town hall, and it is not unusual for as many as one hundred to take part.

The figures indicate that within the two towns there is a relationship between religious fervour and socio-economic status, and support for the Roman Catholic Church and the West Indian pentecostal movement is relatively much stronger than for the traditionally middle-class Church of England.

Attendance at a place of worship is not, however, the only way in which the members of the society are brought into contact with

Table XV—Church Attendance in Hitchin and Letchworth, Spring 1970

	Hitchin (Total population, 26,920)		Letchworth (Total population, 28,950)	
	Number	Percentage	Number	Percentage
Church of England	680	2·5	612	2·1
Non-Conformist	744	2·8	702	2·4
Roman Catholic	1,200	4·5	1,012	3·5
Society of Friends	25	0·1	25	0·1
Salvation Army	—	—	130	0·5
Christian Scientist	—	—	38	0·1
Spiritualist	60	0·2	30	0·1
	2,709	10·10	2,549	8·8

Note : These figures have been rounded off for convenience.

religion. Parents who do not go to any church themselves may nevertheless send their children to Sunday school, although it has been found that the pattern of behaviour relating to Sundays is changing, and fewer people are sending their children to Sunday school for the sake of a peaceful afternoon. According to the compilers of the statistical volume *Facts and Figures about the Church of England* (Central Board of Finance (1959)), "It appears that the decline in Sunday-school attendances is inversely related to the increase in the number of motor cars," which indicates that families are nowadays going for outings together on Sundays.

Once children reach school age they will certainly receive some form of religious instruction since this is still a compulsory part of the curriculum in state-aided schools. Although parents have the right to withdraw their children from such classes if they wish, few exercise this right, and, where they do, the children are bound to absorb something of what is taught from their classmates. They can scarcely avoid becoming involved, directly or indirectly, in the regular decorating of the classroom and singing of carols at Christmas-time, or perhaps in the school ceremonies such as "founders' day" services and harvest festivals.

There is, of course, much discussion taking place at present as to whether or not the provision of religious instruction should remain a statutory obligation in our schools. This partially reflects the decline in the number of staff who are qualified and willing to teach these classes, which is itself a reflection of the decline of at least the more formal aspects of religion. We must remember that, just as pupils have the right to be excused from religious instruction in school, so teachers have the right to refuse to give this instruction if they wish.

The radio and television may also bring people into contact with religion. Religious broadcasting began during the very early days of the British Broadcasting Company, and the provision of religious broadcasts continues to be part of the service of the British Broadcasting Corporation today. The Corporation's official policy on religious broadcasting is as follows:

"The first aim is that it should reflect the worship, thought, and action of those churches which represent the main stream of the Christian tradition in the country. The second is that religious broadcasting should bring before listeners and viewers what is most significant in the relationship between the Christian faith and the modern world. The third aim is that religious broadcasting should seek to reach those on the fringe of the organised life of the churches, or quite outside it."

According to the *Report of the Committee on Broadcasting, 1960* (the Pilkington Report), the aims of religious broadcasting for independent television are essentially the same as for the British Broadcasting Corporation.

Religious programmes are listened to by large numbers of people of all ages and kinds. Many in this vast audience are Christians but many are not, and, since broadcasting can reach them in a way that is impossible for any other medium, it is true to say that it presents the Churches with a very great educational opportunity. David L. Edwards, in *The Honest to God Debate,* remarks upon the danger that relying too much upon mass media and schools holds for the Churches:

". . . Christians are sometimes tempted to hope that their job will be done by the projection through the mass media of a more favourable image. As a matter of fact the great attention given to religion by TV, sound radio and the press has been out of proportion to the vitality of the churches; and as a matter of fact it does not seem to have led to any great increase in churchgoing. And if the TV set cannot do the Church's job for it, neither can the school. It is not enough for Christianity to be taught in the nation's schools, as it is in England through daily acts of worship and through Religious Instruction in class . . . in the England we know it is the fact that religion in schools does not normally lead to active church membership. If the habits and attitudes of English adults are to be transformed, *Christianity has no real hope short of a renewal of the life and the teaching of its local churches.*"

Perhaps the most useful way of trying to establish the place of religion in our society at the present time is to examine the figures available from a number of independent surveys which provide us with some idea of the number of people who claim to have no religious beliefs at all. In a survey of 2189 households in the Rose-worth Estate, Stockton-on-Tees, less than 0·5 per cent of the people questioned had no professed belief; amongst 3473 families in Morpeth, 0·2 per cent were uncommitted, and, to a similar enquiry at Sedgeley in Worcestershire, 4·1 per cent of 537 households gave a negative reply.

A certain amount of bias could easily have been introduced into these findings because not all the field-workers were necessarily trained interviewers, and in enquiries dealing with religious beliefs informants may not always admit their true feelings, particularly if they are questioned by an investigator who wears a clerical collar.

In 1974, a poll undertaken for the B.B.C. found that 64 per cent of the people questioned claimed to believe in the existence of God and 39 per cent believed in life after death. Although this poll showed a downward trend from the findings of a similar poll conducted in 1963, when 71 per cent claimed a belief in God and 53 per cent a belief in life after death, nevertheless there would appear to be good reason for thinking that there is still a very strong element of general religious awareness within the society, although organised religion is declining, and rigid doctrinal observance has less appeal now than it had when people were relatively uneducated and fear of divine retribution was a strong incentive to take part in external observable manifestations of belief. Religious morality has consequently lost much of its meaning, and the sanctions of the Church are no longer of primary importance in influencing behaviour. Colin MacInnes remarked in his article "A Godless Nation":

"It is striking as one listens to hundreds of conversations among persons of all classes, to find how rare is any militant expression of anti-religious feeling. Cordial blasphemy there may indeed often be, yet can one imagine anyone getting up anywhere in public, and seriously denouncing the Almighty without arousing violent resentment and indignation? . . . The fact is, I think, that there exists, in England, a

K

kind of 'church' outside the churches, which consists of hundreds of thousands of persons who are not without belief, who accept certain moral imperatives, who expect the churches to go on functioning like a kind of insurance company for the public conscience, but who are repelled by, or uninterested in, the actual manifestations of organised Christianity."

Colin MacInnes considers that, to a large extent, the Churches are themselves to blame for the decline in organised religion in Britain. He says that all the time the Churches remain class organisations, retain their "indecent obsession" with sex, continue to hold dreary services and do not rediscover their former missionary fervour, they will lose the battle for the minds of men. It is interesting to speculate how long, if Mr MacInnes is right, any religious influences will be available to the society, since the indirect influences of previous generations are probably of greater importance at the present time than direct influences, and they are gradually weakening.

Side by side with the decline in formalised religious practices and beliefs has occurred an increase in the manifestations of the insecurity and *anomie* which have been produced as a result. While it would be too sweeping a generalisation to say that the considerable interest being taken in hallucinatory drugs, transcendental meditation and various forms of mysticism is a symptom of bewildered people looking for some sort of spiritual experience, the need for which is inherent in all human beings, there is no doubt more than a grain of truth in the idea. There are still a number of fundamental questions about life, its origins and purpose, to which science, technology and secular belief systems have so far failed to provide an answer.

The puzzled young man in a conversation with the vicar in H. G. Wells's novel *Babes in the Darkling Wood* remarks:

"At the back of all there surely has to be a creed, a fundamental statement, put in language which does not conflict with every reality we know about the world. We don't want to be put off with serpents and fig-leaves and sacrificial lambs. We want a creed in modern English, sir. And we can't find it."

EXERCISE 11

1. Analyse the social functions of religion in modern Britain. (*A.E.B.*)
2. It has been said that religion is the opiate of the masses. Do you agree?
3. Explain how religion differs from magic.

4. "Religion is a cultural phenomenon, and exemplifies the inventiveness of mankind." Explain and discuss.

5. Examine the ways in which secular ideologies may perform the social functions of religion.

6. "Empty churches, low Sunday-school attendance and the large number of religious buildings now being used for warehouses and other commercial purposes are all indications of the fact that religion is a declining force in Britain." Discuss.

7. "There is a very close relationship between the doctrines of various religious sects and the social condition of the people adhering to them." Explain and discuss.

8. Write notes on the following:

   (*a*) Secular ethics.
   (*b*) Religious morality.
   (*c*) Taboo.
   (*d*) Creeds.
   (*e*) Myths.

9. Examine the notion that the Churches are to blame for the decline in organised religion in Britain.

10. "Britain is now a completely secular society." Examine this statement. (*Oxford*)

11. "Britain is a society without religion." Discuss. (*Oxford*)

12. Account for the divergence between religious observance and religious belief in contemporary Britain. (*London*)

13. Account for the institutional weakness of the Churches in Britain today. (*London*)

FOR FURTHER READING

Sir James Frazer. *The Golden Bough.* (Abridged edition.) Macmillan, 1963.
M. Argyle. *Religious Behaviour.* Routledge and Kegan Paul, 1965.
Leslie Paul. *The Deployment and Payment of the Clergy.* Church Information Office, 1964.
Paul Ferris. *The Church of England.* Penguin Books, 1964.
E. R. Wickham. *Church and People in an Industrial Society.* Lutterworth, 1951.
J. M. Yinger. *Religion, Society and the Individual.* New York, 1957.
R. Robertson (ed.). *Sociology of Religion.* Penguin Books, 1969.
B. R. Wilson. *Religion in a Secular Society.* Penguin Books, 1969.
Michael Hill. *A Sociology of Religion.* Heinemann, 1973.

PART THREE

THE CHANGING SOCIETY

CHAPTER XII

THE MODERN FAMILY

An issue of the *Observer* magazine supplement in September 1967 was devoted almost entirely to the subject of marriage. The front cover of the magazine showed a rather dejected bride sitting in a dustbin beneath the banner headline: *"Are we the last married generation?"* The introductory article began:

"Marriage is changing fast. But what exactly is happening to it? And are we the last married generation? It is nothing new to find marriage attacked or ridiculed: Congreve, Feydeau, Strindberg and Pinter have all dissected its farcical and tragic aspects. (What would drama have done without its essential triangle?) *But what is new is to find marriage ignored or regarded as only one of a number of alternatives.*" [Author's italics].

The pages which followed contained the comments of a number of people upon their own marriage or "avoidance of it," and contained the following selection: an actor and his playwright wife who had been married for seventeen years; an unmarried secretary who was bringing up her 5 year old son alone; a young couple who were living together with no intention of marrying; a divorced woman with two young children; a divorced artist; a young couple who had been living together for six years and "discussing the prospect of getting married on and off during most of that time" (both had been married before); a married couple for whom it was the 35-year-old husband's second marriage; a very young couple who had "had to get married"; a couple who had been married for sixty years; and, finally, a *homosexual* couple who had been living together for sixteen years, both of whom had had wives in the past.

The magazine made interesting reading, and was to some extent provocative. In a journalistic way, it drew attention to the very small but nevertheless increasing number of people within the society who are rejecting the conventional attitudes, and openly forming unions without the formality of marriage. However, the approach to the subject was in no way systematic, and for our purposes it is necessary to consider all the facts which emerge from statistical evidence. Although less colourful than the words of the *Observer*, the words of the Registrar-General paint a more accurate picture: "One of the most striking and important changes in British demography has been the tendency towards younger marriage coupled with the tendency for a larger proportion of people to marry." Table XVI clearly illustrates the Registrar-General's point.

Table XVI—Number Married per 1000 in Each Age-group, 1931, 1951 and 1971: England and Wales

Age-group	Males			Females		
	1931	1951	1971	1931	1951	1971
15–24	70	125	203	140	272	362
25–34	640	720	783	658	798	869
35–44	855	862	873	752	820	888
45–54	847	877	875	720	759	837
55–64	795	850	864	619	624	699
65 and over	619	664	731	341	352	355

Source: *Statistical Review of England and Wales, 1964.* Part III. Commentary, and *Annual Abstract of Statistics, 1974.*

It would appear from the statistical evidence, then, that, far from declining, the society's support for this particular institution is growing all the time. Since marriage is so popular, especially amongst the young, and people whose first (or even second and third) marriages have ended for one reason or another are so frequently prepared to try it again, we can hardly regard marriage as an institution which is "ignored or regarded as only one of a number of alternatives" by any significant portion of the population.

The formation of marriages and the founding of new families depend upon a number of factors, and it would be useful to consider these separately.

The Ratio of the Sexes

Since marriages are unions between two persons of the opposite sex, the number of marriages in existence is determined in the first place by the sex distribution of the population. During the present century there has been a slight rise in the proportion of males in the whole population, and there are now about 94 males for every 100 females.

There has always been an excess of males over females at birth, but this excess has increased slightly from 103 boys to every 100 girls in 1911 to 106 boys to every 100 girls at present. This factor in the past was of relatively minor importance, since the infant mortality rate for boys was always higher than that for girls, as was the male mortality rate in the 5–9 age-group. In 1911 the excess of males at birth had changed to parity of numbers between the sexes by the age of 10, and from then onwards the number of females in each age-group began to exceed the number of males. The effect of this disparity was increased by the very heavy loss of male lives during the First World War, and also by the traditional net loss due to emigration in which males were in a preponderance. Thus, during the 1930s, there was a very considerable excess of females in the marriageable age-group who had no chance of finding a husband at all.

The situation had completely changed by the beginning of the 1960s. The whole generation which was, for the reasons outlined, so short of males had been gradually reduced in size by the natural rate of deaths, and by 1964 it constituted only 10 per cent of the population. There had also been a change to an inward balance of migration, and this had added more men than women to the population. This change, combined with a higher survival rate amongst young males, has meant that parity of numbers is not reached now until a much higher age than ever before. In 1971 it was only among people aged 40 and over that the number of females in the population equalled or exceeded that of males, so there are now more men than women within the reproductive age-groups.

It is interesting to speculate whether this reversal of the traditional pattern will produce any changes in the courtship behaviour of the sexes. Until the present time, the males of this country have been in the fortunate position of having a considerable choice in the matter of selecting a wife, but now the tables have been turned, and there are too few women being chased by too many men. Women can afford to be "choosey" for a change, and they may well be the ones to make the overtures in courting. Perhaps the growing interest being shown by males in dress and cosmetic preparations is an indication of this trend, since, from now on, if a man wants to obtain a wife he will have to make himself more attractive and desirable than his competitors.

One matter that is easily overlooked in any general discussion of the ratio of the sexes in the population as a whole is that, just as there are variations in this ratio within different age-groups in the population, so there are also variations in the distribution of the

sexes geographically. There is a tendency for there to be an excess
of females in urban areas generally, and for this excess to be related
fairly closely to the size of towns—the larger towns and cities containing a greater preponderance of females than smaller ones. A
simple explanation for this may be found in the fact that urban
areas provide more opportunities than rural areas in the types of
employment that are most popular among women, such as secretarial
work, retailing, hairdressing and assembly work in light engineering
factories. The reverse of this is found in very remote rural areas
such as the Highlands of Scotland, where there is a much greater
tendency for younger men to move away to towns for work in the
absence of lucrative employment near their homes.

However, as towns gradually encroach more and more upon the
surrounding countryside, and rural districts within easy travelling
distance of towns become dormitory areas for them, distinctions
between the urban and rural population are becoming less obvious
than before. It may well be that the geographical distribution of the
sexes will become more even in future.

The Age of Marriage

One of the main changes in the pattern of marriage which has
taken place during the present century has been that in the age
at which people marry. The general trend has been for couples to
marry at an earlier age than ever before, as is indicated very clearly
by Table XVII.

Table XVII—Mean Age at Marriage

	All bachelors	All spinsters
1901	27·2	25·6
1951	26·8	24·6
1961	25·6	23·3
1972	24·8	22·8

Source: *Social Trends,* No. 5, 1974.

This trend is probably a reflection of the increased affluence of
the whole society, particularly of its younger members, and also of
the change in attitudes towards marriage. It is no longer taken for
granted that a wedding will be followed by the birth of a child
within the first year, and it is now increasingly common for a young

wife to continue working for some time after her marriage. Nowadays, the period of engagement tends to be much shorter than before, because it is no longer considered necessary to have a fully equipped home ready by the wedding day. Many young couples, after their marriage, furnish their homes jointly, gradually obtaining the things they will need by the time they decide to begin their family.

It is quite frequently suggested that the trend towards earlier marriage has been brought about by a general decline in the moral standard of young people—that the permissive attitude of the society towards premarital intercourse has increased the number of premarital conceptions and consequently the number of "shotgun" weddings. There is little statistical evidence of this, however. The number of teenage brides pregnant at the time of their wedding has remained at about twenty-six per cent of the total since before the Second World War. Of brides aged 20 to 24, the percentage who are pregnant has also remained fairly steady at about 15 per cent during the same period.

In 1951, 55 per cent of legitimate births to mothers under 20 resulted from premarital conceptions, and 12 per cent to mothers aged between 20 and 24 years old. In 1971 the figures were respectively 56 per cent and 10 per cent.

What is of considerable interest in this context, however, is that from 1911 until 1951, illegitimate births as a percentage of all live births remained steady at 5 per cent, but between 1951 and 1971 the percentage increased to eight.

These figures would suggest that changing standards of sexual morality are not so much responsible for earlier marriages as for the growing numbers of children who are being brought up by mothers who have chosen to remain single. In 1971 there were 67,000 unmarried women under the age of 30 bringing up children on their own.

Although the trend towards earlier marriage has occurred in all sections of the society, it has proceeded much further in some sectors than others. In fact, the difference between marriage patterns of different socio-economic groups has widened since the 1930s, earlier marriage being much more marked amongst manual workers than amongst the non-manual, professional and managerial classes. Table XVIII compares the age at marriage of women whose husbands were unskilled manual workers with that of women whose husbands were professional employees.

Some of the differences which occur in the marriage patterns

Table XVIII—Marriage Patterns of Different Socio-Economic Groups

Date of marriage	Age at marriage	Wives of professional employees %	Wives of unskilled manual workers %	Difference %
Married between 24 April 1931 and 23 April 1936	under 20	4·4	13·7	+ 9·3
	20–24	40·2	47·1	+ 6·9
	25–29	41·3	25·8	−15·5
	30–44	14·1	13·5	− 0·6
Married between 24 April 1960 and 23 April 1961	under 20	9·9	40·7	+30·8
	20–24	60·5	42·0	−18·5
	25–29	21·0	9·4	−11·6
	30–44	8·6	7·9	− 0·7

Source: *Statistical Review of England and Wales, 1965*. Part III. Commentary. Table C16.

between the various groups can be accounted for by the fact that professional people generally continue their full-time education beyond their twentieth birthday, but this is not the whole explanation. The Registrar-General states in *The Statistical Review, 1967* that:

"Clearly highly educated men tend to postpone their marriage until well after their twentieth birthday and when they do marry they give more weight to choosing a bride who is relatively close to them in age (as indeed do nearly all men) than they do to choosing a bride who was herself educated beyond her twentieth birthday."

Most men choose brides who are of a similar age to themselves, and the brides of men of professional and managerial status are on average one and a half to two years older than their working-class counterparts.

The Size of Families

One of the most striking changes which has occurred since the Victorian era has been the dramatic fall in the size of families. The average number of live births has fallen from six per woman married in the 1870s to two per woman married in the 1920s. This preference for smaller families is clearly indicated by Table XIX. The change in the size of families has taken place in all social

Table XIX—Distribution of Women Marrying in 1870–9, 1900–9 and 1925, with Varying Number of Live Births

Number of live births	Proportion of women (per 1000) with specified number of births who were first married in:		
	1870–9	1900–9	1925
0	83	113	161
1 or 2	125	335	506
3 or 4	181	277	221
5 to 9	434	246	106
10 or more	177	29	6
All	1000	1000	1000

Source: *Papers of the Royal Commission on Population.* Vol. 6. Table 2.

classes, although the trend towards the smaller family originated in the upper and middle classes during the nineteenth century, and even today manual workers produce on average more children than non-manual workers. The 1971 Census figures show, however, that the overall fall in family size has now been halted, and larger families are becoming more popular. The class differences in the fertility rate remain, however, because, despite the fact that professional people are now producing more children than they have done in the recent past, their families are still smaller than those of working-class parents.

The reasons for the changes in family size are several and varied, but might be summarised as follows:

1. The extension of compulsory education.
2. Increasing affluence and the spread of materialist attitudes.
3. The emancipation of women.
4. The increase in effective contraceptive techniques.

Although we can consider each of these reasons separately, they are all important contributory factors and no hierarchy can be established amongst them. The only distinction that could be made is that, whereas the first three may provide parents with the motives for limiting the size of their families, the fourth provides them with the means to do it.

THE EXTENSION OF COMPULSORY EDUCATION

The appalling conditions under which children were forced to work not only by employers but by their parents during the earlier stages of the Industrial Revolution are too well known to need amplification here. We have become so used to the idea that parents ought to cherish and protect their children that it is difficult to realise that barely a hundred years ago the family wage was, in the majority of cases, dependent upon all its members contributing. Children started working at an extremely early age, and were "financial assets" as far as their parents were concerned.

With the introduction of compulsory education, children ceased to be assets, and became liabilities instead. Parents who had previously come to rely on their children's wages now found themselves in the position of having to feed and clothe their young families out of the money they earned themselves. This factor alone was sufficient, amongst the poorer classes, to make family limitation an economic necessity during the latter years of the nineteenth century.

For all classes in the society, however, the gradual process of educational reform and the extension of the period of compulsory attendance at school have had the effect of increasing the financial responsibilities of parents for their children. Most parents are anxious to ensure that their children "have a good start in life," and it is obviously much easier to provide this for a small family than it is for a large one.

INCREASING AFFLUENCE AND THE SPREAD OF MATERIALIST ATTITUDES

We need only to compare the items which were regarded as essential when the first index for measuring the cost of living was compiled at the beginning of the century with the items included at the present time, to realise that many of the things which we now consider to be almost necessities, and therefore take for granted, were previously looked upon as luxuries. This, perhaps more clearly than anything else, illustrates the changes which have taken place in our standard of living and the attitudes which we have towards our possessions.

It is now agreed among sociologists that poverty exists where the income is less than 40 per cent above the total that would be received by a family if it were receiving social security aid. Using this level as the criterion, a survey conducted recently amongst the families living in a Nottingham council estate found that 22 per cent of the population were living in poverty. Of these "poor" families, however, 90 per cent had television, 85 per cent radio sets,

60 per cent washing machines, 40 per cent vacuum cleaners, 20 per cent record players, 10 per cent refrigerators and 5 per cent cars or motorcycles. The survey established that many consumer goods that were considered luxuries a few years ago are now necessities, and the report on the findings states that:

> "It seems very plain that there are a number of people who would endure malnutrition rather than sacrifice the television set, or even the family car. It is quite pointless to moralise about such matters: new needs have been created." (Department of Adult Education, University of Nottingham. *The Morale of the Poor*. (1968).)

It is apparent that the society as a whole attaches increasing importance to the material possessions which are symbolic of the general rise in the standard of living that has occurred since the Second World War in particular. The expense involved in rearing a large family would make it almost impossible for parents to afford many of the items which are now regarded as essential or as status symbols. Most parents are not prepared to make the sort of sacrifices that would be necessary if they were to have more than two or three children, and, consequently, as the standard of living, assessed in terms of such things as houses, furniture, cars and holidays, has risen, so the size of families has tended to fall.

THE EMANCIPATION OF WOMEN

An important reform, which began towards the end of the nineteenth century and has continued until the present, has been the improvement in the status of women. The methods by which this improvement has been achieved have differed from one sector of the community to another, but in all cases the result has been the same—women have come to possess the same political, educational, occupational and property rights as men. They are quite free to decide for themselves whether to marry or not, and, if they decide to do so, they enter the partnership on the same terms as their husbands. Amongst the labouring classes during the early stages of the Industrial Revolution, women were cruelly exploited in the factories and mines, as they provided an abundant source of cheap labour. The conditions in which they were employed were so atrocious that, together with those of children, they became one of the first great evils of society to attract the attention of Parliament. The number of hours which they were allowed to work was gradually reduced by legislation, and they were eventually forbidden to work at all in the mines. To a considerable extent, therefore, by the end of the last century, women had been freed from the kind of toil to which they had formerly been subjected, and they were in a position to devote more time to their families and their homes.

Higher up the social scale, women were in a very inferior position to men. Those who were married had to submit to the authority of their husbands in almost every sphere of their lives, and, since domestic assistance was readily available in Victorian times, they were virtually useless apart from their child-bearing functions. The unmarried women were obviously denied even this role, and, as a result, fared even worse. Unlike the women of the labouring classes, however, the middle-class women were not ignorant and illiterate. As early as the 1870s they not only were receiving a good secondary education but were also able to enter the universities, and slowly they became eligible to take part in a limited number of local-authority activities, such as sitting on school boards and later on county councils.

This small taste of life outside the confines of their families made them anxious for more, and by the end of the century the feminist movement was gaining momentum—slowly at first but with growing intensity all the time. The first leaders of the movement were able to undertake their public work either because they were un-married or because their families were small or non-existent, and they began to refute the commonly held middle-class view that a woman's place was in the home. Despite all their agitations, which took both militant and non-militant forms, the women's real opportunity to prove themselves was provided by the First World War. With so many of its men leaving their jobs to join the armed forces, the country was in a position in which it had to rely upon women to make good the difference, and, as they successfully undertook a variety of work, they were able to demonstrate that they were not inferior to the men. They were able to justify their claim for higher status and recognition as individuals with minds of their own, who were capable of sharing fully in the responsibilities of citizenship.

As the result of prolonged agitation and the changes in the society brought about by the war, public opinion changed in favour of women having occupations and interests outside the home. Large families were, of course, seen as an impediment to this, and middle-class women, in particular, resented the idea that they should be tied to their homes by too many children. There was a very marked movement towards smaller families amongst women who were married after the First World War ended.

THE INCREASE IN EFFECTIVE CONTRACEPTIVE TECHNIQUES

Since the early nineteenth century there has been a continuous advocacy of birth control in this country. Malthus in his famous *Essay on Population,* written in 1798, put forward "moral restraint" and late marriage as suitable means by which the population as a whole might be kept down, but neither of these suggestions is viewed with favour today. As we have seen, the age at which people marry has been falling steadily, but, at the same time, most people have come to accept that a healthy sexual relationship between husband and wife is one of the essential ingredients in a happy marriage. It is no longer considered right that sexual intercourse should be denied except for purposes of procreation.

Nowadays birth control is advocated on the grounds that it promotes the welfare both of families and of individuals, but the pioneers of the movement for family limitation saw birth control as the only means of averting the threat of over-population and its disastrous consequences which had been so vividly exposed by Malthus. Francis Place first openly proposed the adoption of contraceptive techniques in his book *Some Illustrations of the Principles of Population* (1822), and suggested, in a series of handbills which he published and distributed in the years immediately following, that the sponge might be used as an effective contraceptive. In 1834 *The Fruits of Philosophy,* a book advocating birth control by the American Dr Charles Knowlton, was also published in England, but, although quite a large number of pamphlets and articles on this subject were in circulation during the middle years of the century, the effect on family size was hardly noticeable.

Eventually, in 1877, Charles Bradlaugh and Annie Besant challenged a court decision relating to the publication of literature about family limitation, and deliberately republished *The Fruits of Philosophy.* Their subsequent trial was attended by a great deal of publicity—rather like that which surrounded the trial of the publishers of *Lady Chatterley's Lover* in much more recent times—and, as a result, throughout the country, the subject of birth control was widely discussed. The Malthusian League, which had been founded by Dr Drysdale, Charles Bradlaugh and Mrs Besant, organised branches in many cities and towns, and everywhere trade unions and other associations requested literature and listened to lectures on the subject. Professor Himes, an authority on the history of contraception, has estimated that, in the twenty years following the Bradlaugh–Besant trial, more than a million pamphlets and

L

tracts giving contraceptive advice were sold, and sales of *The Fruits of Philosophy* were exceptionally heavy.

This great wave of propaganda and publicity occurred at a time when there were a number of improvements in the various contraceptive methods available, and these improvements undoubtedly helped to make the idea and practice of birth control more acceptable, particularly to members of the educated classes. These were the people who led the way in the matter of family limitation, and, despite all the amount of information and advice which is available now, middle-class parents are still the ones most interested in, and knowledgeable about, the techniques of birth control.

During the 1920s Dr Marie Stopes and the Malthusian League pioneered the first clinics to give advice and to fit and supply contraceptive appliances under medical supervision, and, in 1930, the Family Planning Association, a voluntary organisation, was founded. The Association has probably done more than any other organisation to gain really widespread recognition for the fact that birth control is of great importance to family welfare, and to break down the taboos and ignorance which have always tended to militate against its wholesale acceptance.

In 1967 the *National Health Service (Family Planning) Act* was passed which granted permissive powers to Local Health Authorities to provide birth control advice and supplies for social as well as medical reasons. In many areas the Family Planning Association acted as agents for Local Health Authorities and provided clinics in hospitals and on local authority premises, and grants were made available to enable the Association to extend its activities. By 1971, there were over one thousand clinics throughout the country.

In April 1974, the *National Health Service Reorganisation Act, 1973*, was implemented, and under this Act it was made the duty of the Secretary of State for Social Services to arrange for the provision of family planning services—this provision being obligatory. As a result the new Area Health Authorities will eventually take over most of the Family Planning Association's clinics and much of its work. The Association, although much reduced in size and scope, will still have a role to play, however, especially in providing information and education services.

These services are extremely important, because, despite all the strides that have been made, the majority of women at risk never seek professional advice about birth control. They rely instead upon information that they can glean from friends or through the "grapevine" in the factory, which is still the main source of knowledge as far as industrial workers are concerned. It has been estimated that not more than one in ten married women in the country attend family planning clinics, and approximately 80 per cent of those who do go are still drawn from the top three socio-economic groups.

The advent of oral contraceptives, with their promise of virtually 100-per-cent effectiveness, might have been expected to spark off a revolution in attitudes towards birth control, but, although they have been widely publicised, many people are as yet reluctant to use them. There is a certain amount of resistance to the idea of taking drugs which have not been in use for long enough for all their possible side effects to be known, since some very tragic mistakes in other spheres of medicine have occurred within the last few years. It is estimated that only one and three-quarter million women use oral contraceptives at present, and the Family Planning Association reports that they are most popular amongst their younger patients, although the pattern of choice of contraceptive is definitely changing.

It would seem, however, that much of the propaganda about birth control fails to influence those who are most in need of advice and guidance. In 1949 the Royal Commission on Population stated that:

> "Measures to promote family welfare and particularly to reduce the inequalities in material circumstances and prospects between different sizes of family are fully justified on grounds of equity and social welfare. . . . Public policy should assume, and seek to encourage, the spread of voluntary parenthood."

Yet today, more than twenty-five years later, one of our society's problems is still that of very large families with small incomes, and the "inequalities in material circumstances" between these families and those which are much smaller, and enjoy so many advantages as a result, are possibly greater now than at any other time in our history.

Divorce and Marriage Breakdown

THE INCREASE IN THE DIVORCE RATE

Since the beginning of the 1960s, there has been a continuing increase in the frequency of divorce. The divorce rate per thousand of the married population quadrupled during the ten-year period 1962–72. Simple consideration of the statistics concerning divorce does not provide us with very much information about changing attitudes to marriage, although it is clear that marriages today are more liable to end in divorce than before.

INTRODUCTION TO SOCIOLOGY

The Registrar-General noted in the *Statistical Review, 1964*:

"In the past, the incidence of divorce seems to have been sensitive to changes in both the permissible grounds for divorce and in the provision of financial assistance to litigants. For example, the Matrimonial Causes Act of 1937 extended the grounds on which divorce was permissible and disturbed the relatively constant level of divorces up to that time. The 1939–45 war brought about a great rise in the frequency of divorce which culminated in the peak figures of 1947. The decline from the 1947 peak was checked by the Legal Aid and Advice Act of 1949, while the start of the latest rise may well have been associated with the introduction of the Legal Aid Act (1960) which changed the income limits for legal aid though the continuing increase, which has now lasted for five years, seems too persistent to be accounted for solely by the effects of that Act."

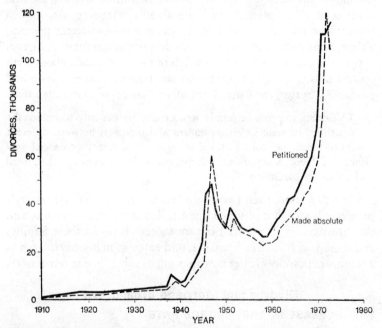

Fig. 5.—Petitions filed and decrees made absolute per 1000 married women
1910–64

The increase was still continuing when the *Divorce Reform Act*, 1969, came into effect in January 1971 and the figures rose even further (*see* Fig. 5). However, changes in the law alone do not explain the greater tendency to divorce, and it would be true to say that the latest change in the law was itself largely brought about by the changing attitudes towards divorce within the population.

The age of marriage is an important factor when considering divorce. The rates for divorce where the wife was under 20 when she married are more than double those where the wife was aged between 20 and 24, and similarly, where the wife was aged 20 to 24, the rates are half as high again as those where the wife was over 25 when she married. The likelihood of a marriage ending in divorce is obviously much higher where couples marry very young (*see* Table XVII). Since the trend towards earlier marriage is continuing, we are likely to see the divorce rate continuing to rise as well.

In all age-groups, there is a relationship between the divorce rate and the *duration of the marriage.* In this country it is not normally possible to file a divorce petition for at least three years after the wedding, and the divorce rate reaches a peak amongst marriages which have lasted between five and nine years. For every year that a marriage lasts beyond the tenth wedding anniversary, the possibility of it ending in divorce is reduced. It would appear, however, that there is a second stage of vulnerability in marriages that have lasted for twenty years or more. It may well be that many couples stay together for the sake of their children, and once the latter have become more or less independent of them they have no wish to continue an unsatisfactory relationship.

THE GROUNDS FOR DIVORCE

Since January 1971 the sole ground for divorce is the irretrievable breakdown of marriage, which includes separation. A divorce may be obtained after two years' separation if both parties consent or after five years if only one party wishes for a divorce.

Before the law was changed, well over half of all divorces were granted on the grounds of adultery. It was much simpler to gain a divorce on this ground than on any other, and many couples were prepared to provide fabricated evidence of adultery in order to be freed from their marriage contract. The new legislation has had the effect of making divorce more honest and reasonable in this respect.

There is no doubt, however, that adultery is a very common cause of marriage breakdown. The factors in society which have influenced the incidence of adultery may well be the same as those which have caused major changes in attitudes towards the whole concept of marriage. Before we consider these changes, however, it is important to remember that, where marriage is concerned, there is perhaps more discrepancy between ideal and actual behaviour than in any other sphere of society. Members of the *Royal Commission on Marriage and Divorce*, which was appointed in 1951, were somewhat unrealistic in making general assumptions related to ideal standards, and came to the conclusion that "marriages are now breaking up which in the past would have held together." It is rather naive to assume that the increase in the number of divorces is a straightforward reflection of the number of marriages which break down, and we should note that religious and social pressures have for generations forced many couples to remain married in the eyes of the law who were quite "divorced" from each other in every other respect. For numerous reasons, unhappy marriages do not by any means all end in divorce.

THE CHANGING ATTITUDES TOWARDS MARRIAGE

The Royal Commission on Marriage and Divorce reported "a tendency to take the duties and responsibilities of marriage less seriously than formerly." It is clearly impossible to measure such changes in attitude with any semblance of accuracy, but it is fairly safe to assume that changes which have occurred in the society as a whole have had some influence on attitudes towards marriage.

The most important function of marriage is the founding of families and the procreation and rearing of children, but as a society we have been steadily attaching more and more importance to the personal relationship between husbands and wives, which, while of great concern, is only one part of family life. As Ronald Fletcher points out in *The Family and Marriage in Britain*:

> "It appears to be a very widespread conception at the present time that love is something one 'falls into'; that it constitutes an immediate and high sublimity of experience which is the central *raison d'être* of, and which should be perpetuated in, marriage; and that if it begins to be somewhat dimmed in the day-to-day stress of family life then the relationship has failed and one should terminate it by divorce. . . . It may be, then, that—with the enhanced emphasis upon *marriage* as something in and for itself—the 'glossy magazine' notion of 'romantic love' is in danger of spreading an altogether superficial and inadequate conception of those qualities of love upon which a successful and happy marital relationship can rest . . . while it is right and proper that the marital relationship should be considered as being worth while in itself, there is perhaps a danger at the present time that this emphasis is being taken too far, and that the other central relationships and duties in the family are receiving too little emphasis."

Marriage in our society is based on the Christian principle of a monogamous union "until death us do part," and the increase in the divorce rate has caused great anxiety, particularly in religious sectors of the community. If marriage is considered as a permanent union to the exclusion of all others until death, then people who share this conviction are bound to oppose any moves made in the direction of reforming our existing divorce laws which might make divorces easier to obtain. There are many people at the present time who feel it would be more sensible to tackle the problem of broken marriages from the other end, as it were, and make marriage more difficult to contract into rather than to contract out of, although there are numerous and obvious obstacles that would make such action almost impossible.

Undoubtedly there is a relationship between the decline in the sanctity of marriage and the decline in religion in our society, but there appears to be very little change in the attitudes of people entering upon marriage, whether they are Christians or not. Despite fears that, as it becomes easier to obtain divorces, people will be tempted to regard the responsibility of marriage less seriously, this does not appear to be borne out by the answers which are given when people are questioned on this point. The truth is that, whatever happens in later years, people when they first get married expect their marriage to last. Thelma Veness's interesting survey *School Leavers* (1962) shows that these young people by no means consider a broken home to be the "norm," but expect marriages to persist.

As far as the society is concerned, the main problem to be faced is that which has to do with the children of broken marriages. It is important to note, therefore, that approximately one-third of all divorces are between couples who have no children, and a further third are between couples who have only one child. A Gallup Poll survey undertaken for the *Daily Telegraph* on the day before the second reading of the new Divorce Bill showed that, where a choice has to be made, 83 per cent of the people questioned believed that "it is better for a child to live with one divorced parent than it is to live with unhappily married parents."

The increase in the divorce rate does not necessarily indicate that marriage as an institution is declining in importance. In fact, the majority of people whose first marriages end in this way, as we have noted before, are likely to marry again within a relatively short time. They obviously do not dislike marriage itself, but only the particular partner they select to try it with.

Working Wives

At the beginning of the 1970s there were approximately 8¾ million women in paid employment in Britain, and of this number more than half were married. There has been a major change in this respect since the beginning of the century, when less than a quarter of the women who worked were married. In the 1930s only 10 per cent of married women were working, and, in the years that have passed since then, the proportion has increased to well over 42 per cent. Married women make a much greater contribution to the labour force than ever before.

Among the lower classes, women have always worked, and they were able to carry out the roles of wife, mother and worker quite easily all the time that industry was of a domestic type. The growth of the factory system during the Industrial Revolution presented working-class women with a new problem, because they now had to choose between staying at home or going out to work in order to earn their money. In those days, the choice was not a realistic one, because economic necessity forced most of these women to take work away from their homes. This created what Myrdal and Klein in *Women's Two Roles* (1956) describe as "one of the blackest spots in the social history of the nineteenth century," and led to the development of "back-street" housing, in the shadow of the factory.

As public opinion over the iniquitous exploitation of women in the factories increased, legislation was introduced which had the effect of gradually putting working-class women back into their homes as their hours and opportunities for employment were controlled. At the same time as this was happening, middle-class women began to agitate for the chance to leave their homes for work and interests outside. This middle-class pressure was largely concerned with unmarried women, however, and there was no real demand for women to take up the dual role of wife and worker.

Thus, at the beginning of this century, although 25 per cent of employable women were actually working, the vast majority of them were unmarried and under the age of 35. Most women in all classes at this time expected to leave their employment when they married. Since the 1900s there have been a number of fundamental alterations in the structure of the female working population which can be partially explained by demographic changes which have occurred during this period.

The percentage of women in the population who do not marry has been falling steadily since 1900, when it was 15 per cent, to the present level of only 5 per cent. The fact that the women who do marry are marrying at an earlier age is also important, because these two changes taken together have caused the number of single women available for employment to be drastically reduced. Occupations which have traditionally been undertaken largely by women, such as nursing and teaching, are now recruiting more and more married women as a result.

Since marriages are beginning earlier, and the size of families has been greatly reduced, the majority of women are now likely to have completed their families and borne their last baby by the time they are 30. Married women clearly are much less tied to their families today, and the great variety of labour-saving devices available also makes them less tied to their homes. Child-bearing and housework are no longer full-time occupations in themselves, and more women than ever before are faced with the prospect of many empty years in the prime of life unless they seek employment elsewhere.

The economic circumstances of the society have also changed considerably since the beginning of the century. During the Second World War, women were recruited to industry and commerce on an even greater scale than during the 1914–1918 war, and the continuation of full employment since 1945 has forced management to offer employment to married women. The rapid growth of new industries, the expansion of the service industries, the introduction of a comprehensive system of social security and health services and the increase in provisions for education have all created demands for labour, and these demands have meant that more and more women are needed to fill the jobs.

We can sum up all this by saying that more married women now go out to work because there are so many jobs available, the number of single women in the population has fallen very sharply, domestic and family responsibilities are less onerous today and the expectancy of life has increased to the extent that women have many more active years to devote to work and interests outside the home.

In *The Science of Society* (1967) Stephen Cotgrove points out that:

"Such changes do not necessarily imply a shift of interest on the part of women away from their traditional role as wives and mothers to a growing interest in and preoccupation with work. Although this may be a trend for women who have a professional training and career, the great majority of working wives use work instrumentally as a source of income to be spent on the home . . . and only secondarily because they are lonely or bored. . . . The increase in working wives is, in fact, perfectly consistent with the growth in home-centredness. Such women put their families first, and are not interested in promotion. This purely instrumental involvement is confirmed by the fact that the peak year for working wives is around age 42, with a steady decline after 45. By age 55–59, only sixteen per cent remain employed."

In her study of housebound mothers, *The Captive Wife* (1966), Hannah Gavron discovered that in the samples of women selected for interviewing:

"By means of education and training over 90% of the middle class wives had some clearly defined occupation by the time they became mothers and 77% of those intended to return to the same kind of work when their children were older.

This reveals clearly that these women no longer saw their lives dominated in the long term by the role of wife and mother.

Only 19% of the working class wives had had any further education, but 29% had acquired some skill while working. Yet 87% were intending to return to work, and many would clearly work in unskilled jobs below their capacity. This indicates that the role of wife and mother had clearly affected their attitudes to training and work before marriage, a situation many now regretted.

37% of the middle class mothers and 29% of the working class mothers continued to work when they had young children. The middle class wives arranged part-time work to fit in with the needs of their children, the working class were less successful at combining home and work.

The main reason for stopping in both cases was that it was wrong to leave the children. 68% of the working class wives who *were* at home would like to have been working, as would have 75% of the middle class wives who were not working.

The main reason for working among the middle class mothers was a combination of emotional and intellectual needs. The main reason for the working class was a combination of financial and emotional and intellectual needs. In both cases, however, the impression given was that the return to work was to some extent an automatic process. The *special* decision was the one to remain at home."

The traditional attitude that a woman's place is in the home is changing, but it has by no means died out completely. As Hannah Gavron found, the main reason given by mothers for leaving work was that "it was wrong to leave the children," and the conflict between the roles of *mother* and worker is now much more evident than that between the roles of *wife* and worker. Many middle-class women in particular experience feelings of guilt about neglecting their families when they take up work outside the home, and some, especially those in very demanding occupations, undoubtedly find they suffer a certain amount of strain. Middle-class women have always been regarded as "ladies of leisure," and to some extent they are still expected by the rest of society to perpetuate this image. Many of them find it extremely difficult to give the impression that they have all the time in the world to devote to gracious entertaining and living a full "social life" when, in reality, they have very little leisure time at all.

It is of importance in any discussion of the conflicting roles undertaken by working mothers to note that social workers and educationalists have failed to find any evidence that the children of these women suffer any disadvantages. School attendance is frequently better amongst these children, since working mothers are not inclined to keep their children at home on the flimsiest of pretexts, and there is no evidence to suggest that delinquency rates are any higher as is sometimes supposed. These children tend to display more self-confidence and a level of independence that are in many ways preferable to the characteristics often noticeable amongst children who are subjected to excessive maternal care and the kind of interference in their lives which results from over-protection.

Illegitimacy and Abortion

The family is of fundamental importance for the functions it performs in the procreation and rearing of chlidren, and anything which threatens to undermine the stability of the family as the reproductive unit is clearly a serious problem for the society as a whole. Any considerable increase in the number of illegitimate births indicates some change in the attitudes towards the family itself, and also towards the norms which support its continuance as the sole reproductive unit and which therefore condemn extramarital intercourse. It is for this reason that the very rapid increase in the illegitimacy rate since the mid 1950s and in the abortion rate since the *Abortion Act*, 1967 came into effect in April 1968 (*see* Fig. 6) has to be considered.

In the decade before the Act became effective the illegitimacy rate doubled, although it is now declining. The decline is not occurring uniformly throughout all age-groups, however, and the number of illegitimate births to mothers under the age of 20 is still increasing. At the same time, the number of abortions to girls under the age of 20 has increased from just over 15,000 in 1970 to above 32,000 in 1973, and quite clearly the frequency with which pregnancy is risked by teenage girls has been rising steeply.

Illegitimacy is largely a problem associated with young women, and more than two-thirds of all illegitimate births are to women under

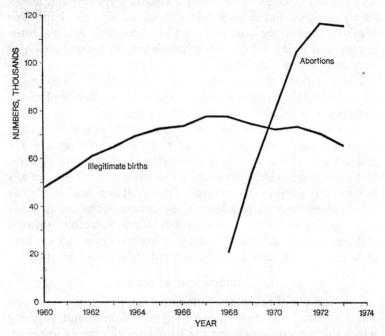

Fig. 6—Illegitimate births and abortions per 1000 women 1960–74

the age of 25. This is, of course, to be expected where more than half of all unmarried women of child-bearing age are teenagers. However, whilst more than a fifth of all births to teenage mothers are illegitimate, only one in fifty births to women between the ages of 25 and 30 are illegitimate births to unmarried women. This suggests that, although teenagers are increasingly risking pregnancy, they are also failing to heed the advice and make use of the services of family planning agencies.

This is substantiated by the findings of two researchers, Arthur and Margaret Wynn, concerning the growing problems of child poverty

("Can family planning do more to reduce child poverty?" (1974)). They pointed out in their report that between 1959 and 1972, the number of fatherless children dependent on supplementary benefits trebled, and many of these children were illegitimate children with very young mothers.

The *Lane Report on the Working of the Abortion Act* (1974) showed that the social class distribution of abortions is quite different from that of illegitimacy or pregnancies in women under 20. The abortion services are used most frequently by women in the top three social classes, whilst illegitimacy and pregnancies in very young women are higher among the women in classes four and five.

The fertility rate of teenaged women increased between 1965 and 1972 by more than enough to compensate for the abortions carried out since the *Abortion Act* became effective, and largely offset the progress made amongst older, better-off women by the family planning services.

Another aspect which has to be considered is that of *all* extra-maritally conceived births, since many of these are legitimated by the marriage of the parents before the child is born. The rate of extra-marital conceptions increased from 11 per cent of all maternities in 1955 to approximately 17 per cent in 1974, which indicates an important change in attitudes towards pre-marital sexual intercourse. At the same time as the number of extra-maritally conceived births has been increasing, the proportion being legitimated by the marriage of the parents has fallen. In 1955, 58 per cent of these maternities were legitimated, but by 1974 the percentage had fallen to below 50, which suggests that there has been not only a change in attitudes towards pre-marital sexual intercourse, but a change in attitudes towards the unmarried mother as well.

McGregor and Rowntree, in *Society: Problems and Methods of Study* (1967), have pointed out that the statistical evidence relating to illegitimacy and extra-marital conceptions:

" . . . may be interpreted as measuring the consequences of either immorality or unreliable contraceptives. From the latter point of view it underlines the importance of the current search for a simple, harmless, and wholly reliable contraceptive. The certainty of ultimate success in this research points the urgency of clarifying the basis and rules of sexual ethics in modern society. Christian doctrine no longer commands universal acceptance, and therefore no code which relies upon supernatural sanctions is likely to command general respect or to become a main determinant of conduct. Inherited rules are customarily justified by two social considerations: first, the risk and consequences of unwanted pregnancies, and second, the dangers to the happiness and stability of marriages established by partners who have indulged, whether with their future spouses or with others, in pre-marital relations. Future developments in contraceptive technique will destroy the cogency of the first consideration; the second invites empirical investigation by the social sciences. At present there is insufficient knowledge to determine the desirable basis for sexual relationships."

There is ample justification for the notion of looking to sociologists to provide the knowledge upon which a rational code of secular morality may be founded. During the last few years there has been a dramatic increase in the interest shown by the lay public in the study of sociology, which suggests that the society may be turning to sociologists to provide the guidance which formerly came from religion. If this is the case, then it becomes a matter of growing urgency that sociologists recognise the new responsibilities which have been thrust upon them in an attempt not only to arrest the symptoms of spreading *anomie* but also to find a cure for this disruptive social disease.

Unfortunately, however, at the present time, sociologists seem to be largely preoccupied with investigating phenomena which need to be changed rather than with those aspects of society which it is desirable to retain.

EXERCISE 12

1. Attempt a sociological explanation of changes in fertility in Britain in the last 100 years. (*A.E.B.*)

2. Give a sociological account of the changing role of married women in modern Britain and examine the problems which they face. (*A.E.B.*)

3. Examine the sociological causes and consequences of the increase in the proportion of wives who work. (*A.E.B.*)

4. Comment on the following statistics and explain their sociological significance.

Petitions for Divorce

1901–5	812 ⎫
1921–5	2,848 ⎬ Annual average
1931–5	4,784 ⎭
1937	5,903
1938	10,233
1947	48,501
1950	29,729
1951	38,382
1956	28,426
1961	31,905
1964	41,468
	(*A.E.B.*)

5. Examine the suggestion that the increase in the divorce rate does not necessarily indicate that marriage as an institution is declining in importance.

6. Discuss the significance for the society of an increase in the illegitimacy rate.

7. "Where marriage is concerned, there is more discrepancy between ideal and actual behaviour than in any other sphere of society." Discuss.

8. Examine the relationship between the decline in the sanctity of marriage and the decline in religion.

9. Attempt a sociological explanation of the fact that between 1955 and 1966 the number of illegitimate births in England and Wales more than doubled.

10. "Changes in family structure and relationships in Britain since 1914 can be explained in terms of the changing role of women in society." Discuss. (*Oxford*)

11. "The 'captive wife' exemplifies the persisting inequalities in the relations of the sexes in Britain today." Discuss. (*London*)

12. What explanations have been offered of the relationships between social class and fertility in Britain since 1870? (*London*)

13. What influences have affected the stability of the family during the twentieth century? (*London*)

FOR FURTHER READING

C. Rosser and C. Harris. *The Family and Social Change*. Routledge and Kegan Paul, 1965.

W. J. Goode. *The Family*. Prentice-Hall, 1964.

W. J. Goode. *Readings on the Family and Society*. Prentice-Hall, 1964.

N. W. Bell and E. G. Vogel. *The Family*. The Free Press, 1960.

V. Wimperis. *The Unmarried Mother and Her Child*. Allen and Unwin, 1960.

Hannah Gavron *The Captive Wife*. Penguin Books, 1972.

A. Myrdal and V. Klein. *Women's Two Roles: Home and Work*. Routledge and Kegan Paul, 1968.

Viola Klein. *Britain's Married Women Workers*. Routledge and Kegan Paul, 1965.

J. and E. Newsom. *Patterns of Infant Care*. Penguin Books, 1972.

J. and E. Newsom. *Four Years Old in an Urban Community*. Allen and Unwin, 1969.

G. Hawthorne. *The Sociology of Fertility*. Collier Macmillan, 1970.

M. P. Fogarty, R. Rapoport and R. N. Rapoport. *Sex, Career and Family*. Allen and Unwin, 1971.

CHAPTER XIII

URBANISATION

What is Urban Sociology?

MORE and more books are coming from the publishers at the present time which proclaim that they are works upon the subject of *urban sociology*, as though this were a subject in its own right and with its own identity. The fact is, of course, that the study of urban life and communities is only one aspect of the encyclopaedic study which is sociology itself, and the term "urban sociology" is used simply as a convenient means of indicating the area of sociology that is being singled out for particular consideration.

Urban sociology is, like its parent, a comprehensive study which may be divided into a number of separate but inter-related parts, and these parts have to do with the phenomena which are peculiar to, or typical of, social life in an urban setting, and also with the setting itself. In the study of urban sociology, then, we find consideration being given to the formulation of policies to control, improve or reform the social conditions of the urban population. Further, there is the analysis of the structure of communities and the nature and functions of neighbourhoods and primary groups, and an assessment of the position of minority groups, particularly of racial minorities, since these are more noticeable in urban areas. Also there is included an examination of the urban setting itself, and an investigation, by means of particular and comparative studies, of different types of urbanisation and their characteristics.

Before we proceed to discuss these phenomena, it is important to note that two different approaches, the *ecological* and the *organisational,* are distinguishable amongst the methods which are employed in the study of urban sociology, although few writers have relied upon one to the complete exclusion of the other. The two approaches do, however, diverge from one another, and raise different questions as a result, which sometimes leads to confusion.

THE ECOLOGICAL APPROACH

The ecological approach is based on the assumption that the main element in urbanisation is the concentration of a very large population within a relatively small space. Sociologists who adopt this approach are interested in discovering the ways in which the size and density of population influence social organisation—the delegation of power and authority, the methods used to reach decisions and formulate policies, the establishment of communications systems, the control of group activities, the regulation of employment and the maintenance of a common sense of purpose. In order to do this, they study and compare the characteristics which are observable amongst people who live in large cities, medium-sized towns, small towns, villages and hamlets, and they define these units in terms of an arbitrarily determined number of inhabitants. As far as the individual is concerned, he is assigned a status according to the type of unit in which he resides, and he may be classified as "urban," "rural" or, possibly, "intermediate," although, if he moves, his status is liable to change.

Sociologists in the ecological school also attempt to discover the ways in which the social organisation of an area changes in response to changes in the size of its population. They regard population size as the causal factor which is responsible for determining the nature of social organisation.

The American Louis Wirth was the first sociologist to make a contribution of real value to the search for a concise theory of urbanism which could be universally applied. Although he managed to avoid committing himself directly on the matter of cause and effect, his approach was that of the ecological school, and in his classic article "Urbanism as a Way of Life" (1938), he isolated three factors—size, density and heterogeneity—which he held were the principal features of urbanism and those upon which a theory of urbanism could be based. Wirth did not claim that such a theory would provide a complete explanation of all the common characteristics of urban life. At this stage he was more concerned to select the minimum number of factors which, in conjunction with each other, would ensure that urbanisation occurred. He argued that large numbers, high density and very noticeable heterogeneity, in combination, are sufficient to ensure the existence of a city in any place at any time. The presence of only one or two of these factors is not enough to do this, but that of any more than these three together is superfluous.

In his later works, Wirth presented numerous arguments to support his contention that areas with large, dense and heterogeneous populations are likely to display a great number of commonly shared characteristics in the nature of their social organisation. He has since been criticised on the grounds that he attempted to generalise far too much, and that many of his propositions and deductions, if they can be applied at all, are only applicable to industrial cities.

THE ORGANISATIONAL APPROACH

The organisational approach could also be referred to as the *behavioural* approach, since it deals with the matter of urbanisation from exactly the opposite direction to that chosen by the ecological sociologists, and regards a particular type of behaviour as the essential ingredient in urban life. For organisational sociologists, it is not where one lives but how one lives which is important. They argue that certain processes in the society will encourage or discourage the development of towns and cities, and that towns in different societies may be organised very differently as a result of behavioural variations. Where the organisational approach is used, an individual is classified as "urban" or "rural," not on the basis of where he lives, but according to the particular set of behaviour patterns which he adopts.

Like the ecological approach, the organisational method seeks to determine the relationship between the size of the population and the nature of social organisation, but, in this case, social organisation is the causal factor and not the effect. Sociologists in this school seek to show that changes in social organisation will be reflected by changes in the size of population units, and they are able to bring a great deal of evidence in support of their argument.

Probably the most notable classical theorist to use this approach was Max Weber, who sought to explain how different types of behaviour, particularly religious behaviour, influenced the development of different types of economic and political systems. He analysed the ways in which Protestantism tended to favour capitalism and the growth of industrialism with its consequential urbanisation in the countries of Western Europe, and emphasised the causal relationship between set patterns of behaviour and the nature of the society as a whole.

FEATURES OF URBAN DEVELOPMENT

The confusion which might result from the fact that these lines of approach are so divergent is less important than the realisation that both have much to offer. They reflect the attempts made by different sociologists to provide a single, simple solution to a problem that is far too complex to be solved so easily, and it could be seriously misleading to concentrate on either the physical grouping or the social organisation in an effort to isolate the essential element in urbanisation.

There are a number of features which are common to all types of urban development, and may have considerable significance for the social system as a whole, particularly in a country like our own, which is now so predominantly urbanised. There is the progressive decline in the strength of the relationship between a person's place of residence and his group affiliations. In an urban community the individual is likely to be very much more mobile, both geographically and socially. For this reason, the importance of the extended family weakens and the primary family group emerges as the basic unit within the society. It is unlikely that the actual physical grouping of people in an area will coincide with the social grouping of people who are bound to each other, not only possibly by ties of kinship, but by common loyalties, common objectives and common patterns of behaviour. The physical groupings that occur will almost certainly be heterogeneous, although, as Wirth suggested, people will tend to respond to this diversity by removing themselves, if they are able, from groups in which the members are very markedly different from themselves. This means that relatively homogeneous areas are likely to develop within a large city or town, and within these areas some slightly stronger bonds may be maintained.

In the course of urbanisation, cities grow and spread out to such an extent that town and countryside tend to merge with one another, and the traditional differences by which urban areas could be distinguished from rural areas are no longer so readily apparent. In many ways, their physical, social and cultural features overlap and become blurred in the process of *urban diffusion*. As Ruth Glass points out in *Society: Problems and Methods of Study* (1967):

" . . . there is one characteristic feature which is visible in all such areas. The same paradox is apparent: the attempt to contain urbanism, or even to escape from it, leads to the spread of urbanism. It is not that the cities themselves reproduce themselves, multiplying in their own city-like forms; it is not that landscapes are transforming into townscapes. Instead, large numbers of the population who previously lived, and who continue to work, in cities are dispersed; and so are many urban functions. The countryside is overrun and festooned with ribbons of pseudo-rural habitations . . . a new configuration of settlements is emerging: most strikingly in the metropolitan regions of Tokyo, of London, of Los Angeles, and along the eastern seaboard of the United

States. Such a metropolitan region is a sprawling expanse, neither town nor country, and here and there submerging the remnants of both. It is so vast and undifferentiated that traces of nucleation are obscured; it appears to be featureless; monotonous; without contours. . . .

It is clear that such conurbations do not reflect a rural revival, despite all their anxious attempts to achieve a semi-rural look. They are the habitat of populations with urban occupations, within the spheres of influence or urban media of communication. Thus the phenomenon which these conurbations represent is undoubtedly that of urban diffusion."

The Formulation of Policy in Urban Areas

At the beginning of the nineteenth century, only about a quarter of the people of Britain lived in towns and cities, but within a hundred years the proportion had increased to over 80 per cent. The proportion has remained constant at this exceptionally high level ever since, and has caused Britain to rank as the most urbanised country in the world.

The changeover from a predominantly rural population to a predominantly urban population occurred for several reasons, amongst which the most notable were, of course, the number of jobs which became available in towns as the Industrial Revolution gained momentum, the very rapid increase in the natural rate of population growth and, during the middle period, the influx of Irish labourers who were driven to this country as a result of the famine in their own land. One important feature of the great spread of urbanisation was the uncontrolled and haphazard manner in which it proceeded, and, unfortunately, ample evidence of this tremendous upsurge of urbanisation with its attendant congestion and overcrowding still remains today in the areas which were the main centres of growth during the Industrial Revolution.

Many contemporary writers described the social conditions of the people during the nineteenth century, but not until its closing years was any attempt made to present a systematic analysis of the situation for the purpose of identifying those aspects of urban life which so urgently needed reforming. The earliest surveys of this type, such as those undertaken by Charles Booth (*Life and Labour of the People in London* (1892–1903)) and B. S. Rowntree (*Poverty: A Study of Town Life* (1901)), were of a general nature, and served to illustrate the numerous problems which had been created by the large-scale urbanisation of the population. They did, however, focus a great deal of attention on poverty and employment, since these were the problems which became so overwhelmingly apparent.

The situation has now changed. These original problems have largely been overcome as a result of the introduction of the welfare state and the policies of successive governments which have aimed at securing conditions of full employment. Today, therefore, surveys conducted in urban areas are not of such a general nature as their predecessors, but tend instead to concentrate on particular problems such as housing, immigration, public health, local administration, town planning, traffic control and so on—the list is, in fact, a seemingly endless one. Most of these enquiries are carried out at the local level and are motivated by the desire to obtain information in order to determine local policy. These surveys are not usually undertaken for any purpose other than that of assessing the size of a particular problem in a given area. However, they are not purely descriptive, as they generally attempt to determine the cause or causes of the problem as the basis for finding solutions to them. Because these surveys are essentially practical, the findings are not normally made available to sociologists who might wish to make use of them for comparative study, nor are the surveys conducted in a standardised manner which would facilitate comparison of the results.

Occasionally, where it is considered that the information obtained from a survey may be indicative of the situation in other areas because of the similarity between them, the report may be published. This may happen if the data are required by an agency outside the area, rather than by the actual local authority concerned, and if the area is selected because it happens to be fairly representative for the purposes of the study. An example of this kind of survey was that undertaken by the Calouste Gulbenkian Foundation, *The Needs of Youth in Stevenage* (1959). The terms of reference for this enquiry were "to discover, define and plan for the needs of the disproportionately high number of young people in Stevenage and other New Towns," but the committee which undertook the investigation confined themselves to Stevenage, because they felt that the conditions there were similar to those encountered in all new towns, and to study the one would be sufficient.

Sometimes public attention is directed towards a certain area, because, for one reason or another, it "makes the headlines" in the national press. In this case, the local authority or a voluntary organisation may decide to investigate the matter, and, on account of the wave of publicity surrounding the area, the findings are likely to be of interest to a wide audience. Many of the people who have read of the "goings on" in a certain place in their newspapers, or

seen programmes about it on television, may like to read a more
objective account of the situation if a survey report is published in
the form of a book with a challenging title. Such studies also provide good ammunition for local or national pressure groups.

This happened fairly recently when the area known as Notting
Hill had been "in the news" on a number of occasions. Pearl Jephcott was appointed as the investigator for a project set in motion
by the City Parochial Foundation and given financial backing by
it. The project was referred to officially as the North Kensington
Family Study, but Pearl Jephcott later wrote a book about her findings which bore the title *A Troubled Area* (1964). The reasons why
Notting Hill attracted the attention of the public are outlined by
the author in the first chapter of the book.

> "The more recent history of trouble in this area is not a savoury one.
> It includes the sordid story of the murders of 10 Rillington Place which
> date from the mid-1940s; the outbreak of violence between white and
> coloured in the late 1950s; the sporadic activities of the National Socialist
> Movement and kindred bodies in the early 1960s; and, in 1963, the expo-
> sure of landlord scandals—the Rachmanism which has been going on for
> years. The local press reflects with dreary monotony the extent and
> variety of troubles which afflict the district."

Within a short space of time it became apparent to those involved
in the investigation that many of the problems derived from housing, in particular multi-occupied houses, and a noticeable lack of
self-help amongst the people living in the area. The main conclusions reached at the completion of the survey were summarised
by Pearl Jephcott as follows:

> "A trouble-prone area like Notting Dale* requires an intensive and
> sustained programme of help from both official and voluntary agencies.
> It is essential that any such programme should enlist the goodwill (for
> which there is plenty of evidence) and the active support of residents
> at all social levels. It would be sound to stress the potential assets of
> the cosmopolitan population and to make the approach positive and
> popular—'New North Kensington' perhaps, or even 'It's nice in Notting
> Hill.' "

Because of the interest shown by so many outsiders in the problems of Notting Hill, the Town Clerk of Kensington added his

---

* Notting Dale is the area of North Kensington to which the survey was
confined, but the names Notting Dale and Notting Hill are frequently used
interchangeably.

official comments on the study, and outlined the methods being used by the council to improve the conditions of the residents in that area:

" . . . not with a view to criticising Miss Jephcott's survey . . . but to correct an impression which might otherwise be gained that the authorities are either unaware of or inactive in seeking, within the limits of their powers, a solution to the many human problems presented by North Kensington."

The very obvious practical bias of recent urban investigations for the purposes of providing various bodies, whether local authorities or voluntary organisations, with the background information necessary for policy forming, has been reflected in the general decline of attention being paid to the processes of urbanisation and the features of urbanism as matters of academic interest to sociologists specialising in urban sociology. This type of academic interest inspired sociologists such as Weber, and, later, theorists like Louis Wirth and his colleagues in the "Chicago" School of the 1920s and 1930s, but no contribution was made by British sociologists in the form of a structural analysis of urbanism until quite recently, despite the fact that Britain is the most urbanised society of all.

In 1957 the Committee for Urban Studies was formed, which gave top priority to research into the economic and social features of urbanism in Britain. Under the auspices of the committee, C. A. Moser and Wolf Scott undertook a statistical study of urban typology, and, in 1961, a report of their findings was published under the title British Towns: A statistical study of their social and economic differences. Moser and Scott introduced their report by remarking that:

"Hitherto in this country no systematic and general research has been done into the ways in which British towns differ from or resemble one another. One is all too ready to speak of the urban dweller, the urban pattern, the urban way of life, without appreciating the variations found both within and between cities. . . . The two main objectives were, first to assemble and collate material, pointing out the similarities and contrasts, and secondly to classify towns on the basis of their social, economic and demographic characteristics. . . . In spite of the notable diversity between the towns, it is obvious that many of them have features in common and that they could be grouped into rough categories. . . . It is obvious that the many series used to describe the towns are not independent, that they overlap in the story they tell. Towns with a high proportion of heavy industry tend, on the whole, to have 'low social class' proportions, to have a substantial labour vote, high infant mortality, and so on."

Comparative studies of this type suggest that, where problems which are common to all urban areas are found to exist and the contributory factors underlying them become apparent, wholesale action at national level may well be necessary to improve the situation, rather than piecemeal action at the local level. This is particularly important when it is recognised that the availability of funds to deal with these problems varies considerably from one authority to another, and those with the greatest amount of money to spend frequently have the smallest number of problems needing to be solved.

Perhaps one explanation why there has been so little interest shown in the systematic study of urbanism in this country is that, for emotional and ideological reasons, a traditional *anti-urban* attitude has developed. It is as though, as a society, we have tried to delude ourselves into believing that urbanism does not exist simply by ignoring it and refusing to come to terms with it. During the period of rapid urbanisation in the nineteenth century, no effort was made to control or direct the expansion of the cities and towns, and the results of this *laissez-faire* growth were both ugly and unhealthy. The conditions in the urban areas were so bad that they promoted social disorder and chaos. All that was least desirable in society was nurtured in these places, which were generally nothing better than overgrown slums. Large cities were seen as the centres of social disorder and the breeding-grounds of dissension and rebellion. As the dislike of the cities intensified, those who were able to do so moved to the outskirts, and many areas were neglected and left to decay as a result. In the course of time, the outskirts became further removed from the centres of these industrial cities until they began to merge with each other, causing vast conurbations to develop. At the same time, the "nastiness" of cities was emphasised, and their reputation was seen to be one that was deserved.

This anti-urban movement has led to the general feeling that small-scale development is decidedly preferable to large-scale settlement patterns, and a great deal of attention has therefore been given to the study of small-scale developments within the wider field. A major and fashionable branch of urban sociology at the present time is the investigation of communities and small groups, such as neighbourhood groups, in an urban setting, and the emphasis in any investigation of this type appears to be placed on the problems and defects produced by urbanism, notably the problems associated with *anomie*. In this branch of urban sociology, the anti-urban tendencies of the society as a whole are very apparent.

Community Studies

Since the end of the Second World War, many sociologists have been encouraged to climb aboard the bandwagon of urban sociology, and most of them have found a seat amongst those specialising in community studies. The result of this has been the production of a large number of detailed accounts of social life in places that had often been known previously only to the people who actually lived in them. The investigations have been undertaken, not for the purposes of social engineering, but rather as a series of academic exercises, and, although the main theme of these studies usually centres round the roles and rituals which make up the social life of these communities, they do not themselves fit into any organised or integrated pattern. The information gained from them is not obtained for any particular purpose other than that of satisfying the interest of the investigator, and little attempt has been made to bring the results of all the studies together, or to collate the vast amount of material and use it for the development of sociological theory.

In the large area of urban sociology which is devoted to the study of communities, there is, therefore, a great wealth of material, which has been collected, and is still being collected, in a sporadic and disjointed fashion, and it does not readily lend itself to generalisations for this reason. Its most useful purpose at the present time would seem to be that of providing people who are considering changing their place of residence with some very detailed information about which areas of the country to move to, and which ones to avoid. This may sound rather cynical, but it does underline the fact that social scientists are not immune to the same sort of dangers that face all scientists who become carried away by the more "gimmicky" aspects of their chosen subject.

In Chapter II, we noted that knowledge is only of scientific value if it is organised in such a way that relationships are established, and it has some well-defined objective, or objectives. At the moment, these relationships and objectives are largely lacking in the field of social science which is concerned with community studies. This fact has been recognised by Ronald Frankenberg, who has made use of the material provided by a number of these studies, and attempted to bring it together in such a way that some general trends and patterns could be distinguished. Ronald Frankenberg, in *Communities in Britain* (1966), describes a community in the following way:

> "Community implies having something in common. In the early use of the word it meant having goods in common. Those who live in a community have overriding economic interests which are the same or complementary. They work together and also play and pray together. Their common interest in things gives them a common interest in each other. They quarrel with each other but are never indifferent to each other. They form a group of people who meet frequently face-to-face, although this may mean they end up back-to-back. That people in such an area of social life turn their backs on each other is not a matter of chance. In a community even conflict may be a form of co-operation."

The actual communities which have been the object of study, and the quasi-communities such as neighbourhoods and small groups, cover a very wide range from villages with well under 1000 inhabitants to places like Bethnal Green with a population of 54,000. In Britain, there can be no hard and fast dividing line between rural and urban communities, because the process of urban diffusion and the growth of communications, education, health services and even of retail distribution on a nationwide scale have all combined to reduce the divisions between town and country that once existed. It is therefore necessary to think in terms of a continuum with rural communities, in which the ties linking members together are very numerous and personal, at one end of the scale, and urban groups, in which the ties are fewer and less personal, at the other end. In between these two extremes will be many intermediate stages which may be inclined more to one or more to the other.

In all social groups the concepts of status and role are of fundamental importance, and when the findings of the many community studies are brought together this emerges very clearly. In those communities where one generation is succeeded by another and people are bound to each other by ties of kinship or by virtue of the economic functions which form the basis of the community's existence, everyone not only knows everyone else but recognises their status within the group. There is little need for any overt status symbols, because status is taken for granted, and unconsciously recognised by everyone concerned. In communities where ties of kinship are numerous, and the extended family group is of importance, family origin is the factor which gives a person a social position. The individual's family background will determine the way in which he is regarded by others.

It might well be expected that in a small village where the economy is largely based on agriculture, the status of any single individual is determined by who he is—that is, by his family background—and how he fits into the established pattern. The author's own observations, over a long period, of a fairly isolated community in the Western Highlands of Scotland would certainly support this. There is no formal organisation within the community in order to create *sociability,* because the numerous roles of the villagers constantly overlap and interweave and the same group of people meet each other in all the different spheres of life—at home, at work and in their leisure-time pursuits. Co-operation and self-help are not only necessary but almost inevitable in this kind of situation.

This does not mean that there are no organised activities of any kind in a village. There usually are. In the village studied by the author, while there are no regular meetings of any kind during the summer months when the people have little time to spare for anything that does not have to do with the land, during the winter, when the days are short and the evenings are long, the badminton club and the drama society are very popular. However, the fact still remains that the people are sociable without them, and these organised activities only provide additional opportunities for sociability.

A similar type of social behaviour has also been found to exist in the Bethnal Green area of London. Willmott and Young have found a number of aspects of social life which correspond closely to those of the rural community. In *Family and Class in a London Suburb,* they write:

> "The informal ties that abound in the East End—ties with relatives who are also neighbours, with neighbours who are former schoolmates or present workmates, with a whole host of people familiar in one way or another—all make for easy, unforced sociability. Of course, there are clubs in Bethnal Green—the place is well supplied with University Settlements and youth clubs, and there are the usual British Legion branches, political organisations and the rest—but for most people these are not essential for meeting others and mixing with them. The Bethnal Greener can do enough of that without joining anything. Sociability, in such a setting, needs no organisation."

One important factor to be considered in any discussion of the similarities between such apparently different types of community as exist in the Highlands of Scotland and the East End is that they are both basically single-class communities. This is clearly of great significance, as other studies have shown, and such informal sociability is less noticeable in the more heterogeneous groups.

Willmott and Young, who went on to study the London suburb of Woodford, and compared their findings here with those obtained in Bethnal Green, discovered that in this area, which has a high proportion of middle-class people, the working-class members of the community frequently try to adapt themselves by "accepting middle-class views and setting out to become middle class themselves, in attitude, in house and furniture, and in politics."

However much this seeming conformity exists in the respect of class, there are few other ties to bind the people together. Most of the people who live in Woodford do not work there, but travel backwards and forwards each day to their place of employment, which is usually in Central London.

Nor do the people of Woodford attach any great importance to living near the older generation, and:

" . . . whichever generation they belonged to, this was a common refrain—that the children had their own lives to lead, that their independence should be welcomed and indeed encouraged, and that it was wrong for parents to try to hang on to their children after marriage. . . . Far less people in Woodford live very close to parents and other relatives, and there is less day-to-day interaction. Meetings between relatives are much less casual, much more dependent upon definite appointments. . . . The immediate family—the married couple with their dependent children—is much more on its own, more independent, more self-sufficient."

The people of Woodford have relatively few ties, then, other than place of residence and predominantly middle-class attitudes. Who you *are* is obviously of little importance here; it is rather who you *know* that determines status in this community, and this is reflected in the large number of organisations such as clubs, societies and churches to which so many Woodford residents belong. Membership of one or more of these organisations enables people to meet each other and make friends, and friendship is important in this area. The people of Woodford feel that they belong to a very friendly, helpful community, although most of them appear to seek out those whom they consider to be of their own social class, so that "sometimes consciously, sometimes not, the middle class who predominate keep others out" of various social organisations. The working-class people of Woodford seldom belong to clubs or go to church, probably because they are not made to feel welcome.

Although friendliness is important, Willmott and Young noted that the character of the friendliness found in Woodford differed from the rather casual, taking-each-other-for-granted, type of relationship found in Bethnal Green.

"In Woodford relations are not so easy going. Standards are harsher. A newcomer to a street—and, of course, there are far more 'newcomers' in the suburb than in Bethnal Green—will not necessarily be accepted into a neighbourhood group. She has to show she is worthy of it, be the right sort of person, have a decently furnished home of her own, speak with the right accent, be neatly dressed, enjoy living in Woodford but not so much that she would greatly mind moving, have a readiness to engage in conversation, and, above all, be rather extroverted, able to march out and meet people without being too shy about it. Sociability becomes a sort of profession. To get on well, people have to some extent to put on a front of *bonhomie*, and maybe leave out some part of their personality in the process. They have to conform—in a typical Woodford avenue there seems more uniformity of gardens, attitudes and opinions than in an East End 'turning.' Maybe uniformity is one of the prices we have to pay for sociability in a more mobile society."

The *idea of conformity* is clearly of importance in any community. In areas with a long history and well-established behaviour patterns, it is relatively easy for the individual to understand, maybe almost unconsciously, what is required of him if he wishes to be accepted by the other members of the group. What happens, however, in those areas which have no such established norms? Of these, there are more and more as completely new towns are built, and housing estates mushroom all over the country, covering land which was formerly used only for agricultural purposes.

These areas do not really justify being called "communities," since any sense of community would appear to be lacking. J. M. Mogey found that the people of Barton, a housing estate three miles from the centre of Oxford, tended to keep themselves to themselves and were unwilling to become involved in any social activity. This unwillingness to become identified with any group was seen by Mogey as a sign of social insecurity, and signs of the same kind were noted by Willmott and Young in their study of "Greenleigh," a new council estate where people from Bethnal Green have been rehoused. They, too, found the people keeping themselves to themselves, and many of their informants considered that "Greenleigh" was an unfriendly place. One person summed up the situation by saying that there was no reason to be friendly, because "they come from different neighbourhoods, they were different sorts of people, and they didn't mix." As Ronald Frankenberg remarks about such estates in *Communities in Britain*:

> "Although active interaction with neighbours is at a minimum, their presence is felt. They are perceived as watchful eyes looking for faults in the housewife's craftsmanship as wife, housekeeper and mother. The husband's job, often far removed from the estate, is no longer the main criterion of status. A family is judged (or thought to be judged) by its mother and its mother is judged by the appearance and affluence of her home and her children's appearance. The standards to which the neighbours are thought to impel one are paradoxically not local but national—the standards of the women's magazines, newspapers, and television commercials."

The new town and the new estate, in these days of greater geographical mobility, are almost certain to provide an essentially anomic social environment, and it is hardly surprising that the people who live in them are frequently restless and unhappy. Perhaps one of the most notable characteristics of the private estates is the "turnover" of their population, and the resultant increase in anomie as the repercussions have a multiplying effect. The nationally sanctioned standards, as portrayed by the mass media, will be influential where people are unduly concerned about "what the neighbours will think." Where local norms are lacking, it is probably fairly safe to assume that Mrs Smith down the road will not quarrel with what the television commercials say is right.

There is another aspect of the housing estate and new town which is significant, and this is that their lack of norms makes them unsatisfactory as far as the young people who grow up in them are concerned. They are frequently referred to by adolescents as "boring" and they rarely provide many social facilities, so that the more obvious symptoms of frustration and discontent are likely to be found. Deviance and delinquency are by no means unheard of in these places, although anxious parents often fail to understand what it is that is lacking for the children who are brought up in the seemingly idyllic surroundings of neat, clean and well-appointed houses with plenty of fresh air and space in which to move about.

In the past villages and towns were allowed to develop "naturally" in a haphazard, *laissez-faire* manner. The results have in many cases been aesthetically displeasing, and in most the inheritance from the past causes great inconvenience in these days of more enlightened attitudes towards housing standards and public-health requirements, not to mention traffic congestion and chaos. However, the older towns and villages do possess something which we can best refer to as "character" and this ingredient is sadly lacking in suburbia, new towns and newly developed villages. The uniformity and monotony of these areas may perhaps be responsible to some extent for the feelings of frustration and discontent which are so frequently encountered in them. It is worth remembering that the inhabitants are all individuals with an innate desire to have an opportunity to express their own personalities, and this opportunity may not be available in the "paradise" which has been planned by someone else with a different idea of what life is all about.

Many of us would agree with Professor Sprott, who has remarked in his book *Human Groups*:

> "It is never easy to discover exactly what dream is in the minds of those planners who talk so fervently about the 'sense of community,' which they seem to think so desirable. They want people to be 'neighbourly'; they do not seem quite to approve of people just having a few friends in remote parts whom they like to visit, they want them to take an interest in the affairs of the locality in which they live. Perhaps they envisage a community as a kind of purée, mashed strawberries and cream, strongly flavoured with the 'we-feeling'. . . . Perhaps they are just lonely and think everybody else is. Anyway, they certainly aim at making the new towns and new housing estates into 'real communities.' "

It may well be that eventually, when time has eroded the newness of the new towns, these areas will develop traditions of their own. When Willmott and Young made a study of Dagenham forty years after its original conception they found that *length of residence* is important, but they were careful to point out in their book *The Evolution of a Community* that Dagenham is largely one class, and that "neighbourly relationships are more likely to develop in the *street* if people are similar to each other in social background."

Length of residence may not, however, be an influential factor in determining the social life in a housing estate, particularly a private estate. The author has herself been interested in this particular problem, and, in the light of what she discovered from an admittedly rather superficial observation of one such estate on the outskirts of Hitchin in Hertfordshire and another a few miles from Chatham in

Kent, she wonders whether they will ever evolve any social life of their own, if this is considered desirable.

In both the estates mentioned, the author found that when they were first built the new residents were drawn from all parts of the British Isles; families from Glasgow, Leeds, London, Truro, Derby, Manchester, Eastbourne and many other such widely scattered places were all living in the same road. Both of the estates are within fairly easy reach of London, where a large number of the men have their work, although some are employed locally. The range of occupations varies very widely, from the factory worker who regards owning his own house as a sign of having "bettered himself" and his wife who is generally exceedingly "house-proud" as a result, to the ex-public-school man in a junior executive position at the start of a promising career.

A feature of both of the estates is the very fast rate at which the houses change hands. In the course of ten to twelve years many of them now have a third or even fourth set of occupants. On one of the estates, in a street of thirty-nine houses, only five are still owned by their original purchasers after twelve years, and the average length of occupancy is between three and four years. The people whom the author has questioned about this do not, in most cases, move right away from the area, but generally buy another house within a radius of ten miles. These people quite readily explain that they regard living on an estate like this as a purely temporary measure. They are usually young married couples who state that a house on a new estate is all they can afford at first, that there are rarely any difficulties in the way of obtaining a mortgage, and that these properties always appreciate in value. One couple did not put any pictures, mirrors or ornaments on the walls when they moved in because they felt that they would be marked, and that might make their house more difficult to sell. Although the gardens may be filled with flowers and shrubs, their owners do not seem to put down many roots themselves. The only noticeable collective activity was that, in the early years, of the "Residents' Association," a pressure group directed mainly against the builders and the council.

This type of estate tends to attract a very heterogeneous population, and the whole series of community studies have shown how very widespread is the desire of people to live with others like themselves—in fact, in homogeneous groups.

The Study of the Urban Setting

NEW TOWNS

Many centuries before the birth of Christ, the Greeks were actively planning and developing their towns along the lines which we think of as "modern" and "new" in Britain today. The Greeks were concerned to prevent disorganised growth and congestion, and they followed the practice of relieving congestion by colonising new centres to which the excess population was removed. The colonies, or "overspill areas" as we should call them now, were, however, limited in area and population, and it was therefore possible to maintain a balance between urban and rural communities which prevented the kind of urban diffusion which has been the source of many of the problems of more modern civilisations.

Aristotle conceived that there was an optimum size for a city, and maintained that it needed to be large enough to comprise all the functions of a city, but not so large that these functions were obstructed. This idea was later restated by Leonardo da Vinci in sixteenth-century Italy when he set out his proposals for the re-organisation of Milan. Da Vinci, however, was more precise than Aristotle, because he stated the actual number of citizens which he regarded as suitable to form the population of the ideal city at thirty thousand.

This number was reiterated by Sir Ebenezer Howard, who was the first person in our own society to seek an answer to the problems of "megalopolis" by creating entirely new cities, planned and built with the definite objective of overcoming the ever-encroaching sprawl of suburbia. Howard was the idealist behind the garden city movement in Britain, which began with the building of Letchworth Garden City, founded in 1903–4, and developed into the new-town movement which began after the Second World War.

Howard's ideas, which he set out in his book *Garden Cities of Tomorrow*, were essentially simple, but they were nevertheless regarded as audacious and revolutionary. His concept of the new city was governed by four principles: growth by means of colonisation; control of the land as a matter of public interest; a limitation of area and numbers; and the provision of a sufficient variety of economic and social opportunities for the population.

It has been suggested that, although Howard envisaged a garden city as a comprehensive and well-balanced entity, it was unfortunate that in his plans for Letchworth he was so much influenced by the pattern of middle-class, suburban development which was evolved during the nineteenth century. On the face of it, there appears to be very little to distinguish the early garden city, built on an open plan with ample private gardens much in evidence, from the rather exclusive suburbs of a large city. However, any suburb is primarily a residential area, and it should not be confused in any way with the new city which Howard envisaged, because this was designed to encompass industry, commerce, government, education and all the social activities, as well as housing, which are necessary within a largely self-contained and integrated unit.

The new towns which have been built since Letchworth Garden City have followed the same sort of pattern, even though the materials used in their construction have reflected the changing techniques of the building industry, so that Stevenage New Town, which is only a few miles away from Letchworth, has a distinctly more modern appearance. Appearances are deceptive, however, and many town-planners consider that, as well as a change in the conception of the city relating to area and population, we should by now have moved away from the traditional patterns of suburban development which have so much influenced the design of our new towns—notably the conventional types of house, each with its own garden.

Howard recognised that no small city could be completely self-contained. Some specialised functions, such as the provision of a symphony orchestra, a professional theatre company, a technical college and large retail stores, rely upon the resources of a very large and varied population and access to capital funds which the small city could not possess. It is largely because of the many advantages to be gained from living in an area with a vast population that more and more people are attracted to the big cities and metropolitan growth still continues unabated. To provide the same kind of advantages for the people of the new garden cities, Howard envisaged, not that each of these cities would be an isolated unit, but that they would be built in clusters of at least ten and that these *town-clusters* would have a speedy public transport system to link them to each other. In this way, all the advantages of a large population could become available within a region, but the disadvantages of existing metropolitan areas and conurbations would not be found in them.

There is no inviolable law which governs the number of people needed to form the population of a city, and there was no special reason for Howard's suggested thirty thousand. Letchworth itself functioned for many years with less than fifteen thousand, and some of the recently built new towns will eventually hold more than one hundred thousand. What is important is that we should think in terms of a completely new municipal structure, which can create the conditions under which urban development can proceed in an orderly and harmonious way.

The overcrowding and over-extension of our existing cities has led to many of them becoming places to which people go only to work, for shopping or for entertainment, and they are not places for living in at all. People pour into them from the overcrowded commuters' trains in the morning and pour out of them again in the evening, leaving many parts completely deserted and lifeless. This is an undesirable situation for a number of reasons. Many people are forced to spend a considerable portion of their time travelling backwards and forwards, and this time is neither productive nor enjoyable—it is a hiatus between work and leisure. In order to make it possible for people to travel, a great deal of capital has to be devoted to providing transport systems which are over-employed for a few hours during the whole course of a twenty-four-hour day, but which for the majority of the time have a great deal of excess capacity which is grossly under-employed. This is obviously wasteful and inefficient in terms of the deployment of economic resources.

It is only within recent years that the planned redevelopment of existing towns and the creation of entirely new towns have become matters of social and public concern. Any attempts by the national government to introduce further controls or enter new spheres are generally regarded as serious infringements of the democratic principles, and for this reason successive governments have been somewhat wary of broadening their field of influence except where such interference is seen to be necessary in order to ameliorate very obvious social evils or to satisfy the demands of really vocal and powerful pressure groups. Consequently, as a society, our attitudes towards urban development and policy have tended to lack coherence, and no rational or clear objective has been discernible, despite the fact that Britain is a predominantly urban country.

Any policy that gains the support of the society must be explained in terms of its attempts to increase the extent of human happiness and its promise to reduce misery and frustration. A policy which will have the effect of raising the overall standard of living by increasing the value of real incomes, improving housing conditions, health and employment, and providing better opportunities for the enjoyment of leisure-time activities and interests, will almost certainly meet with the approval of most people. But the ways in which the policy seeks to achieve these desirable advantages must be clearly expressed and supported by convincing arguments. It is not enough to make statements in cold, impersonal terms about the possibilities of greater industrial output, the redeployment of labour and increased efficiency in commerce and administration which new urban policies might promote. Individuals think in terms of their own satisfaction and enjoyment, and they will not be won over unless they can see the personal advantages to be gained from the changes that are envisaged. It is important to realise, also, that a great deal of satisfaction and pleasure is to be found in the appearance of our surroundings, and the aesthetic aspects of any new developments must always be considered. Towns need to be beautiful as well as functional, and this beauty has to be a kind that is recognised by as many as possible of the beholders.

Under the *New Towns Act* of 1946, the Minister of Housing and Local Government and the Secretary of State for Scotland were given the power to designate any area of land as the site of a proposed new town. The same power was extended to the Secretary of State for Wales in 1965. Once an area has been designated, a development corporation is appointed which is given the task of creating the town and controlling its progress from the time the first plans are drawn up until all the building is substantially completed. The corporation of each new town receives general instructions from the Government about the size of the population which has to be planned for, and the main purposes of the particular development for which it is responsible. The role of the corporation is an extremely important one, because it has to interpret the general instructions and bring into existence an entirely new community within which thousands of people can live, work and spend their leisure time.

The development corporations are financed initially by the Government, although some of the factories, shops and houses eventually built in the towns may be provided by private enterprise on land leased by the corporations. Government loans for capital expenditure in the new towns are made from the Exchequer Funds, and repayment is provided for over a period of sixty years from the date the advance is made. So far nearly £1,500 million has been invested in the development of our new towns, and many of the earlier ones to be established are now beginning to show an annual surplus. This particular type of investment shows promise of being a very remunerative proposition for the country.

The availability of land is, of course, as important as the availability of capital, and the development corporations are empowered to acquire, either by agreement or by compulsory purchase, the land or other property which they require for their purposes. Once the necessary acreage has been obtained, the corporations have to ensure that, in addition to houses, flats, offices, shops, schools and other essential buildings, the main services such as roads, water supplies, sewage works, gas and electricity are provided. These services have to be planned so that they can keep pace with the rapidly expanding domestic and industrial needs of the new population.

Under the terms of the *New Towns Act* of 1959, the Commission for the New Towns was established. This is a central agency to which the assets and liabilities of each development corporation are transferred once its task of creating a new town is virtually completed. When the corporation is dissolved, the work of supervising the final stages of a town's growth is undertaken by a local committee appointed by the Commission. To ensure the necessary continuity, these committees are mainly staffed by officers who originally served the development corporations. By March 1968 four new towns—Crawley, Hatfield, Hemel Hempstead and Welwyn Garden City—had been handed over to the Commission.

At all stages in the progress of a new town, there must be close and detailed collaboration between those responsible for its development and the local authority within whose area it is situated. Only in this way is it possible for educational, social and other essential public services to be provided and expanded to meet the demands of the new community.

We hear a great deal about the "blues and bloomers" of our existing new towns, and they have acquired a reputation for being characterless and depressing. This may well be because they are so obviously "planned" and their layouts are all so similar. At least, they all appear very similar to the architecturally uninformed eye, and are superficially little more than glorified council estates, possessing none of the charm or interest of many towns with a long history. It would not be possible or even desirable to produce towns which were mere reproductions of antiques, but it would perhaps be possible to introduce less regimentation and homogeneity into the planning of them. In *The New Towns* (1969), Sir Frederick Osborn and Arnold Whittick argue that to complain about the similarity of the new towns is stupid:

"They are products of the same period, the same country and the same economic and social circumstances. Of course they cannot differ in scenic effects as widely as Venice differs from San Francisco, New York from Granada, or Rothenburg from Bath. But a town is not a stage set to amuse on a single occasion a playgoer seeking a novel thrill. The perambulating aesthete who, once in a lifetime, sees a town, values it as a spectacle. He wants a change from his own town. But the resident sees the same buildings day by day for years. They ought to be pleasing to him of course. But they cannot produce a continual sense of variation. That however can be given to him by the seasonal changes in vegetative surroundings—which is one reason why ample space, gardens and generous landscaping are not less important than architectural design."

Complaints about the similarity of our new towns may be illogical or founded upon unreasonable premises, but many of the residents do, nevertheless, mention the monotony themselves. This is not simply a criticism levelled at these towns by "perambulating aesthetes." The seasonal changes which occur in vegetative surroundings are too slow and undramatic to alleviate the symmetry and lack of variation in the streets and houses which are seen by residents every day.

However, against the disadvantages of monotony and lack of character, have to be set all the numerous advantages and successes of the first experiments in planned urban developments. The new towns provide their populations with houses of a good standard in healthy surroundings. The people nearly all live close to their place of employment, and the open countryside is within easy reach, as are modern schools, shops, public buildings, churches and places of entertainment (*see* Table XX).

According to a progress report on the new towns issued by the Department of Economic Affairs (January 1967):

"The most important factor in the success of the new towns is the availability of jobs within easy reach of home. Over 21 million sq. ft of new factory space have been built, and offices, research laboratories and branches of government departments are established in many of the towns. The new towns receive preferential treatment in the granting of industrial development certificates by the Board of Trade, but their main attraction for industrialists is the opportunity they offer for expansion. . . . Consequently, there is a steady stream of new industries to

Table XX—Progress of the New Towns (to June 30, 1973)

Town	New Industries		New Shops	New Houses and Flats	Net + Expenditure for all purposes £
	Number of firms	Number Employed			
Basildon	173	21,173	374	19,775	91,519,973
Bracknell	44	9,263	192	12,330	46,064,824
Central Lancashire	—	—	—	—	1,549,000
Crawley	92	22,109	294	15,302	39,110,000
Harlow	113	15,642	340	21,957	64,552,000
Hatfield	20	1,450	117	4,478	12,559,000
Hemel Hempstead	73	13,126	308	14,060	45,500,000
Milton Keynes	32	960	5	1,004	38,039,000
Northampton	34	939	6	1,114	18,491,000
Peterborough	32	646	19	891	15,879,000
Stevenage	82	18,058	356	19,604	69,386,000
Welwyn Garden City	23	3,981	133	6,640	18,869,000
Aycliffe	—	—	92	6,763	17,851,000
Corby	28	4,737	253	8,176	25,578,000
Peterlee	28	3,971	158	7,259	28,222,000
Redditch	160	4,799	81	3,943	37,980,000
Runcorn	62	2,756	95	4,409	38,997,000
Skelmersdale	76	8,889	126	7,260	59,012,000
Telford	71	3,477	33	4,593	51,081,000
Warrington	—	—	—	150	15,289,000
Washington	109	5,380	31	5,703	28,752,000
Cwmbran	70	1,671	224	8,419	30,972,000
Newtown (Mid-Wales)	14	403	1	375	3,456,000
Cumbernauld	101	5,652	108	9,913	59,641,000
East Kilbride	269	16,364	190	10,596	71,344,000
Glenrothes	110	7,151	102	9,272	37,356,000
Livingstone	24	2,907	38	5,362	32,999,000
Irvine	15	848	12	1,382	13,885,000
Total	1,865	176,272	3,588	219,730	£1,013,810,797

Source: *Whitaker's Almanack*, 1975.

the new towns, and in most of them there is very little unemployment. There is generally a wide variety of industry, and in those towns where one industry predominates ... the development corporations are striving to introduce alternative employment. An increasing number of commercial and service businesses are moving to the new towns and helping to provide a wider range of employment for the growing numbers of school leavers, but most of the towns want more office firms, and several of the development corporations have built offices to let. . . ."

We have not yet reached the stage of creating the "town-clusters" envisaged by Sir Ebenezer Howard, and not one of our separate new towns can be expected to provide all the different services and functions which are required by a very varied population. However, as the new towns mature, and the artificiality of the age structure of their populations is reduced by the process of time, they may become more widely accepted as the prototypes of satisfactory solutions to the problem of uncontrolled urbanisation.

THE MODERNISATION OF TOWNS

As well as planning and building new towns, we have to consider what must be done to modernise our existing large towns and cities so that they can satisfactorily provide for the needs of a growing population. It has been estimated that by the year 2000 the population will have increased to almost 60 million, and, in real terms, this means that we shall have to provide for an addition which is approximately equivalent to the combined populations of England's eight largest cities outside London in 1970—about 5 million. As well as aggravating existing problems associated with housing and employment, probably four out of five families will own cars, and the congestion of our roads will also get worse as each year passes.

The difficulties which stand in the way of providing adequately for growing numbers in an overcrowded island have for a long time been recognised. As a nation, however, we have been somewhat dilatory in taking the necessary action to alleviate the ever-increasing pressure, and to control the very serious regional imbalance which has become more and more marked since the 1930s.

The *Town and Country Planning Act* of 1947 introduced a system by means of which development plans were prepared for the whole country and had to be approved by the Minister of Housing and Local Government before any new undertakings could be commenced. The local planning authorities have to control all major developments strictly in accordance with these plans, and, as a result, there has been rather more stability and consistency throughout the country in the years since 1947 than there was previously. It has unfortunately proved extremely difficult not only to keep the development plans up to date but also to keep them forward looking and responsive to the rapid changes which have taken place since they were originally produced. They have generally failed to take

into account with sufficient speed changes in population forecasts
and traffic growth as well as other important economic and social
trends. Most local authorities therefore now find that they are
fighting a rearguard battle using yesterday's ammunition against
tomorrow's problems.

According to the report of the Planning Advisory Group, which
was set up in May 1964:

> "The dominant task of urban planning over the next twenty years
> will be the physical reshaping of the large towns and cities, the moderni-
> sation of their road and transport systems, the redevelopment of town
> centres and the wholesale renewal, whether by comprehensive improve-
> ment or redevelopment, of obsolescent housing. This process will call
> for a radical re-appraisal of the town's functions and of the distribution
> of activities within the town. The attempt to establish a reasonable
> balance between accessibility and environmental standards will be a
> major pre-occupation. It will involve not only a massive programme
> of road improvement (which includes improving the traffic capacity of
> the existing 'embryo network' as well as the construction of entirely new
> routes), but also the maintenance and improvement of public transport
> and a critical assessment of the scope for obtaining a better distribution
> of major traffic generating uses throughout the urban area and a positive
> policy of relocation to achieve this."

The rapidly changing appearance of Britain's landscape provides
the most tangible evidence available to us all of the effects of technological progress, and it should act as a constant reminder to us that
we can no longer ignore the social implications of increasing industrialisation and economic development.

EXERCISE 13

1. Assess the importance of Louis Wirth's theory of urbanism to the study
of urban sociology.
2. Considerable differences have been reported between family life in traditional working-class areas of industrial cities and that in newer housing estates
or in middle-class areas. Give a brief account of these differences, and attempt
a sociological explanation of them. (*A.E.B.*)
3. "The attempt to contain urbanism, or even to escape from it, leads to the
spread of urbanism" (Ruth Glass). Explain and discuss.
4. To what extent does the present state of urban development in Britain
reflect a traditional "anti-urban" attitude in the society?
5. Account for the fact that informal sociability is less noticeable in heterogeneous than in single-class communities.
6. "Maybe uniformity is one of the prices we have to pay for sociability in
a more mobile society" (Willmott and Young). Discuss.

7. What contribution might be made by sociologists to an understanding of the discontent to be found amongst residents in new private housing estates?

8. Outline the principles on which Sir Ebenezer Howard based his plans for garden cities. To what extent might these principles provide a solution to the problems of "megalopolis"?

9. What do you consider to be the main lessons that have been learned as a result of the experiments in planned urban development that have taken place since the *New Towns Act* 1946 was passed?

10. Examine the reasons why the new policies in urban development have so far failed to prevent more and more people being attracted to the big cities and to check metropolitan growth.

11. What are the main bases of social segregation in urban areas in Britain? (*Oxford*)

12. Discuss the town planning problems of any *one* urban area with which you are familiar. (*Oxford*)

13. What features, if any, distinguish the culture and social structure of rural communities from those of urban society? (*London*)

14. "The doctrine of *laissez faire* could not long survive in an age of great cities". Discuss. (*London*)

FOR FURTHER READING

R. N. Morris. *Urban Sociology.* Allen and Unwin, 1968.

P. Willmott and M. Young. *Family and Class in a London Suburb.* Routledge and Kegan Paul, 1960.

Pearl Jephcott. *A Troubled Area.* Faber and Faber, 1964.

M. Young and P. Willmott. *Family and Kinship in East London.* Routledge and Kegan Paul, 1957.

P. Willmott. *The Evolution of a Community.* Routledge and Kegan Paul, 1963.

J. M. Mogey. *Family and Neighbourhood—Two Studies in Oxford.* Oxford University Press, 1956.

R. Frankenberg. *Communities in Britain.* Penguin Books, 1966.

C. A. Moser and W. Scott. *British Towns.* Oliver and Boyd, 1961. (Originally Report No. 2, *Report Series, Centre for Urban Studies.*)

Sir Frederick Osborn and A. Whittick. *The New Towns: The Answer to Megalopolis.* Leonard Hill, 1969.

Council of Europe Social Committee, Strasbourg. *Social Aspects of Regional Development: Urban Areas.* 1967.

Pearl Jephcott. *Homes in High Flats.* Oliver and Boyd, 1971.

The Needs of New Communities. H.M.S.O., 1967.

Jeremy Seabrook. *City Close-Up.* Allen Lane, 1971.

CHAPTER XIV

MINORITY GROUPS AND RACIAL DISCRIMINATION

THE study of minority groups and race relations is conventionally covered by urban sociology, because the process of urbanisation itself has caused minorities to become more prominent, and the related problems of migration, divisiveness and social disorganisation to become more pronounced.

Minority Groups in Britain
ATTITUDE TOWARDS MINORITY GROUPS

Minority groups are by no means a new phenomenon within our society. Our population is extremely mixed as a result of successive waves first of invaders and later of immigrants which began in pre-historic times and have continued until the present day. A glance around you in any crowded place will be sufficient to show how well assorted we are on the superficial basis of appearance alone—blondes, brunettes and redheads; blue eyes, grey eyes and brown eyes; short ones, tall ones, fat ones and thin ones; broad shoulders and narrow shoulders; long noses and snub noses. In fact it is quite impossible to produce a description that fits a "typically British" man or woman. Another glance, this time at a telephone directory, will give a quick guide, on the basis of surnames, as to where many of our ancestors came from originally, and will provide numerous examples of the anglicised forms of Norman, German, Dutch and other foreign names borne by people who came, for one reason or another, to settle in Britain in the past.

Two factors should be considered in this context, however. Firstly, until quite recently, all the people who came to this country had *a broadly similar colour of skin*, and they were not therefore easily distinguishable from the people amongst whom they were living. Differences in language, religion or other aspects of culture cannot be recognised simply by looking at a person, and this has generally proved to be an advantage.

Secondly, in nearly every case in the past, newcomers to Britain brought with them *some particular skill or expertise* which they contributed to the society, and from which we benefited as a result.

Not only was the culture of this society enriched, but many economic advantages ensued. Banking and finance, retail distribution, the clothing industry, art and music provide just a few examples of the many spheres of social life which have gained a great deal from the abilities and aptitudes of various groups of immigrants who have come to Britain in the past.

This does not mean that minority groups have always been welcomed, nor does it mean that they have not encountered discrimination. In most cases, they have found it necessary to seek the anonymity of large towns, and form small communities of their own within them. Some minority groups rapidly became assimilated by the society and no longer exist; the only evidence of them which still remains today is that of the surnames they added to our own list. These people really only needed to learn our language before they were accepted, and, within one generation, they were no different from the majority.

Where differences of religion are concerned, assimilation is more difficult, if not impossible, and the communities formed by minority groups have therefore tended to perpetuate themselves. Many large towns still have flourishing Jewish communities within them today, despite the fact that very few Gentiles are actively anti-Semitic in their attitudes. Many Jews who do not wish to perpetuate their "Jewishness" live perfectly ordinary lives by our standards, and are scattered throughout the whole society. However, for those who still think of themselves as "Jewish" rather than "British," and who wish to reinforce and continue their own way of life, it is obviously far easier to do this in a community which comprises other Jews. Any minority group which wishes to preserve its separate identity is really forced to rely on its own resources in order to provide what is needed to do this, whether it be religious buildings, schools, youth clubs or old people's homes, and only by group co-operation is this possible.

This idea of coming together in order to reinforce shared beliefs and attitudes and to gain recognition for common objectives is of fundamental importance to any minority regardless of the extent and intensity with which it happens to differ from the majority.

The way in which minority groups are treated by the rest of the society is largely determined by whether or not they are seen to constitute a threat to that society. Any minority which might undermine the established social system, and endanger the accepted behaviour patterns of the majority, will not be willingly tolerated.

If the minority becomes large enough and powerful enough to make its presence felt in a way that adversely affects the larger group, the underlying differences between them may cause open conflicts. The open conflict may not be more serious than a battle of words between a vociferous few who try, usually without success, to change the mental attitude of their numerous opponents. On the other hand it may take the form of a brawl in the street like the not infrequent scuffles between groups of Irishmen and Scots outside public houses in Glasgow, or, in its most extreme form, it may cause the kind of race riots which occur in the United States and have also now occurred in Britain, particularly in Notting Hill.

THE QUESTION OF COLOUR

A great deal of public attention has been focused upon the problems of minority groups, particularly racial minorities, since 1945 and especially since the early 1950s. During this period, *race* has come to be virtually synonymous with *colour*, because a different colour of skin makes the individual instantly recognisable.

Although small numbers of coloured immigrants have found their way to Britain for a long time, and have settled in enclaves in some dockland areas and ports such as Cardiff, Hull and London, set up as restaurateurs in big cities or travelled the countryside peddling a variety of goods, their arrival in any significant number has been a fairly recent phenomenon. Migration is not, however, a one-way process, and more people leave Britain each year as emigrants than enter it as immigrants. However, the coloured population in this country has been growing steadily and the increase has been seen in many quarters as a threat to the indigenous population. Some members of the society feel that their own standard of living may fall, or at least fail to rise, because of the extra pressure put upon housing, hospital accommodation, educational facilities and employment as the numbers grow. Some may feel that there is a threat to the existence or continuation of the British "way of life."

These fears are not necessarily justified, although, in a period of economic crisis such as we are experiencing at the present time, coloured immigrants are likely to be used as scapegoats, and they will be blamed for everything that is wrong in the society. In some areas, because the coloureds outweigh the whites, it is quite understandable that the whites consider that they have been "taken over."

Of the population as a whole, coloured people account for slightly more than 2 per cent, but they are not evenly distributed. In some towns and cities the proportion is nearer 10 per cent, while in particular neighbourhoods more than half the population is now coloured. The majority of the coloured immigrants have moved into industrial cities, because they come for economic reasons and settle where they are able to find work. According to the 1971 Census, nearly half the immigrants from India, Pakistan and the West Indies live in our ten largest cities—London, Birmingham, Liverpool, Manchester, Bristol, Leeds, Coventry, Sheffield, Nottingham and Bradford.

The Social Problems of Immigrants

THE RATIO OF THE SEXES

The ratio of the sexes among immigrants shows a considerable imbalance, there being far too many men and far too few women, and this alone can create difficulties. For example, venereal disease has always been associated with communities of men without their womenfolk, particularly where the men have been in a strange country, and it has also always been an illness which has been regarded by the general public as a symptom of vice and immorality. It is hardly surprising, therefore, that the higher rate of venereal disease amongst immigrants has caused a certain amount of agitation, as have the other diseases, typhoid and smallpox, which, rightly or wrongly, immigrants have been blamed for bringing to Britain.

The ratio of women to men is highest amongst the West Indians and lowest amongst the Pakistanis, which partially helps to explain the varying propensity the different groups have for settling down in this country. There are signs that this imbalance is now being corrected, and many of the more recent immigrants have come to Britain in family groups, particularly in those cases where they have been forced to leave the country in which they were previously living.

COMMUNICATION

The problems associated with language differences are too well known to require enlargement here. In this respect, the West Indians have a considerable advantage, because their native tongue is English, although not necessarily the English of an Englishman. There may well be difficulties as a result of misunderstandings and the fact that West Indians do not always have an adequate grasp of the language and the vocabulary, but they are not nearly so isolated by virtue of a language barrier as the majority of Indians and Pakistanis.

The fact that the West Indian women are quite free to mix socially with other people in the same way that British women are means also that they have more opportunity to learn and use the language of Britain as it is used by the host population. Indian and Pakistani women, on the other hand, are usually very restricted, and may not learn English at all. It is quite common for them to use their children as interpreters when they need to communicate with people outside their own community. This sometimes creates problems in schools attended by immigrant children where teachers find that their pupils are kept away from classes in order to accompany their mothers on visits to the doctor, the hospital, the social security office or the housing department.

The ability to communicate is at the root of all human relationships, and is an essential ingredient of social life and interaction. Where there is no shared language, different groups will have great difficulty in co-operating with each other, and it is unfortunate that so many immigrants find it so difficult to learn English. It is quite unrealistic to expect many British people to learn any of the numerous and diverse languages spoken by the immigrants in order to overcome this important obstacle.

As the second generation, in the form of the immigrant children, grows up, the language barrier will begin to crumble. Many of the coloured children in Britain already speak English fluently, and often have strong regional accents, but not all the English-speaking children will necessarily remain in Britain when they grow up. Some of these very important links in the communications network will therefore be lost just at a time when their presence might have proved really valuable.

Most Pakistani parents, for example, would like their children to marry Pakistanis, and many send their children back to Pakistan when they reach marriageable age. They find that in Britain the whole concept of family loyalties, particularly loyalty to the extended family, differs from their own, and they feel that for a son or daughter to marry a European, or even a Pakistani who has been brought up in Britain, may seriously undermine the stability of the family. This is understandable if it is realised that most Pakistanis are Mohammedans and their family units are therefore very closely knit. The Koran contains strict orders for children to look after their parents when they become old or sick:

"Do good to your parents, whether one of them or both of them attain old age, and do not show the least disgust with them, and reproach them not, but speak kindly to them and act permissively and humbly towards them out of tender affection, and say, O Lord, have mercy on them both, as they nursed me when I was a child."

Children are a form of insurance against old age and infirmity in Pakistan, but in our society, where this is no longer the case, Pakistani parents may be apprehensive that their children will not take these responsibilities seriously unless they are sent back to their own homeland.

The duration of the immigrants' stay in Britain is clearly of importance where learning English is concerned. It has been estimated that between 1955 and 1960, 19 per cent of the West Indians re-emigrated, as did 40 per cent of the Indians and 69 per cent of the Pakistanis. By the 1970s the high rate of return of the Indians and Pakistanis had begun to fall, as many of the married men who arrived here without their families had been joined by their wives and children, and intend to stay. As the sex ratio becomes nearer to unity, and the children grow up, more unmarried immigrants will find wives in Britain, and will be less likely to return home. Many unmarried Indians, however, still have their marriages arranged in the villages or towns they originate from, and come to Britain with the intention of earning as much money as they can before returning to India again within a few years.

At present the immigrants who are most likely to stay in Britain, whose children can most easily communicate with members of the host society when they arrive, and who, in their turn, will most probably marry and bring up families of their own here, are the West Indians. About half of the coloured population in Britain comes from the West Indies.

CULTURAL DIFFERENCES

We have already seen how differences in language may present difficulties when different racial groups are brought together, but there are many other cultural phenomena—religion, family, dress, dietary habits and so on—which will have established patterns of behaviour and strongly held attitudes to support them. These behaviour patterns and attitudes will almost certainly produce conflict between the separate immigrant groups and the host society, but there will also be conflict between the various racial minorities themselves.

The West Indians have often been described as "more British than the British," and there is something essentially English about life in the West Indies if it is judged at the superficial level of language, religion, place-names in the islands and cricket. But, as Sheila Patterson points out in *Dark Strangers*, it is misleading to carry any comparisons too far:

"The bulk of West Indian migrants to Britain are drawn from a semi-rural colonial proletariat with a background of slavery, poverty and frustration which has left a distinctive mark on working habits, family organization, religious practice, and attitudes to authority."

Despite the fact that, to an outsider, the West Indians who come to this country appear to be a fairly homogeneous group drawn from a working-class background, they regard themselves very differently. They are very conscious of differences in colour, class and status which cannot be obvious to anyone else.

West Indians are very much influenced by the fact that they have become accustomed to the idea of there being one law for the rich and another for the poor. Their whole background of West Indian history and experience bears evidence of the fact. As a result, many of their attitudes reflect these traditional assumptions. Most working-class West Indians, for example, look upon marriage as very desirable, but only for those who can afford a formal wedding. A marriage ceremony, like a baptism or a funeral, is an elaborate and expensive social occasion in the West Indies, and is quite beyond the pocket of many. However, the procreation of children is generally expected of people, whatever their social class, so that common-law unions—in which a man and woman live together as man and wife without any legal ties—are quite frequent.

The West Indians, therefore, have very different attitudes to marriage from those of our own society, and also from those of the Indians or Pakistanis. As Dilip Hiro points out in *The Indian Family in Britain* (1967):

"Marriage in India is a highly respected institution and is taken seriously by both partners. Attitudes towards sex and sexual matters tend to be prudish. Sexual matters are not discussed openly, or even mentioned. Physical demonstration of love in public, even between man and wife, is rare. Extra-marital adventure is very uncommon.

Indians admire and respect a woman who is a conscientious housewife and mother. They greatly value modesty in a woman. It is generally thought indecent for a woman to expose her body immodestly. It is rare to see an Indian woman drinking in a pub, or eating in a restaurant, even when the place may be owned and managed by Indians or Pakistanis. . . . In general, outside of the family, contacts between Indian men and women are minimal. Social functions where men and women mix freely, dance and drink are non-existent in the Indian community. Whenever there are gatherings for marriages, cremations or religious festivals, men and women group separately."

Pakistanis regard marriage and sexual relationships in very much the same way as Indians. However, while Mohammedans of the different race or colour may marry because Islam strongly prohibit any distinction being made between people on the grounds of colour or race, Pakistani parents would not wish to see their children marry any followers of an idol-worshipping religion, such as Hindus. In fact, Christians and Jews, who are looked upon as "People of the Book" are more acceptable to Pakistanis as marriage partners than most Indians.

These rather brief comparisons of some of the attitudes held by different racial groups are enough to indicate that in any society where several racial groups are represented there are bound to be elements of tension and conflict. The complete integration of all minority groups into a unified whole with the majority is an ideal which even time cannot be expected to make a reality. It is, therefore, more important to concentrate, not upon the problems of assimilation and integration, but upon trying to protect minority groups against discrimination which threatens their rights as individuals. These are the rights upon which our democratic system is founded. The majority needs to recognise the minority groups and be tolerant of them, and, in their turn, the minorities have to respect the beliefs and attitudes of the majority.

The Psychological Aspects of Colour

In many instances, it is quite possible for mutual toleration to exist, and many racial minorities in Britain are not subjected to the kind of discrimination which is frequently practised against coloured minorities, despite the legislation which has been introduced to prevent it. After three major surveys had been conducted to investigate problems of discrimination in Britain, Political and Economic Planning released a report on *Racial Discrimination in Britain* (1967). A summary of this report has been published and in its opening paragraph this report states:

"The study has revealed substantial discrimination against coloured immigrants in the main aspects studied—employment, housing and the provision of services. The differential treatment and experiences of coloured immigrants as against other minority groups (such as Cypriots and Hungarians) leave no doubt that the discrimination is largely based on colour."

There is a considerable amount of evidence to indicate that *colour*, quite independently of any other characteristics, may be the cause of prejudice and discrimination for psychological reasons. We need only to consider the connotations of the words "black" and "white" to realise that, even in everyday language, these words are used to symbolise distinctions between wrong and right, evil and good, contamination and purity. Also, there are many superstitions and deep-rooted traditional beliefs associated with these colours.

The idea of "black" has come to be correlated with many personal characteristics such as lower intelligence, a tendency to violence, unduly prominent sexual behaviour and "primitiveness," which, although quite unfounded, cannot easily be eradicated or ignored. In many cases the behaviour of coloured immigrants appears to support these correlations, and they are therefore continued. The differences between the educational background of the white population and that of the immigrants may cause the immigrants to be labelled as "less intelligent"; the publicity given to any violence in which coloured people are involved may earn them the reputation of being "more violent." It is worth noting that we are very liable to ignore or take a more lenient view of violence between white people than we are of that between coloured people.

The sexual adventures of coloured men who live in a strange society with far too few of their own women-folk may be looked upon as a sign of their general "sexiness," although it is not uncommon for any group of men in a similar situation to behave in this way. Any culture which differs from our own tends to be thought of as inferior to some extent at least, and people who have a different cultural background might be thought of as primitive even though they are highly sophisticated. Unfortunately, all societies in the world do not reach the same stage in the process of civilisation at the same time, and the fact that many immigrants come from backward and underdeveloped countries tends to reinforce the image of "primitiveness." This does not mean, however, that such characteristics are innate and that the individual who comes from such a society is genetically incapable of being "civilised."

As well as the superstitions and traditional beliefs about the characteristics associated with colour, there has also developed a homespun racialist theory which militates against intermarriage. There seems to be a strongly held belief that it is biologically wrong to mate black with white, and children of mixed marriages sometimes experience emotional difficulties because they do not have the security of knowing that they are "either one thing or the other." They are outsiders as far as each racial group is concerned, and it is sometimes believed that such children inherit, not the best, but the worst of the two races. All the arguments put forward by biologists and geneticists which disprove these ideas appear to make little impression on these irrational beliefs. In the earliest periods of human evolution, there was extensive migration and hybridisation, which eventually crystallised into distinctive ethnic groupings as a consequence of man's biological adaptation to different physical environments. This could, perhaps, be thought of as selection of the fittest for survival under very different conditions, and it may well be that during this process human populations gradually developed "protective" mechanisms which served to obviate the more serious consequences of the kind of genetic intermingling which reduced the chances of survival. If this is so, then some of the expressed assumptions about the "facts" of racial cross-breeding could be the remnants of a mechanism which was at one time essential for the perpetuation of man as a being. There are, after all, other vestigial mechanisms of this kind, but of a type which are more easy to comprehend. For example, the appendix is an organ for which man now has no use, but which at one stage in the evolutionary process made it possible for the originators of this particular species of animal to live on a diet of grass and thus to survive.

Psychologists have been able to show that there are numerous motives for prejudice which no legislation can satisfactorily overcome. A fundamental characteristic of group behaviour is the attitude of group members to outsiders. The outgroup may be seen as a threat to the established norms of the group, or it may be blamed by the group for its own failures or insecurities. We have already discussed these aspects of group behaviour in Chapter V, but it is important to note in the context of coloured racial minorities that these groups are instantly recognisable and are therefore very obviously different from the rest of the society.

People who are disliked and who are the objects of discrimination will develop their own defence mechanisms. They may tend to accentuate the ways in which they differ from the majority in order to preserve their self-respect and their separate identity. These minority groups may form their own dislikes and prejudices, and may even become aggressive in their behaviour towards the majority, and the majority will be given further reason to dislike them as a result. This means that a vicious circle is created which it is very difficult to break, and a problem exists in the society which cannot easily be solved.

In his book *Racial Discrimination in England*, based on the Political and Economic Planning report of the same name, W. W. Daniel writes:

". . . as immigrants become more accustomed to English ways of life, as they acquire higher expectations and higher qualifications, so they experience more personal direct discrimination. This is apparent in the local differences between Areas with established communities as opposed to new communities. It is evident in the relative experiences of discrimination among people with English vocational training as opposed to people with no formal qualifications. It is inherent in the attitudes of employers to accepting coloured people for jobs for which there might be competition or from which they might aspire to a position of responsibility or authority. . . . This is shown both by the problems facing qualified coloured school-leavers now, in those Areas where they exist in any numbers, and by employers' attitudes to taking them on for traineeships and apprenticeships, which reflect general attitudes to the recruitment of coloured people: that they should be accepted only in the absence of sufficient numbers of white applicants. . . . This is of crucial importance because the type of job that people do in an industrial society more than anything else determines their identity in that society. . . . As long as coloured people tend to be employed in a limited range of jobs largely at the lowest end of the scale a consistent set of attitudes and prejudices will be attached to them . . . the second general conclusion is that awareness of discrimination, hostility and prejudice reinforces any tendency on the part of the people to withdraw into their own closed communities where they can insulate themselves against its effects and regulate their lives to avoid its most overt manifestations. Not only does this create increasingly separate communities but it also limits the coloured people's expectations, ambitions and awareness of the range of opportunity which British society would provide. In short it will mean that coloured people will, themselves, increasingly come to accept the inferior role that is allotted them in society, until the gap between black and white, the disparity between national social equality and hard reality, becomes so great that the main outlet for the talents of able coloured people is the leadership of revolt."

In direct and personal discrimination against the coloured immigrants are sown the seeds of alienation and the creation of embittered groups of new second-class citizens in Britain. The problem is one which constitutes a very real danger for the white population as the immigrant population grows and becomes more powerful. At present there are only about a million coloured people in Britain, but it is estimated that this number will have trebled by the end of the century even if no more immigrants are allowed to enter.

EXERCISE 14

1. Explain why the existence of minority groups is more prominent in urban than in rural areas.
2. Examine the reasons why *race* has come to be virtually synonymous with *colour* in Britain.
3. What social problems does the coloured immigrant encounter at the present time? Is there any possibility that these problems will be lessened in the future?
4. The West Indians have often been described as "more British than the British." To what extent is this description meaningful and appropriate?
5. "Legislation is of little value in overcoming racial discrimination." Discuss.
6. Cultural differences not only produce conflict between the separate immigrant groups and the host society, but between the various immigrant groups themselves. Compare the cultural background of the West Indian immigrants with that of *either* the Indians *or* the Pakistanis.
7. What dangers are there to a society in which a second-class citizenship develops?
8. Examine the superstitions and traditional beliefs still widely held in Britain which influence attitudes towards coloured immigrants.
9. The type of job that a person does in an industrial society largely determines his status within that society. In what ways is this fact likely to create problems in the future as the number of qualified coloured school-leavers increases?
10. Describe and comment on immigration to Britain since 1950. (*Oxford*)
11. Is there evidence of widespread colour prejudice in contemporary Britain? (*Oxford*)
12. "It is the scale and rapidity of post-war immigration, rather than prejudice, which accounts for the 'colour problem' in Britain today." Discuss. (*London*)
13. "Discrimination in the sphere of immigration, far from reducing tension between different racial groups in Britain can only intensify it." Discuss. (*London*)

FOR FURTHER READING

W. W. Daniel. *Racial Discrimination in England.* Penguin Books, 1968.
Report of the Race Relations Board for 1966–67. H.M.S.O.
Sheila Patterson. *Dark Strangers.* Penguin Books, 1965.
Donald Hinds. *Journey to an Illusion.* Heinemann, 1966.
Robin Oakley (ed.). *New Backgrounds: The Immigrant Child at Home and at School.* Published for the Institute of Race Relations. Oxford University Press, 1968.
Martin Luther King. *Chaos or Community.* Hodder & Stoughton, 1968.

Peter Griffiths. *A Question of Colour*. Leslie Frewin, 1966.
Stuart Hall. "Black Britons: Some Teenage Problems." *Community*, No. 3, July 1970.
A. John. *Race in the Inner City*. Runnymede Trust, 1970.
J. Rex and R. Moore. *Race, Community and Conflict*. Oxford University Press, 1966.
R. S. P. Elliott and J. Hickie. *Ulster: A Case Study in Conflict Theory*. Longmans, 1971.

CHAPTER XV

DELINQUENCY AND ANTI-SOCIAL BEHAVIOUR

ALL societies are concerned with the problems of deviance and crime, which could loosely be described as anti-social behaviour, and with the need to induce conformity amongst the individuals who might be inclined to deviate. Punishment, therefore, is the means not only by which a society avenges itself against offenders, but also by which it is hoped that people will be prevented from ever engaging in anti-social activities.

The whole concept of deviance and crime is a very difficult one to analyse, because there is no single criterion which can be universally applied to distinguish between good and bad. If we define crime as "a breach of the established criminal law," we have to consider the fact that the criminal law is relative to both time and place. What is illegal in one society may not be illegal in another, and, even within a particular society, the law may change from one year to the next and may be completely transformed within a few generations. There is obviously little within such a changeable affair as the criminal law which might provide the basis for any systematic investigation of crime.

Many attempts have been made by theorists to find the essential elements which constitute crime, and the universal concept which might be referred to as *natural crime* has been suggested. Natural crimes would be those crimes which offend against certain basic characteristics of human nature and human society. Unfortunately, any standards by which natural characteristics, such as honesty or compassion, might be measured tend to be entirely subjective, because human nature is as variable as the institutions through which social life finds expression. The existence of natural crime presupposes the existence of some ultimate ethical criterion, and the search for a determinant by which behaviour may be judged good or bad according to some intrinsic value is an endless one.

There is no general agreement about what is right or wrong, and therefore the most satisfactory solution to the problem of understanding crime is to take into consideration only offences against the prevailing laws of the particular society under investigation.

In this way an objective standard is made available, and the discussions about ethical and moral considerations, which are confusing and unlikely to produce many agreed principles, need not cloud the issue.

The Measurement of Crime

Any investigation of the amount of crime, the general trends or particular types of crime in Britain is bound to rely heavily upon the statistical evidence which is available. Each year the Home Office publishes the figures relating to crime, and these are classified under two main headings: "crimes known to the police" and "number of persons dealt with." The ways in which the crimes have been dealt with—whether by imprisonment, fines, probation, etc.—are given, and the figures are also cross-classified to show the relationships between crimes, age and sex. These statistics are of obvious importance to the sociologist as well as the criminologist.

It must be remembered, however, that these statistics cannot provide a completely accurate account. Under the heading "crimes known to the police" will appear all the figures relating to "undetected crimes," or those for which it has proved impossible to secure a conviction, as well as to the crimes committed by the "persons dealt with." Not all crimes become known to the police anyway, and these statistics are therefore likely to underestimate quite considerably the actual amount of crime which has occurred. Many breaches of the law may be dealt with by members of the public themselves, and the offences are "hushed up" for the sole purpose of "keeping the police out of it." An employer may deal with dishonesty on the part of an employee by giving him the sack; many cases of assault are not reported, and quite frequently, for the sake of preserving their good name and reputation, families may "cover up" the activities of their black sheep.

The statistics relating to "persons dealt with" may be similarly misleading, because one offender may have committed a number of crimes, and, although these will have been taken into account, he may have been dealt with by means of a single conviction. The statistics are useful, however, when any enquiry is made into the characteristics of persons who commit crimes, because, while the figures may be an underestimate of the total number of offenders, they provide a great deal of information about numerical trends and the distribution of crime according to sex and age.

The ways in which the behaviour of the public may cause statistical errors to occur are not the only sources of inaccuracy. Some quite serious errors may be introduced by the police themselves. This is obviously not done intentionally, but is a direct consequence of the very noticeable lack of uniformity between different forces in the methods employed by them to deal with the less serious types of crime such as prostitution, drunkenness and traffic offences. The variations which are found in crime figures from one area to another might indicate nothing more sinister than the different attitudes held by their respective Chief Constables. It may well be, for example, that the police in one area are much less tolerant of prostitution than the police in another. One force may be instructed to issue warnings to people in the case of first offences being committed, while another force is less lenient. This of course can only occur in the case of relatively minor offences, but these offences are all symptoms of anti-social behaviour and deviance, so they are of great interest to the sociologist. However, the comparison of statistics relating to different areas cannot be a strict one, nor can any comparison made over a period of time, although Tables XXI–XXIII, which relate to indictable offences, do provide an indication of certain trends within the society.

The Departmental Committee on Criminal Statistics reported in 1967 that:

> "The total number of indictable offences known to the police tends to be used as an index of crime as if it were analogous to, for example, the cost of living index. This practice, although not openly encouraged, is insufficiently discouraged by the present Criminal Statistics. We think it important to discourage it, because the figure of total indictable offences has two main defects that rule it out as a satisfactory index of crime: it gives as much weight to a trivial larceny of goods worth a few pence as it gives to a robbery, rape or murder, and it includes many offences in which the fluctuation in the number of offences known to the police may bear little relationship to the fluctuation in the number of offences committed."

If we remain aware of the pitfalls in using the statistics as an index of crime, we can use them, nevertheless, as the basis of broad generalisations. It is most unlikely, for example, that the great increase in the number of persons found guilty is entirely the result of improved efficiency on the part of the police, and it is therefore reasonable to believe that there has been an overall increase in crime during recent years. Furthermore, the statistics indicate clearly

Table XXI—Persons Found Guilty of Indictable Offences:
Analysis by Type of Offence (England and Wales)

	1969	1970	1971	1972	1973
Total offences	304,070	322,898	321,836	340,035	337,446
Violence against the person:					
Total	20,855	23,443	26,266	28,230	33,041
Murder	75	97	97	79	90
Manslaughter	164	190	195	217	223
Wounding	19,563	22,013	24,724	26,667	31,222
Other offences against the person	1,053	1,143	1,250	1,267	1,496
Sexual offences	6,497	6,656	6,758	6,475	7,169
Burglary	66,898	68,064	65,441	60,901	54,362
Robbery	2,526	2,614	2,999	3,415	3,159
Theft and handling stolen goods	186,818	199,177	193,508	188,979	180,875
Fraud and forgery	14,530	15,866	16,616	17,537	16,105
*Criminal damage	1,409	1,675	3,934	26,783	33,223
*Other indictable offences	4,537	5,403	6,314	7,715	9,512

* In October 1971, as a result of the *Criminal Damage Act* 1971, most non-indictable offences of malicious damage became indictable offences of criminal damage.

Source: *Annual Abstract of Statistics, 1974.*

Table XXII—Persons Found Guilty of Indictable Offences:
Analysis by Sex and Age (thousands)

	1960	1970	1971	1972	1973
Males					
All ages	143·9	280·2	277·3	293·4	292·3
Under 17 years	52·4	66·6	62·1	69·1	71·9
17 and under 21 years	25·1	69·6	71·2	75·0	75·9
21 years and over	66·4	144·0	144·0	149·3	144·5
Females					
All ages	19·6	42·7	44·5	46·6	45·2
Under 17 years	5·0	7·8	6·8	6·9	7·2
17 and under 21 years	2·7	7·3	8·1	8·4	8·4
21 years and over	11·9	27·6	29·6	31·4	29·6

Source: *Annual Abstract of Statistics, 1974.*

Table XXIII—Persons under 17 Found Guilty of Indictable Offences

	1969	1970	1971	1972	1973
Total	72,445	74,397	68,855	75,962	79,135
Violence against the person	2,249	2,827	3,574	4,598	5,283
Sexual offences	895	869	749	730	804
Burglary	25,015	25,892	24,471	23,898	23,459
Robbery	1,334	745	880	1,256	1,312
Theft and handling stolen goods	41,598	42,594	37,155	36,752	37,476
Fraud and forgery	606	659	716	726	744
*Criminal damage	597	658	1,090	7,662	9,661
Other indictable offences	151	153	230	340	396

* See Table XXI.
Source: *Annual Abstract of Statistics, 1974.*

that males are more likely to commit offences than females, and that the rate of crime has increased most rapidly amongst young people between the ages of 17 and 21. This is the generation which is now reaching adulthood, and which has been born since the Second World War ended. It is therefore tempting to assume that the society itself, which has undergone many rapid changes in a relatively short space of time, is at fault—that the social system is perhaps unsatisfactory, because it does not provide the conditions which are necessary if its members are to become fully integrated.

Forms of Anti-Social Behaviour

Any form of crime represents a rejection of the established norms, for one reason or another, and rejection occurs if the norms are not sufficiently meaningful to the individual for them to become internalised. The process by which the individual becomes socialised through the internalisation of social norms was regarded by Durkheim as the essential process in social organisation and stability. Socialisation and selection are the processes which reduce the distance between individual needs and individual satisfaction in social groups, whether the group is a small primary group or the society as a whole. If the distance between needs and satisfaction is a wide one, individuals will tend to reject the group. They may be able to gain satisfaction within another group, and resolve their feelings of frustration and tension successfully by simply moving from one group to another. In the most extreme form, this could be achieved by emigrating to a different country, and choosing the country which offers the most opportunity as far as the emigrant is concerned, or, on a smaller scale, it could be achieved by changing jobs or moving to a different neighbourhood. In all these cases, the individual is selecting the group which he feels is most able to satisfy his needs and with which he can identify himself, so that its norms are acceptable to him and become, in fact, his own.

If the tensions and strains experienced by the individual cannot be resolved by the process of self-selection, he may respond to the situation in which he finds himself by non-conformity. This non-conformity, however, need not take the form of deviant behaviour, because reformers and inventors are all non-conformists to some extent and only through non-conformity is change or progress possible. A society which contained no non-conforming members would in fact be a stagnant society. However, reformers and inventors do not attempt to violate the moral norms of the group. They may introduce new ideas, or they may attempt to change the internal organisation of the group to which they belong, but the ideas have to be acceptable, and the changes have to be brought about in ways approved by the group, if the stability of the group is to be preserved. Non-conformity which is deviant is not tolerated by society, because it seeks to achieve ends which are not socially valued by means which are not socially approved.

The non-conformist who responds to frustration in a deviant way may refuse to perform the roles which the society expects him to perform. The deliberate withdrawal from the performance of roles is referred to as *retreatism*, and the most extreme form of retreatism is, of course, *suicide*. But, in a less conclusive and dramatic way, drug-taking and alcohol consumption which may lead to the negation of roles in *addiction* and *alcoholism*, can also become forms of retreatism.

The deviant who retreats from the performance of roles and "contracts out" of society directs his aggressive responses to frustration against himself, whilst the criminal, who may perform quite satisfactorily some of the roles required of him, turns his aggression towards others. Both types of behaviour might well be different responses to the same kind of situation. For this reason, the investigator who suspects that something in the social system itself may be conducive to deviance will look not only at the statistics relating to crime but also at those relating to suicide, drug addiction and alcoholism to see whether any comparable trends are to be observed.

SUICIDE

Durkheim was the first sociologist to undertake a systematic study of suicide, and his classic work on this subject, *Du suicide* (1897), still remains the most important single contribution to the sociological understanding of the problem. Durkheim argued that although suicide appears to be a very personal action it can properly be explained only in terms of the society to which the individual who commits suicide belongs. By means of detailed statistical analysis, he demonstrated the relationship between suicide rates and the level of integration of individuals into social groups. He found that the most highly integrated individuals are the least likely to commit suicide, and argued that this could explain why, for example, suicide rates are higher amongst the single, widowed and divorced than amongst the married. Also this might explain why the rates are much lower among members of large families, and very tightly knit religious groups.

Durkheim reasoned that a certain number of suicides was to be expected in any social group, and that the collective tendency of the society towards suicide could be measured by means of its suicide rate. This rate would remain fairly constant if the character of the society did not change.

In his study, Durkheim distinguished three types of suicide, but saw each of them as a reflection of the relationship between the individual and society.

The first type, which he referred to as *egoistic suicide,* he saw as a result of an abnormal degree of individualism. This had the effect of reducing the individual's ability to withstand the collective inclination of the society against suicide, and weakening the society's control over him. The person who committed this type of suicide would have little concern for the society, and would therefore be inadequately involved with it. Durkheim included most suicides due to physical or mental illness in this category, as well as those due to bereavement or deprivation.

Durkheim argued that, while egoistic suicide could be regarded as the result of too little social control over the individual, *altruistic suicide* was committed by people over whom the society had too strong a hold. In this case, people who had too little individualism might be driven to take their own lives by an excessive sense of social duty and altruism. Into this category he placed people who strongly believed themselves to be a burden to the society—perhaps the aged and the chronically sick—or who sacrificed themselves because the society, far from abrogating suicide, actually favoured it in certain special circumstances. For example, for many generations Hindu widows were expected to throw themselves on to the funeral pyres of their husbands, and, more recently, the Japanese encouraged many of their young men to pilot "suicide" dive-bombers during the Second World War. In all cases, Durkheim pointed out, altruistic suicide inspired the respect and admiration of the rest of the society.

Durkheim identified the third type of suicide as *anomic suicide*, which occurred if the society, because of a disruption in its values and norms, could not control the behaviour of individuals. If the stability of the social structure was disturbed by rapid changes individuals would find themselves in an insecure social environment where relationships with others were disorganised and unregulated. A decline in religious beliefs, the relaxation of moral codes or a change in the importance attached by the society to any of its basic institutions such as marriage would be manifestations of anomie, and would tend to be reflected in a higher incidence of suicide. Durkheim argued that suicide was much more frequent in comparatively flexible and liberal societies than in those which were rigid and stricter, and demonstrated this by comparing the suicide rate among Roman Catholics with that among Protestants.

It should, however, be remembered that the statistics relating to suicide in Roman Catholic communities cannot be regarded as very reliable. This is because suicide is held to be a "mortal sin" for which there is no chance of repentance, and consequently a deliberate effort is made to avoid recording deaths as "suicides" wherever possible. In fact, all statistics which are concerned with suicides have to be treated with a certain amount of caution. These figures are derived from the verdicts of coroners, and the proof of suicide which is required by a coroner's court differs somewhat from the proof of the cause of death which is provided by a post-mortem examination. It is also frequently difficult to distinguish between suicides and accidental deaths or even murder. It has been estimated that the number of suicides recorded may be one-fourth to one-third lower than the actual number of deaths by suicide which occur.

Studies which have been undertaken since Durkheim made his analysis of suicide have led to some aspects of his work being challenged—for example, his assumption that secularisation leads to an increase in the rate of suicide. However, in western countries, it has been found that there is a significant correlation between increasing suicide rates and the following criteria: male sex, single and divorced state, widowhood, increasing age, childlessness, dense population, living in a large town, a high standard of living and an unsatisfactory emotional environment during childhood. This strongly supports Durkheim's theory that suicide is socially engendered, and that variations in suicide rates reflect differing degrees of integration of the individual into social groups. A sociological explanation of suicide seems to be more satisfactory than a psychological explanation which attributes suicide to some form of mental abnormality. The incidence of suicide is certainly much higher in mental hospitals than in the general population, and some forms of mental illness may have a high suicidal risk, but the development of personal abnormalities can frequently be attributed to factors in the social environment.

It is well known that traumatic experiences in childhood play a part in causing several types of abnormal behaviour such as delinquency, and it is possible that the emotional and social instability which might result from a broken home in childhood could predispose an individual to be unable to cope later in life with the kind of crises which are associated with suicide. P. Bruhn's study of patients in Edinburgh who had attempted suicide supports this possibility. Bruhn compared this group of patients with a control group of out-patients who were receiving psychiatric treatment, and he found a significantly greater incidence of broken homes in childhood amongst the suicidal group. He found also that the individuals within this group had all experienced at least one of four types of disturbance in their social environment either just before or at the time that they attempted to commit suicide. The four types of disturbance Bruhn distinguished were instability resulting from the loss of a member of the household, unemployment, moving the place of residence and serious marital problems. This would therefore suggest that an individual's experiences during the formative childhood years are influential in determining the way in which he is able to cope with emotional stresses later in life.

The suicide rate of the population of England and Wales reached a peak in the years preceding the outbreak of the Second World

War, and then it fell rapidly. After the war ended it rose once more, but did not reach the pre-war level again.

It is important to note that, although the total number of suicides reached a peak of 6247 in 1963, and has since fallen very considerably (to 3823 in 1973), the fall has not taken place in all age-groups or amongst both sexes. It can be seen that any reduction can be accounted for by a fall in the suicide rate amongst the older age-groups, particularly amongst older men. In the lower age-groups, however, the rates have continued to rise. The overall fluctuations during the period 1963 to 1973 may well be due in part tò changes in the economic conditions in the society, which affect some age-groups more than others, and may not indicate any distinctive trends in the population as a whole. If we attempt to generalise, however, we can say that the tendency to commit suicide is higher amongst males than females, and, in the case of both sexes, the proportional increase has been highest in the age-groups which have also shown an increase in their crime rates.

DRUG ADDICTION

Before considering the extent to which drug-taking as a form of retreatism has become a problem in Britain, it is necessary to remark that, while suicide and alcoholism may be regarded as responses made by individuals to a situation which can be analysed only in personal terms, drug-taking is largely associated with the growth of a sub-culture within the society.

The use of alcohol is socially acceptable, and the majority of people therefore take it and approve of it, although the individual who indulges in excessive drinking may sometimes be regarded with disfavour. More often, however, he is treated with a certain tolerant amusement, and his exploits will not usually cause him to become an outcast from his group of friends and acquaintances. However, in any society at a given time, people whose usage of drugs differs from the socially acceptable patterns will be looked upon by the rest of the society as deviants. They will be treated differently. The drug-taker's perception of himself will be influenced by this, and, as he will also see himself as being different, he will be likely to withdraw deliberately from the rest of society. He will seek out others like himself with whom he can be identified, and, in this way, a sub-culture will be established which is quite separated from the wider society.

In the United States two types of sub-cultures associated with drug-taking have emerged. The first of these is made up of poverty-stricken groups of urban slum dwellers, which contain large numbers of Negroes, Puerto Ricans and Mexicans, many of whom are unemployed and have unsatisfactory and insecure backgrounds. The second type is made up of "beatnik" and more recently "hippy" groups whose members are neither economically nor culturally deprived, but who are drawn to each other because they feel a need to express resentment against the established social system.

In Britain, however, drug-taking has never been associated with extreme poverty and deprivation, and the sub-culture which is now developing is more akin to the second American type. It has been suggested that the emergence of drug-taking in Britain was largely caused by American and Canadian addicts coming here to take advantage of the system, which, until very recently, placed the responsibility for treating addicts on general practitioners. The addicts came in the hopes of obtaining heroin and cocaine through the National Health Service, and they frequently earned money to pay for essentials—food, shelter and clothing—by illegally selling a portion of their supply of drugs to others.

Because of the difficulties generally encountered in obtaining drugs—the majority of addicts have always been reluctant to "register" with a doctor—and the limited sources of supply, addicts have been forced to establish a network of communications amongst themselves in order to ensure a steady supply. The sub-culture of drug addicts became established in London, and in this way a social locus developed towards which people susceptible to addiction were drawn. It would appear that the original group of these addicts, during the 1950s, had certain interests in common apart from drugs, and the British addicts were perhaps also attracted by American movements in jazz, art and poetry with which drugs were strongly connected in the United States. Certainly the addicts in Britain—who were mostly middle-aged people earning their living within the fields of jazz, art and literature—were somewhat older than the members of the second wave of drug addicts and drug abusers which became apparent during the early 1960s and which showed more affinity to amphetamines than to heroin.

The teenage movement in drug-taking is associated with the development of what amounts to a youth sub-culture in the society, which is symbolised by its own mode of dress, its own music, its own entertainments and its own meeting-places. It is likely that the majority of youngsters who first took stimulant drugs did so in order to keep them awake and to boost their energy during the hectic week-ends of parties and dancing which started to become popular with teenagers during the early years of the 1960s. Some drug-taking, however, is probably associated with an attempt to repudiate the values and attitudes of older generations and the desire to prove independence. The use of amphetamines was quickly followed by the introduction of cannabis, LSD and other "psychedelic" drugs which promise, in the words of Aldous Huxley's *The Doors of Perception*:

". . . a world that human beings had never had before . . . eons of blissful experience miraculously telescoped into a single hour . . . human beings will be able to achieve effortlessly what in the past could only be achieved with difficulty by means of self-control and spiritual exercises."

To a generation which appears to be very much preoccupied with avoiding boredom, there is obvious temptation in the idea of using hallucinatory drugs in order to escape from the mundane realities of everyday life.

There is a great deal of controversy at the present time over the desirability of using cannabis. An increasingly vociferous minority within the population does not consider this drug to be dangerously harmful, and quite a number of people would like to see the regulations and controls which prohibit its use relaxed. Few people would question that the use of heroin is undesirable, but at this stage there is insufficient scientific evidence to prove conclusively that the use of cannabis involves serious risks, although there is no doubt that some heroin addicts were first introduced to drugs through cannabis. The increase in the number of addicts, particularly young addicts, in Britain in recent years is a matter of concern, and, because addicts rapidly spread their "infection" to others, they constitute a very real threat both socially and economically.

The figures in Table XXIV are of use in that they provide some indication of the way in which the problem developed during the 1960s. By no means all addicts were then registered with a doctor, and of those who were there is no complete record. These statistics provide only a very conservative estimate of the true situation which existed.

The Government did not remain unaware of the growing amount of illicit dealing in dangerous drugs. In 1961/62 the number of convictions for the misuse of cannabis, notably for its illegal possession, more than doubled—increasing from 288 cases to 588. In 1963/64 the number of convictions involving manufactured drugs,

Table XXIV—The Age of Drug Addicts Known to the Home Office, 1959–66

Age	1959	1960	1961	1962	1963	1964	1965	1966
Under 20	—	1	2	3	17	40	145	329
20–34	50	62	94	132	184	257	347	558
35–49	92	91	95	107	128	138	134	162
50 and over	278	267	272	274	298	311	291	286
Unknown	34	16	7	16	8	7	10	14
Total	454	437	470	532	635	753	927	1,349

mainly heroin and cocaine, rose from 63 to 101—an increase of approximately sixty per cent. In order to control this spread, the *Drugs (Prevention of Misuse) Act* and the *Dangerous Drugs Act* were passed in 1964 and 1965 respectively. The first covered the use of amphetamines and LSD, and the second the use of heroin, morphine and cocaine. Both these Acts increased the powers of the police to search premises, seize drugs and prosecute people who were found to have obtained drugs illegally. However, neither of these Acts had the effect of altering in any way the system which had been used for treating addicts in Britain since 1926.

In that year the Rolleston Committee defined a drug addict as a patient who:

". . . while capable of leading a useful and relatively normal life when a certain minimum dose is regularly administered becomes incapable of this when the drug is entirely discontinued."

In Britain drug addiction has always been regarded as a medical problem, and, until recently, general practitioners had the main responsibility for the treatment of people who had for therapeutic or non-therapeutic reasons become dependent on drugs. It has now become evident that this system is open to abuse, and could itself make it possible for supplies of drugs to become available to others besides the patients for whom they were originally prescribed. Despite the Acts of 1964 and 1965, the number of convictions involving dangerous drugs increased by more than fifty per cent between 1965 and 1966. As a result, doctors, social workers, teachers, youth leaders, police and parents all put pressure on the Government to introduce really effective legislation to combat the menace of drug abuse. Progress in this field is slow because governmental responsibility is divided; the Home Secretary is responsible for regulating the possession of dangerous drugs, the Department of Health and Social Security for the treatment of addicts, and the Department of Education and Science for the spreading of information and education in our schools.

The Department of Health and Social Security is now charged with implementing the *Dangerous Drugs Act*, 1967, and is responsible for putting into effect the recommendations of the Second Inter-departmental Committee on Drug Addiction (Brain Committee) which reported its findings in 1965. This committee had no doubt that new addicts were being produced because established addicts were obtaining from their doctors more drugs than they needed for their own use, and were then selling or giving away their surpluses. It has been estimated that an addict can support himself by supplying drugs from his own prescriptions to five or six un-registered addicts, which is the reason why addiction is regarded as a "contaminative" phenomenon, and addicts have a compulsion to introduce other people to the habit. The Brain Committee, in their report of 1965, urged that the system which had "independent doctors treating addicts in their consulting-rooms" should be brought to an end in order to prevent the over-prescription which the members blamed for the spread of addiction:

"From the evidence before us, we have been led to the conclusion that the major source of supply has been the activity of very few doctors who have prescribed excessively for addicts. Thus we were informed that in 1962 one doctor alone prescribed almost 600,000 tablets of heroin (*i.e.* 6 kilogrammes) for addicts. The same doctor, on one occasion, prescribed 900 tablets of heroin (9 grammes) to one addict, and three days later, prescribed for the same patient another 600 tablets (6 grammes) 'to replace pills lost in an accident.' Further prescriptions of 720, *i.e.* 7·2 grammes, and 840, *i.e.* 8·4 grammes, of tablets followed later to the same patient. Two doctors each issued a single prescription for 1000 tablets (*i.e.* 10 grammes). These are only the more startling examples. We heard of other instances of prescriptions for considerable, if less spectacular, quantities of dangerous drugs over a long period of time. Supplies on such a scale can easily provide a surplus that will attract new recruits to the ranks of the addicts. The evidence further shows that not more than six doctors have prescribed these very large amounts of dangerous drugs for individual patients and these doctors have acted within the law and according to their professional judgement."

Under the *Dangerous Drugs Act* of 1967, which is concerned only with the "hard" drugs, general practitioners are prevented from prescribing heroin and cocaine except in cases where treatment is not related to addiction. This has had the effect of reducing the supply of drugs, which are only available in special treatment centres, so that addicts are forced to register. The general aim of this Act was to provide the necessary legislation to control the spread of addiction while at the same time not imposing such severe restrictions that an organised illegal market would develop in the way that an underworld black market appeared in the United States during the Prohibition era (1920–33). In moving the second reading of the *Dangerous Drugs Bill* in April 1967, Miss Alice Bacon, Minister of State at the Home Office, remarked: "The addict must feel that his future lies with the doctor and not the drug pedlar, and society must be assured that the addict cannot become a pedlar of his own medicine." Miss Bacon also demonstrated the need for further research, because "we still know too little about the motivation of addicts and the most effective ways of dealing with them."

Table XXV provides statistical evidence of the trends in drug

Table XXV—Dangerous Drugs: Addicts (United Kingdom)

	1969	1970	1971	1972	1973
Number taking drugs on 31st December	1,466	1,430	1,555	1,619	1,818
Males	1,067	1,053	1,135	1,197	1,371
Females	399	377	420	422	447
Age distribution					
Under 20 years	224	142	118	96	84
20 and under 25	590	631	722	728	751
25 and under 30	225	238	289	376	530
30 and under 35	82	90	112	117	134
35 and under 50	116	112	112	120	137
50 and over	204	195	179	165	181
Age not stated	25	22	23	17	1

Source: *Social Trends, 1974.*

addiction since the 1967 Act became effective. Although the total number of addicts shows no sign of decreasing, it appears that the Act has had a marked effect in curbing addiction amongst teenagers.

One of the major problems encountered in attempts to cure drug addiction is that the treatment itself does nothing to alleviate the pressures put on the individual which caused him to practise this form of retreatism in the first place. Recidivism is consequently very high, because, as a result of his drug-taking, the addict will most probably have become alienated from the wider society and emotionally and socially dependent on the group of addicts and drug-abusers of which he has become a member. This means that, not only has the addict to be helped to give up drugs, but he must also undergo a prolonged period of rehabilitation. A large number of addicts will continue to relapse unless the community is able to provide them with a variety of different means of continuing support.

ALCOHOLISM

The World Health Organisation has defined alcoholics as:

". . . those excessive drinkers whose dependence on alcohol has attained such a degree that they show a noticeable mental disturbance or an interference with their mental and bodily health, their interpersonal relations and their smooth social and economic functioning; or who show the prodromal signs of such development."

As Dr Lincoln Williams has pointed out in his book *Alcoholism Explained*:

"Alcoholism is not synonymous with drunkenness. Although all alcoholics may show signs of drunkenness yet many who get drunk are far from being alcoholics. Many men, for example, take 'one over the eight' on festive occasions like parties, regimental dinners or Old Boys' reunions, but it does not follow from this that they are suffering from true addiction, although of course they may be. When as the years go by alcohol becomes of paramount importance to the individual, when he cannot visualize his life without it, and furthermore, when he cannot voluntarily abstain from it, then alcoholism has supervened and he is now addicted."

It has been estimated that there are probably over half a million alcoholics in Britain at the present time, although any estimate of figures relating to alcoholism is bound to be unreliable. Alcoholism is not notifiable, and only a small proportion of the people affected ever seek or receive treatment. While we cannot, therefore, gauge accurately the size of this particular problem, it is nevertheless a serious one, and the alcoholic presents difficulties not only as far as he himself is concerned but also to his family and the whole community. Alcoholism leads to absenteeism, unemployment, the incurring of debt and, possibly in consequence, to crime, and to general social decline. There is also a great deal of evidence to suggest that alcoholics are responsible for many accidents which occur on our roads, and they also help to swell the ranks of those arrested for drunkenness. In most, if not in all, of our large cities, there are to be found small groups of alcoholics who, in the final stages of degeneration, have come together, and are existing in the most deplorable and degrading circumstances.

Alcoholism can only begin with drinking, and it is for this reason

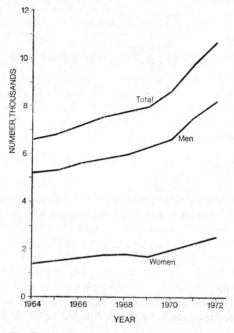

Fig. 7—Number of alcoholics by sex 1964–72

that the steep rise in convictions for drunkenness is viewed with concern, especially as this rise has been reflected by an increase in the number of established alcoholics (*see* Fig. 7). Many of the people convicted were young people under the age of 21, and more known alcoholics than before are in their twenties. (*see* Table XXVI).

Drinking is a form of retreatism in many respects, and the decline in the number of convictions for drunkenness which has occurred since the peak year of 1962 does not necessarily indicate a general improvement in the social conditions likely to favour retreatism.

*Table XXVI—Offences of Drunkenness in England and Wales,
1960–1973*

1960	1962	1964	1966	1968	1970	1972	1973
65,170	80,798	73,167	66,599	75,225	78,748	88,236	96,779

Source: *Annual Abstract of Statistics, 1974.*

Probably the most interesting factor in the study of drinking
behaviour is that, whilst the majority of adults in our society use
alcohol, and all are subjected to the same pressures in the form of
advertising and social attitudes towards drinking, most people are
able to control satisfactorily the amount of alcohol that they con-
sume. Relatively few become alcoholics. Dr Williams refers to
alcoholism as "a constitutional disease allied to a personality disorder," and regards the alcoholic as a person who is "intellectually
and physically adult but emotionally immature." Thus the person
who is unable to cope with the stresses and strains of life, either at
work or within his family, may use alcohol in the first place as
means of relieving his frustration and depression. If he continues
to do this over a period of time—this period varies from person
to person—he will eventually be compelled to drink because his
body will adapt itself so that it will require alcohol. It is on account
of the physical reactions produced after a certain amount of alcohol
has been consumed that alcoholism can be considered as a disease
with its own characteristic symptoms. If the alcoholic does not
receive treatment and advice while the disease is still in its early
stages, the chances of a recovery are slight.

Unfortunately the prevailing social attitude towards alcoholism
is one which encourages alcoholics to conceal their condition. By
the time the disease has progressed to the stage at which the individual is no longer able to do this, it is frequently too late for him
to benefit from any treatment. Fortunately our attitudes are beginning to change, although the change is slow, and we are gradually
learning to show more compassion towards those members of the
society who are in many ways inadequate.

That alcoholism is a symptom of inadequacy and incomplete
socialisation is becoming increasingly apparent. Investigations into
the home life and background of alcoholics all confirm that a

significant number have a history of broken homes during childhood, or have been brought up in emotionally unsatisfactory circumstances. Their parents were often extremely strict and domineering or else far too lenient and inclined to over-protect or spoil the children, so that, later in life, these children found themselves incapable of establishing normal, stable relationships with others. Their emotional immaturity and dependence frequently causes them to select "mother substitutes" or "father substitutes" as marriage partners.

However successful the treatment of the physical symptoms of alcoholism may be, no permanent cure will be brought about unless the patient can be given a great deal of emotional support in the form of functional alternatives to alcohol in times of stress. The alcoholic needs to be dependent on someone, whether that person is a doctor, a husband or wife, a social worker or a sponsor in an Alcoholics Anonymous group. Rehabilitation through group therapy has been found to be most successful amongst alcoholics who are extroverted and gregarious, and least successful amongst those who cannot tolerate any pressure put upon them to form continuous and intimate relationships with any number of other people.

All of this shows very clearly that since the responses of alcoholics are *superficially* similar, in order to cope with the problems they create, the personality of the individual displaying the symptoms has to be considered in isolation before a method of treatment can be devised.

CRIMINALITY

In this dicussion of anti-social or deviant behaviour, it has become apparent that the process of socialisation is of fundamental importance. During the socialisation process a very influential part is played by the *peer group*—the group of people who are looked upon by the individual as equal to and like himself and with whom he will identify himself—and the people who are particularly significant as far as the individual is concerned. These are the *significant others* to whom the individual refers and upon whose norms and attitudes his own standards are based.

Whilst anti-social behaviour is generally regarded as a type of non-conformity for which blame can be laid at the door of faulty or incomplete socialisation, this does not provide a complete theory of the nature of deviance. For example, if a sub-culture develops, it will produce norms and attitudes of its own, and a great deal of pressure may be put on individuals to conform to these even though they are at variance with the norms of the wider society. Thus, a person anxious to become identified with and part of a group which he regards as a peer group may deliberately set out to gain recognition by the group by copying the behaviour of its members. Adolescents may start smoking or drinking because they want to be treated as adults, and, for them, this behaviour symbolises adulthood; they may not wish to smoke or drink for the sake of any direct satisfaction they derive from doing so, and they may even find it unpleasant. Some youngsters may like or admire others who are members of a delinquent group, and they may commit offences in order to gain entry to that group. Within delinquent groups status and respect are achieved by means of committing "bigger and better" offences, and possibly by incurring heavier penalties as a result.

The fact that deviant roles may be learned in the same way that non-deviant roles are learned provides the basis of E. H. Sutherland's theory of *differential association*. Sutherland has suggested that people become criminals because they are in frequent contact with other criminals and therefore are more likely to adopt their behaviour patterns than those of non-criminals from whom they are largely isolated. This imitative element in behaviour was treated in a light-hearted way by the radio dramatist L. du Garde Peach, who used it as the theme of his comedy, *The White Sheep of the Family,* in which the nonconformity of one member of the family to the criminal behaviour of the rest caused them a considerable amount of consternation and worry.

Theories such as Sutherland's are valuable because they make a contribution to our understanding of the etiology of crime and deviance—that is the study of the causal factors involved in these phenomena—but they do not provide us with an explanation of its distribution. R. K. Merton has suggested that the distribution of crime reflects variations in the number of opportunities available within the society which enable individuals to achieve goals that are socially approved. He argues that crime rates are highest amongst the working classes in industrial areas, because the discrepancies are greatest in this case. Critics of Merton's theory have pointed out, however, that working-class people are more likely to be discovered if they commit offences, and their activities are more likely to be recorded officially, because they do not have the same opportunities to cover up their behaviour and use influence to keep themselves out of the courts as their middle- and upper-class counterparts.

These approaches to the study of deviance and delinquency are sociological and attempt to analyse the factors within society itself which are conducive to conformity as well as to deviance. Both of these elements are equally important if we are to reach a full understanding of the nature of the problems associated with deviance. However, as well as the sociological approaches, some recent research which has been carried out in Scotland and in maximum security hospitals in England has revived the controversy which originated with the constitutional theory of crime put forward by the Italian criminologist Lombroso.

Lombroso suggested that criminality is inborn, and is the result of atavistic reversion to an earlier evolutionary type; he regarded criminals as throwbacks to a more ape-like form of being. He also considered that there were basic hereditary flaws which in later generations could cause the deterioration in physique and behaviour which is frequently observable amongst criminals. Lombroso based his theory on the findings he obtained when he recorded the physical measurements of a large number of criminals. He claimed that there was a "criminal type" which could be recognised because the individuals concerned would possess at least five of the following "degenerative stigmata": a small cranium, projecting ears, a receding forehead, a thin upper lip, a plentiful head of hair but no beard, and certain actual defects of physique.

Lombroso's theory has been strongly criticised, particularly on the grounds that he did not have an adequate control group drawn from the non-criminal population with which he could make comparisons. His theory has been refuted by later students of criminology, and the idea of there being a distinguishable "criminal type" has largely been neglected as a result of the growing enthusiasm for psychological and sociological theories.

The revival of interest in the constitutional aspects of delinquency was occasioned by the discovery that there is a very suggestive parallel between abnormal results obtained when the electrical activity of the brain is studied by means of the electro-encephalograph (E.E.G.) and abnormal behaviour. For example, Sessions Hodge and Grey Walter made E.E.G. studies of 100 boys admitted to an approved school in 1950, and found that 84 per cent of them showed some abnormality. Hill, Stafford-Clark and Taylor reported to the Royal Commission on Capital Punishment (1949) that E.E.G.

abnormalities had been found in forty-four out of ninety-four murderers studied in this way. Whilst only a minority of those who had committed purely incidental or clearly motivated murders displayed these abnormalities, a majority of those who had committed apparently motiveless, sexual and other "abnormal" murders provided abnormal E.E.G. results.

More recently it has been found that a significant number of male offenders have abnormal chromosome patterns. Of the chromosomes present in the nucleus of every cell in the body, one pair determines the sex of the individual. The chromosome designated Y is responsible for maleness and that designated X for femaleness. The normal male has the genetic structure XY and the normal female XX. It has now been reliably established that a number of male prisoners have chromosome patterns XYY, XXYY or a combination of XY with XXYY. These men are characteristically over six feet in height, and they generally have a long history of delinquent behaviour which started at an early age, although they are not usually very skilled at committing crimes.

It is as yet too soon to assess fully the import of these constitutional studies. However, they do provide us with evidence which suggests that there is a hard core of delinquents in the society whose behaviour is quite involuntary. Any attempts to repress this behaviour or to rehabilitate the offenders are unlikely to achieve even the slightest success. It would clearly be both unethical and inhumane to punish these unfortunate individuals, and it would also be wasteful of energy and resources to try to reform them.

The complexity of deviance is such that the search for systematic theories to explain it has largely been abandoned. It is now generally acknowledged that an understanding of the nature of deviance is more likely to be reached if emphasis is placed not on the formulation of a single general theory but upon the causal factors involved. Since, in any given case or group of cases, a number of causal factors—some major and some minor or contributory—are certain to be operative, there is nothing to be gained by studying any one in isolation from the rest. Those who are concerned with the problems of deviance will therefore advisedly adopt a *multi-factorial approach* in which the constitutional, psychological and sociological aspects of this particular phenomenon are all taken into consideration and related to each other.

The Control of Deviance

Whilst deviance itself is a very complex phenomenon, attitudes towards the treatment and control of deviance are no less so. We continue to use the words "punishment" and "penal" in connection with the treatment of delinquents, and, as a result, the real nature of the subject is obscured. The punitive elements in treatment are important, but these are by no means the only factors involved which influence our attitudes towards offenders. A number of motives—deterrence, retribution, prevention, reformation, restitution and expiation—are to be discerned, and these are not all punitive. When we are faced with a real situation rather than a philosophical or academic exercise, these different motives are not usually separated from each other in our minds, and we tend therefore to respond to the particular situations in a rather confused and illogical manner. Where our emotions are concerned it is not always easy to disentangle fact from fantasy and analyse a situation in an objective way.

The way in which delinquents are treated does, however, require a rational approach to the problems they present both to the society as a whole and also as far as they are themselves affected as individuals. In the past, penal policy tended to alter in response to changes in social and economic pressures put upon the policy makers, and did not reflect progressive changes in attitudes engendered by a growing knowledge of the nature and causes of crime.

Durkheim argued that as a society moved towards *organic* stability, based on division of labour, and away from *mechanical* solidarity, based on similarity of function, its attitudes towards the treatment of criminals would necessarily become concerned more with restitution than with punishment alone. With restitution, the criminal is expected to compensate his victim for the damage that has been done to him. Social anthropologists have found that, in small, primitive communities where personal interests are directly and clearly involved, restitution is the most important element in penal actions.

More recently, Rusche and Kirchheimer have put forward an explanation of penal attitudes based simply on economic considerations (*Punishment and Social Structure* (1939)). In their view, when labour is in plentiful supply, the reactions to crime will be almost entirely punitive, but, when it is harder to come by, more constructive attitudes will prevail and the labour force will be increased by making productive use of criminal labour. This could explain why, in the past, offenders were put to work as galley-slaves, or, nearer our own times, prisoners were transported to Botany Bay and other territories to fill the demand for labour, which was created by growing colonialism. As free labour became more readily available in these areas, the practice of deporting convicts declined, but, as there was also a plentiful supply of labour in this country, prisoners had no productive use at home either. It therefore became accepted that they would be kept in close confinement on a meagre subsistence diet, without being given anything constructive to do. These conditions remained virtually unchanged until the early years of the present century.

Men, women and children, whatever the nature of their offence, all used to be treated in the same way. The first reformers attempted to improve the prisoners' conditions by agitating for separate accommodation to be provided for women and children, being primarily motivated by a strong sense of moral rectitude derived from their religious beliefs. They were mostly concerned about the ways in which the overcrowded conditions in the prisons fostered sexual licence and corruption, and, with few exceptions, they were generally more interested in reforming the prisons than the prisoners.

During the nineteenth century, a new penal philosophy began to make its influence felt, and the idea that prisoners should be kept apart from each other gradually became accepted. The main feature of the prisons built during the middle period of the century was the provision of separate cells in which it was possible to isolate offenders from each other. Solitary confinement was regarded as a deterrent in these institutions, and when prisoners were brought together to work, or for exercise, strict silence was observed. To strengthen the deterrent nature of the new penal system, useless and monotonous forms of toil were devised, such as the "treadmill," since the principle of preventing the prisoners from communicating with each other ruled out the possibility of providing a workshop and more constructive forms of employment.

When Dickens visited the United States in 1842, he was taken to see the house of correction in South Boston which had served as one of the models for the new British system of separate confinement, and in his *American Notes* he wrote:

"America, as a new and not over-populated country, has in all her prisons, the one great advantage, of being enabled to find useful and profitable work for the inmates; whereas, with us, . . . honest men who have not offended against the laws are frequently doomed to seek employment in vain. . . .

. . . our best prisons would seem at the first glance to be better conducted than those in America. The treadmill is conducted with little or no noise; five hundred men may pick oakum in the same room, without a sound; and both kinds of labour admit of such keen and vigilant superintendence, as will render even a word of personal communication amongst the prisoners almost impossible. On the other hand, the noise of the loom, the forge, the carpenter's hammer, or the stonemason's saw, greatly favour those opportunities of intercourse—hurried and brief no doubt, but opportunities still—which these several kinds of work, by rendering it necessary for men to be employed very near to each other, and often side by side, without any barrier or partition between them, in their very nature present. . . . In an American state prison or house of correction, I found it difficult at first to persuade myself that I was really in a jail: a place of ignominious punishment and endurance. And to this hour I very much question whether the humane boast that it is not like one, has its root in the true wisdom or philosophy of the matter."

Support for the new "separate system" grew rapidly, and at the same time there was a movement towards centralisation and uniformity within the penal system. In 1877 the control of all prisons was placed in the hands of the Prison Commission, which was set up to administer the national policy, and Edmund du Cane was appointed to be its first chairman. Du Cane was an able administrator, and under his guidance a very rigid system was introduced and enforced throughout the country. Detailed schemes for the treatment and discipline of prisoners were drawn up, and isolation and unconstructive hard labour became the order of the day.

Du Cane remained chairman of the Prison Commission for just over twenty years, and during this period he assumed increasing influence, until the rigidity and lack of sensitivity to the human aspects of imprisonment drew a number of attacks from the press. As a result, in 1895, a Departmental Committee on Prisons (the Gladstone Committee) carried out an enquiry into the whole system and recommended that:

". . . the system should be made more elastic, more capable of being adapted to the special cases of individual prisoners; that prison discipline should be more effectually designed to maintain, stimulate or awaken the higher susceptibilities of prisoners, to develop their moral instincts, to train them in orderly and industrious habits and whenever possible, to turn them out of prison better men and women physically and morally than when they came in."

The Gladstone Committee urged that changes be made immediately and that the standardised pattern which had been developed should be replaced by a system which took into consideration the individuality of the prisoners. In consequence, the twentieth century saw the introduction of a more progressive attitude towards penal policy. Two new trends were to be observed within the prison system which are still being developed at the present time. The first was concerned with the classification of offenders and the provision of different forms of treatment for the various classes; the second was the movement away from the idea that imprisonment was the only solution to the problem of criminal behaviour.

Ruggles-Brise succeeded du Cane as Chairman of the Prison Commission, and he not only furthered the development of a more flexible and individualistic treatment of adult offenders, but also took a particular interest in adolescents. He had the idea of setting up special training establishments for youthful offenders, and, after some early experiments at Bedford Prison had produced satisfactory results, a new type of institution was developed to deal with them. The first of these new institutions was founded at Borstal in Kent, and this small village gave its name to the system of dealing with adolescent offenders which has become famous throughout the world.

In 1908 the *Prevention of Crimes Act* made provision for the extension of the borstal system, and also introduced *preventive detention*, the aim of which was the protection of the public against the habitual criminal who seemed to be completely incapable of responding to any treatment. Under the *Criminal Justice Act*, 1961, the law now provides two types of sentence for persistent offenders. *Preventive detention* may be imposed only on people aged 30 and over who are found guilty of an offence which is punishable by at least two years' imprisonment and who have had at least three similar convictions since the age of 17. People over the age of 21 may be sentenced to *corrective training* if they have been convicted of an offence punishable by imprisonment for at least two years and have had two similar convictions since they were 17.

The *Probation of Offenders Act* of 1907 put on a proper footing the work which had for some time been carried out by the Church of England Temperance Society. The Society's workers, who were known as Court Missionaries, had attempted to prevent first offenders from being brought into contact with more hardened criminals in the prisons by attempting reform and rehabilitation on an informal basis. Until the 1907 Act was passed the Court Missionaries had no official status, but from 1887 magistrates had been permitted to recommend that, in suitable cases, the sentences of first offenders be suspended to enable the missionaries to work with them in the hope of keeping them from committing further misdemeanours.

Probation is now a well-established part of our penal system, and is the only means the society has of rehabilitating offenders without sending them to an institution. It has been estimated that the cost of putting a person on probation is less than one-twentieth that of keeping him in prison. While cost may not be the only factor for consideration, and clearly we cannot expect prisons and other penal establishments to become redundant, there is a strong case to be made for improving the probation service. Effective alternatives to imprisonment are not only more economical but generally more desirable, since they help to reduce the risk of contamination by more serious offenders. Also, despite all the money and effort that has been devoted to it, the prison system is still grossly overcrowded, and this militates against any radical overhaul and reform of the prisons themselves. Between 1962 and 1972, the daily average population in our prisons increased from 31,000 to 38,300. It is therefore a matter of some urgency to reduce the number by all possible means, because a system which has to cope with too many offenders with inadequate facilities may well create more problems than it solves. It is quite impossible to keep such a large number of prisoners fully and usefully employed, and lengthy periods of enforced idleness will almost inevitably make them less fit for work when they are released.

Pauline Morris, who undertook a survey of prisoners and their dependants, has, in *Prisoners and their Families* (1965), pointed out that:

"The experience of imprisonment does not occur in isolation for a man with a family, and the prison wall can never be a complete barrier to the emotional currents which flow between a man and his wife and children. Too often in prison work, the family is thought of as some external appendage, remote and irrelevant to the processes of treatment and training, rather than as a continuous influence upon the man in custody. For the family, the sense of isolation from the prison world is often greater than the isolation of the prisoner from the world outside. He has newspapers, radio and often television to keep him in touch; wives and children see little of the prison world save what is glimpsed during brief visits. . . . The families of prisoners, like those of mental patients, suffer disabilities which stem from situations which they themselves have not, for the most part, brought about. Their condition of less eligibility for social support ought to be a moral affront to an affluent civilized society. But more than that, every stress suffered by such families weakens the family and increases the likelihood of other family members, especially the children, becoming social casualties, thus adding not only to the charge upon the community but to the sum of human unhappiness."

The desirability of keeping as many offenders as possible out of prison, and, by means of other forms of supervision, assisting them to earn their own living and remain in contact with their families, is quite obvious, particularly when it is remembered that a considerable number of people who are sent to prison each year to serve short-term sentences are more of a nuisance than a serious menace to the society.

Where juveniles and young people are concerned, the penal system has been considerably altered during the present century. At first there was a general movement towards keeping these offenders out of the prisons as far as possible, and we are now attempting to establish new ways of dealing with juveniles which will also keep them out of the courts except in the most serious circumstances. The main emphasis is placed on rehabilitation and the prevention of further offences. The minimum age for committal to prison is now 17, and even then a court cannot send anyone to prison under the age of 21 unless it establishes that there is no other appropriate treatment available. Any prison sentence that is imposed must be either of less than six months or of over three years.

In April 1968 a Government white paper, *Children in Trouble*, was published, which set out specific proposals for changing legislation for dealing with young offenders. The aim of the envisaged changes was:

". . . to increase the effectiveness of the measures available to deal with juvenile delinquency. Effectiveness means helping children whose behaviour is unacceptable to grow up, to develop personal relationships and to accept their responsibilities towards their fellows, so that they become mature members of society; in some cases it also means firm control of anti-social behaviour. In order to achieve this aim, it is necessary to develop further our facilities of observation and assessment, and to increase the variety of facilities for continuing treatment, both residential and non-residential. Increased flexibility is needed so as to make it easier to vary the treatment when changed circumstances or fuller diagnosis suggest the need for a different approach. Organisational changes are also desirable so as to provide a setting for closer co-operation between the services concerned."

In 1969 the *Children and Young Persons Act* was passed and it came into effect in January 1971. Under this Act, many of the responsibilities for young offenders passed from the Home Office to the children's departments of local authorities. Magistrates no longer have the power to send delinquents to approved schools, and young offenders are now committed to the care of a local authority. They may remain with their parents, be sent to live with foster parents or be placed in a community school, according to what is considered most appropriate in each case. Approved schools were abolished under the Act, and the new community schools that have replaced them provide care for all types of children in need, not only those who have committed an offence.

It is too early at this stage to make any assessment of how the new legislation is working, although considerable anxiety is already being expressed that the "softer" approach to delinquents may be encouraging them to think that they can "get away with it" when they commit an offence. Certainly, the crime rates amongst juveniles are still increasing steadily, and should not be viewed with complacence.

The new methods for dealing with young offenders, however, throw a very considerable burden on to the local authorities, and in many areas they have neither the staff nor the facilities to cope with the influx of children that are now being added to those already in care. It could therefore well be the case that the new legislation is not as effective as was hoped, not because the legislation itself was ill-conceived, but because as yet the agencies that have to implement it do not have adequate resources available to them.

In recognising the importance of the treatment of offenders as individuals, and particularly the role that the treatment of juveniles can play in our attempts to control and reduce anti-social behaviour within the community as a whole, we have made considerable progress during this century. However, crime figures continue to rise, as do the figures relating to other forms of deviance and retreatism. The more progress that is made, the further the horizon appears to recede, and it would seem that the society itself, for a variety of reasons, is placing increasingly intolerable pressures on the individual. There is a very obvious lack of any common feeling of objective and purpose, and people are finding it more and more difficult to find a satisfactory answer to the questions "Why am I here?", "What am I doing?" and "Where am I going?" This uncertainty produces symptoms of disorder and disorganisation within the community, and this in turn is reflected in the growing number of social casualties in the form of deviants and delinquents who can find no satisfactory *functional alternatives* through which they can express themselves and find relief from feelings of tension.

The Committee on Children and Young Persons summed up the situation in their report (1960):

"During the past fifty years there has been a tremendous material, social and moral revolution in addition to the upheaval of two wars. While life has in many ways become easier and more secure, the whole future of mankind may seem frighteningly uncertain. Everyday life may be less of a struggle, boredom and lack of challenge more of a danger, but the fundamental insecurity remains with little the individual can do about it. The material revolution is plain to see. At one and the same time it has provided more desirable objects, greater opportunities for acquiring them illegally, and considerable chances of immunity from the undesirable consequences of so doing. It is not always so clearly recognised what a complete change there has been in social and personal relationships (between classes, between the sexes and between individuals) and also in the basic assumptions which regulate behaviour. These major changes in the cultural background may well have replaced the disturbances of war as factors which contribute in themselves to instability within the family. In such a climate it is no wonder that many young people are bewildered or that some parents become uncertain what standards they should insist on or what ideals they should put before their children. It is more a matter of surprise that so few young people get into real trouble and that there are, on the whole, so few families which break down or otherwise fail their children. It seems probable, however, that those families which have themselves failed to achieve a stable and satisfactory family life will be the most vulnerable, and that the children brought up in them will be those most likely to succumb to whatever adverse influences there may be in the outside world."

EXERCISE 15

1. What can sociological study contribute to an understanding of any *two* of the following: drug addiction; suicide; delinquency; illegitimacy; strikes? (*A.E.B.*)

2. "The fact that the behaviour of young people differs from that of adults does not justify the conclusion that there is a distinctive 'youth culture.'" Explain and discuss. (*A.E.B.*)

3. *Either*: (*a*) "Researchers have, in general, failed to account for the fact that crime is mainly a characteristic of young males." Discuss.

Or: (*b*) What light can sociological researches throw on the causes of crime and delinquency? (*A.E.B.*)

4. "The behaviour of a non-conformist is not necessarily deviant behaviour." Explain and discuss.

5. What social factors contribute to the development of a *sub-culture*? Illustrate your answer with references to any one sub-culture which exists in Britain at the present time.

6. Assess the importance of *peer groups* in the process of socialisation.

7. Outline any two theories of criminality, and examine the value of their contribution to our understanding of criminal behaviour.

8. Examine the changes which have taken place in the treatment of offenders during the last hundred years.

9. "The use of the words 'punishment' and 'penal' in connection with the treatment of delinquents tends to obscure its real nature and purpose." Discuss.

10. What evidence is there that juvenile delinquency is a serious social problem in Britain today? (*Oxford*)

11. What is "crime"? Is there any evidence to indicate that crime is increasing? (*Oxford*)

12. In what ways can clinical and statistical studies of delinquency complement each other? Discuss this in the light of examples of each kind of study. (*London*)

13. *Either*: (*a*) Retribution and reform are the horns of society's dilemma in framing its penal system. Critically examine possible ways of resolving this dilemma.

Or: (*b*) Would it be accurate to say that "the real problem in dealing with young offenders is the inadequacy or absence at present, of facilities for treatment"? (*London*)

FOR FURTHER READING

M. E. Wolfgang and F. Ferracuti. *The Subculture of Violence*. Tavistock, 1967.

Pauline Morris. *Prisoners and their Families*. Allen and Unwin, 1965.

Erwin Stengal. *Suicide and Attempted Suicide*. Penguin Books, 1964.

M. M. Glatt *et al*. *The Drug Scene in Great Britain*. Edward Arnold, 1967.

Drug Addiction. Office of Health Economics, 1967.

N. Kessel and H. Walton. *Alcoholism*. Penguin Books, 1965.

Lincoln Williams. *Alcoholism Explained*. Evans Brothers, 1967.

Children in Trouble. H.M.S.O., 1968.

Sewell Stokes. *Our Dear Delinquents*. Heinemann, 1965.

D. J. West. *The Young Offender*. Penguin Books, 1967.

Mary Morse. *The Unattached*. Penguin Books, 1965.

T. R. Fyvel. *The Insecure Offenders: Rebellious Youth in the Welfare State*. Penguin Books, 1963.

David M. Downes. *The Delinquent Solution*. Routledge and Kegan Paul, 1966.

M. Wolff. *The Prison System in Britain*. Eyre and Spottiswoode, 1967.

M. Philipson. *Sociological Aspects of Crime and Delinquency*. Routledge and Kegan Paul, 1971.

W. G. Carson and P. Wiles. *Crime and Delinquency in Britain*. Robertson, 1971.

CHAPTER XVI

COMMUNICATIONS AND THE
MASS MEDIA

MOST of our working hours are spent communicating either directly
or indirectly with each other. If we are not actually transmitting or
receiving messages in the form of speech either amongst a group of
friends, in the classroom, or in the office, factory or shop, we may
be listening to the radio, watching television, reading newspapers
or books, or writing down the ideas that we want to pass on to someone else. We have moved a long way since the days when speech
was virtually the only means of communication, but, despite man's
long history, almost everything which is associated with large-scale
communication has been developed within a relatively short period.
Until the nineteenth century, such books and journals as were
printed by hand were the privileged reading of the wealthy and the
educated—a very small minority of the people.

The invention of the steam press, which enabled printing to be
done at speed, started a revolutionary process in communications,
and this process is still continuing today. The development of the
telegraph and telephone, cameras and projectors, the microphone
and broadcasting, television and communications satellites have all
helped to change, for better or worse, the whole aspect of life. Not
only is what happens in one part of the country known almost
immediately to the people in every other part, but also we are kept
constantly aware of what is happening throughout the world. For
this reason the dimensions and perspectives of our lives are continually altering. The way in which we think and live is being
modified all the time as our access to information, education and
entertainment is increased.

The development of the machinery of communications has, however, created new problems at the same time that it has brought
many benefits. All forms of mass communication are extremely
expensive to provide, and they can only be maintained if they
attract a very large audience. In some countries they are provided
as a state enterprise, in which case the population is subjected to
and conditioned by the policies of its ruling élite, and in others they
are dependent upon advertising and commercial interests. This is

just as dangerous, since, in order to attract as wide an audience as possible, advertisers will have to pander to the majority, and neglect the needs of the highly educated and more thoughtful element in the community. It is most unusual for any of the various media of communications to be kept apart from both political and commercial influence, and we are fortunate that in Britain most of our sound radio and much of our television is organised as a public service through the British Broadcasting Corporation.

Much of what is published, televised and broadcast is undoubtedly of great value, and many people have been stimulated into following new interests as a result of having attractive paperback books so readily available and watching programmes of high quality on television. Many subjects and pleasures which used to be experienced and appreciated by only a small minority are now gaining a much wider audience as a result of the increased publicity that is given to them.

Against such advantages, however, we have to balance the disadvantages that result from the necessary standardisation which inevitably occurs in any form of mass production, whether it be of cars and furniture or entertainment and education. Because of the economic factors which are of fundamental importance, there is a very real risk that this standardisation will mean a process of levelling down rather than of levelling up. Purveyors of mass communication are bound to take popular demand into consideration when they are planning what to provide, or else they must use professional skill and expertise first to create a popular demand and then to satisfy it, and this can be very costly.

There are two possible alternatives open to the society in how it uses the channels of mass communication available. Either we can use these channels to produce a "cultural democracy," or we can use them in such a way that a "cultural class system" emerges. The problem of deciding whether we want a genuine democracy with all that this implies, or a high-brow versus low-brow class system, is one which cannot satisfactorily be solved. Because we cannot solve the problem, as in so many other areas where there is a conflict between aims and interests, we have to attempt to reach some form of compromise. This is certain, at times, to provoke controversy and dissension of the kind with which we are all so familiar today.

It is therefore both interesting and important to analyse the progress that we have made in attempting to reach a satisfactory compromise in Britain. We can then better understand how our beliefs and attitudes are likely to be influenced by, or, perhaps, how they will themselves help to influence, the multiplicity of communications media which are available to us.

Newspapers and the Press

The people of Britain are the most newspaper-conscious people in the world. In proportion to the size of our population we read more newspapers than any other nation at the same stage of almost total literacy, but this does not mean that our reading is very varied. Both our national and our local newspapers have been considerably reduced in number since the First World War, so that, as our overall readership increased, we came to concentrate on fewer papers (*see* Table XXVII).

Table XXVII—The Number of Daily Papers in England, Wales and Scotland

	1921	1948	1966	1974
National morning	13	10	10	9
Provincial—morning and evening	130	100	93	90
London evening	4	3	2	2
Sundays—national and provincial	21	16	13	13

The main reason why a newspaper may be forced to cease publication is, ironically, the same one which encourages us to read the number of papers that we do—they are very inexpensive to buy. Newspapers are not, however, cheap to produce and distribute, and the selling price to the public is only kept as low as it is because advertisers are prepared to pay heavily to use this medium to reach the millions of potential customers which readers represent (*see* Table XXVIII). No newspaper could survive without advertisers, as was shown by the closure of the *News Chronicle* in 1960. Over a million copies of that paper were sold each day, but large sums of money were lost because the advertisers would not buy space, and so the paper was forced to close down.

Without the presence of advertisers, a paper could be kept in existence only if it were either state sponsored and supported or else heavily subsidised. The implications of control of this sort are obvious, and, as a nation which jealously guards the right to a free

Table XXVIII—Newspapers: Percentage of Total Revenue Attributable to Sales and Advertising

Class of publication	Sales %	Advertising %
National mornings—quality	25	73
—popular	54	45
National Sundays —quality	21	79
—popular	51	46
London evenings	38	61
Provincial mornings	41	58
Provincial evenings	37	62
Provincial weeklies	21	79

Source: Report of the Royal Commission on the Press, 1962.

press, we would naturally be unwilling to have our newspapers controlled by a central agency.

THE FREEDOM OF THE PRESS

The fact that we have no direct censorship does not mean that there is complete freedom of the press in Britain at all times. During the First and Second World Wars, for example, censorship was applied in order to ensure that the enemy did not come into possession of information which might have proved useful. On the other hand, even during peacetime, some form of censorship is needed to protect official secrets and documents, and, since the passing of the *Official Secrets Act* of 1911, the freedom of the press has always been limited to some extent. Section 2 of this Act makes it an offence to communicate or receive secret or confidential information. Although the main purpose of the Act was to prevent espionage, it also had the effect of curtailing the reporting of certain items which could be regarded as matters of national concern. These include the provision of detailed information about military equipment and coverage of espionage trials.

In 1920 a further *Official Secrets Act* made it the legal duty of every person to give any information which he possessed relating to offences, or suspected offences, under that Act and the one of 1911. Journalists feared that, under Section 6 of the 1920 Act, they could be compelled to disclose the sources of any information they obtained which was covered by the *Official Secrets Acts*. The fact that there is a certain amount of ambiguity about the news that ought, or ought not, to be printed has presented reporters with some problems. For example, in 1962 a Tribunal of Inquiry was set up to investigate the case of the spy William Vassall, and the way in which this case had been handled by the press. Brendan Mulholland, a journalist who had written an article on Vassall for the *Daily Mail*, was asked by the Tribunal to state where he had obtained the information he included in the closing paragraphs of the article. This he refused to do, as did Reginald Foster, another journalist who was questioned by the Tribunal. Later proceedings were taken against both men in the High Court, and they were sentenced to a term of imprisonment.

In an attempt to clarify the situation the Services, Press and Broadcasting Committee was established. This committee, which consists of government officials and representatives of the press, radio and television, is an advisory body with the task of ensuring that defence secrets are not published. It is this committee which issues the Defence ("D") Notices to editors, advising them of the items of news that the defence officials regard as secret and asking them not to make these publicly known. The "D" Notice system has no legal sanctions to enforce it, and only provides for a voluntary form of censorship. However, editors rarely disregard a "D" Notice, since to do so might cause charges to be brought against a newspaper under the *Official Secrets Acts*.

The main difficulty encountered under the present system is that newspapers frequently find that their ability to provide the public with information is considerably restricted in cases where it would be desirable for this information to be made known. For example, the mishandling of a situation by a government department or the serious inefficiency of certain officials might be kept from public knowledge and scrutiny by claiming that the information is "confidential." If too broad an interpretation is put on the notion of "official secrets," the freedom of the press to inform the public and to appraise government actions will be undermined.

The press is jealous of its freedom, and rightly so, but the liberties of the individual must also be safeguarded. Certain standards of integrity and decency have to be maintained by journalists if they are to respect the privacy and rights of members of the public. Following upon the recommendations made by the Royal Commission on the Press in 1949, the Press Council was first established as a voluntary body in 1953. Ten years later, in 1963, it was re-established as a statutory body with an independent chairman and

INTRODUCTION TO SOCIOLOGY

with a fifth of its members drawn from amongst laymen. The purposes of the Press Council include the investigation of complaints from individuals or groups of the general public who feel that their affairs have been mishandled, as well as the preservation of the freedom of the press. The findings of all investigations undertaken by the Press Council are published.

THE FUNCTIONS OF THE PRESS

The dissemination of news and the printing of advertisements are not the only functions of the press. Editors have also to take into consideration the role of newspapers as a medium for education and entertainment, and it is on the basis of the relative emphasis which is placed upon the different aspects—news, education and entertainment—that the papers may be classified as *quality* or *popular*. The quality newspapers are not merely skimmed through by their readers and then discarded, but are generally closely studied and used for reference by people who demand a great deal from them. Of course, these papers also make demands upon their readers because the information is not set out in such a way that it can be casually collected by being read at a glance as it is in the popular press.

Table XXIX—Newspapers: Approximate Percentage Distribution of Space Allocated to Material Other than Advertising

Newspaper	News	Features and miscellaneous material	Pictures
News of the World	67	27	6
People	52	35	13
Sunday Mirror	50	26	24
Daily Mirror	45	26	29
Sunday Express	40	40	20
Daily Express	62	20	18
Daily Mail	55	19·5	25·5
Sun	48	35	17
Daily Telegraph	61	25	14
Sunday Times	50	36	14
Observer	49	40	11
Sunday Telegraph	55	31	14
Guardian	64	26	10
Times	74	15	11

Source: Roger Manvell. *This Age of Communication.*

Table XXX—Newspapers: Approximate Percentage
Distribution of News

Newspaper	Political, social, economic, arts	Personalities	Disaster and crime	Sport
News of the World	20	5	36	39
People	13	4	38	45
Sunday Mirror	25	11	13	51
Daily Mirror	31	17	14	38
Sunday Express	43	11	11	35
Daily Express	38	3	17	42
Daily Mail	45	8	12	35
Sun	51·5	19	9·5	20
Daily Telegraph	57	5	3·5	34·5
Sunday Times	61	9	1	29
Observer	71	6	1	22
Sunday Telegraph	64	3	2	31
Guardian	70	1	1	28
Times	70	6	1	23

Source: Roger Manvell. *This Age of Communication.*

Tables XXIX and XXX show quite clearly why it is important that editors should consider the nature as well as the number of their readers. It is obvious that people expect the newspapers which they read to satisfy very different requirements, and the person who reads *The Times* concentrates much more upon the political, economic and cultural aspects of the news than does the reader of the *Daily Mirror*, who is as interested in the more sensational aspects of crimes, disasters and personalities as he is in serious matters. The difference between the Sunday quality and popular papers is even more marked, and readers of the latter clearly prefer being entertained to being educated.

A great deal of interest has been shown—particularly by advertisers, to whom it is of importance—in the social class and occupational background of readers. According to the Institute of Practitioners in Advertising the adult population of this country has been divided as shown on page 386 and following this classification Table XXXI shows how the readership of our national newspapers is distributed.

The most popular papers of all, according to circulation figures,

Grade	Social status	Estimated percentage of adult population
A	Upper middle class ⎱	
B	Middle class ⎰	12
C1	Lower middle class	22
C2	Skilled working class	31
D	Working class ⎱	
E	Lowest subsistence level, *e.g.* some old-age pensioners ⎰	35

are the *Daily Mirror*, the *News of the World*, the *People* and the *Sunday Mirror*, and these certainly attract the largest proportion of their readers from people with a working-class background. (*See* Table XXXI.) It is a fallacy to believe that the popular press is followed only by working-class readers and the quality press only by members of the upper classes. The papers which have the largest

Table XXXI—The Social Grade of Adult Readers of National Newspapers

(Percentage of adults in each social grade)

Newspaper	A	B	C1	C2	D	E
Daily Mirror	7	13	26	42	42	24
Sun	6	9	21	36	37	16
Daily Express	22	24	27	21	19	20
Daily Mail	14	15	17	11	10	10
Daily Telegraph	37	25	13	4	3	2
Daily Record	1	2	3	5	6	4
The Times	20	10	4	1	1	1
Guardian	11	8	5	1	1	*
The Financial Times	12	6	3	1	1	*
Any national daily	83	77	77	79	77	63
News of the World	9	15	28	47	52	33
Sunday Mirror	8	17	28	41	38	19
Sunday People	8	14	26	38	39	27
Sunday Express	47	41	36	22	15	17
Sunday Post	5	8	10	12	13	13
Sunday Times	44	28	14	6	3	2
Observer	20	16	10	4	2	1
Sunday Mail	2	2	5	7	7	5
Sunday Telegraph	23	14	8	3	2	1
Any Sunday paper	88	86	86	89	87	74

Source: JICNARS *National Readership Survey, July 1973–June 1974.*

circulation figures attract readers from a whole cross-section of the community and may therefore be regarded as generally popular, whilst the smaller readerships of quality papers similarly cut across class groupings. It therefore would appear that the choice of newspaper is not entirely governed by the educational level, social background or occupation of readers, but reflects instead the attitudes of readers towards a newspaper and their different conceptions of its functions.

Broadly speaking, the people who choose the popular papers require entertainment more than do the readers of the quality papers, and they prefer to have the news presented to them in a way that is quickly and easily assimilated. As a result, the popular press is less likely to create or alter public opinion directly, and more likely simply to reflect the views of its readers. At times, the influence of the popular press on social matters may be considerable where serious news items can be seen by readers to have obvious personal and emotional implications to which they respond immediately, sometimes strongly enough to demand that some action be taken by those in authority. But, as Roger Manvell has remarked in *This Age of Communication*: "The popular press . . . like its readers is more interested in personalities than in policies, in events than evaluations."

The quality papers, on the other hand, may have considerable power politically, economically and socially. The sources of information, expert knowledge and advice which they have developed in order to satisfy the demands of their general readers are also available to people in positions of authority. Through their correspondence columns they are also able to provide an indication of the views and reactions of the more serious and thoughtful members of the public. Collectively, they provide an invaluable forum for debate and are important "sounding boards" for the opinions of national leaders. The functions of the popular and the quality newspapers are therefore somewhat different.

The approach of the popular papers is largely subjective, whilst that of the quality papers is more objective, appealing to the intellect rather than to the emotions. Although the combined circulation figures of *The Times*, the *Daily Telegraph* and the *Guardian* are less than half the figure of the *Daily Mirror*, the influence of the quality papers is out of all proportion to the number of copies sold each day. The chief aim of the popular press today would seem to be to put over in a stimulating and often sensational way the anticipated or potential viewpoint of the relatively uninformed man in the street. It is well known that, in contrast to this, people in executive positions and those who hold political power and responsibility rely heavily upon the information which is contained within the pages of the quality newspapers, and they pay considerable attention to the manner in which their activities and ideas are reported and commented upon by the more serious journalists.

We have already noted that a major source of revenue of newspapers is provided by advertising (*see* Table XXVIII). During the last few years, the popular newspapers have suffered as a result of the relatively greater flow of advertising to commercial television. The latter may be regarded as being in direct competition with the newspapers, and the growth of this form of communication has had a considerable impact on the press. Of recent years, expenditure on advertising as a percentage of the gross domestic product has remained constant, but the proportion attracted by the national daily newspapers has dropped. This has affected the popular newspapers more than the quality papers, since advertisers wishing to promote commodities with a mass appeal see commercial television as a better medium than the press. Goods and services advertised in the quality papers tend to have a more limited appeal, and for this reason there is nothing to be gained from transferring to television, which is considerably more expensive. This means, however, that the economic viability of the popular press has been seriously threatened, and, so long as the present system of financing our newspapers is continued, the welfare of the whole industry is at stake. Several important national newspapers are experiencing financial difficulties at present and may be forced to close unless some far-reaching changes are introduced very soon.

Statistics show that it is not only the advertisers who regard television as an alternative to newspapers. Some former readers do as well and the overall number of copies of national daily newspapers sold shows signs of shrinking. It is significant that it is the popular press which has suffered most as a result of the decline, and since 1960 the quality papers have actually been expanding their circulation and increasing their share of the total market. In 1950 the quality daily papers' share of the national circulation was 8·2 per cent, by 1960 it had increased to 10·5 per cent and by 1974 it was about 15 per cent. The growth of the quality week-end papers' share of circulation has been even more spectacular, rising from 3·2 per cent of the total in 1950 to 16·5 per cent in 1974.

This seems surprising at first, but the quality papers may have achieved their improved circulation figures as a result of changing their standards, if not lowering them, and also by introducing the coloured magazine supplements as a means of challenging the movement of advertising towards commercial television. It may well be true, also, that the quality papers still are able to satisfy the need for information of a type that is largely outside the field of television, particularly commercial television, which at all times has to consider the size of its audience. Television has certain limitations, despite its many attractions, as a medium of communications. It is very much a "once-for-all" medium in which pictures and words are purely transitory, and have little use as reference material. Scientific developments have made it possible for television programmes to be recorded on video-tape machines, but these are not yet so cheap as to be widely available. The general viewer still cannot set his own pace, or pause to give extra attention to items he selects himself.

The information given on television tends to be brief and at times even superficial, because it is aimed at such a wide and varied audience, and much that is of importance has of necessity to be omitted by the programme editors. Although the "magazine" type of programme can examine a selected range of topics in greater depth than is possible in news broadcasts, it is interesting to note that if the editorial matter contained in one issue of the *Sunday Times* were to be read aloud on television at least twenty hours of viewing time would be required.

The newspapers, particularly the quality papers, now tend to concentrate on those areas in which television cannot, or does not, provide an adequate service. They give a much broader coverage of the news, and offer more in the way of analysis, comment and features. The popular papers are now noticeably more serious in their approach and style today than they were at the beginning of the 1960s, although they do not give the same expression of minority views as do the quality papers, which regard this as an important function.

A major difference between television (and sound broadcasting) and the newspapers as channels for disseminating news and views, which is of considerable importance where the *political* influence of the two media is compared, is their relative impartiality. According to the charters which control the operation of the broadcasting corporations, the onus on television and sound broadcasting is that they should remain impartial and as a result, they tend to be

o

Table XXXII—The General Political Tendency, Control and Circulation of the National Newspapers

Title	General political tendency	Controlled by	Circulation average Jan–June 1973
The Times	Independent	The Thomson Organisation Ltd.	345,044
Daily Telegraph	Conservative	Daily Telegraph Ltd.	1,423,031
Guardian	Independent	Guardian Newspapers Ltd.	344,356
Daily Express	Independent; stresses importance of British Commonwealth	Beaverbrook Newspapers Ltd.	3,296,988
Daily Mail	Independent	Associated Newspapers Ltd.	1,703,215
Sun	Left of centre	News International Ltd.	2,931,466
Morning Star	Communist	People's Press Printing Society Ltd.	49,241
Daily Mirror	Left of centre	International Publishing Corporation Ltd.	4,261,683
The Financial Times	Independent	Pearson Longman Ltd.	194,651
Observer	Independent	The Observer Trust	795,076
Sunday Times	Independent	The Thomson Organisation Ltd.	1,504,515
Sunday Telegraph	Conservative	Daily Telegraph Ltd.	755,326
News of the World	Independent	News International Ltd.	5,950,645
People	Independent	International Publishing Corporation Ltd.	4,428,598
Sunday Express	As for Daily Express	Beaverbrook Newspapers Ltd.	4,086,482
Sunday Mirror	Left of centre	International Publishing Corporation Ltd.	4,496,082

unadventurous in their approach to news and ideas. The press, on the other hand, tends to be much more biased, and newspaper editors have much more freedom in the expression of opinions. Unfortunately, however, the weakening position of the newspaper industry as a whole, the process of closures and the concentration of ownership in the hands of a few men such as Lord Thomson may be leading to a situation where the variety of opinions is so reduced that the idea of an independent press becomes a mere myth.

The left-wing press has suffered as a result of closures and mergers more than the right-wing press. The *News Chronicle*, the *Evening Star*, the *Daily Sketch* and the *Sunday Citizen* have all collapsed and the communist paper, the *Morning Star*, is able to continue only because it is heavily subsidised by contributions made by its readers. The emergence of a more right-wing press as time goes by is a matter for concern to the whole community, whatever the political sympathies of individuals may be. The functions of the press can only be satisfactorily performed in a free society where there is variety and competition. Collectively, our newspapers provide our most important medium for the expression of new ideas, new arguments and widely varying opinions. The press can also act as an effective opposition to the government of the day, particularly when the official opposition party is small or ineffective.

Apart from its political functions, the press acts as a guardian of all public interests. It keeps a continual watch on the activities of numerous bodies and individuals whether they be concerned with business and trade, military affairs, religion, education, foreign matters, recreation or any of the myriad institutions and organisations which together form and affect the social system to which we belong. An energetic, thriving and independent newspaper industry is a very valuable part of a democracy, and it is therefore essential to safeguard its stability.

Magazines and Books

MAGAZINES

The market for magazines has developed along with that for newspapers and has many of the same characteristics. There is a very large output of periodicals of all kinds in Britain, and 4300 are currently published, of which about 2000 are technical and trade journals. All manner of interests is catered for, and there are magazines for women, for children, for the different religious denominations, for sports enthusiasts, for gardeners, for anglers, for photographers and so on. Whilst the trade and technical journals are of importance to the people who have specialist interests, it is the magazines which are intended for a more general readership with which we are concerned.

The general magazines can be roughly divided into four categories: those for children which contain a large number of pictures and a comparatively small amount of advertising; those for women which have between one-third and one-half of their space devoted to advertising; the periodicals associated with broadcasting and television which also contain a considerable amount of advertising; and the weekly journals such as *The Economist* and *New Society* for the more serious-minded readers. These also have about one-third of their space occupied by advertisements. Although the demand for the more serious magazines has greatly increased since the war, and reflects the growing interest in the quality newspapers, the most prominent periodicals in terms of circulation figures are the popular women's weeklies and the television journals.

The editorial content of the serious weeklies is wholly taken up by comment and opinion on political, economic, social and cultural matters, and even *Punch*, which is by tradition the leading humorous magazine, is now devoting an increasing amount of space to the review of public affairs. These periodicals attempt to stimulate and influence the ideas and opinions of their readers, as do the quality newspapers. The popular magazines, however, characteristically limit the range of interests which they develop, and concentrate upon confirming established ideas rather than creating new ones. The women's weeklies are concerned chiefly with fiction, articles on domestic activities, fashion and personal appearance, and gossip and advice columns. There is a tacit assumption that the interests of women are chiefly in the home, and most of the articles are designed to assist them to be good housekeepers, wives and mothers. The advice offered in answer to letters addressed to the "problems page" tends to be conservative and to be based on traditional and ideal standards of morality. The fiction is easy to read, and makes no demands upon the intellect of the reader, but offers instead a way of escape from the monotony and more humdrum life of the average housewife. The romantic element is obvious.

It is interesting to note that in a television programme about women's magazines, when a hundred regular readers were questioned about the type of heroes they liked to find in short stories, they voted overwhelmingly in favour of characters who were unlike their husbands and boyfriends. Although the sample of women selected for questioning was very small, it probably provided a reasonable indication that for most women the popular magazines offer an innocuous means of escaping from reality for a short time each week.

The popular women's magazines have very little to offer to the growing number of professional women who have many interests outside the home, and the increasing readership of the serious periodicals probably includes more of this group. They are also likely to turn to such magazines as *New Society*, which has rapidly established its reputation for covering the sociological aspects of current affairs.

One category of magazines which has assumed considerable importance is that aimed at young people. The teenage market now means big business, and commercial enterprises have not been slow to exploit it. Connie Alderson, who undertook a study of teenage reading habits (*Magazines Teenagers Read*), discovered that:

"... boys appear to have far more interest in hobbies and sports than do girls. Judging from the reading habits, the girls appear to read juvenile comics and teenage magazines from the age of 11. They pass on to teenage magazines and pop music magazines in the middle groups, and reach *Woman* and *Woman's Own* in the last age group. After the first age group the boys' reading shows a variety of interests. ... The striking fact which emerges from the analysis is that apart from the 17 plus grammar school girls, the girls' figures show that their interests appear to be concentrated on romance, pop and clothes. ... It is not possible to compare the serious/hobbies type of magazines for boys and girls because it would be a one-sided affair. The long lists of magazines taken from the boys' questionnaires would produce blanks from the girls."

The difference in the attitudes of young boys and young girls towards reading reflects very strongly the inequalities in educational and career opportunities which still persist for the two sexes. Whilst the boys read widely and the magazines they choose help them to pursue a great variety of hobbies and interests, girls in the same age-groups concentrate on three or four magazines with a very limited scope. Connie Alderson made a detailed analysis of the contents of the three most popular magazines, *Trend, Jackie* and *Valentine*, over a period of eight months, and produced the statistics shown in Table XXXIII.

Connie Alderson suggests that, as a society, we may underestimate the "pernicious influence" of the popular teenage and women's magazines, which is the consequence of their "persistent

Table XXXIII—Ration of Contents of Three Popular Teenage Magazines

	Trend	Jackie	Valentine
	%	%	%
Picture strip stories	20	30	40
Advertisements	15	10	3
Pictures of pop stars	10	10	10
Printed stories	10	5	5
Printed historical serial	5	—	—
Pop gossip with pictures	5	17	17
Letters dealing with pop stars	5	—	10
Problem letters	3	5	4
Humorous letters from readers	—	5	—
Fashion, beauty and shopping hints	17	12	4
Competitions, illustrations for printed stories, astrology, poems, miscellaneous	10	6	7
	100	100	100

Source: Connie Alderson. *Magazines Teenagers Read.*

encouragement to 'dream' rather than to 'do' or to participate." As she points out:

"The wide adherence to the magazines is another reflection of women's limited role and opportunity for careers. Feeling little incentive to study, girls, especially the 'Newsom' girl, turn to them; and once they get used to 'easy' reading, progress is further impeded. As well as reflecting the limited life, the magazines serve to further limit life, for they present existing life as having attractions if approached correctly; they do not encourage expanding interests. A regrettable point to note is that the readers seek not only escapism but practical help which they accept wholeheartedly. The whole attachment shows a preoccupation with entertainment and fun, and with the mode of life, instead of life itself. The magazines support, confirm and perpetuate the restricted lives and ideas of the typical reader; the 15-year-old school-leaver who is engaged, perhaps by 16 or 17, and married by 20."

The three teenage magazines which Connie Alderson studied are most popular with girls aged 13 to 15, but they are also very widely read by those in the 11–13 and 15–17 age-groups, although the older girls enjoy their mothers' periodicals as well. From this it can be seen that these magazines are likely to influence girls from an early age, and the process of social conditioning to which they lend much support is a continuing and far-reaching one. It is of a stultifying rather than a stimulating nature.

BOOKS

Books, especially those in hard covers, are associated in the minds of many with school, and this is quite natural, since so much of our education is still based on books. It is a somewhat sad thought that, after all the struggles to achieve universal literacy, books cease to be of real importance to a great number of people once schooldays are left behind. For those who have learned to enjoy good literature, those who wish to add to their store of knowledge and those who seek the satisfaction that comes from sustained reading on subjects of interest to them, books will always find a place in their homes and lives. However, books are regarded by a large section of the community simply as a form of easy entertainment and a means of killing time. Judging by the amount of poor-quality material which now finds its way on to the market, there is a great deal of boredom to be banished and a lot of time that people would prefer dead.

The revolution in popular reading in the form of books began during the mid 1930s, when Allen Lane (later Sir Allen) launched Penguin Books. The history of paperbacks is a long one, dating from the eighteenth century, but it was on 30th July 1935 that the movement towards mass publication as we know it today really began. On that day ten new paperbacks in orange, green and blue covers were first displayed by bookshops, bookstalls and Woolworths and the black and white penguin, which is now so familiar, appeared. The Second World War added a special impetus to the reading of paperback books, because the United States Government, realising that much of war consists of waiting and boredom, distributed $132\frac{1}{2}$ million copies of such books amongst its armed forces. The demand for further titles grew as a result of the new interest being shown by many who had previously done little reading, and American publishers quickly increased their output in response. Many of the American books eventually reached Britain, and so stimulated the market and our own publishers.

Paperback books are cheap, and Sir Allen Lane once said that his chief aim was to provide good books in an attractive form for the same price as a packet of cigarettes. Although both cigarettes and paperbacks are today very much more expensive than they were in

1935, the two do still cost approximately the same. The price of paperbacks is only kept low, however, by the fact that large numbers are printed and sold. Whilst an average-priced hardback book will begin to make a profit when between 2500 and 3000 copies have been sold, ten times that number of copies must be sold before a paperback becomes profitable. In order to safeguard themselves against a loss, publishers have two courses open to them; either they can bring out in paperback form a book which has previously enjoyed large sales as a hardback, or they can concentrate on publishing the type of book that can almost be guaranteed to sell well because it has a massive ready-made market. The latter type of book includes thrillers, romances and the "TV/film tie-ins."

As with the popular papers and magazines, the creation of new ideas and interests is largely outside the realms of the cheap paperback, and publishers tend to confine themselves to presenting a combination of what was popular in the past and what is mediocre in the present. Good literature is mostly confined to providing cheap editions of the books selected as "set" works in examinations for the General Certificate of Education. It is perhaps worth noting at this point that the growing awareness of matters of general social concern, evidenced by the current interest being shown in the study of sociology, has encouraged paperback publishers to produce a spate of books on sociological topics. Here, of course, the publishers are entering the field of educational works, and works of this nature will, it may be hoped, enjoy a wider readership as time goes by.

Mass readership is the most important factor in the publication of paperbacks, and, both in the number of titles and in total sales, murder and mystery stories lead all other categories. The authors of the most popular stories write to more or less the same formula, and the ingredients which they use include a considerable amount of sensationalism—exaggerated accounts of violence, murder, horror and sexual adventures are always apparently enjoyed—strong but relatively uncomplicated characterisation, a fast-moving plot and a contemporary or possibly futuristic setting. This formula provides all the elements of escapism and remoteness from reality which seem to be so overwhelmingly desirable at the present time, and the influence of the United States is obvious. The list of best-selling murder stories is headed by the books of Mickey Spillane, and this author specialises in lurid descriptions of physical violence and brutality.

Apart from books about murder and mystery, historical romances, novels with a religious or Biblical character as the hero and books about "ordinary" people have a considerable appeal. Whether or not a book is well written, however, has little connection with its sales, and, from the point of view of literature, a large number of books which enjoy enormous sales are very third rate. This is the apparently inevitable consequence of what the distinguished publisher Michael Joseph referred to as "the folly of over-production," and it would no doubt have caused the early educationalists to have second thoughts about the advisability of striving to ensure that everyone was given the opportunity of learning to read.

Whilst the idea that a very low standard is accepted unquestioningly by so many presents a somewhat gloomy and negative picture, there is a more encouraging side to the trends in reading. Approximately 11,000 branches of public libraries hold between them a stock of over ninety-one million books, and the section of the community which uses the library services is growing all the time. The demand for non-fiction is increasing, and the paperback industry is responding by expanding its production of books of this kind. Public librarians have, within recent years, stressed the importance of ensuring that the books available in the children's section of libraries are carefully selected to encourage the reading of better-quality works. Most habits are acquired quite early in life, and, if the youngest readers can be taught to discriminate in their choice of books, the standards of material presented may be raised in the future. The process will inevitably be a slow one, and in the meantime much that is crude, primitive and even sometimes obscene will continue to reach the homes of millions.

Radio and Television

SOUND RADIO

The first broadcast of the British Broadcasting Corporation was transmitted on 1st January 1927. The Corporation had existed for four years previously as the British Broadcasting Company, which was founded by the radio industry and had J. C. W. Reith as managing director. When the Company became a public corporation Reith was appointed as Director-General, a position he held until 1938, and in which he brought a very strong influence to bear upon broadcasting in Britain. Reith, as he stated in a speech at the time the Corporation was formed, saw the task of the Governors as giving "a conscious social purpose to the exploitation of this medium."

The first Director-General was an authoritarian who was determined to establish firmly the principle of broadcasting as a public service free from either commercial or state control, and the attitude held by the people of Britain towards broadcasting today has largely been shaped by the pattern which Reith originated. He believed that the public interest could best be served in broadcasting through a monopoly, and the monopoly remained unbroken in sound and, later, in vision as well until the Independent Television Authority was created in 1954. Reith was anxious to set the standards as high as possible, and because of the Corporation's monopolistic position he was able to offer a strong middle-class culture to the listeners. Broadcasting has therefore developed along very different lines from publishing.

By the time competition entered the field of sound broadcasting and, for a brief period, "pirate" radio stations issued a challenge, the pattern and standards of the medium were so well established in Britain that little impact was made. It is true that the B.B.C. responded to the challenge by introducing a fourth network in 1967 to provide a continuous service of popular music, but the effect of this has largely been to give a yardstick with which the other programmes may be compared. It also acts as a reminder of the standards which might be expected if the use made of broadcasting were to be decided by majority opinion rather than by firm leadership.

Commercially, competition may lead customers to select the best from amongst commodities offered to them at a similar price, but culturally this idea is not a tenable one. As the Committee on Broadcasting (the Pilkington Committee) pointed out in their report (1960):

"The broadcasting authorities have certainly a duty to keep sensitively aware of the public's tastes and attitudes as they now are and in all their variety; and to care about them. But if they do more than that, this is not to give the public 'what someone thinks is good for it.' It is to respect the public's right to choose from the widest possible range of subject matter and so to enlarge worthwhile experience. Because in principle, the possible range of subject matter is inexhaustible, all of it can never be presented, nor can the public know what the range is. So, the broadcaster must explore it, and choose from it first. This might be called 'giving a lead': but it is not the lead of the autocratic or arrogant. It is the proper exercise of responsibility by public authorities duly constituted as trustees for the public interest."

The constitution of the B.B.C. charges it with providing enlightenment as well as entertainment, and the way in which the available time is allocated reflects the attempts made by the Corporation to discharge its responsibilities in both of these areas (see Table XXXIV).

Apart from the provision of enlightenment and entertainment, broadcasting has an important part to play in the preservation, development and transmission of the society's culture. Viewed as a whole, the services provided by sound radio satisfactorily perform this particular role, but it should be remembered that listeners are likely to switch off their sets or turn to another programme if they do not like what they hear. Whilst the B.B.C. itself regards its sound services as an integrated whole, listeners, on the other hand, tend to develop allegiances to a particular network. The segregation of material into four distinctive types of programme encourages this, and, as the Pilkington Committee remarked, the content of programmes is classified very much according to "height-of-brow."

In the words of the B.B.C. Handbook, 1968, Radio 1 caters, at least between 7 a.m. and 7.30 p.m., for an audience mainly consisting of "under-25-year-olds avid for 'pop' and more 'pop' " and "the image is designed to be youthful, friendly and fast-moving." Radio 2 caters for "those many millions who are not attracted by a continuous diet of 'pop'," but prefer instead light music and general light entertainment. Radio 3, which consists of the Third Programme, the Music Programme, Study Session and the Sports Service, caters for serious music-lovers, intelligent laymen with an interest in the arts, philosophy, history and science and specialist or minority groups. Radio 4 provides a comprehensive coverage of the news and comment on it. It also gives listeners a large variety of plays, talks, orchestral concerts and serial readings, and aims to satisfy the requirements of the "broad middle section of the community." Radio 4 also caters for important minority groups such as farmers, gardeners and motorists, carries programmes for schools and offers second chances to hear certain items selected from Study Session.

The Pilkington Committee recognised certain dangers inherent in the B.B.C.'s policy of segregating the programmes in this way:

"From segregating programmes into classes, the next step might well be to segregate listeners into classes, to assume that there are large numbers of people who like only one sort of programme and different people who like only another, to think not of overlapping majority and minority tastes, but to distinguish sharply between 'majorities'

Table XXXIV—B.B.C. Radio Programme Analysis, 1973–74

	Radio 1		Radio 2		Radio 3		Radio 4		Total	
	Hours	%	Hours	%	Hours	%	Hours	%	Hours	%
Music	4,603	92·2	5,920	78·6	4,768	71·6	345	4·9	15,636	59·7
Current affairs, features and documentaries	74	1·5	160	2·1	312	4·7	3,272	46·6	3,818	14·6
News	88	1·8	513	6·8	191	2·9	803	11·4	1,595	6·1
Drama			125	1·7	143	2·1	872	12·4	1,140	4·4
Sport	13	0·3	420	5·6	226	3·4	47	0·7	706	2·7
Light entertainment	20	0·4	226	3·0	6	0·1	339	4·8	591	2·3
Religion	28	0·5	107	1·4	39	0·6	257	3·7	431	1·6
Schools							444	6·3	444	1·7
Further education	156	3·1			272	4·1	76	1·1	348	1·3
Children's programmes	10	0·2			48	0·7	111	1·6	315	1·2
Continuity			60	0·8	172	2·6	209	3·0	451	1·7
	4,992	100·0	7,531	100·0	6,177	92·8	6,775	96·5	25,475	97·3
Open University	—	—	—	—	477	7·2	243	3·5	720	2·7
	4,992	100·0	7,531	100·0	6,654	100·0	7,018	100·0	26,195	100·0

Source: B.B.C. Handbook, 1975.

and 'minorities,' to think of present tastes rather than of capacities. We believe that the B.B.C. has not altogether avoided this danger."

Lord Reith's idea of programme planning was to combine all kinds of material at all levels on one channel, and he strongly criticised the creation of the Third Programme, which he felt was a serious mistake. He felt that it was better to over-estimate the mentality of the public than to under-estimate it, and considered that to present people with a variety of strongly contrasting items was the most likely method to stimulate new interests and new pleasures. There is certainly always a possibility, however remote, that the listener who keeps his radio set permanently switched on may discover the delights of Beethoven despite the fact that he really hopes to hear the top twenty records in the hit parade. Since available evidence suggests that the limits to appreciation and discrimination are likely to be determined by educational and social background, it would be too optimistic to expect broadcasting alone to raise the cultural standards of the society by any great amount. But these standards are more likely to be raised if the B.B.C. avoids emphasising cultural differences by an undue amount of segregation.

There is no doubt that at the present time the policy of the B.B.C. is based on a more "take it or leave it" attitude than it was originally, and Sir Ian Jacob, the Director-General at the time the system of stratification was introduced, declared that it was not the aim of the Corporation "to force education down people's throats." J. Scupham, in *Broadcasting and the Community*, comments upon the idea that listeners should be asked to decide for themselves which network appeals to them if public service broadcasting has any cultural and educational purpose to achieve:

"It is a type of invitation which is realistic enough for the better-educated groups, and wholly unrealistic for the rest. . . . It is blind to the fact that selectivity is itself a product of education, and it takes no adequate account of the existence of insurmountable educational barriers. To tell the audience of the Light Programme that they must look for anything further that they want on the Home Service or the Third Programme is to tell them that if they do not like the fare at Lyons, the Ritz is open to all. They cannot pay the educational price."

The B.B.C. has rightly earned itself a high reputation for the manner in which it has consistently ensured that serious material is available for everyone who wants it and provided for all tastes, abilities and interests. Lord Reith's avowed ambition was to bring "the best of everything into the greatest number of homes" through a form of "paternal" leadership, but it is now widely argued that even the most kindly paternalism is out of accord with the temper of the times and is undemocratic. It implies the imposition of ideas and tastes from above and the denial of freedom. Those who advocate changes in the system, however, are most likely to be found amongst the better-educated and more ideological sections of the community, and they would have nothing to lose themselves if sound broadcasting were to be reorganised in such a way that the majority of the people were given what they wanted. The fact is frequently ignored that a benign dictator may be able to lead people to want something which, if left to their own devices, they would have had no opportunity of discovering for themselves.

If we wish to continue the trend towards educating more and more people to share and enjoy all the advantages which come from a rich culture and to feel that they are personally involved in the society's development, then it would be dangerous to submit to pressure from those who prefer the idea of a cultural democracy to an imposed system. Cultural freedom might be defined as "the right of the people to choose for themselves which parts of the society's culture they will accept and which parts they will reject." It might also be defined as "the right of the people to remain as illiterate and ignorant as they like for as long as they like." It is worth bearing this in mind when we are considering the nature and purposes of public-service broadcasting.

Local and Commercial Radio

In July 1972 the *Sound Broadcasting Act* came into effect. This Act extended the functions of the Independent Television Authority to include the provision of local commercial radio stations and renamed it the *Independent Broadcasting Authority*. Nineteen commercial stations are due to be established by the end of 1975.

Local radio had already been started by the B.B.C., which opened stations in eight towns in 1967. By March 1971 the number of stations had been increased to twenty, providing coverage to approximately 75 per cent of the population. The plans for commercial radio provide for the eventual establishment of up to sixty stations covering about 70 per cent of the country but catering for recognisable communities.

After eight years, however, it is still difficult to assess the extent to which there is a real demand for local radio in Britain. The Centre for Mass Communication Studies at Leicester University undertook a survey in Leicester in 1968, and it was found that although 40 per cent of the adult population had the VHF facilities with which to receive local radio, only about 17 per cent listened to Radio Leicester regularly. Radio Leicester was considered, at the time the survey was made, to be one of the most successful stations. The researchers made the point, however, that the people who listened to the local station were generally satisfied with what they heard. The research also revealed that support for local radio is greater from people towards the bottom of the social scale.

Before local sound broadcasting was introduced, it was feared in some quarters that it might adversely affect the circulation figures of local newspapers. There is, however, little evidence of this happening, and this may well be because local radio attracts its audience from a sector of the population which does not include the most avid readers of local newspapers.

The B.B.C. anticipated that local radio would stimulate greater participation in community activities, but it appears that in this respect there was an undue amount of optimism. Whilst some organisations make considerable use of the broadcasting facilities available, and many prefer radio to the press, there is little indication of any real impact having been made in the field of community activities. The B.B.C. has also had difficulty in attracting financial assistance from local sources towards the cost of providing the services. It has had to cover not only the entire capital cost involved but more than half the operating cost as well.

Commercial radio is still very much in its infancy, but the two London stations, Capital Radio and the London Broadcasting Company, claim that their audiences are growing steadily. It is estimated that, of the eight and a half million people who lived within the area covered by the stations in January 1974, two million listened to Capital and over one million listened to L.B.C. at some point each week. Capital, which emphasises pop music, has a larger proportion of younger listeners than L.B.C., which specialises in news and sport.

The medium of commercial sound broadcasting is not yet fully understood, and, according to the I.B.A., "Radio advertising is still a developing craft in this country." It appears that the B.B.C. has a formidable rival in commercial radio, however, and the economy cuts which it introduced in January 1975 may restrict its local broadcasting services. This can only benefit commercial radio, which is concerned more to attract audiences by giving the listeners what they want to hear, than to provide a local service with social and community considerations very much to the fore. As the I.B.A. stations learn by experience how to gauge their audiences and how best to handle advertising, the B.B.C. may find it has a serious challenger not only at the local level but also at the national network level, as has occurred in television.

TELEVISION

The growth of television has been one of the most striking and influential developments in a century that has witnessed many far-reaching scientific and technological achievements. Unlike sound broadcasting, however, television has not enjoyed the same lengthy period during which it could establish firmly its own traditions and standards with relatively little effective opposition.

Television broadcasting, which began with sound broadcasting as a rival, has a considerable advantage as a medium of communication in that it has the additional element of vision, and has, consequently, an even greater power to persuade and influence. Television's chief disadvantage is that it has considerably less time at its disposal in which to cover a really wide range of material. Although the B.B.C. was allocated a second channel, which opened in the London area in 1964 and by 1974 was available to more than 90 per cent of the population, it still has only about one-third of the number of hours that sound broadcasting has. What is perhaps even more important is the fact that the B.B.C. has a very strong competitor in the Independent Broadcasting Authority.

Before the passing of the *Television Act* of 1954, which introduced an alternative independent television service, a great deal of controversy was aroused in the country about the desirability of breaking the B.B.C.'s monopoly. Whilst it was apparent that a large section of the community was anxious for a greater amount of freedom, it was equally clear that many people also feared that uncontrolled sponsored television on American lines would lead to a very drastic decline in standards. A television service is extremely expensive to provide, and the scope of the B.B.C. was limited by the fact that its revenue was dependent upon licence fees. Although the number of licences issued had increased each year, these did not allow the services to be expanded to meet the market that was available. There was, therefore, a strong case to be made in favour of creating an independent service, which would derive its revenue from a source other than licence fees. Commercial organisations, which were an obvious source to turn to for this purpose, had long been lobbying for a television channel.

In order to avoid the pitfalls of direct commercial control of television as exists in the United States, where the advertiser through his agents is responsible for presenting the programme in the time he buys, we adopted an indirect system in Britain. Advertisers buy time or space from the Programme Companies (of which there are now fifteen covering fourteen areas), but they do not have any say in the way programmes are planned or any share in their production. The rates charged to the advertisers are determined by the time at which their "commercials" are shown, and by the size of the audience which it is estimated will view them. The Programme Companies are controlled by the Independent Broadcasting Authority, to which they pay an annual rent for the privilege of providing a service in the area allocated to them and obtaining an income from the sale of advertising space.

The *Television Act*, 1954, and the subsequent 1964 Act under which the Authority was renewed, charged the Independent Television Authority with providing information, education and entertainment in similar terms to that laid down for the B.B.C. For this reason, the Programme Companies have to seek the approval of the Authority before they can transmit any programme, and four times a year they are obliged to submit their proposals for the following quarter to the Authority. The ultimate responsibility for policy planning and general supervision of standards and material thus rests with the Authority.

The advocates of a monopoly in television as in sound broadcasting expected that the introduction of an independent television service would bring about a sharp decline in broadcasting standards. The independent Programme Companies were naturally anxious to gain as large a share of the television audience as possible, and a majority of the public certainly switched over to I.T.V. at "peak" viewing time when programmes of a widely popular appeal were shown.

The first years of the new relationship between the B.B.C. and I.T.V. were tense and uneasy, and it rather looked as though the fears of the "pro-monopoly" camp would be realised. The Pilkington Committee reported a considerable amount of disquiet about the standard of television programmes and noted that:

". . . for the sake of easy appeal, television portrayed too often a world in which the moral standards normally accepted in society were either ignored or flouted, and that for a similar reason it showed excessive violence."

The Pilkington Committee blamed the Independent Television Authority for failing to enforce the standards required of it when it was created, and remarked that:

> "The disquiet about and dissatisfaction with television are, in our view, justly attributed very largely to the service of independent television. This is so despite the popularity of the service, and the well-known fact that many of its programmes command the largest audiences. Our enquiries have brought us to appreciate why this kind of success is not the only, and is by no means the most important, test of a good broadcasting service. Indeed, it is a success which can be obtained by abandoning the main purpose of broadcasting."

The Independent Television Authority was established initially for a ten-year term. During its first six years the new service effectively demonstrated its ability to secure and retain a majority of the viewing audience, but the Pilkington Committee were less sure of its ability to further the social purposes of broadcasting and recognise the responsibilities of a medium which had so much power to influence and persuade. The adverse publicity given to television, and, in particular, commercial television, caused a great deal of controversy before the *Television Act, 1964,* was passed, and this controversy is still continuing at the present time. As a nation we have not been able to reach a decision which is completely acceptable. Despite much philosophic discussion about the formulation of policies, there is insufficient strength of conviction about what is the right policy, and we have merely achieved a compromise which, while it works fairly well, is not completely satisfactory. The powers of the Independent Broadcasting Authority have been increased, and are more strongly upheld, and the anxieties about the decline in broadcasting standards have been somewhat diminished. The anxiety about whether anything is being done to raise standards still remains.

Since the *Television Act* of 1964 was passed, both B.B.C. and I.B.A. have settled down to a more stable relationship, and each has tended to concentrate on the type of programme in which it has proved successful in terms of audience ratings (*see* XXXV and XXXVI).

It is in their approach rather than in the allocation of material that the two services differ. Anxious to avoid the sort of criticism which it received from the Pilkington Committee, the I.B.A. has apparently decided that it is safer to conform and work to the pattern

Table XXXV—B.B.C. Television Programme Analysis, 1973–74

	B.B.C.-1		B.B.C.-2		Total	
	Hours	%	Hours	%	Hours	%
B.B.C. productions:						
Current affairs, features and documentaries	1,080	21·7	799	25·0	1,879	23·1
Sport	677	13·7	307	9·6	984	12·1
Children's programmes	488	9·8	119	3·7	607	7·4
Light entertainment	355	7·2	197	6·2	552	6·8
Drama	295	5·9	206	6·5	501	6·1
News	242	4·9	175	5·5	417	5·1
Schools	360	7·3			360	4·4
Further education	166	3·3	95	3·0	261	3·2
Religion	138	2·8	24	0·7	162	2·0
Music	35	0·7	74	2·3	109	1·3
Programmes in Welsh	78	1·6			78	1·0
Continuity	249	5·0	127	4·0	376	4·6
	4,163	83·9	2,123	66·5	6,286	77·1
British and foreign feature films and series	796	16·1	449	14·1	1,245	15·3
	4,959	100·0	2,572	80·6	7,531	92·4
Open University	—	—	618	19·4	618	7·6
	4,959	100·0	3,190	100·0	8,149	100·0

Source: *B.B.C. Handbook, 1975.*

which had more or less been set by the B.B.C. when it had the
monopoly in television broadcasting. The approach of commercial
television has been rather akin to that of the popular press, and it
is sometimes content to obtain large audiences by planning programmes on the principle that the public knows what it likes and
likes what it knows. Commercial television, for this reason, tends not
to perform the role of innovator.

Somewhat surprisingly, it was the B.B.C. under the Director-
Generalship of Sir Hugh Greene which loosened television's former
very close links with the Establishment. When Dr Joseph Treneman
questioned a sample of 1500 people in 1958, he discovered that a
large number of them regarded the B.B.C. as being socially distant
from them, representing the Government, employers, the most

Table XXXVI—I.T.V. Weekly Programme Pattern, 1974

	Hours (approx.)	%
Plays, serials and series	22·7	23·6
Children's programmes	11·5	12·0
Feature films	10·65	11·1
Current affairs and documentaries	10·6	11·0
Entertainment and music	10·25	10·7
Sport	9·6	10·0
News and news magazines	9·4	9·8
Schools programmes	6·2	6·5
Adult education	2·7	2·8
Religion	2·4	2·5
Total	96·0	100

Source: *I.T.V. 75: A Guide to Independent Television.*

privileged and the élites rather than ordinary people. Competition from independent television forced the B.B.C. to reappraise its policy and approach, and rid itself of its rather staid, conservative image in order to win and hold an audience. In fact, as J. Scupham writes in *Broadcasting and the Community*:

"The older attitudes slipped too readily into the rigid postures of a 'good form' instinct with the values of what was then the governing class; the new attitudes can be theatrical gestures of revolt, and as empty as the old, produced with less regard for the long-term impact on society than for the short-term impact on the ratings. In its least happy offerings the B.B.C. used to play to the stalls; now to the gallery. Moral shock tactics encourage the shock troops. They rarely make converts, and always harden the opposition. The story of the B.B.C.'s excursion into a *genre* that is still by the abuse of a useful word called satire is perhaps a cautionary tale. Political satire with a cutting edge calls for a committed political passion; *saeva indignatio* is not to be had weekly for the asking; social comment must be urbane and polished to earn the name of satire. *Not so much a Programme* . . . and its successors found one brilliant mimic with a gift for puncturing the pomposities of politicians of whatever party; one good amusing comedienne. With far too much space to fill the programme had not 'wit enough to keep it sweet.' It was reduced to charades about clergymen, headmasters, and other Aunt Sallys of the Left; to interminable and disorderly conversation pieces; and to increasingly crude attempts to shock the *bourgeoisie*. B.B.C. apologies followed indecencies, and grosser indecencies the apologies. The public was left in doubt whether a recurring nastiness was part of a campaign of provocation which the Director General welcomed as socially imperative, or whether it simply revealed a disciplinary incompetence which would have seemed ridiculous to any previous B.B.C. régime.

The new freedom is a clear gain, but not an end in itself if it means only that 'anything goes.' However hardly won or greatly cherished, it is no more than a condition for the realisation of values, which lie beyond the battlefield itself."

Now that the B.B.C. has established that it can be less conformist, less conservative and more adventurous than its competitor, and since, unlike commercial television, it has no advertisers breathing down its neck scrutinising the audience ratings, it should perhaps use its greater freedom to reinforce its status as a cultural and educative force within the community. At the moment too little emphasis is placed on the fact that, of the two services, the B.B.C. is in a stronger position than I.B.A. to persevere and build up an audience for programmes of a high quality. The public may respond slowly at first, and be reluctant to change its viewing habits, but, given time and ingenuity, it is possible to achieve considerable success. The very wide acclaim given to the dramatisation of *The Forsyte Saga* effectively demonstrated the power of gentle persuasion.

We are inclined to forget that television is a young medium, and there is still a great deal to be learned about its use. It is difficult to think creatively if there is too strong an element of tradition in formulating policy, and this is in no case more apparent than it is in the use that is made of the medium of television. However, as Durkheim clearly recognised, a society depends for its stability and continuity upon the transmission of well-established and tested values, and probably the most important means of transmitting values today is television. It is therefore clearly essential that those who are responsible for planning the programmes should have a very real sense of purpose and an understanding of the tremendous power which they have to influence their audiences, to shape or strengthen attitudes and opinions, and to develop the ability to discriminate. To the programme planners, the society has delegated the responsibility for selecting on its behalf what will be placed before it, and people have a right to the best that is available.

Innovation and experiment can take place against a background of well-tried values; the two concepts are not mutually exclusive,

as many people seem mistakenly to believe. Greater freedom and
a movement away from an authoritarian structure with its imposed
system need not lead necessarily to a decline in standards. The
freedom that is looked for should be the kind of freedom which
enables all shades and varieties of interests to be represented, and
which recognises the right of humanists to express their views as
well as Anglicans or Roman Catholics, anarchists as well as totali-
tarians—in fact, minorities as well as majorities. This can be done
in such a way that the traditional beliefs and assumptions which
underlie the social system are not abused or wilfully cast aside. It
is not necessary, for example, to ridicule or pour scorn on the
institutions of marriage or the monarchy when discussing their
relevance in society at the present time. Nor is it necessary to
shock people in an attempt to make them think, as this is more
likely to make them antagonistic and resistant to new ideas.

The authoritarian system vests in an individual or a group of
people the power to decide what the rest of the society shall be
given in the way of education, enlightenment and entertainment;
to limit arbitrarily the extent and nature of the material made available. This is neither democratic nor acceptable in this day and age,
but, having gained the freedom that comes from recognising the
right of all groups within the society to be represented, it is important to ensure that they are represented in the best possible way.

Stuart Hall and Paddy Whannel, in their comprehensive study *The
Popular Arts* (1964), suggest that in the past somewhat limiting
standards were set by what was considered "respectable" by the
"great" rather than by the "humble." They point to the kind of
hierarchy in tastes that has developed in the minds of many people
which makes it impossible for them to recognise that all forms of
are and entertainment have their own values:

> "We must stop talking about the various kinds of art and entertain-
> ment as if they were necessarily competitive. Popular music, for
> example, has its own standards. Ella Fitzgerald is a highly polished
> professional entertainer who within her own sphere could hardly be
> better. Clearly it would be inappropriate to compare her to Maria
> Callas; they are not aiming at the same thing. . . . Different kinds
> of music offer different sorts of satisfaction. If we can begin to recog-
> nise different aims and to assess varying achievements with defined
> limits we shall get rid of much of the mish-mash in between."

The ability to recognise aims and to assess achievements presupposes the ability to compare and to discriminate. This ability is

obtained as a result of training, and, as yet, not everyone has had the education which enables him to discriminate for himself. To this extent, if the society is to be presented with the best that is available, the majority of its members will need to rely on the ability of someone else to discriminate for them. In the case of television broadcasting, it is the programme planners who should rightly be expected to do this. It is essential that those people who have been delegated the responsibility for making decisions and acting on behalf of others should *respect* the audience for whom they are catering. They should at all times ask, "Is this good enough for them?" and not complacently think, "They do not know any better, so this will be good enough for them." Only in this way can we be certain that the very best use is made of our newest and most effective medium of communication.

In a modern industrial society based on mass production, mass consumption and mass communications there is inevitably a risk of mass mediocrity destroying the society's cultural values. It is perhaps in television broadcasting that the problem of avoiding mediocrity is greatest, because, by the vast majority of people, television is regarded primarily as a source of entertainment. As Philip Abrams has written in *Discrimination and Popular Culture*:

> "Broadcasters themselves tend to believe that broadcasting can do anything. Specifically the media exist to provide services of three kinds, services of information, education and entertainment. In effect, wherever the broadcaster tries to fill the first or second of these roles the chances are he will succeed and that radio and television will prove superior media of communication to most others; wherever he tries to fill the third role, that of entertainer, the chances are he will fail and that radio and television will prove less adequate media than many others."

The problem is not an easy one to solve. The Pilkington Committee saw the development of mass-mediocrity as the consequences of "trivialisation," and explained that:

> "Triviality resides in the way the subject matter is approached and the manner in which it is presented. A trivial approach can consist in a failure to respect the potentialities of the subject matter no matter what it be, or in a too ready reliance on well-tried themes, or in a habit of conforming to established patterns or in a reluctance to be imaginatively adventurous . . . in a failure to take full and disciplined advantage of the artistic and technical facilities which are relevant to a particular subject, or in an excessive interest in smart packaging

at the expense of the contents of the package, or in a reliance on gimmicks so as to give a spurious interest to a programme at the cost of its imaginative integrity, or in too great a dependence on hackneyed devices for creating suspense or raising a laugh or evoking tears."

With cinema audiences sharply diminished in size and numerous local repertory theatres being forced to close through lack of support, there is plenty of evidence to show that, for the majority of people, television is today their main form of entertainment. It has been estimated that, on average, people view television for between one and a half and three hours each day—the actual time being fairly closely associated with the educational background of viewers, and tending to increase as the level of educational achievement declines. One B.B.C. survey also established that, the more people watch, the less discriminating they are about what they watch, and this, of course, underlines the considerable responsibility in the hands of the programme planners.

The Pilkington Committee referred to the failure of the planners to take "disciplined advantage" of the facilities and techniques available to them. Discipline can only exist where there is also a commonly recognised and upheld sense of purpose, and at this stage in time there is a considerable amount of controversy over the social purposes of broadcasting and which of these are the most important. There are, indeed, many people who do not believe that there has to be any purpose at all. Perhaps it is for this reason that television is at present rather inclined to dominate the society. We have not yet learned how to control and use to its best advantage this particularly powerful and influential medium.

EXERCISE 16

1. "Mass production, mass consumption and mass communications produce a mass culture and mass mediocrity." Discuss.
2. Discuss the notion that commercialism has no respect for cultural values.
3. Account for the fact that readership of "popular" newspapers has declined since 1960, whilst that of the "quality" newspapers has increased.
4. The reading habits of boys are considerably different from those of girls. Explain the factors within the society which might cause these differences, and the likely consequences of them.
5. Make an appraisal of the "paperback revolution."
6. "The attitude of a public corporation must be paternalistic in the last resort." Discuss this statement with reference to broadcasting and television.
7. "The main purpose of broadcasting is to make the microphone and the television screen available to the widest possible range of subjects and to the best exponents available of the differing views on any given subject" (Sir Hugh

Greene, Director-General of the B.B.C.). How far do you consider that this purpose is being achieved at the present time?

8. "The universality, continuity and domesticity of radio and television have made them substitutes for thinking and doing." Discuss.

9. To what extent do the controllers of the mass media shape the nature of society?

FOR FURTHER READING

R. B. Heath. *The Mass Media: Newspapers.* Bodley Head, 1968.

Frank Huggett. *The Newspapers.* Heinemann, 1968.

National Board for Prices and Incomes. Report No. 43. *Costs and Revenue of National Daily Newspapers.* H.M.S.O., 1967.

Connie Alderson. *Magazines Teenagers Read.* Pergamon, 1968.

B.B.C. Handbook 1975. B.B.C. Publications.

I.T.V. 1975: A Guide to Independent Television. Independent Television Authority, 1975.

Denys Thompson (ed.). *Discrimination and Popular Culture.* Penguin Books, 1964.

Stuart Hood. *The Mass Media.* Macmillan, 1972.

Jeremy Tunstall (ed.). *Media Sociology: A Reader.* Constable, 1970.

Denis McQuail (ed.). *Readings in the Sociology of Mass Communications.* Penguin Books, 1972.

James Halloran (ed.). *The Effects of Television.* Panther Books, 1970.

Jeremy Tunstall. *Journalists at Work.* Constable. 1971.

B.B.C. Audience Research Department Report. *Violence on Television: Programme Content and Viewer Perception,* 1972.

INDEX

A

abortion, 303
Abrams, Mark, 241
Abrams, Philip, 411
absenteeism, 221
accident-proneness, 222
acquisitiveness, 218
advertising, 381, 385, 388, 405
  Institute of Practitioners in Advertising, 385
age of marriage, 286, 297
aggression, 219
alcohol, 357
alcoholism, 353, 363
Alderson, Connie, 393
Allport, G. W., 54, 99
altruistic suicide, 354
anomic suicide, 354
anomie, 13, 135, 278, 306, 355
anthropologists, 144, 161
anti-urbanism, 316
archaeologists, 51
Argyle, M., 101, 270
Aristotle, 4, 167, 325
Aron, Raymond, 119
associations, 41
attitudes, 94, 95, 236, 367, 408, 409
  measurement of, 72
  towards education, 257
  towards marriage, 298

B

Bacon, Alice, 362
Barton, 321
B.B.C. See British Broadcasting Corporation
behaviour, 13, 24, 35, 97, 111
  as a determinant of class, 126
behaviourists, 35
beliefs, 236, 263
belief systems, 263
Benedict, Ruth, 94
Berg, Leila, 244
Besant, Annie, 293
Bethnal Green, 319, 321

bias, 23, 25, 61, 78
Bird, Charles, 107
birth-rate, 158
Blondel, Jean, 187
Bogardus, E., 79
books, 395
Booth, Charles, 312
borstal system, 373
Bowlby, John, 113
Bowley, A. L., 71
Bradlaugh, Charles, 293
breakthrough, 18
British Broadcasting Corporation, 125, 380, 397, 402, 403, 404
broadcasting, 125, 397
  and religion, 276
  sound radio, 397
  See also local and commercial radio, and television
Brown, J. A. C., 220
Bruhn, P., 356
Butler, David, 175

C

cabinet, 173
cannabis, 359
capital, 198
case-histories, 58
castes, 116
Central Advisory Committee on Education, 231, 243
central government, 173
Certificate of Secondary Education, 251
charisma, 18
Chatham, 323
"Chicago" school, 315
Christianity. See religion
chromosomes, 91, 369
church attendance, 273
Church of England Temperance Society, 373
Cicero, 5
civilisation, 48
civil service, 129, 165, 239
clan system, 145

415

F

factors of production, 199
family, 93, 94, 137, 144, 283
  functions of, 149
  size of, 288
Family Planning Association, 294
feudalism, 19, 116, 163, 167
fixation, 220
Fletcher, R., 149, 298
Frankenberg, Ronald, 317, 322
Frazer, Sir James, 265, 271
freedom of the press, 382
frustration, 219, 322, 353
  relief through religion, 269
functional alternatives, 377

G

Gallup, George, 74
Gavron, Hannah, 302
General Elections, 175
Gittins, J., 113
Gladstone Committee, 372
Glass, Ruth, 311
Goldthorpe, J. H., 132
Gottschalk, L., 56
Griffith, S., 259
groups, 41, 99, 344
  quasi-groups, 41
Gulbenkian Foundation, 313
Guttman, L., 81

H

Hall, Stuart, 410
Harris, L., 172
Hawthorne investigations, 200, 216
Henriques, F., 224, 269
heredity, 91
heroin, 359
hierarchy, development of, 109
Highlands, Scottish, 146, 319
Hill, J. M. M., 221
Himes, N., 293
Hiro, Dilip, 341
historians, 52
historical method in social investigation,
  36, 51
Hitchin, 274, 323
Hobbes, Thomas, 7
Hodge, R. Sessions, 368
holidays, 227
housing estates, private, 323

Howard, Sir Ebenezer, 325
Huxley, Aldous, 359
Hyndman, Henry, 19

I

I.B.A. See Independent Broadcasting
  Authority
ideal patterns of behaviour, 43, 97, 268
ideal type, 17
ideology, 271
illegitimacy, 147, 303
immigrants, 102, 121, 142, 335
incentives, 216
incest, 142, 147
incomes, 201
  as a determinant of class, 121
Independent Broadcasting Authority,
  398, 402, 403, 404
instincts, 92
institutions, 42, 230
integration, 12, 39, 101
  religion and, 267
inter-personal perception, 95, 99
isolates, 86, 111

J

Jephcott, Pearl, 314
judiciary, 166
juvenile delinquents, 375

K

Kalinin, M. I., 237
Kalton, Graham, 248
Kelley, H. H., 110
Kirchheimer, O., 370
Knowles, K. G. J. C., 224
Knowlton, Charles, 293

L

Labour Party, 181, 183, 186, 193, 210
labour turnover, 221
Lane, Sir Allen, 395
language, 47
Latent Structure Analysis, 79, 80
Lavers, G. R., 158, 273
laws, 165
  ecclesiastical, 272
Lazarsfield, P. F., 80
leaders
  motivation of, 108
  training of, 238